KV-638-440

# PART 2

# Paper 2.4

# Financial Management and Control

# EXAM KIT

Approved Publisher

**KAPLAN**

**PUBLISHING**

FOULKS LYNCH

## SCENARIO-BASED QUESTIONS

*Page number*

| | | Question | Answer | Exam |
|---|---|---|---|---|
| 1 | Franctic Ltd | 55 | 249 | *Pilot 01* |
| 2 | Jack Geep | 56 | 255 | *Dec 02* |
| 3 | Doe Limited | 58 | 262 | *Dec 03* |
| 4 | Nespa | 60 | 268 | *Jun 04* |
| 5 | Spender Construction plc | 62 | 274 | *Jun 00* |
| 6 | Stadium Eats | 64 | 280 | *Jun 98* |
| 7 | Water Supply Services plc | 66 | 283 | *Jun 02* |
| 8 | Tower Railways plc | 68 | 287 | *Dec 01* |
| 9 | Amber plc | 69 | 292 | *Dec 00* |
| 10 | Springbank plc | 71 | 296 | *Jun 03* |
| 11 | The Independent Film Company | 72 | 301 | *Jun 99* |
| 12 | Sassone plc | 74 | 304 | *Dec 04* |
| 13 | ARG Co | 76 | 309 | *Jun 05* |

# SYLLABUS AND EXAM FORMAT

---

## Format of the exam

|  |  | *Number of marks* |
|---|---|---|
| Section A: | One compulsory scenario-based question | 50 |
| Section B: | Choice of 2 from 4 questions (25 marks each) | 50 |
|  |  | —— |
|  |  | 100 |
| Total time allowed: 3 hours |  | —— |

---

## Aim

To develop knowledge and understanding of financial management methods for analysing the benefits of various sources of finance and capital investment opportunities, and of the application of management accounting techniques for business planning and control.

## Objectives

On completion of this paper candidates should be able to:

- explain the role and purpose of financial management

- evaluate the overall management of working capital

- evaluate appropriate sources of finance for particular situations

- appraise capital investment through the use of appropriate methods

- identify and discuss appropriate costing systems and techniques

- prepare budgets and use them to control and evaluate organisational performance

- understand the basic principles of performance management

- critically assess the tools and techniques of financial management and control

- demonstrate the knowledge, understanding, skills, abilities and critical evaluation expected in Part 2.

# Position of the paper in the overall syllabus

Students must have a thorough knowledge of the material in Paper 1.2 Financial Information for Management and a good knowledge of other Part 1 papers.

Financial Management and Control is integrated with other Part 2 papers by providing a management decision framework within which some aspects of the Part 2 syllabus are developed. The effects of capital allowances and corporation tax on capital investment appraisal are examinable. Knowledge gained from Paper 2.3 Business Taxation (UK) will be useful in this respect.

Financial Management and Control is developed in Part 3 into advanced study of Performance Management (Paper 3.3) and Strategic Financial Management (Paper 3.7).

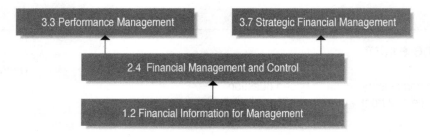

# Syllabus content

## 1 Financial management objectives

(a) The nature, purpose and scope of financial management.

(b) The relationship between financial management, management accounting and financial accounting.

(c) The relationship of financial objectives and organisational strategy.

(d) Problems of multiple stakeholders in financial management and the consequent multiple objectives.

(e) Objectives (financial and otherwise) in not-for-profit organisations.

## 2 The financial management environment

(a) Financial intermediation and credit creation.

(b) Money and capital markets

    (i) Domestic and international

    (ii) Stock markets (both major markets and small firm markets).

(c) The Efficient Markets Hypothesis.

(d) Rates of interest and yield curves.

(e) The impact of fiscal and monetary policy on business.

(f) Regulation of business (for example, pricing restrictions, green policies and corporate governance).

## 3 Management of working capital

(a) The nature and scope of working capital management.

(b) Funding requirements for working capital.

(c) Working capital needs of different types of business.

(d) The relationship of working capital management to business solvency.

(e) Management of stock, debtors, short term funds, cash, overdrafts and creditors.

(f) Techniques of working capital management (including ratio analysis, EOQ, JIT, credit evaluation, terms of credit, cash discounts, factoring and invoice discounting, debtors cycles, efficient short-term fund investing, cash forecasting and budgets, Miller-Orr model, basic foreign exchange methods, probabilities and risk assessment, terms of trade with creditors).

## 4 Sources of finance

(a) Sources and relative costs (including issue costs) of various types of finance and their suitability to different circumstances and organisations (large and small, listed and unlisted) including:

(i) access to funds and the nature of business risk

(ii) the nature and importance of internally generated funds

(iii) capital markets (types of share capital, new issues, rights issues, loan capital, convertibles, warrants)

(iv) the effect of dividend policy on financing needs

(v) bank finance (short, medium and long term, including leasing)

(vi) trade credit

(vii) government sources: grants, regional and national aid schemes and tax incentives

(viii) problems of small company financing (collateral, maturity funding gap, risk)

(ix) problems of companies with low initial earnings (R&D, Internet, and other high-technology businesses)

(x) venture capital and financial sources particularly suited to the small company

(xi) international money and capital markets, including an introduction to international banking and the finance of foreign trade.

(b) Requirements of finance (for what purpose, how much and for how long) in relation to business operational and strategic objectives.

(c) The importance of the choice of capital structure: equity versus debt and basic analysis of the term profile of funds.

(d) Financial gearing and other key financial ratios and analysis of their significance to the organisation.

(e) Appropriate sources of finance, taking into account:

(i) cost of finance

(ii) timing of cash payments

(iii) business risk and financial risk

(iv) effect on gearing and other ratios

(v) effect on company's existing investors.

## 5 Capital investment appraisal

(a) Discounted cash flow techniques

(i) simple and compound interest

(ii) net present value

(iii) annuities and perpetuities

(iv) internal rate of return

(v) future value

(vi) nominal interest

(b) Appraisal of domestic capital investment opportunities for profit making and not-for-profit organisations through the use of appropriate methods and techniques

(i) the risk / return relationship

(ii) return on capital employed

(iii) payback

(iv) internal rate of return

(v) net present value

(vi) single and multi-period capital rationing

(vii) lease or buy decisions

(viii) asset replacement using equivalent annual cost. Including (in categories (i)-(viii)) the effects of taxation, inflation, risk and uncertainty (probabilities, sensitivity analysis, simulation).

## 6 Costing systems and techniques

(a) The purpose of costing as an aid to planning, monitoring and control of business activity.

(b) Different approaches to costing.

(c) Costing information requirements and limitations in not-for-profit organisations.

(d) Behavioural implications of different costing approaches including performance evaluation.

(e) Implications of costing approaches for profit reporting, the pricing of products and internal activities/ services.

## 7 Standard costing and variance analysis

(a) Standard costing

(i) determination of standards

(ii) identification and calculation of sales variances (including quantity and mix), cost variances (including mix and yield); absorption and marginal approaches

(iii) significance and relevance of variances

(iv)   operating statements

(v)   interpretation and relevance of variance calculations to business performance.

(b)   Planning and operational variances.

(c)   Behavioural implications of standard costing and variance reporting.

## 8   Budgeting and budgetary control

(a)   Objectives of budgetary planning and control systems including aspects of behavioural implications.

(b)   Evaluation of budgetary systems such as fixed and flexible, zero based and incremental, periodic, continuous and activity based.

(c)   Development, implementation and coordination of budgeting systems: functional, subsidiary and master/ principal budgets (including cash budgeting); budget review.

(d)   Calculation and cause of variances as aids to controlling performance.

(e)   Quantitative aids to budgeting and the concepts of correlation, basic time series analysis (seasonality) and forecasting; use of computer based models.

(f)   Behavioural implications of budgeting and budgetary control.

## 9   Performance measurement

(a)   Measurement of productivity, activity, profitability and quality of service

(b)   Relationship of measure to type of entity and range of measures, both monetary and non-monetary

(c)   Indices to allow for price and performance changes through time

(d)   Evaluating performance against objectives and plans, and identifying areas of concern from the information produced

(e)   The impact of cost centres, revenue centres, profit centres and investment centres on management appraisal

(f)   Difference between business performance and management performance

(g)   Benchmarking

# Excluded topics

The following topics are specifically excluded from the syllabus:

- Calculations involving the derivation of cost of capital in discounting problems. Candidates will always be supplied with an appropriate discount rate.

- Calculations relating to Modigliani and Miller propositions.

# Additional information

Present value and annuity tables will be provided in the exam.

# ANALYSIS OF PAST PAPERS

## June 2003

### Section A

1    NPV calculation with writing down allowances and sensitivity analysis. Ratio analysis. Method of financing proposed investment.

### Section B

2    Sales forecasting: trend line and seasonal variations. Top-down and bottom-up budgeting.

3    Early settlement discount (evaluation). Financing working capital.

4    Stock market efficient. Value for money (VFM) and maximisation of shareholder wealth.

5    Limiting factor analysis. Make-or-buy decision. Limitations of marginal costing for decision-making.

## December 2003

### Section A

1    Working capital management: overtrading, using a factor. Lease or buy decision.

### Section B

2    Budgeting. Production and cash budgets. Periodic and continuous budgets. Budgetary slack.

3    Capital rationing.

4    Problems of monopoly. Raising long-term finance.

5    Variance analysis, including materials mix and yield variances.

## June 2004

### Section A

1    NPV, IRR and accounting rate of return, with inflation and taxation (including capital allowances) and the use of investment appraisal methods. Assessing risk and uncertainty for investment decision-making. Sources of finance for a machine.

### Section B

2    Factors affecting loan interest rates. Long-term and short-term funding to finance working capital. Cash operating cycle and working capital investment.

3    Activity-based costing and its uses

4    Financing an expansion with debt capital or equity capital: financial and operational gearing, interest cover, earnings per share; business risk and financial risk

5    Planning and operational variances. Factors in a decision whether or not to investigate a variance.

## December 2004

### Section A

1    Planning and operational variances.

DCF: equivalent annual cost, investment appraisal with taxation and inflation.

Conflicting corporate objectives.

Lifecycle costing and target costing.

### Section B

2    Flexible budget. Variance analysis. Purpose of budgeting.

3    Rights issue. Effect of a rights issue on EPS, shareholder wealth, gearing and interest cover.

4    Activity-based costing. Financial and non-financial performance measures for organisational and management performance.

5    Risk and uncertainty in investment appraisal: payback, sensitivity analysis, expected NPV.

## June 2005

### Section A

1    A wide-ranging question covering NPV with inflation and taxation (including capital allowances), limitations of the method used, evaluation of financing method, ABC, forward contracts and bills of exchange.

### Section B

2    Applying costing methods to not-for-profit organisations, including ZBB. Using ABB in a manufacturing business.

3    Variances, including sales mix. Standard costing.

4    Performance appraisal of a quoted company, total shareholder return and directors' remuneration.

5    Inventory management, including EOQ. Evaluation of a discount.

## December 2005

### Section A

1    (a) Investment appraisal calculation – NPV

(b) Investment appraisal decision – discussion aspects

(c) Additional NPV calculations

(d) Analysis of current financial position and likelihood of raising a bank loan

(e) Variances – calculation and comment

### Section B

2    Discussion question on divisional performance appraisal

3    Activity based costing – calculations and discussion

4    Finance – buy v lease and calculations for a bank loan

5    Cash management

## *Note:*

The syllabus for paper 2.4 changed from June 2004. Some additional topics were introduced to the syllabus, but it is still not yet clear how they might be examined. New topics include performance measurement (including index numbers).

It seems possible that some questions on relevant costing may continue to appear. This has been the case in the past, when decision-making had only a small mention in the syllabus. Some questions on this topic have therefore been included here, although it is likely that relevant costing will be examined within the context of investment appraisal and DCF analysis.

# REVISION GUIDANCE

## Planning your revision

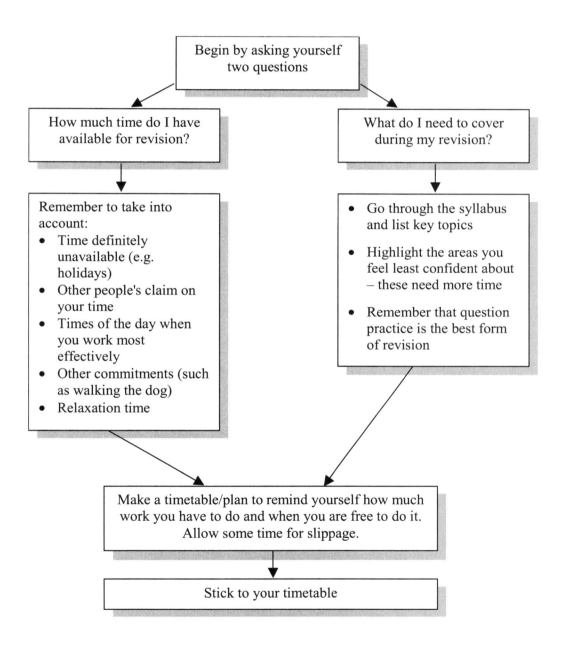

Begin by asking yourself two questions

How much time do I have available for revision?

What do I need to cover during my revision?

Remember to take into account:
- Time definitely unavailable (e.g. holidays)
- Other people's claim on your time
- Times of the day when you work most effectively
- Other commitments (such as walking the dog)
- Relaxation time

- Go through the syllabus and list key topics
- Highlight the areas you feel least confident about – these need more time
- Remember that question practice is the best form of revision

Make a timetable/plan to remind yourself how much work you have to do and when you are free to do it. Allow some time for slippage.

Stick to your timetable

# Revision techniques

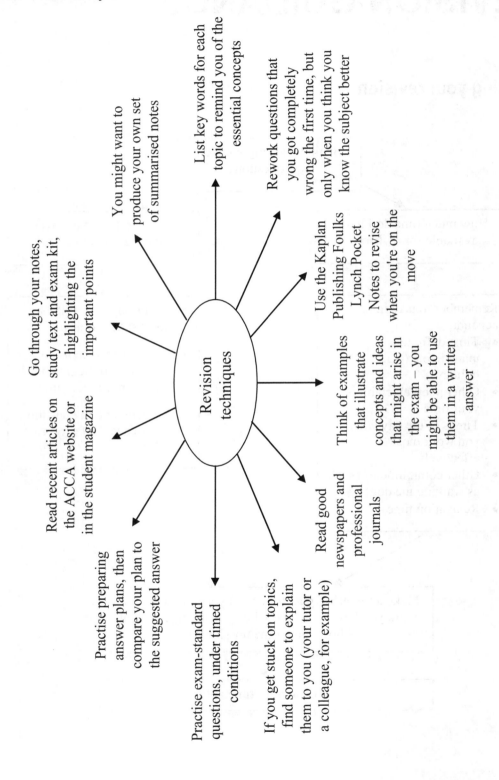

List key words for each topic to remind you of the essential concepts

Rework questions that you got completely wrong the first time, but only when you think you know the subject better

You might want to produce your own set of summarised notes

Use the Kaplan Publishing Foulks Lynch Pocket Notes to revise when you're on the move

Go through your notes, study text and exam kit, highlighting the important points

Revision techniques

Think of examples that illustrate concepts and ideas that might arise in the exam – you might be able to use them in a written answer

Read recent articles on the ACCA website or in the student magazine

Read good newspapers and professional journals

Practise preparing answer plans, then compare your plan to the suggested answer

Practise exam-standard questions, under timed conditions

If you get stuck on topics, find someone to explain them to you (your tutor or a colleague, for example)

# EXAM TECHNIQUES

- You might want to spend the first few minutes of the exam **reading the paper**.

- Where you have a **choice of question**, decide which questions you will do.

- Unless you know exactly how to answer the question, spend some time **planning** your answer.

- **Divide the time** you spend on questions in proportion to the marks on offer. One suggestion is to allocate 1½ minutes to each mark available, so a 10 mark question should be completed in 15 minutes.

- Spend the last **five minutes** reading through your answers and **making any additions or corrections**.

- **Essay questions**: Your essay should have a clear structure. It should contain a brief introduction, a main section and a conclusion. Be concise. It is better to write a little about a lot of different points than a great deal about one or two points.

- If you **get completely stuck** with a question, leave space in your answer book and **return to it later.**

- Stick to the question and **tailor your answer** to what you are asked. Pay particular attention to the verbs in the question.

- If you do not understand what a question is asking, **state your assumptions**. Even if you do not answer in precisely the way the examiner hoped, you should be given some credit, if your assumptions are reasonable.

- You should do everything you can to make things easy for the marker. The marker will find it easier to identify the points you have made if your **answers are legible**.

- **Computations**: It is essential to include all your workings in your answers. Many computational questions require the use of a standard format: company profit and loss account, balance sheet and cash flow statement for example. Be sure you know these formats thoroughly before the exam and use the layouts that you see in the answers given in this book and in model answers.

- **Case studies**: To write a good case study, first identify the area in which there is a problem, outline the main principles/theories you are going to use to answer the question, and then apply the principles/theories to the case.

- **Reports, memos and other documents**: Some questions ask you to present your answer in the form of a report or a memo or other document. So use the correct format - there could be easy marks to gain here.

# MATHEMATICAL TABLES

## Formulae sheet

**Economic order quantity** $= \sqrt{\dfrac{2C_oD}{C_H}}$

**Discount factor** $= \dfrac{1}{(1 + r)^n}$

### Annuities

Future value $= A\left(\dfrac{(1 + r)^n - 1}{r}\right)$

Present value $= \dfrac{A}{r}\left(1 - \dfrac{1}{(1 + r)^n}\right)$

### Dividend growth model

$$P_0 = \left(\dfrac{D_0(1 + g)}{(r - g)}\right)$$

### Miller Orr Model

Return point = Lower limit $+ \left(\frac{1}{3} \times \text{spread}\right)$

$$\text{Spread} = 3\left[\dfrac{\frac{3}{4} \times \text{transaction cost} \times \text{variance of cashflows}}{\text{interest rate}}\right]^{\frac{1}{3}}$$

### Linear regression

$y = a + bx$

$$b = \dfrac{n\sum xy - \sum x\sum y}{n\sum x^2 - \left(\sum x\right)^2}$$

$$a = \dfrac{\sum y}{n} - \dfrac{b\sum x}{n}$$

$$r = \dfrac{n\sum xy - \sum x\sum y}{\sqrt{\left(n\sum x^2 - \left(\sum x\right)^2\right)\left(n\sum y^2 - \left(\sum y\right)^2\right)}}$$

### Indices

Laspeyre price index $= \dfrac{\sum(p_1 \times q_0)}{\sum(p_0 \times q_0)} \times 100$

Paasche price index $= \dfrac{\sum(p_1 \times q_1)}{\sum(p_0 \times q_1)} \times 100$

Laspeyre quantity index $= \dfrac{\sum(q_1 \times p_0)}{\sum(q_0 \times p_0)} \times 100$

Paasche quantity index $= \dfrac{\sum(q_1 \times p_1)}{\sum(q_0 \times p_1)} \times 100$

KAPLAN PUBLISHING

# Present value table

Present value of 1 i.e. $(1 + r)^{-n}$

Where    r = discount rate

           n = number of periods until payment

| Periods | | | | | *Discount rate (r)* | | | | | | |
|---|---|---|---|---|---|---|---|---|---|---|---|
| (n) | 1% | 2% | 3% | 4% | 5% | 6% | 7% | 8% | 9% | 10% | |
| 1 | 0.990 | 0.980 | 0.971 | 0.962 | 0.952 | 0.943 | 0.935 | 0.926 | 0.917 | 0.909 | 1 |
| 2 | 0.980 | 0.961 | 0.943 | 0.925 | 0.907 | 0.890 | 0.873 | 0.857 | 0.842 | 0.826 | 2 |
| 3 | 0.971 | 0.942 | 0.915 | 0.889 | 0.864 | 0.840 | 0.816 | 0.794 | 0.772 | 0.751 | 3 |
| 4 | 0.961 | 0.924 | 0.888 | 0.855 | 0.823 | 0.792 | 0.763 | 0.735 | 0.708 | 0.683 | 4 |
| 5 | 0.951 | 0.906 | 0.863 | 0.822 | 0.784 | 0.747 | 0.713 | 0.681 | 0.650 | 0.621 | 5 |
| 6 | 0.942 | 0.888 | 0.837 | 0.790 | 0.746 | 0.705 | 0.666 | 0.630 | 0.596 | 0.564 | 6 |
| 7 | 0.933 | 0.871 | 0.813 | 0.760 | 0.711 | 0.665 | 0.623 | 0.583 | 0.547 | 0.513 | 7 |
| 8 | 0.923 | 0.853 | 0.789 | 0.731 | 0.677 | 0.627 | 0.582 | 0.540 | 0.502 | 0.467 | 8 |
| 9 | 0.914 | 0.837 | 0.766 | 0.703 | 0.645 | 0.592 | 0.544 | 0.500 | 0.460 | 0.424 | 9 |
| 10 | 0.905 | 0.820 | 0.744 | 0.676 | 0.614 | 0.558 | 0.508 | 0.463 | 0.422 | 0.386 | 10 |
| 11 | 0.896 | 0.804 | 0.722 | 0.650 | 0.585 | 0.527 | 0.475 | 0.429 | 0.388 | 0.350 | 11 |
| 12 | 0.887 | 0.788 | 0.701 | 0.625 | 0.557 | 0.497 | 0.444 | 0.397 | 0.356 | 0.319 | 12 |
| 13 | 0.879 | 0.773 | 0.681 | 0.601 | 0.530 | 0.469 | 0.415 | 0.368 | 0.326 | 0.290 | 13 |
| 14 | 0.870 | 0.758 | 0.661 | 0.577 | 0.505 | 0.442 | 0.388 | 0.340 | 0.299 | 0.263 | 14 |
| 15 | 0.861 | 0.743 | 0.642 | 0.555 | 0.481 | 0.417 | 0.362 | 0.315 | 0.275 | 0.239 | 15 |
| (n) | 11% | 12% | 13% | 14% | 15% | 16% | 17% | 18% | 19% | 20% | |
| 1 | 0.901 | 0.893 | 0.885 | 0.877 | 0.870 | 0.862 | 0.855 | 0.847 | 0.840 | 0.833 | 1 |
| 2 | 0.812 | 0.797 | 0.783 | 0.769 | 0.756 | 0.743 | 0.731 | 0.718 | 0.706 | 0.694 | 2 |
| 3 | 0.731 | 0.712 | 0.693 | 0.675 | 0.658 | 0.641 | 0.624 | 0.609 | 0.593 | 0.579 | 3 |
| 4 | 0.659 | 0.636 | 0.613 | 0.592 | 0.572 | 0.552 | 0.534 | 0.516 | 0.499 | 0.482 | 4 |
| 5 | 0.593 | 0.567 | 0.543 | 0.519 | 0.497 | 0.476 | 0.456 | 0.437 | 0.419 | 0.402 | 5 |
| 6 | 0.535 | 0.507 | 0.480 | 0.456 | 0.432 | 0.410 | 0.390 | 0.370 | 0.352 | 0.335 | 6 |
| 7 | 0.482 | 0.452 | 0.425 | 0.400 | 0.376 | 0.354 | 0.333 | 0.314 | 0.296 | 0.279 | 7 |
| 8 | 0.434 | 0.404 | 0.376 | 0.351 | 0.327 | 0.305 | 0.285 | 0.266 | 0.249 | 0.233 | 8 |
| 9 | 0.391 | 0.361 | 0.333 | 0.308 | 0.284 | 0.263 | 0.243 | 0.225 | 0.209 | 0.194 | 9 |
| 10 | 0.352 | 0.322 | 0.295 | 0.270 | 0.247 | 0.227 | 0.208 | 0.191 | 0.176 | 0.162 | 10 |
| 11 | 0.317 | 0.287 | 0.261 | 0.237 | 0.215 | 0.195 | 0.178 | 0.162 | 0.148 | 0.135 | 11 |
| 12 | 0.286 | 0.257 | 0.231 | 0.208 | 0.187 | 0.168 | 0.152 | 0.137 | 0.124 | 0.112 | 12 |
| 13 | 0.258 | 0.229 | 0.204 | 0.182 | 0.163 | 0.145 | 0.130 | 0.116 | 0.104 | 0.093 | 13 |
| 14 | 0.232 | 0.205 | 0.181 | 0.160 | 0.141 | 0.125 | 0.111 | 0.099 | 0.088 | 0.078 | 14 |
| 15 | 0.209 | 0.183 | 0.160 | 0.140 | 0.123 | 0.108 | 0.095 | 0.084 | 0.074 | 0.065 | 15 |

# Annuity table

Present value of an annuity of 1 i.e. $\dfrac{1-(1+r)^{-n}}{r}$

Where        r = discount rate

                n = number of periods

| Periods (n) | 1% | 2% | 3% | 4% | 5% | 6% | 7% | 8% | 9% | 10% | |
|---|---|---|---|---|---|---|---|---|---|---|---|
| 1 | 0.990 | 0.980 | 0.971 | 0.962 | 0.952 | 0.943 | 0.935 | 0.926 | 0.917 | 0.909 | 1 |
| 2 | 1.970 | 1.942 | 1.913 | 1.886 | 1.859 | 1.833 | 1.808 | 1.783 | 1.759 | 1.736 | 2 |
| 3 | 2.941 | 2.884 | 20829 | 2.775 | 2.723 | 2.673 | 2.624 | 2.577 | 2.531 | 2.487 | 3 |
| 4 | 3.902 | 3.808 | 3.717 | 3.630 | 3.546 | 3.465 | 3.387 | 3.312 | 3.240 | 3.170 | 4 |
| 5 | 4.853 | 4.713 | 4.580 | 4.452 | 4.329 | 4.212 | 4.100 | 3.993 | 3.890 | 3.791 | 5 |
| 6 | 5.795 | 5.601 | 5.417 | 5.242 | 5.076 | 4.917 | 4.767 | 4.623 | 4.486 | 4.355 | 6 |
| 7 | 6.728 | 6.472 | 6.230 | 6.002 | 5.786 | 5.582 | 5.389 | 5.206 | 5.033 | 4.868 | 7 |
| 8 | 7.652 | 7.325 | 7.020 | 6.733 | 6.463 | 6.210 | 5.971 | 5.747 | 5.535 | 5.335 | 8 |
| 9 | 8.566 | 8.162 | 7.786 | 7.435 | 7.108 | 6.802 | 6.515 | 6.247 | 5.995 | 5.759 | 9 |
| 10 | 9.471 | 8.983 | 8.530 | 8.111 | 7.722 | 7.360 | 7.024 | 6.710 | 6.418 | 6.145 | 10 |
| 11 | 10.37 | 9.787 | 9.253 | 8.760 | 8.306 | 7.887 | 7.499 | 7.139 | 6.805 | 6.495 | 11 |
| 12 | 11.26 | 10.58 | 9.954 | 9.385 | 8.863 | 8.384 | 7.943 | 7.536 | 7.161 | 6.814 | 12 |
| 13 | 12.13 | 11.35 | 10.63 | 9.986 | 9.394 | 8.853 | 8.358 | 7.904 | 7.487 | 7.103 | 13 |
| 14 | 13.00 | 12.11 | 11.30 | 10.56 | 9.899 | 9.295 | 8.745 | 8.244 | 7.786 | 7.367 | 14 |
| 15 | 13.87 | 12.85 | 11.94 | 11.12 | 10.38 | 9.712 | 9.108 | 8.559 | 8.061 | 7.606 | 15 |

| (n) | 11% | 12% | 13% | 14% | 15% | 16% | 17% | 18% | 19% | 20% | |
|---|---|---|---|---|---|---|---|---|---|---|---|
| 1 | 0.901 | 0.893 | 0.885 | 0.877 | 0.870 | 0.862 | 0.855 | 0.847 | 0.840 | 0.833 | 1 |
| 2 | 1.713 | 1.690 | 1.668 | 1.647 | 1.626 | 1.605 | 1.585 | 1.566 | 1.547 | 1.528 | 2 |
| 3 | 2.444 | 2.402 | 2.361 | 2.322 | 2.283 | 2.246 | 2.210 | 2.174 | 2.140 | 2.106 | 3 |
| 4 | 3.102 | 3.037 | 2.974 | 2.914 | 2.855 | 2.798 | 2.743 | 2.690 | 2.639 | 2.589 | 4 |
| 5 | 3.696 | 3.605 | 3.517 | 3.433 | 3.352 | 3.274 | 3.199 | 3.127 | 3.058 | 2.991 | 5 |
| 6 | 4.231 | 4.111 | 3.998 | 3.889 | 3.784 | 3.685 | 3.589 | 3.498 | 3.410 | 3.326 | 6 |
| 7 | 4.712 | 4.564 | 4.423 | 4.288 | 4.160 | 4.039 | 3.922 | 3.812 | 3.706 | 3.605 | 7 |
| 8 | 5.146 | 4.968 | 4.799 | 4.639 | 4.487 | 4.344 | 4.207 | 4.078 | 3.954 | 3.837 | 8 |
| 9 | 5.537 | 5.328 | 5.132 | 4.946 | 4.772 | 4.607 | 4.451 | 4.303 | 4.163 | 4.031 | 9 |
| 10 | 5.889 | 5.650 | 5.426 | 5.216 | 5.019 | 4.833 | 4.659 | 4.494 | 4.339 | 4.192 | 10 |
| 11 | 6.207 | 5.938 | 5.687 | 5.453 | 5.234 | 5.029 | 4.836 | 4.656 | 4.486 | 4.327 | 11 |
| 12 | 6.492 | 6.194 | 5.918 | 5.660 | 5.421 | 5.197 | 4.988 | 4.793 | 4.611 | 4.439 | 12 |
| 13 | 6.750 | 6.424 | 6.122 | 5.842 | 5.583 | 5.342 | 5.118 | 4.910 | 4.715 | 4.533 | 13 |
| 14 | 6.982 | 6.628 | 6.302 | 6.002 | 5.724 | 5.468 | 5.229 | 5.008 | 4.802 | 4.611 | 14 |
| 15 | 7.191 | 6.811 | 6.462 | 6.142 | 5.847 | 5.575 | 5.324 | 5.092 | 4.876 | 4.675 | 15 |

KAPLAN PUBLISHING

# Section 1

# PRACTICE QUESTIONS

## FINANCIAL MANAGEMENT OBJECTIVES AND ENVIRONMENT

### 1    TAGNA

Tagna is a medium-sized company that manufactures luxury goods for several well-known chain stores. In real terms, the company has experienced only a small growth in turnover in recent years, but it has managed to maintain a constant, if low, level of reported profits by careful control of costs. It has paid a constant nominal (money terms) dividend for several years and its managing director has publicly stated that the primary objective of the company is to increase the wealth of shareholders. Tagna is financed as follows:

|  | £m |
|---|---|
| Overdraft | 1.0 |
| 10 year fixed-interest bank loan | 2.0 |
| Share capital and reserves | 4.5 |
|  | 7.5 |

Tagna has the agreement of its existing shareholders to make a new issue of shares on the stock market but has been informed by its bank that current circumstances are unsuitable. The bank has stated that if new shares were to be issued now they would be significantly under-priced by the stock market, causing Tagna to issue many more shares than necessary in order to raise the amount of finance it requires. The bank recommends that the company waits for at least six months before issuing new shares, by which time it expects the stock market to have become strong-form efficient.

The financial press has reported that it expects the Central Bank to make a substantial increase in interest rate in the near future in response to rapidly increasing consumer demand and a sharp rise in inflation. The financial press has also reported that the rapid increase in consumer demand has been associated with an increase in consumer credit to record levels.

**Required:**

(a) Discuss the meaning and significance of the different forms of market efficiency (weak, semi-strong and strong) and comment on the recommendation of the bank that Tagna waits for six months before issuing new shares on the stock market.   **(9 marks)**

(b) On the assumption that the Central Bank makes a substantial interest rate increase, discuss the possible consequences for Tagna in the following areas:

    (i)    sales

    (ii)   operating costs, and

    (iii)  earnings (profit after tax).   **(10 marks)**

(c)    Explain and compare the public sector objective of 'value for money' and the private sector objective of 'maximisation of shareholder wealth'.    **(6 marks)**

**(Total: 25 marks)**

## 2    STAKEHOLDERS

Private sector companies have multiple stakeholders who are likely to have divergent interests.

**Required:**

(a)    Identify five stakeholder groups and briefly discuss their financial and other objectives.    **(12 marks)**

(b)    Examine the extent to which good corporate governance procedures can help manage the problems arising from the divergent interests of multiple stakeholder groups in private sector companies in the UK.    **(13 marks)**

**(Total: 25 marks)**

## 3    MANAGEMENT ACCOUNTING

(a)    Some writers have suggested that the purposes of management accounting systems are costing and management control.

**Required:**

Briefly discuss whether this satisfactorily describes the purposes of management accounting systems.    **(6 marks)**

(b)    A company, which is engaged in retailing food and household products, has stores in many towns.  These stores, whilst managed locally, report to a Head Office and are served from a few strategically located warehouses by the company's own transport fleet.

**Required:**

Discuss the management accounting information which is likely to be provided in such a company.    **(14 marks)**

**(Total: 20 marks)**

## 4    NEWS FOR YOU

News For You operate a chain of newsagents and confectioner's shops in the south of England, and are considering the possibility of expanding their business across a wider geographical area. The business was started in 20X2 and annual turnover grew to £10 million by the end of 20X6. Between 20X6 and 20X9 turnover grew at an average rate of 2% per year.

The business still remains under family control, but the high cost of expansion via the purchase or building of new outlets would mean that the family would need to raise at least £2 million in equity or debt finance. One of the possible risks of expansion lies in the fact that both tobacco and newspaper sales are falling. New income is being generated by expanding the product range stocked by the stores, to include basic foodstuffs such as bread and milk. News For You purchases all of its products from a large wholesale distributor which is convenient, but the wholesale prices leave News For You with a relatively small gross margin. The key to profit growth for News For You lies in the ability to generate sales growth, but the company recognises that it faces stiff competition from large food retailers in respect of the prices that it charges for several of its products.

## 9    BLIN

Blin is a company listed on a European stock exchange, with a market capitalisation of €6m, which manufactures household cleaning chemicals. The company has expanded sales quite significantly over the last year and has been following an aggressive approach to working capital financing. As a result, Blin has come to rely heavily on overdraft finance for its short-term needs. On the advice of its finance director, the company intends to take out a long-term bank loan, part of which would be used to repay its overdraft.

**Required:**

(a)    Discuss the factors that will influence the rate of interest charged on the new bank loan, making reference in your answer to the yield curve.          **(9 marks)**

(b)    Explain and discuss the approaches that Blin could adopt regarding the relative proportions of long- and short-term finance to meet its working capital needs, and comment on the proposed repayment of the overdraft.          **(9 marks)**

(c)    Explain the meaning of the term 'cash operating cycle' and discuss its significance in determining the level of investment in working capital. Your answer should refer to the working capital needs of different business sectors.          **(7 marks)**

**(Total: 25 marks)**

## 10    VELM PLC

Velm plc sells stationery and office supplies on a wholesale basis and has an annual turnover of £4,000,000. The company employs four people in its sales ledger and credit control department at an annual salary of £12,000 each. All sales are on 40 days' credit with no discount for early payment. Bad debts represent 3% of turnover and Velm plc pays annual interest of 9% on its overdraft. The most recent accounts of the company offer the following financial information:

**Velm plc: Balance Sheet as at 31 December 20X2**

|  | £000 | £000 | £000 |
|---|---|---|---|
| Fixed assets |  |  | 17,500 |
| Current assets |  |  |  |
| Stock of goods for resale |  | 900 |  |
| Debtors |  | 550 |  |
| Cash |  | 120 |  |
|  |  | 1,570 |  |
| Creditors: amounts falling due within one year |  |  |  |
| Trade creditors | 330 |  |  |
| Overdraft | 1,200 |  |  |
|  |  | 1,530 |  |
|  |  |  | 40 |
|  |  |  | 17,540 |
| Creditors: amounts falling due after more than one year |  |  |  |
| 12% Debenture due 20X9 |  |  | 2,400 |
|  |  |  | 15,140 |
| Ordinary shares |  |  | 3,500 |
| Reserves |  |  | 11,640 |
|  |  |  | 15,140 |

Velm plc is considering offering a discount of 1% to customers paying within 14 days, which it believes will reduce bad debts to 2.4% of turnover. The company also expects that offering a discount for early payment will reduce the average credit period taken by its customers to 26 days. The consequent reduction in the time spent chasing customers where payments are overdue will allow one member of the credit control team to take early retirement. Two -thirds of customers are expected to take advantage of the discount.

**Required:**

(a)     Using the information provided, determine whether a discount for early payment of one per cent will lead to an increase in profitability for Velm plc.          **(5 marks)**

(b)     Discuss the relative merits of short-term and long-term debt sources for the financing of working capital.          **(6 marks)**

(c)     Discuss the different policies that may be adopted by a company towards the financing of working capital needs and indicate which policy has been adopted by Velm plc.
          **(7 marks)**

(d)     Outline the advantages to a company of taking steps to improve its working capital management, giving examples of steps that might be taken.          **(7 marks)**

**(Total: 25 marks)**

## 11    SPECIAL GIFT SUPPLIES PLC

Special Gift Supplies plc is a wholesale distributor of a variety of imported goods to a range of retail outlets. The company specialises in supplying ornaments, small works of art, high value furnishings (rugs, etc) and other items that the chief buyer for the company feels would have a market in the UK. In seeking to improve working capital management, the financial controller has gathered the following information.

|  | *Months* |
| --- | --- |
| Average period for which items are held in stock | 3.5 |
| Average debtors collection period | 2.5 |
| Average creditors payment period | 2.0 |

**Required:**

(a)     Calculate Special Gift Supplies' funding requirements for working capital measured in terms of months.          **(2 marks)**

(b)     In looking to reduce the working capital funding requirement, the financial controller of Special Gift Supplies is considering factoring credit sales. The company's annual turnover is £2.5m of which 90% are credit sales. Bad debts are typically 3% of credit sales. The offer from the factor is conditional on the following:

   (1)     The factor will take over the sales ledger of Special Gift Supplies completely.

   (2)     80% of the value of credit sales will be advanced immediately (as soon as sales are made to the customer) to Special Gift Supplies, the remaining 20% will be paid to the company one month later. The factor charges 15% per annum on credit sales for advancing funds in the manner suggested. The factor is normally able to reduce the debtors' collection period to one month.

   (3)     The factor offers a 'no recourse' facility whereby they take on the responsibility for dealing with bad debts. The factor is normally able to reduce bad debts to 2% of credit sales.

   (4)     A charge for factoring services of 4% of credit sales will be made.

   (5)     A one-off payment of £25,000 is payable to the factor.

The salary of the Sales Ledger Administrator (£12,500) would be saved under the proposals and overhead costs of the credit control department, amounting to £2,000 per annum, would have to be reallocated. Special Gift Supplies' cost of overdraft finance is 12% per annum. Special Gift Supplies pays its sales force on a commission only basis. The cost of this is 5% of credit sales and is payable immediately the sales are made. There is no intention to alter this arrangement under the factoring proposals.

**Required:**

Evaluate the proposal to factor the sales ledger by comparing Special Gift Supplies' existing debtor collection costs with those that would result from using the factor (assuming that the factor can reduce the debtors' collection period to one month).

**(8 marks)**

(c) As an advisor to Special Gift Supplies plc, write a report to the financial controller that outlines:

(i) how a credit control department might function

(ii) the benefits of factoring and

(iii) how the financing of working capital can be arranged in terms of short and long term sources of finance.

In particular, make reference to: the financing of working capital or net current assets when short term sources of finances are exhausted; and the distinction between fluctuating and permanent current assets. **(15 marks)**

**(Total: 25 marks)**

## 12 TNG

TNG Co expects annual demand for product X to be 255,380 units. Product X has a selling price of £19 per unit and is purchased for £11 per unit from a supplier, MKR Co. TNG places an order for 50,000 units of product X at regular intervals throughout the year. Because the demand for product X is to some degree uncertain, TNG maintains a safety (buffer) stock of product X which is sufficient to meet demand for 28 working days. The cost of placing an order is £25 and the storage cost for Product X is 10 pence per unit per year.

TNG normally pays trade suppliers after 60 days but MKR has offered a discount of 1% for cash settlement within 20 days.

TNG Co has a short-term cost of debt of 8% and uses a working year consisting of 365 days.

**Required:**

(a) Calculate the annual cost of the current ordering policy. Ignore financing costs in this part of the question. **(4 marks)**

(b) Calculate the annual saving if the economic order quantity model is used to determine an optimal ordering policy. Ignore financing costs in this part of the question.

**(5 marks)**

(c) Determine whether the discount offered by the supplier is financially acceptable to TNG Co. **(4 marks)**

(d) Critically discuss the limitations of the economic order quantity model as a way of managing stock. **(4 marks)**

(e) Discuss the advantages and disadvantages of using just-in-time stock management methods. **(8 marks)**

**(Total: 25 marks)**

# SOURCES OF FINANCE

## 13 ASSOCIATED INTERNATIONAL SUPPLIES LTD

The following are summary financial statements for Associated International Supplies Ltd.

|  | 20X4 £000 | 20X9 £000 |
|---|---|---|
| Fixed assets | 115 | 410 |
| Current assets | 650 | 1,000 |
| Current liabilities | 513 | 982 |
| Long-term liabilities | 42 | 158 |
| Total | 210 | 270 |
| Capital and reserves | 210 | 270 |

|  | 20X4 £000 | 20X9 £000 |
|---|---|---|
| Sales | 1,200 | 3,010 |
| Cost of sales, expenses and interest | 1,102 | 2,860 |
| Profit before tax | 98 | 150 |
| Tax and distributions | 33 | 133 |
| Retained earnings | 65 | 17 |

*Notes:* Cost of sales was £530,000 for 20X4 and £1,330,000 for 20X9.

Debtors are 50% of current assets and trade creditors are 25% of current liabilities for both years.

**Required:**

(a) You are a consultant advising Associated International Supplies Ltd. Using suitable financial ratios, and paying particular attention to growth and liquidity, write a report on the significant changes faced by the company since 20X4. The report should also comment on the capacity of the company to continue trading, together with any other factors considered appropriate.

An appendix to the report should be used to outline your calculations. **(17 marks)**

(b) Explain and evaluate the sources of finance available to small businesses for fixed assets. **(8 marks)**

**(Total: 25 marks)**

## 14 ARWIN

Arwin plans to raise £5m in order to expand its existing chain of retail outlets. It can raise the finance by issuing 10% debentures redeemable in ten years' time, or by a rights issue at £4.00 per share. The current financial statements of Arwin are as follows.

| **Profit and loss account for the last year** | £000 |
|---|---|
| Sales | 50,000 |
| Cost of sales | 30,000 |
| Gross profit | 20,000 |
| Administration costs | 14,000 |
| Profit before interest and tax | 6,000 |
| Interest | 300 |

| | |
|---|---|
| Profit before tax | 5,700 |
| Taxation at 30% | 1,710 |
| Profit after tax | 3,990 |
| Dividends | 2,394 |
| Retained earnings | 1,596 |

| **Balance sheet** | £000 |
|---|---|
| Net fixed assets | 20,100 |
| Net current assets | 4,960 |
| 12% debentures (redeemable in six years) | 2,500 |
| | 22,560 |
| Ordinary shares, par value 25p | 2,500 |
| Retained profit | 20,060 |
| | 22,560 |

The expansion of business is expected to increase sales revenue by 12% in the first year. Variable cost of sales makes up 85% of cost of sales. Administration costs will increase by 5% due to new staff appointments. Arwin has a policy of paying out 60% of profit after tax as dividends and has no overdraft.

**Required:**

(a) For each financing proposal, prepare the forecast profit and loss account after one additional year of operation. **(5 marks)**

(b) Evaluate and comment on the effects of each financing proposal on the following:

(i) Financial gearing;

(ii) Operational gearing;

(iii) Interest cover;

(iv) Earnings per share. **(12 marks)**

(c) Discuss the dangers to a company of a high level of gearing, including in your answer an explanation of the following terms:

(i) Business risk;

(ii) Financial risk. **(8 marks)**

**(Total: 25 marks)**

## 15 JERONIMO PLC

Jeronimo plc currently has 5 million ordinary shares in issue, which have a market value of £1.60 each. The company wishes to raise finance for a major investment project by means of a rights issue, and is proposing to issue shares on the basis of 1 for 5 at a price of £1.30 each.

James Brown currently owns 10,000 shares in Jeronimo plc and is seeking advice on whether or not to take up the proposed rights.

**Required:**

(a) Explain the difference between a rights issue and a scrip issue. Your answer should include comment on the reasons why companies make such issues and the effect of the issues on private investors. **(6 marks)**

(b) Calculate:

    (i) the theoretical value of James Brown's shareholding if he takes up his rights

    (ii) the theoretical value of James Brown's rights if he chooses to sell them. **(4 marks)**

(c) Using only the information given below, and applying the dividend growth model formula, calculate the required return on equity for an investor in Jeronimo plc.

**Jeronimo plc:**

| | |
|---|---|
| Current share price: | £1.60 |
| Number of shares in issue: | 5 million |
| Current earnings: | £1.5 million |
| Dividend Paid | (Pence per share): |
| 20X5: | 8 |
| 20X6: | 9 |
| 20X7: | 11 |
| 20X8: | 11 |
| 20X9: | 12 |

The formula for the dividend growth model is as follows: $R = \left( \dfrac{D_1}{MV} + g \right) \times 100$

**(4 marks)**

Where R = Percentage required return on equity

(d) If the stock market is believed to operate with a strong level of efficiency, what effect might this have on the behaviour of the finance directors of publicly quoted companies? **(6 marks)**

**(Total: 20 marks)**

## 16 TECHFOOLS

Techfools.com has just issued convertible debentures with an 8% per annum coupon to the value of £5 million. The nominal value of the debentures is £100 and the issue price was £105. The conversion details are that 45 shares will be issued for every £100 convertible debentures held with a date for conversion in five years exactly. Redemption, should the debenture not be converted, will also take place in exactly five years. Debentures will be redeemed at £110 per £100 nominal convertibles held. It is widely expected that the share price of the company will be £4 in five years' time.

Assume an investor required return of 15%.

Ignore taxation in your answer.

**Required:**

(a) Briefly explain why convertibles might be an attractive source of finance for companies. **(4 marks)**

(b) (i) Estimate the current market value of the debentures, assuming conversion takes place, using net present value methods and assess if it is likely that conversion will take place. **(5 marks)**

    (ii)    Identify and briefly comment on a single major reservation you have with your evaluation in part b (i). **(2 marks)**

(c)    Explain why an issuing company seeks to maximise its conversion premium and why companies can issue convertibles with a high conversion premium. **(4 marks)**

(d)    Explain what is meant by the concept of intermediation (the role of a banking sector) and how such a process benefits both investors and companies. **(10 marks)**

**(Total: 25 marks)**

## 17   TIRWEN PLC

Tirwen plc is a medium-sized manufacturing company which is considering a 1 for 5 rights issue at a 15% discount to the current market price of £4.00 per share. Issue costs are expected to be £220,000 and these costs will be paid out of the funds raised. It is proposed that the rights issue funds raised will be used to redeem some of the existing debentures at par. Financial information relating to Tirwen plc is as follows:

**Current balance sheet**

|  | £000 | £000 | £000 |
|---|---|---|---|
| Fixed assets |  |  | 6,550 |
| Current assets |  |  |  |
|   Stock |  | 2,000 |  |
|   Debtors |  | 1,500 |  |
|   Cash |  | 300 |  |
|  |  | 3,800 |  |
| Current liabilities |  |  |  |
|   Trade creditors | 1,100 |  |  |
|   Overdraft | 1,250 |  |  |
|  | 2,350 |  |  |
| Net current assets |  |  | 1,450 |
| Total assets less current liabilities |  |  | 8,000 |
| 12% debentures 2012 |  |  | 4,500 |
|  |  |  | 3,500 |
| Ordinary shares (per value 50p) |  |  | 2,000 |
| Reserves |  |  | 1,500 |
|  |  |  | 3,500 |

**Other information:**

| | |
|---|---|
| Price/earnings ratio of Tirwen plc: | 15.24 |
| Overdraft interest rate: | 7% |
| Corporation tax rate: | 30% |
| Sector advantages:   debt/equity ratio (book value): | 100% |
|         interest cover: | 6 times |

**Required:**

(a)   Ignoring issue costs and any use that may be made of the funds raised by the rights issue, calculate:

    (i)   the theoretical ex rights price per share;

    (ii)  the value of rights per existing share. **(3 marks)**

(b)   What alternative actions are open to the owner of 1,000 shares in Tirwen plc as regards the rights issue? Determine the effect of each of these actions on the wealth of the investor. **(6 marks)**

(c)   Calculate the current earnings per share and the revised earnings per share if the rights issue funds are used to redeem some of the existing debentures. **(6 marks)**

(d)   Evaluate whether the proposal to redeem some of the debentures would increase the wealth of the shareholders of Tirwen plc. Assume that the price/earnings ratio of Tirwen plc remains constant. **(3 marks)**

(e)   Discuss the reasons why a rights issue could be an attractive source of finance for Tirwen plc. Your discussion should include an evaluation of the effect of the rights issue on the debt/equity ratio and interest cover. **(7 marks)**

**(Total: 25 marks)**

# CAPITAL INVESTMENT APPRAISAL

## 18   INVESTMENT APPRAISAL

(a)   Explain and illustrate (using simple numerical examples) the Accounting Rate of Return and Payback approaches to investment appraisal, paying particular attention to the limitations of each approach. **(6 marks)**

(b)   (i)   Explain the differences between NPV and IRR as methods of Discounted Cash Flow analysis. **(6 marks)**

    (ii)  A company with a cost of capital of 14% is trying to determine the optimal replacement cycle for the laptop computers used by its sales team. The following information is relevant to the decision:

The cost of each laptop is £2,400. Maintenance costs are payable at the end of *each full year* of ownership, but not in the year of replacement, e.g. if the laptop is owned for two years, then the maintenance cost is payable at the end of year 1.

| Interval between replacement (years) | Trade-in value (£) | Maintenance cost |
|---|---|---|
| 1 | 1,200 | Zero |
| 2 | 800 | £75 (payable at end of Year 1) |
| 3 | 300 | £150 (payable at end of Year 2) |

**Required:**

Ignoring taxation, calculate the equivalent annual cost of the three different replacement cycles, and recommend which should be adopted. What other factors should the company take into account when determining the optimal cycle? **(8 marks)**

**(Total: 20 marks)**

## 19 BREAD PRODUCTS LTD

Bread Products Ltd is considering the replacement policy for its industrial size ovens which are used as part of a production line that bakes bread. Given its heavy usage each oven has to be replaced frequently. The choice is between replacing every two years or every three years. Only one type of oven is used, each of which costs £24,500. Maintenance costs and resale values are as follows:

| Year | Maintenance per annum £ | Resale value £ |
|------|------|------|
| 1 | 500 | |
| 2 | 800 | 15,600 |
| 3 | 1,500 | 11,200 |

Original cost, maintenance costs and resale values are expressed in current prices. That is, for example, maintenance for a two year old oven would cost £800 for maintenance undertaken now. It is expected that maintenance costs will increase at 10% per annum and oven replacement cost and resale values at 5% per annum. The money discount rate is 15%.

**Required:**

(a) Calculate the preferred replacement policy for the ovens in a choice between a two-year or three-year replacement cycle. **(12 marks)**

(b) Identify the limitations of Net Present Value techniques when applied generally to investment appraisal. **(13 marks)**

**(Total: 25 marks)**

## 20 HOWDEN PLC

(a) Explain how inflation affects the rate of return required on an investment project, and the distinction between a real and a nominal (or 'money terms') approach to the evaluation of an investment project under inflation. **(6 marks)**

(b) Howden plc is contemplating investment in an additional production line to produce its range of compact discs. A market research study, undertaken by a well-known firm of consultants, has revealed scope to sell an additional output of 400,000 units p.a. The study cost £0.1 m but the account has not yet been settled.

The price and cost structure of a typical disc (net of royalties), is as follows:

| | £ | £ |
|------|------|------|
| Price per unit | 12.00 | |
| Costs per unit of output | | |
| Material cost per unit | 1.50 | |
| Direct labour cost per unit | 0.50 | |
| Variable overhead cost per unit | 0.50 | |
| Fixed overhead cost per unit | 1.50 | |
| | | (4.00) |
| Profit | | 8.00 |

The fixed overhead represents an apportionment of central administrative and marketing costs. These are expected to rise in total by £500,000 pa as a result of undertaking this project. The production line is expected to operate for five years and require a total cash outlay of £11m, including £0.5m of materials stocks. The equipment will have a residual value of £2m. Because the company is moving towards a JIT stock management policy, it is expected that this project will involve steadily reducing working capital needs, expected to decline at about 3% pa by volume. The production line will be accommodated in a presently empty building for which an offer of £2m has recently been received from another company. If the building is retained, it is expected that property price inflation will increase its value to £3m after five years.

While the precise rates of price and cost inflation are uncertain, economists in Howden's corporate planning department make the following forecasts for the average annual rates of inflation relevant to the project:

| | |
|---|---|
| Retail Price Index | 6% pa |
| Disc prices | 5% pa |
| Material prices | 3% pa |
| Direct labour wage rates | 7% pa |
| Variable overhead costs | 7% pa |
| Other overhead costs | 5% pa |

*Note:* you may ignore taxes and capital allowances in this question.

### Required:

Given that Howden's shareholders require a real return of 8.5% for projects of this degree of risk, assess the financial viability of this proposal. **(13 marks)**

(c)   Briefly discuss how inflation may complicate the analysis of business financial decisions. **(6 marks)**

**(Total: 25 marks)**

## 21   FILTREX PLC

(a)   Distinguish between 'hard' and 'soft' capital rationing, explaining why a company may deliberately choose to restrict its capital expenditure. **(6 marks)**

(b)   Filtrex plc is a medium-sized, all equity-financed, unquoted company which specialises in the development and production of water- and air-filtering devices to reduce the emission of effluents. Its small but ingenious R & D team has recently made a technological breakthrough which has revealed a number of attractive investment opportunities. It has applied for patents to protect its rights in all these areas. However, it lacks the financial resources required to exploit all of these projects, whose required outlays and post-tax NPVs are listed in the table below. Filtrex's managers consider that delaying any of these projects would seriously undermine their profitability, as competitors bring forward their own new developments. All projects are thought to have a similar degree of risk.

| Project | Required outlay | NPV |
|---|---|---|
| | £ | £ |
| A | 150,000 | 65,000 |
| B | 120,000 | 50,000 |
| C | 200,000 | 80,000 |
| D | 80,000 | 30,000 |
| E | 400,000 | 120,000 |

The NPVs have been calculated using as a discount rate the 18% post-tax rate of return which Filtrex requires for risky R & D ventures. The maximum amount available for this type of investment is £400,000, corresponding to Filtrex's present cash balances, built up over several years' profitable trading. Projects A and C are mutually exclusive and no project can be sub-divided. Any unused capital will either remain invested in short-term deposits or used to purchase marketable securities, both of which offer a return well below 18% post-tax.

**Required:**

(i)     Advise Filtrex plc, using suitable supporting calculations, which combination of projects should be undertaken in the best interests of shareholders.

(ii)    Suggest what further information might be obtained to assist a fuller analysis.

**(12 marks)**

(c)   Explain how, apart from delaying projects, Filtrex plc could manage to exploit more of these opportunities.                                                  **(7 marks)**

**(Total: 25 marks)**

## 22   ARMCLIFF LTD

Armcliff Ltd is a division of Shevin plc which requires each of its divisions to achieve a rate of return on capital employed of at least 10% pa. For this purpose, capital employed is defined as fixed capital and investment in stocks. This rate of return is also applied as a hurdle rate for new investment projects. Divisions have limited borrowing powers and all capital projects are centrally funded.

The following is an extract from Armcliff's divisional accounts:

**Profit and loss account for the year ended 31 December 20X4**

|  | £m |
|---|---|
| Turnover | 120 |
| Cost of sales | (100) |
| Operating profit | 20 |

**Assets employed as at 31 December 20X4**

|  | £m | £m |
|---|---|---|
| Fixed (net) |  | 75 |
| Current assets (including stocks £25m) | 45 |  |
| Current liabilities | (32) |  |
|  |  | 13 |
| Net capital employed |  | 88 |

Armcliff's production engineers wish to invest in a new computer-controlled press. The equipment cost is £14m. The residual value is expected to be £2m after four years operation, when the equipment will be shipped to a customer in South America.

The new machine is capable of improving the quality of the existing product and also of producing a higher volume. The firm's marketing team is confident of selling the increased volume by extending the credit period. The expected additional sales are:

| Year 1 | 2,000,000 units |
|---|---|
| Year 2 | 1,800,000 units |
| Year 3 | 1,600,000 units |
| Year 4 | 1,600,000 units |

Sales volume is expected to fall over time due to emerging competitive pressures. Competition will also necessitate a reduction in price by £0.5 each year from the £5 per unit proposed in the first year. Operating costs are expected to be steady at £1 per unit, and allocation of overheads (none of which are affected by the new project) by the central finance department is set at £0.75 per unit.

Higher production levels will require additional investment in stocks of £0.5m, which would be held at this level until the final stages of operation of the project. Customers at present settle accounts after 90 days on average.

**Required:**

(a)    Determine whether the proposed capital investment is attractive to Armcliff, using the average rate of return on capital method, as defined as average profit-to-average capital employed, ignoring debtors and creditors.

   *Note:* Ignore taxes.                                                          **(10 marks)**

(b)    (i)    Suggest three problems which arise with the use of the average return method for appraising new investment.                                    **(3 marks)**

       (ii)   In view of the problems associated with the ARR method, why do companies continue to use it in project appraisal?                                **(3 marks)**

(c)    Briefly discuss the dangers of offering more generous credit, and suggest ways of assessing customers' creditworthiness.                                    **(9 marks)**

                                                                      **(Total: 25 marks)**

## 23    SLUDGEWATER PLC

Sludgewater plc, a furniture manufacturer, has been reported to the anti-pollution authorities on several occasions in recent years, and fined substantial amounts for making excessive toxic discharges into the air. Both the environmental lobby and Sludgewater's shareholders have demanded that it clean up its operations.

If no clean up takes place, Sludgewater estimates that the total fines it would incur over the next three years can be summarised by the following probability distribution (all figures are expressed in present values.)

| Level of fine | Probability |
|---|---|
| £1.0m | 0.3 |
| £1.8m | 0.5 |
| £2.6m | 0.2 |

A firm of environmental consultants has advised that spray painting equipment can be installed at a cost of £4m to virtually eliminate discharges. Unlike fines, expenditure on pollution control equipment is tax-allowable via a 25% writing-down allowance (reducing balance, based on gross expenditure). The rate of corporation tax is 30%, paid with a one-year delay. The equipment will have no scrap or resale value after its expected three year working life. The equipment can be in place ready for Sludgewater's next financial year.

A European Union grant of 25% of gross expenditure is available, but with payment delayed by a year. The consultant's charge is £200,000 and the new equipment will raise annual production costs by 2% of sales revenue. Current sales are £15 million per annum, and are expected to grow by 5% per annum compound. No change in working capital is envisaged.

Sludgewater applies a discount rate of 10% after tax on investment projects of this nature. All cash inflows and outflows occur at year ends.

**Required:**

(a)    Calculate the expected net present value of the investment.

       Briefly comment on your results.                                           **(12 marks)**

(b)    Write a memorandum to Sludgewater's management in respect of the potential investment taking into account both financial and non-financial criteria.    **(8 marks)**

                                                                      **(Total: 20 marks)**

## 24    LEAMINGER PLC

Leaminger plc has decided it must replace its major turbine machine on 31 December 20X2. The machine is essential to the operations of the company. The company is, however, considering whether to purchase the machine outright or to use lease financing.

**Purchasing the machine outright**

The machine is expected to cost £360,000 if it is purchased outright, payable on 31 December 20X2. After four years the company expects new technology to make the machine redundant and it will be sold on 31 December 20X6 generating proceeds of £20,000. Capital allowances for tax purposes are available on the cost of the machine at the rate of 25% per annum reducing balance. A full year's allowance is given in the year of acquisition but no writing down allowance is available in the year of disposal. The difference between the proceeds and the tax written down value in the year of disposal is allowable or chargeable for tax as appropriate.

**Leasing**

The company has approached its bank with a view to arranging a lease to finance the machine acquisition. The bank has offered two options with respect to leasing which are as follows:

|                          | Finance lease      | Operating lease    |
| ------------------------ | ------------------ | ------------------ |
| Contract length (years)  | 4                  | 1                  |
| Annual rental            | £135,000           | £140,000           |
| First rent payable       | 31 December 20X3   | 31 December 20X2   |

**General**

For both the purchasing and the finance lease option, maintenance costs of £15,000 per year are payable at the end of each year. All lease rentals (for both finance and operating options) can be assumed to be allowable for tax purposes in full in the year of payment. Assume that tax is payable one year after the end of the accounting year in which the transaction occurs. For the operating lease only, contracts are renewable annually at the discretion of either party. Leaminger plc has adequate taxable profits to relieve all its costs. The rate of corporation tax can be assumed to be 30%. The company's accounting year-end is 31 December. The company's annual after tax cost of capital is 10%.

**Required:**

(a)    Calculate the net present value at 31 December 20X2, using the after tax cost of capital, for:

   (i)    purchasing the machine outright

   (ii)    using the finance lease to acquire the machine

   (iii)    using the operating lease to acquire the machine.

   Recommend the optimal method.                                                          **(12 marks)**

(b)    Assume now that the company is facing capital rationing up until 30 December 20X3 when it expects to make a share issue. During this time the most marginal investment project, which is perfectly divisible, requires an outlay of £500,000 and would generate a net present value of £100,000. Investment in the turbine would reduce funds available for this project. Investments cannot be delayed.

   Calculate the revised net present values of the three options for the turbine given capital rationing. Advise whether your recommendation in (a) would change.

                                                                                          **(5 marks)**

(c)   As their business advisor, prepare a report for the directors of Leaminger plc that assesses the issues that need to be considered in acquiring the turbine with respect to capital rationing. **(8 marks)**

**(Total: 25 marks)**

## 25   PRIME PRINTING PLC

(a)   Explain the cash flow characteristics of a finance lease, and compare it with the use of a bank loan or cash held on short-term deposit. Your answer should include some comment on the significance of a company's anticipated tax position on lease versus buy decisions. **(10 marks)**

(b)   Prime Printing plc has the opportunity to replace one of its pieces of printing equipment. The new machine, costing £120,000, is expected to lead to operating savings of £50,000 per annum and have an economic life of five years. The company's after tax cost of capital for the investment is estimated at 15%, and operating cash flows are taxed at a rate of 30%, one year in arrears.

The company is trying to decide whether to fund the acquisition of the machine via a five-year bank loan, at an annual interest rate of 13%, with the principal repayable at the end of the five-year period.  As an alternative, the machine could be acquired using a finance lease, at a cost of £28,000 p.a. for five years, payable in advance. The machine would have zero scrap value at the end of five years.

*Note:*  due to its current tax position, the company is unable to utilise any capital allowances on the purchase until year one.

### Required:

Assuming that writing-down allowances of 25% p.a. are available on a reducing balance basis, recommend, with reasons, whether Prime Printing should replace the machine, and if so whether it should buy or lease. **(15 marks)**

**(Total: 25 marks)**

## 26   CAPITAL RATIONING

Basril plc is reviewing investment proposals that have been submitted by divisional managers. The investment funds of the company are limited to £800,000 in the current year. Details of three possible investments, none of which can be delayed, are given below.

### Project 1

An investment of £300,000 in work station assessments. Each assessment would be on an individual employee basis and would lead to savings in labour costs from increased efficiency and from reduced absenteeism due to work-related illness. Savings in labour costs from these assessments in money terms are expected to be as follows:

| Year | 1 | 2 | 3 | 4 | 5 |
|---|---|---|---|---|---|
| Cash flows (£000) | 85 | 90 | 95 | 100 | 95 |

### Project 2

An investment of £450,000 in individual workstations for staff that is expected to reduce administration costs by £140,800 per annum in money terms for the next five years.

### Project 3

An investment of £400,000 in new ticket machines. Net cash savings of £120,000 per annum are expected in current price terms and these are expected to increase by 3.6% per annum due to inflation during the five-year life of the machines.

Basril plc has a money cost of capital of 12% and taxation should be ignored.

**Required:**

(a) Determine the best way for Basril plc to invest the available funds and calculate the resultant NPV:

    (i)     on the assumption that each of the three projects is divisible;

    (ii)    on the assumption that none of the projects are divisible. **(10 marks)**

(b) Explain how the NPV investment appraisal method is applied in situations where capital is rationed. **(3 marks)**

(c) Discuss the reasons why capital rationing may arise. **(7 marks)**

(d) Discuss the meaning of the term 'relevant cash flows' in the context of investment appraisal, giving examples to illustrate your discussion. **(5 marks)**

**(Total: 25 marks)**

## 27 UMUNAT PLC

Umunat plc is considering investing £50,000 in a new machine with an expected life of five years. The machine will have no scrap value at the end of five years. It is expected that 20,000 units will be sold each year at a selling price of £3·00 per unit. Variable production costs are expected to be £1·65 per unit, while incremental fixed costs, mainly the wages of a maintenance engineer, are expected to be £10,000 per year. Umunat plc uses a discount rate of 12% for investment appraisal purposes and expects investment projects to recover their initial investment within two years.

**Required:**

(a) Explain why risk and uncertainty should be considered in the investment appraisal process. **(5 marks)**

(b) Calculate and comment on the payback period of the project. **(4 marks)**

(c) Evaluate the sensitivity of the project's net present value to a change in the following project variables:

    (i)     sales volume;

    (ii)    sales price;

    (iii)   variable cost;

and discuss the use of sensitivity analysis as a way of evaluating project risk.

**(10 marks)**

(d) Upon further investigation it is found that there is a significant chance that the expected sales volume of 20,000 units per year will not be achieved. The sales manager of Umunat plc suggests that sales volumes could depend on expected economic states that could be assigned the following probabilities:

| Economic state | Poor | Normal | Good |
|---|---|---|---|
| Probability | 0.3 | 0.6 | 0.1 |
| Annual sale volume (units) | 17,500 | 20,000 | 22,500 |

Calculate and comment on the expected net present value of the project. **(6 marks)**

**(Total: 25 marks)**

# COSTING SYSTEMS AND TECHNIQUES

## 28   BUD PLC

A division of Bud plc is engaged in the manual assembly of finished products F1 and F2 from bought-in components. These products are sold to external customers. The budgeted sales volumes and prices for Month 9 are as follows:

| Product | Units | Price |
|---|---|---|
| Fl | 34,000 | £50.00 |
| F2 | 58,000 | £30.00 |

Finished goods stockholding budgeted for the end of Month 9, is 1,000 units of F1 and 2,000 units of F2, with no stock at the beginning of that month. The purchased components C3 and C4 are used in the finished products in the quantities shown below. The unit price is for just-in-time delivery of the components; the company holds no component stocks.

| | Component | |
|---|---|---|
| Product | C3 | C4 |
| F1 (per unit) | 8 units | 4 units |
| F2 (per unit) | 4 units | 3 units |
| Price (each) | £1.25 | £1.80 |

The standard direct labour times and labour rates and the budgeted monthly manufacturing overhead costs for the assembly and finishing departments for Month 9 are given below:

| Product | Assembly | Finishing |
|---|---|---|
| Fl (per unit) | 30 minutes | 12 minutes |
| F2 (per unit) | 15 minutes | 10 minutes |
| Labour rate (per hour) | £5.00 | £6.00 |
| Manufacturing overhead cost for the month | £617,500 | £204,000 |

Every month a predetermined direct labour hour recovery rate is computed in each department for manufacturing overhead and applied to items produced in that month.

The selling overhead of £344,000 per month is applied to products based on a predetermined percentage of the budgeted sales value in each month.

**Required:**

(a)   Prepare summaries of the following budgets for Month 9:

   (i)   component purchase and usage (units and value)

   (ii)   direct labour (hours and value)

   (iii)   departmental manufacturing overhead recovery rates

   (iv)   selling overhead recovery rate

   (v)   stock value at the month-end.   **(8 marks)**

(b)   Tabulate the standard unit cost and profit of each of F1 and F2 in Month 9.   **(3 marks)**

(c)   Prepare a budgeted profit and loss account for Month 9 which clearly incorporates the budget values obtained in (a) above.   **(3 marks)**

(d)   Explain clearly the implications of the company's treatment of manufacturing overheads, i.e. computing a monthly overhead rate, compared to a predetermined overhead rate prepared annually.   **(6 marks)**

**(Total: 20 marks)**

## 29    ABC

(a)    Discuss the conditions under which the introduction of ABC is likely to be most effective, paying particular attention to:

- product mix

- the significance of overheads and the ABC method of charging costs

- the availability of information collection procedures and resources, and

- other appropriate factors.                                                    **(17 marks)**

(b)    Explain why ABC might lead to a more accurate assessment of management performance than absorption costing.                                       **(8 marks)**

**(Total: 25 marks)**

## 30    ABKABER PLC

Abkaber plc assembles three types of motorcycle at the same factory: the 50cc Sunshine; the 250cc Roadster and the 1000cc Fireball. It sells the motorcycles throughout the world. In response to market pressures Abkaber plc has invested heavily in new manufacturing technology in recent years and, as a result, has significantly reduced the size of its workforce.

Historically, the company has allocated all overhead costs using total direct labour hours, but is now considering introducing Activity Based Costing (ABC). Abkaber plc's accountant has produced the following analysis.

|  | Annual output (units) | Annual direct labour hours | Selling price (£ per unit) | Raw material cost (£ per unit) |
|---|---|---|---|---|
| Sunshine | 2,000 | 200,000 | 4,000 | 400 |
| Roadster | 1,600 | 220,000 | 6,000 | 600 |
| Fireball | 400 | 80,000 | 8,000 | 900 |

The three cost drivers that generate overheads are:

| Deliveries to retailers | – | the number of deliveries of motorcycles to retail showrooms |
|---|---|---|
| Set-ups | – | the number of times the assembly line process is re-set to accommodate a production run of a different type of motorcycle |
| Purchase orders | – | the number of purchase orders. |

The annual cost driver volumes relating to each activity and for each type of motorcycle are as follows:

|  | Number of deliveries to retailers | Number of set-ups | Number of purchase orders |
|---|---|---|---|
| Sunshine | 100 | 35 | 400 |
| Roadster | 80 | 40 | 300 |
| Fireball | 70 | 25 | 100 |

The annual overhead costs relating to these activities are as follows:

|  | £ |
|---|---|
| Deliveries to retailers | 2,400,000 |
| Set-up costs | 6,000,000 |
| Purchase orders | 3,600,000 |

All direct labour is paid at £5 per hour. The company holds no stocks.

At a board meeting there was some concern over the introduction of activity based costing.

The finance director argued: 'I very much doubt whether selling the Fireball is viable but I am not convinced that activity based costing would tell us any more than the use of labour hours in assessing the viability of each product.'

The marketing director argued: 'I am in the process of negotiating a major new contract with a motorcycle rental company for the Sunshine model. For such a big order they will not pay our normal prices but we need to at least cover our incremental costs. I am not convinced that activity based costing would achieve this as it merely averages costs for our entire production'.

The managing director argued: 'I believe that activity based costing would be an improvement but it still has its problems. For instance if we carry out an activity many times surely we get better at it and costs fall rather than remain constant. Similarly, some costs are fixed and do not vary either with labour hours or any other cost driver.'

The chairman argued: 'I cannot see the problem. The overall profit for the company is the same no matter which method of allocating overheads we use. It seems to make no difference to me.'

**Required:**

(a)     Calculate the total profit on each of Abkaber plc's three types of product using each of the following methods to attribute overheads:

    (i)      the existing method based upon labour hours

    (ii)     activity based costing.                                                  **(13 marks)**

(b)     Write a report to the directors of Abkaber plc, as its management accountant. The report should:

    (i)      evaluate the labour hours and the activity based costing methods in the circumstances of Abkaber plc; and

    (ii)     examine the implications of activity based costing for Abkaber plc, and in so doing evaluate the issues raised by each of the directors.

    Refer to your calculations in requirement (a) above where appropriate.     **(12 marks)**

**(Total: 25 marks)**

## 31     ADMER

Admer owns several home furnishing stores. In each store, consultations, if needed, are undertaken by specialists, who also visit potential customers in their homes, using specialist software to help customers realise their design objectives. Customers visit the store to make their selections from the wide range of goods offered, after which sales staff collect payment and raise a purchase order. Customers then collect their self-assembly goods from the warehouse, using the purchase order as authority to collect. Administration staff process purchase orders and also arrange consultations.

Each store operates an absorption costing system and costs other than the cost of goods sold are apportioned on the basis of sales floor area.

Results for one of Admer's stores for the last three months are as follows:

| Department | Kitchens £ | Bathrooms £ | Dining Rooms £ | Total £ |
|---|---|---|---|---|
| Sales | 210,000 | 112,500 | 440,000 | 762,500 |
| Cost of goods sold | 63,000 | 37,500 | 176,000 | 276,500 |
| Other costs | 130,250 | 81,406 | 113,968 | 325,624 |
| Profit | 16,750 | (6,406) | 150,032 | 160,376 |

The management accountant of Admer is concerned that the bathrooms department of the store has been showing a loss for some time, and is considering a proposal to close the bathrooms department in order to concentrate on the more profitable kitchens and dining rooms departments. He has found that other costs for this store for the last three months are made up of:

|  | £ | Employees |
|---|---|---|
| Sales staff wages | 64,800 | 12 |
| Consultation staff wages | 24,960 | 4 |
| Warehouse staff wages | 30,240 | 6 |
| Administration staff wages | 30,624 | 4 |
| General overheads (light, heat, rates, etc.) | 175,000 | |
|  | 325,624 | |

He has also collected the following information for the last three months:

| Department | Kitchens | Bathrooms | Dining Rooms |
|---|---|---|---|
| Number of items sold | 1,000 | 1,500 | 4,000 |
| Purchase orders | 1,000 | 900 | 2,500 |
| Floor area (square metres) | 16,000 | 10,000 | 14,000 |
| Number of consultations | 798 | 200 | 250 |

The management accountant believes that he can use this information to review the store's performance in the last three months from an activity-based costing (ABC) perspective.

**Required:**

(a) Discuss the management accountant's belief that the information provided can be used in an activity-based costing analysis. **(4 marks)**

(b) Explain and illustrate, using supporting calculations, how an ABC profit statement might be produced from the information provided. Clearly explain the reasons behind your choice of cost drivers. **(8 marks)**

(c) Evaluate and discuss the proposal to close the bathrooms department. **(6 marks)**

(d) Discuss the advantages and disadvantages that may arise for Admer from introducing activity-based costing in its stores. **(7 marks)**

**(Total: 25 marks)**

## 32 BML

BML has three product lines: P1, P2 and P3. Since its creation the company has been using a single direct labour cost percentage to assign overhead costs to products.

Despite P3, a relatively new line, attracting additional business, increasing overhead costs and a loss of market share, particularly for P2, a major product, have convinced the management that the costing system is in need of some development. A team, led by the management accountant was established to develop an improved system of costing based on activities. The team spent several weeks collecting data (see tables below) for the different activities and products. For the accounting period in question, given in the tables below is data on BML's three product lines and overhead costs:

|  | P1 | P2 | P3 |
|---|---|---|---|
| Production volume | 7,500 units | 12,500 units | 4,000 units |
| Direct labour cost per unit | £4 | £8 | £6.40 |
| Material cost per unit | £18 | £25 | £16 |
| Selling price per unit | £47 | £80 | £68 |
| Materials movements (in total) | 4 | 25 | 50 |
| Machine hours per unit | 0.5 | 0.5 | 0.2 |
| Set-ups (in total) | 1 | 5 | 10 |
| Proportion of engineering work | 30% | 20% | 50% |
| Orders packed (in total) | 1 | 7 | 22 |

| Activities | Overhead cost |
|---|---|
|  | £ |
| Material receiving and handling | 150,000 |
| Machine maintenance and depreciation | 390,000 |
| Set-up labour | 18,688 |
| Engineering | 100,000 |
| Packing | 60,000 |
| Total | 718,688 |

**Required:**

(a)  Calculate the overhead rate and the product unit costs under the existing costing system. **(4 marks)**

(b)  Identify for each overhead activity, an appropriate cost driver from the information supplied, and then calculate the product unit costs using a system that assigns overheads on the basis of the use of activities. **(9 marks)**

(c)  Comment on the results of the two costing systems in (a) and (b) above. **(7 marks)**

**(Total: 20 marks)**

## 33    BRUNTI PLC

The following budgeted information relates to Brunti plc for the forthcoming period:

|  | Products | | |
|---|---|---|---|
|  | XYI | YZT | ABW |
|  | (000) | (000) | (000) |
| Sales and production (units) | 50 | 40 | 30 |
|  | £ | £ | £ |
| Selling price (per unit) | 45 | 95 | 73 |
| Prime cost (per unit) | 32 | 84 | 65 |
|  | Hours | Hours | Hours |
| Machine department (machine hours per unit) | 2 | 5 | 4 |
| Assembly department (direct labour hours per unit) | 7 | 3 | 2 |

Overheads allocated and apportioned to production departments (including service cost centre costs) were to be recovered in product costs as follows:

Machine department at £1.20 per machine hour

Assembly department at £0.825 per direct labour hour

You ascertain that the above overheads could be re-analysed into 'cost pools' as follows:

| Cost pool | £000 | Cost driver | Quantity for the period |
|---|---|---|---|
| Machining services | 357 | Machined hours | 420,000 |
| Assembly services | 318 | Direct labour hours | 530,000 |
| Set up costs | 26 | Set ups | 520 |
| Order processing | 156 | Customer orders | 32,000 |
| Purchasing | 84 | Suppliers' orders | 11,200 |
| | 941 | | |

You have also been provided with the following estimates for the period:

| | Products | | |
|---|---|---|---|
| | XYI | YZT | ABW |
| Number of set-ups | 120 | 200 | 200 |
| Customer orders | 8,000 | 8,000 | 16,000 |
| Suppliers' orders | 3,000 | 4,000 | 4,200 |

**Required:**

(a) Prepare and present profit statements using:

    (i) conventional absorption costing **(5 marks)**

    (ii) activity-based costing. **(10 marks)**

(b) Comment on why activity-based costing is considered to present a fairer valuation of the product cost per unit. **(5 marks)**

**(Total: 20 marks)**

## 34 ABC PLC

ABC plc, a group operating retail stores, is compiling its budget statements for 20X8. In this exercise revenues and costs at each store A, B and C are predicted. Additionally, all central costs of warehousing and a head office are allocated across the three stores in order to arrive at a total cost and net profit of each store operation.

In earlier years the central costs were allocated in total based on the total sales value of each store. But as a result of dissatisfaction expressed by some store managers alternative methods are to be evaluated.

The predicted results before any re-allocation of central costs are as follows:

| | A | B | C |
|---|---|---|---|
| | £000 | £000 | £000 |
| Sales | 5,000 | 4,000 | 3,000 |
| Costs of sales | 2,800 | 2,300 | 1,900 |
| Gross margin | 2,200 | 1,700 | 1,100 |
| Local operating expenses | | | |
|   Variable | 660 | 730 | 310 |
|   Fixed | 700 | 600 | 500 |
| Operating profit | 840 | 370 | 290 |

The central costs which are to be allocated are:

|  | £000 |
|---|---|
| Warehouse costs: | |
| Depreciation | 100 |
| Storage | 80 |
| Operating and despatch | 120 |
| Delivery | 300 |
| Head office: | |
| Salaries | 200 |
| Advertising | 80 |
| Establishment | 120 |
| | |
| Total | 1,000 |

The management accountant has carried out discussions with staff at all locations in order to identify more suitable 'cost drivers' of some of the central costs. So far the following has been revealed.

|  | A | B | C |
|---|---|---|---|
| Number of despatches | 550 | 450 | 520 |
| Total delivery distances (thousand miles) | 70 | 50 | 90 |
| Storage space occupied (%) | 40 | 30 | 30 |

1    An analysis of senior management time revealed that 10% of their time was devoted to warehouse issues with the remainder shared equally between the three stores.

2    It was agreed that the only basis on which to allocate the advertising costs was sales revenue.

3    Establishment costs were mainly occupancy costs of senior management.

This analysis has been carried out against a background of developments in the company, for example, automated warehousing and greater integration with suppliers.

**Required:**

(a)    As the management accountant prepare a report for the management of the group which:

(i)    computes the budgeted net profit of each store based on the *sales value* allocation base originally adopted *and* explains 'cost driver', 'volume' and 'complexity' issues in relation to cost allocation commenting on the possible implications of the dissatisfaction expressed                **(7 marks)**

(ii)    computes the budgeted net profit of each store using the additional information provided, discusses the extent to which an improvement has been achieved in the information on the costs and profitability of running the stores and comments on the results.                **(14 marks)**

(b)    Explain briefly how regression analysis and coefficient of determination ($r^2$) could be used in confirming the delivery mileage allocation method used in (a) above.

**(4 marks)**

**(Total: 25 marks)**

## 35    PARSER LTD

The managing director of Parser Ltd, a small business, is considering undertaking a one-off contract and has asked her inexperienced accountant to advise on what costs are likely to be incurred so that she can price at a profit. The following schedule has been prepared:

| Costs per special order: | Notes | £ |
|---|---|---|
| Direct wages | 1 | 28,500 |
| Supervisor costs | 2 | 11,500 |
| General overheads | 3 | 4,000 |
| Machine depreciation | 4 | 2,300 |
| Machine overheads | 5 | 18,000 |
| Materials | 6 | 34,000 |
| | | 98,300 |

### Notes

1    Direct wages comprise the wages of two employees, particularly skilled in the labour process for this job, who could be transferred from another department to undertake work on the special order. They are fully occupied in their usual department and sub-contracting staff would have to be brought in to undertake the work left behind. Sub-contracting costs would be £32,000 for the period of the work. Different sub-contractors who are skilled in the special order techniques are available to work on the special order and their costs would amount to £31,300.

2    A supervisor would have to work on the special order. The cost of £11,500 is comprised of £8,000 normal payments plus £3,500 additional bonus for working on the special order. Normal payments refer to the fixed salary of the supervisor. In addition, the supervisor would lose incentive payments in his normal work amounting to £2,500. It is not anticipated that any replacement costs relating to the supervisor's work on other jobs would arise.

3    General overheads comprise an apportionment of £3,000 plus an estimate of £1,000 incremental overheads.

4    Machine depreciation represents the normal period cost based on the duration of the contract. It is anticipated that £500 will be incurred in additional machine maintenance costs.

5    Machine overheads (for running costs such as electricity) are charged at £3 per hour. It is estimated that 6,000 hours will be needed for the special order. The machine has 4,000 hours available capacity. The further 2,000 hours required will mean an existing job is taken off the machine resulting in a lost contribution of £2 per hour.

6    Materials represent the purchase cost of 7,500 kg bought some time ago. The materials are no longer used and are unlikely to be wanted in the future except on the special order. The complete stock of materials (amounting to 10,000 kg), or part thereof, could be sold for £4.20 per kg. The replacement cost of material used would be £33,375.

Because the business does not have adequate funds to finance the special order, a bank overdraft amounting to £20,000 would be required for the project duration of three months. The overdraft would be repaid at the end of the period. The company uses a cost of capital of 20% to appraise projects. The bank's overdraft rate is 18%.

The managing director has heard that, for special orders such as this, relevant costing should be used that also incorporate opportunity costs. She has approached you to create a revised costing schedule based on relevant costing principles.

**Required:**

(a)   Briefly explain what is meant by opportunity cost.                    **(2 marks)**

(b)   Adjust the schedule prepared by the accountant to a relevant cost basis, incorporating appropriate opportunity costs.                    **(11 marks)**

(c)   Explain why very Small to Medium-sized Enterprises (SMEs), such as Parser Ltd, might face problems in obtaining appropriate sources of finance. In your answer pay particular attention to problems and issues associated with:

   (i)    uncertainty concerning the business

   (ii)   assets available to offer as collateral or security, and

   (iii)  potential sources of finance for very new SMEs excluding sources from capital markets.                    **(12 marks)**

**(Total: 25 marks)**

## 36   ALBION PLC

The managers of Albion plc are reviewing the operations of the company with a view to making operational decisions for the next month. Details of some of the products manufactured by the company are given below.

| Product | AR2 | GL3 | HT4 | XY5 |
|---|---|---|---|---|
| Selling price (£/unit) | 21.00 | 28.50 | 27.30 | |
| Material R2 (kg/unit) | 2.0 | 3.0 | 3.0 | |
| Material R3 (kg/unit) | 2.0 | 2.2 | 1.6 | 3.0 |
| Direct labour (hours/unit) | 0.6 | 1.2 | 1.5 | 1.7 |
| Variable production overheads (£/unit) | 1.10 | 1.30 | 1.10 | 1.40 |
| Fixed production overheads (£/unit) | 1.50 | 1.60 | 1.70 | 1.40 |
| Expected demand for next month (units) | 950 | 1,000 | 900 | |

Products AR2, GL3 and HT4 are sold to customers of Albion plc, while Product XY5 is a component that is used in the manufacture of other products. Albion plc manufactures a wide range of products in addition to those detailed above.

Material R2, which is not used in any other of Albion's products, is expected to be in short supply in the next month because of industrial action at a major producer of the material. Albion plc has just received a delivery of 5,500 kg of Material R2 and this is expected to be the amount held in stock at the start of the next month. The company does not expect to be able to obtain further supplies of Material R2 unless it pays a premium price. The normal market price is £2.50 per kg.

Material R3 is available at a price of £2.00 per kg and Albion plc does not expect any problems in securing supplies of this material. Direct labour is paid at a rate of £4.00 per hour.

Folam Limited has recently approached Albion plc with an offer to supply a substitute for Product XY5 at a price of £10.20 per unit. Albion plc would need to pay an annual fee of £50,000 for the right to use this patented substitute.

**Required:**

(a)   Determine the optimum production schedule for Products AR2, GL3 and HT4 for the next month, on the assumption that additional supplies of Material R2 are not purchased.                    **(8 marks)**

(b)   If Albion plc decides to purchase further supplies of Material R2 to meet demand for Products AR2, GL3 and HT4, what should be the maximum price per kg that the company is prepared to pay?                                    **(3 marks)**

(c)   Discuss whether Albion plc should manufacture Product XY5 or buy the substitute offered by Folam Limited.

Your answer must be supported by appropriate calculations.        **(7 marks)**

(d)   Discuss the limitations of marginal costing (variable costing) as a basis for making short-term decisions.                                    **(7 marks)**

**(Total: 25 marks)**

## 37   THROUGHPUT

MN Ltd manufactures automated industrial trolleys, known as TRLs. Each TRL sells for £2,000 and the material cost per unit is £600. Labour and variable overhead are £5,500 and £8,000 per week respectively. Fixed production costs are £450,000 per annum and marketing and administrative costs are £265,000 per annum.

The trolleys are made on three different machines. Machine X makes the four frame panels required for each TRL. Its maximum output is 180 frame panels per week. Machine X is old and unreliable and it breaks down from time to time. It is estimated that, on average, between 15 and 20 hours of production are lost per month. Machine Y can manufacture parts for 52 TRLs per week and machine Z, which is old but reasonably reliable, can process and assemble 30 TRLs per week.

The company has recently introduced a just-in-time (JIT) system and it is company policy to hold little work-in-progress and no finished goods stock from week to week. The company operates a 40-hour week, 48 weeks a year (12 months × 4 weeks) but cannot meet demand. The demand for the next year is predicted to be as follows. This is expected to be typical of the demand for the next four years:

| *Units per week* | | *Units per week* | |
| --- | --- | --- | --- |
| January | 30 | July | 48 |
| February | 30 | August | 45 |
| March | 33 | September | 42 |
| April | 36 | October | 40 |
| May | 39 | November | 33 |
| June | 44 | December | 30 |

The production manager has suggested that the company replaces machine Z with machine G. Machine G can process 45 TRLs per week and costs £550,000. It is estimated that the variable overhead cost per week will increase by £4,500 if TRLs are made on machine G. The maintenance manager is keen to spend £100,000 on a major overhaul of machine X – he says this will make it 100% reliable.

**Required:**

(a)   Calculate the throughput accounting ratio for MN (defined below) for the key resource for an average hour next year.

$$\text{Throughput accounting ratio} = \frac{\text{Return per factory hour}}{\text{Cost per factory hour}}$$

Where

$$\text{Return per factory hour} = \frac{\text{Sales price - material cost}}{\text{Time on key resource}}$$                                    **(6 marks)**

(b)     Explain the concept of throughput accounting.                              **(4 marks)**

(c)     To what use might the throughput accounting the ratio be put? Use the case of MN Ltd where appropriate to illustrate your answer.                    **(4 marks)**

(d)     Explain how the concept of contribution in throughput accounting differs from that in marginal costing.                                             **(6 marks)**

(e)     If MN Ltd has decided to purchase machine G and spend £100,000 on a major overhaul of machine X, the accountant and the production manager should collaborate to ensure a new focus for monitoring and reporting production activities.  What is the new focus? Explain what should be monitored and reported.

**(5 marks)**

**(Total: 25 marks)**

## 38   SPRING PLC

At a recent board meeting of Spring plc, there was a heated discussion on the need to improve financial performance. The Production Director argued that financial performance could be improved if the company replaced its existing absorption costing approach with an activity-based costing system. He argued that this would lead to better cost control and increased profit margins. The Managing Director agreed that better cost control could lead to increased profitability, but informed the meeting that he believed that performance needed to be monitored in both financial and non-financial terms. He pointed out that sales could be lost due to poor product quality or a lack of after-sales service just as easily as by asking too high a price for Spring plc's products. He suggested that while the board should consider introducing activity-based costing, it should also consider ways in which the company could monitor and assess performance on a wide basis.

### Required:

(a)     Describe the key features of activity-based costing and discuss the advantages and disadvantages of adopting an activity-based approach to cost accumulation.

**(14 marks)**

(b)     Explain the need for the measurement of organisational and managerial performance, giving examples of the range of financial and non-financial performance measures that might be used.                                               **(11 marks)**

**(Total: 25 marks)**

# STANDARD COSTING AND VARIANCE ANALYSIS

## 39   STANDARD COSTING

(a)     Outline the uses of standard costing and discuss the reasons why standards have to be reviewed.                                                      **(13 marks)**

(b)     Standard costs are a detailed financial expression of organisational objectives. What non-financial objectives might organisations have? In your answer, identify any stakeholder group that may have a non-financial interest.           **(12 marks)**

**(Total: 25 marks)**

## 40   MATERIAL VARIANCES

A company makes a product using two materials, X and Y, in the production process. A system of standard costing and variance analysis is in operation. The standard material requirement per tonne of mixed output is 60% material X at £30 per tonne and 40% material Y at £45 per tonne, with a standard yield of 90%.

The following information has been gathered for the three months January to March:

|  | January | February | March |
|---|---|---|---|
| Output achieved (tonnes) | 810 | 765 | 900 |
| Actual material input: |  |  |  |
| X (tonnes) | 540 | 480 | 700 |
| Y (tonnes) | 360 | 360 | 360 |
| Actual material cost (X plus Y) (£) | 32,400 | 31,560 | 38,600 |

The actual price per tonne of material Y throughout the January to March period was £45.

### Required:

(a)   Prepare material variance summaries for each of January, February and March which include yield and mix variances in total plus usage and price variances for each material and in total. **(15 marks)**

(b)   Prepare comments for management on each variance including variance trend.

**(6 marks)**

(c)   Discuss the relevance of the variances calculated above in the light of the following additional information. The company has an agreement to purchase 360 tonnes of material Y each month and the perishable nature of the material means that it must be used in the month of purchase and additional supplies in excess of 360 tonnes per month are not available. **(4 marks)**

**(Total: 25 marks)**

## 41   PERSEUS CO LTD

The Perseus Co Ltd a medium sized company, produces a single product in its one overseas factory. For control purposes, a standard costing system was recently introduced and is now in operation.

The standards set for the month of May were as follows:

| | |
|---|---|
| Production and sales | 16,000 units |
| Selling price (per unit) | £140 |

*Materials*

| | |
|---|---|
| Material 007 | 6 kilos per unit at £12.25 per kilo |
| Material XL90 | 3 kilos per unit at £3.20 per kilo |

*Labour*

4.5 hours per unit at £8.40 per hour

*Overheads (all fixed)*

£86,400 per month. They are not absorbed into the product costs.

The actual data for the month of May, is as follows.

Produced 15,400 units which were sold at £138.25 each.

*Materials*

Used 98,560 kilos of material 007 at a total cost of £1,256,640 and used 42,350 kilos of material XL90 at a total cost of £132,979.

*Labour*

Paid an actual rate of £8.65 per hour to the labour force. The total amount paid out, amounted to £612,766.

*Overheads (all fixed)*

£96,840

**Required:**

(a) Prepare a standard costing profit statement, and a profit statement based on actual figures for the month of May. **(6 marks)**

(b) Prepare a statement of the variances which reconciles the actual with the standard profit or loss figure. (Mix and yield variances are not required.) **(9 marks)**

(c) Explain briefly the possible reasons for inter-relationships between material variances and labour variances. **(5 marks)**

**(Total: 20 marks)**

## 42 WOODEEZER LTD

Woodeezer Ltd makes quality wooden benches for both indoor and outdoor use. Results have been disappointing in recent years and a new managing director, Peter Beech, was appointed to raise production volumes. After an initial assessment Peter Beech considered that budgets had been set at levels which made it easy for employees to achieve. He argued that employees would be better motivated by setting budgets which challenged them more in terms of higher expected output.

Other than changing the overall budgeted output, Mr. Beech has not yet altered any part of the standard cost card. Thus, the budgeted output and sales for November 20X2 was 4,000 benches and the standard cost card below was calculated on this basis:

|  |  | £ |
|---|---|---|
| Wood | 25 kg at £3.20 per kg | 80.00 |
| Labour | 4 hours at £8 per hour | 32.00 |
| Variable overheads | 4 hours at £4 per hour | 16.00 |
| Fixed overhead | 4 hours at £16 per hour | 64.00 |
|  |  | 192.00 |
| Selling price |  | 220.00 |
| Standard profit |  | 28.00 |

Overheads are absorbed on the basis of labour hours and the company uses an absorption costing system. There were no stocks at the beginning of November 20X2. Stocks are valued at standard cost.

Actual results for November 20X2 were as follows:

|  |  | £ |
|---|---|---|
| Wood | 80,000 kg at £3.50 | 280,000 |
| Labour | 16,000 hours at £7 | 112,000 |
| Variable overheads |  | 60,000 |
| Fixed overhead |  | 196,000 |

|  | £ |
|---|---|
| Total production cost (3,600 benches) | 648,000 |
| Closing stock (400 benches at £192) | 76,800 |
|  | 571,200 |
| Sales (3,200 benches) | 720,000 |
| Actual profit | 148,800 |

The average monthly production and sales for some years prior to November 20X2 had been 3,400 units and budgets had previously been set at this level. Very few operating variances had historically been generated by the standard costs used.

Mr. Beech has made some significant changes to the operations of the company. However, the other directors are now concerned that Mr. Beech has been too ambitious in raising production targets. Mr. Beech had also changed suppliers of raw materials to improve quality, increased selling prices, begun to introduce less skilled labour, and significantly reduced fixed overheads.

The finance director suggested that an absorption costing system is misleading and that a marginal costing system should be considered at some stage in the future to guide decision-making.

**Required:**

(a)   Prepare an operating statement for November 20X2. This should show all operating variances and should reconcile budgeted and actual profit for the month for Woodeezer Ltd.                                                                                      **(14 marks)**

(b)   In so far as the information permits, examine the impact of the operational changes made by Mr. Beech on the profitability of the company. In your answer, consider each of the following:

(i)     motivation and budget setting

(ii)    possible causes of variances.                                                               **(6 marks)**

(c)   Re-assess the impact of your comments in part (b), using a marginal costing approach to evaluating the impact of the operational changes made by Mr Beech.

Show any relevant additional calculations to support your arguments.      **(5 marks)**

**(Total: 25 marks)**

## 43   BICYCLES

It is the quarter-end at a UK company which sells bicycles throughout Europe. One model produced in a dedicated plant had a budgeted column of 20,000 units of production and sales for the quarter. The budgeted/standard manufacturing and selling costs, applicable to this one model, for the quarter are shown in Table 1 below:

**Table 1**

|  | Per unit £ | Total £000 |
|---|---|---|
| *Manufacturing:* |  |  |
| Material | 45 | 900 |
| Labour and variable overhead | 15 | 300 |
| Fixed overhead |  | 1,200 |
| Total manufacturing cost |  | 2,400 |

*Selling:*

| | | |
|---|---|---|
| Variable overhead | 15 | 300 |
| Fixed overhead | | 340 |
| Total selling overhead | | 640 |

1   The fixed manufacturing overheads are recovered, at a rate per unit, based on the budgeted volume levels.

2   Variable selling overheads are incurred in proportion to units sold.

3   The standard selling price is £190 per unit.

For reporting purposes and identifying stock values the company operates a standard absorption costing system. For the quarter in question the production was 16.800 units, however sales were only 11,800 units.

In order to undertake some basic sales and marketing planning, costs are analysed into variable and fixed elements in order to compute the break-even point and profits at various sales volumes. The Sales Manager had calculated the break-even point as 1,339 units and for the 11,800 units sold in this quarter had predicted a loss. He was surprised therefore to see that the statement of actual profit/loss just produced for the quarter (Table 2) revealed a small profit as follows:

**Table 2**

| Production | 16,800 units | | |
|---|---|---|---|
| Sales | 11,800 units | | |

| | £000 | £000 |
|---|---|---|
| Sales: | | 2,242 |
| Manufacturing costs | | |
| Standard cost of production | | |
| 16,800 units | 2,016 | |
| *Less:* increase in stock 5,000 units | 600 | |
| Cost of sales | | 1,416 |
| Manufacturing margin | | 826 |
| *Less:* Manufacturing variances | | |
| Fixed overhead volume | 192 | |
| Expenditure | 48 | |
| | | 240 |
| | | 586 |
| Selling overheads | | |
| Variable | 138 | |
| Fixed | 376 | |
| | | 514 |
| Net profit | | 72 |

**Required:**

(a)   Using marginal costing:

(i)   illustrate the calculation of the break-even point undertaken by the Sales Manager

(ii)   calculate the loss predicted by the Sales Manager based on the actual units sold of 11,800.

For part (a) use the budgeted/standard costs given for the quarter in Table 1. **(4 marks)**

(b) (i) Demonstrate how the value of the manufacturing fixed overhead volume variance, shown in Table 2, has been computed and briefly explain its significance. **(5 marks)**

(ii) Calculate the expenditure and volume variances which apply to the selling overheads in this quarter. **(3 marks)**

(c) Reconcile the loss calculated in (a) (ii) with the profit for the quarter shown in Table 2 indicating all relevant differences. Briefly explain why an actual profit is revealed when a loss was anticipated by the Sales Manager. **(8 marks)**

**(Total: 20 marks)**

## 44    PAN-OCEAN CHEMICALS

Pan-Ocean Chemicals has one product which requires inputs from three types of material to produce batches of product Synthon. Standard cost details for a single batch are shown below:

|  | *Materials* | | *Labour* | |
| --- | --- | --- | --- | --- |
| *Material type* | *Standard kgs* | *Standard price per kg (£)* | *Standard hours* | *Standard rate per hour (£)* |
| S1 | 8 | 0.3 | 1 | 5.00 |
| S2 | 5 | 0.5 | | |
| S3 | 3 | 0.4 | | |

A standard loss of 10% of input is expected. Actual production was 15,408 kgs for the previous week. Details of the materials used were:

*Actual material used (kg)*
S1    8,284
S2    7,535
S3    3,334

Total labour cost for the week was £6,916 for 1,235 hours worked.

**Required:**

(a) Calculate:

(i) total material mix, yield and usage variances **(9 marks)**

(ii) labour rate and efficiency variances. **(2 marks)**

(b) Explain why the sum of the mix variances for materials measured in kg should be zero. **(3 marks)**

(c) Write a report to management which explains and interprets your results in part (a). The report should pay particular attention to:

– explaining what is meant by mix and yield variances in respect of materials, and

– possible reasons for all the results you have derived. **(11 marks)**

**(Total: 25 marks)**

## 45    CARAT

Carat plc, a premium food manufacturer, is reviewing operations for a three-month period of 20X3. The company operates a standard marginal costing system and manufactures one product, ZP, for which the following standard revenue and cost data per unit of product is available:

| | |
|---|---|
| Selling price | £12.00 |
| Direct material A | 2.5 kg at £1.70 per kg |
| Direct material B | 1.5 kg at £1.20 per kg |
| Direct labour | 0.45 hrs at £6.00 per hour |

Fixed production overheads for the three-month period were expected to be £62,500.

Actual data for the three-month period was as follows:

| | |
|---|---|
| Sales and production | 48,000 units of ZP were produced and sold for £580,800. |
| Direct material A | 121,951 kg were used at a cost of £200,000. |
| Direct material B | 67,200 kg were used at a cost of £84,000. |
| Direct labour | Employees worked for 18,900 hours, but 19,200 hours were paid at a cost of £117,120. |
| Fixed production overheads | £64,000 |

Budgeted sales for the three-month period were 50,000 units of Product ZP.

**Required:**

(a)    Calculate the following variances:

   (i)    sales volume contribution and sales price variances

   (ii)    price, mix and yield variances for each material

   (iii)    labour rate, labour efficiency and idle time variances.    **(8 marks)**

(b)    Prepare an operating statement that reconciles budgeted gross profit to actual gross profit with each variance clearly shown.    **(5 marks)**

(c)    Suggest possible explanations for the following variances:

   (i)    material price, mix and yield variances for material A

   (ii)    labour rate, labour efficiency and idle time variances.    **(5 marks)**

(d)    Critically discuss the types of standard used in standard costing and their effect on employee motivation.    **(7 marks)**

**(Total: 25 marks)**

## 46    FOOD MANUFACTURER

A food manufacturer specialises in the production of frozen cakes and sweet products, selling mainly to supermarkets. The following monthly budget applies to one of its products.

*Original budget*

| | £000 | £000 |
|---|---|---|
| Sales | | 1,000 |
| Costs: | | |
| Ingredients | 400 | |
| Labour and energy | 100 | |
| Fixed overheads | 300 | |
| | | 800 |
| Profit | | 200 |

For the ingredients, a standard quantity of 5 kg per pack is required; a standard price of 40p per kg applies in the original budget.

Considerable attention has been given to increasing the market share of this product whilst attempting to maintain its profitability. Consequently, since the preparation of the budget the management team implemented some changes to the manufacture and sale of this product. These changes were as follows:

(i)     The product was budgeted to sell for £5.00 per pack but, to promote sales, a price reduction on all sales to £4.50 per pack was made.

(ii)    The supplier of ingredients was changed and this secured a price reduction to 37.5p per kg on all ingredient supplies in return for a long-term contract.

(iii)   The method of working was changed in order to reduce the direct labour and energy costs which are regarded as variable.

All of the above changes applied for the whole of the month just ended and are reflected in the actual results shown below. The management intend, however, to use the original budget, for both cost and volume, as a reference point until the effect of the changes has been evaluated.

The following actual results have just been reported for the month:

*Actual results*

|  | £000 | £000 |
|---|---|---|
| Sales |  | 1,080 |
| Costs: |  |  |
| Ingredients | 520 |  |
| Labour and energy | 110 |  |
| Fixed overheads | 340 |  |
|  |  | 970 |
| Profit |  | 110 |

**Required:**

(a)     Prepare a flexible budget (for the actual quantity sold in the month just ended) based on the original budgeted unit costs and selling price.     **(3 marks)**

(b)     Using variances, reconcile the original budget profit with the actual profit. You should use a contribution approach to variance analysis.     **(9 marks)**

(c)     Provide a commentary on the variances you have produced. Within this commentary refer to possible interrelationships between the variances and how the level of fixed overheads may be reduced.     **(8 marks)**

**(Total: 20 marks)**

47    **LINSIL**

Linsil has produced the following operating statement reconciling budgeted and actual gross profit for the last three months, based on actual sales of 122,000 units of its single product:

| **Operating statement** | £ | £ | £ |
|---|---|---|---|
| Budgeted gross profit |  |  | 800,000 |
| Budgeted fixed production overhead |  |  | 352,000 |
| Budgeted contribution |  |  | 1,152,000 |
| Sales volume contribution variance |  | 19,200 |  |
| Sales price variance |  | (61,000) |  |
|  |  |  | (41,800) |
| Actual sales less standard variable cost of sales |  |  | 1,110,200 |

**Planning variances**

| Variable cost variances | Favourable | Adverse | |
|---|---|---|---|
| Direct material price | | 23,570 | |
| Direct material usage | 42,090 | | |
| Direct labour rate | | 76,128 | |
| Direct labour efficiency | | 203,333 | |
| | 42,090 | 303,031 | (260,941) |

**Operational variances**

| Variable cost variances | Favourable | Adverse | |
|---|---|---|---|
| Direct material price | | 31,086 | |
| Direct material usage | 14,030 | | |
| Direct labour rate | | 19,032 | |
| Direct labour efficiency | 130,133 | | |
| | 144,163 | 50,118 | 94,045 |

| | | | |
|---|---|---|---|
| Actual contribution | | | 943,304 |
| Budgeted fixed production overhead | | (352,000) | |
| Fixed production overhead expenditure variance | | 27,000 | |
| Actual fixed production overhead | | | (325,000) |
| Actual gross profit | | | 618,304 |

The standard direct costs and selling price applied during the three-month period and the actual direct costs and selling price for the period were as follows:

| | Standard | Actual |
|---|---|---|
| Selling price (£/unit) | 31.50 | 31.00 |
| Direct material usage (kg/unit) | 3.00 | 2.80 |
| Direct material price (£/kg) | 2.30 | 2.46 |
| Direct labour efficiency (hrs/unit) | 1.25 | 1.30 |
| Direct labour rate (£/hr) | 12.00 | 12.60 |

After the end of the three-month period and prior to the preparation of the above operating statement, it was decided to revise the standard costs retrospectively to take account of the following:

1    A 3% increase in the direct material price per kilogram

2    A labour rate increase of 4%

3    The standard for labour efficiency had anticipated buying a new machine leading to a 10% decrease in labour hours; instead of buying a new machine, existing machines had been improved, giving an expected 5% saving in material usage.

**Required:**

(a)    Using the information provided, demonstrate how each planning and operational variance in the operating statement has been calculated.    **(11 marks)**

(b)    Calculate direct labour and direct material variances based on the standard cost data applied during the three-month period.    **(4 marks)**

(c)   Explain the significance of separating variances into planning and operational elements, using the operating statement above to illustrate your answer.   **(5 marks)**

(d)   Discuss the factors to be considered in deciding whether a variance should be investigated.   **(5 marks)**

**(Total: 25 marks)**

## 48   MERMUS PLC

Mermus plc is comparing budget and actual data for the last three months.

|  | Budget £ | Budget £ | Actual £ | Actual £ |
|---|---|---|---|---|
| Sales |  | 950,000 |  | 922,500 |
| Cost of sales |  |  |  |  |
| Raw materials | 133,000 |  | 130,500 |  |
| Direct labour | 152,000 |  | 153,000 |  |
| Variable production overheads | 100,700 |  | 96,300 |  |
| Fixed production overheads | 125,400 |  | 115,300 |  |
|  |  | 511,100 |  | 495,100 |
|  |  | 438,900 |  | 427,400 |

The budget was prepared on the basis of 95,000 units produced and sold, but actual production and sales for the three-month period were 90,000 units.

Mermus uses standard costing and absorbs fixed production overheads on a machine hour basis. A total of 28,500 standard machine hours were budgeted. A total of 27,200 machine hours were actually used in the three-month period.

**Required:**

(a)   Prepare a revised budget at the new level of activity using a flexible budgeting approach.   **(4 marks)**

(b)   Calculate the following:

(i)    raw material total cost variance;

(ii)   direct labour total cost variance;

(iii)  fixed overhead efficiency variance;

(iv)   fixed overhead capacity variance;

(v)    fixed overhead expenditure variance.   **(8 marks)**

(c)   Suggest possible explanations for the following variances:

(i)    raw materials total cost variance;

(ii)   fixed overhead efficiency variance;

(iii)  fixed overhead expenditure variance.   **(6 marks)**

(d)   Explain three key purposes of a budgeting system.   **(7 marks)**

**(Total: 25 marks)**

## 49   BRK

BRK Co operates an absorption costing system and sells three products, B, R and K which are substitutes for each other. The following standard selling price and cost data relate to these three products:

| Product | Selling price per unit | Direct material per unit | Direct labour per unit |
|---|---|---|---|
| B | £14.00 | 3.00 kg at £1.80 per kg | 0.5 hrs at £6.50 per hour |
| R | £15.00 | 1.25 kg at £3.28 per kg | 0.8 hrs at £6.50 per hour |
| K | £18.00 | 1.94 kg at £2.50 per kg | 0.7 hrs at £6.50 per hour |

Budgeted fixed production overhead for the last period was £81,000. This was absorbed on a machine hour basis. The standard machine hours for each product and the budgeted levels of production and sales for each product for the last period are as follows:

| Product | B | R | K |
|---|---|---|---|
| Standard machine hours per unit | 0.3 hrs | 0.6 hrs | 0.8 hrs |
| Budgeted production and sales (units) | 10,000 | 13,000 | 9,000 |

Actual volumes and selling prices for the three products in the last period were as follows:

| Product | B | R | K |
|---|---|---|---|
| Actual selling price per unit | £14.50 | £15.50 | £19.00 |
| Actual production and sales (units) | 9,500 | 13,500 | 8,500 |

### Required:

(a)   Calculate the following variances for overall sales for the last period:

   (i)   sales price variance;

   (ii)   sales volume profit variance;

   (iii)   sales mix profit variance;

   (iv)   sales quantity profit variance and reconcile budgeted profit for the period to actual sales less standard cost.   **(13 marks)**

(b)   Discuss the significance of the sales mix profit variance and comment on whether useful information would be obtained by calculating mix variances for each of these three products.   **(4 marks)**

(c)   Describe the essential elements of a standard costing system and explain how quantitative analysis can assist in the preparation of standard costs.   **(8 marks)**

**(Total: 25 marks)**

# BUDGETING, BUDGETARY CONTROL AND DECISION-MAKING

## 50   ALL PREMIER SERVICES PLC

All Premier Services plc is a fee charging hospital that has two specialist wards, X and Y. A third ward, Z, is used for patients who are well enough to leave Wards X and Y but who require a short period of hospital rest before being discharged. It is intended that Ward Z will be only occupied by patients transferred from the other wards. Budgeted details relating to the wards are as follows (fixed and variable costs are for a complete week).

| Ward: | X | Y | Z |
|---|---|---|---|
| Number of beds | 60 | 40 | 45 |
| Budgeted fee per bed per night (£) | 225 | 200 | 170 |
| Budgeted occupancy % | 65 | 80 | 100 |

| Budgeted costs: | £ |
|---|---|
| Fixed overheads | 127,300 |
| Variable overheads | 42,412 |

Fixed overheads are allocated to the wards on the basis of the number of beds available in each ward. Variable overheads are allocated to beds in proportion to the fees earned per ward.

**Required:**

(a) (i) Prepare a budgeted profit/loss statement (based on one week) for each of the wards and for the three wards combined. Calculate the total cost incurred per bed occupied per week (seven nights). **(5 marks)**

(ii) A proposal has been put forward to increase the number of beds in ward Z to 75. This proposal would be expected to increase occupancy in wards X and Y to 80% and 95%, respectively. Budgeted occupancy in ward Z will remain at 100%. It is expected that total variable overheads would increase to £57,881 as a result.

Evaluate this proposal on the same basis as your answer to part (a) (i).

**(5 marks)**

(b) (i) In making decision about expanding Ward Z, comment on the fact that it is only occupied by patients from wards X and Y. **(2 marks)**

(ii) Briefly assess the relevance of the allocation bases for fixed and variable overheads. **(3 marks)**

(c) Describe the characteristics of a responsibility accounting system and discuss what factors exist in non-profit organisations that make responsibility accounting difficult to implement. **(10 marks)**

**(Total: 25 marks)**

## 51 ACRED LIMITED

Acred Ltd manufactures a single product. It is preparing monthly budgets for the six months from July to December 20X4. The following standard revenue and cost data is available:

| Selling price | £12.00 per unit |
|---|---|
| Materials | 2 kg per unit at £2.40 per kg |
| Labour | £1.80 per unit |
| Direct expenses | £1.20 per unit |

Sales in June 20X4 and July 20X4 are forecast to be 10,000 units in each month. As a direct result of marketing expenditure of £95,000 in August 20X4, sales are expected to be 11,000 units in August 20X4 and to increase by 1,000 units in each month from September to December. Sales after December 20X4 are expected to remain at the December 20X4 level.

25% of sales are paid for when they occur and 75% of sales are paid for in the month following sale. Stocks of finished goods at the end of each month are required to be 20% of the expected sales for the following month. Stocks of materials at the end of each month are required to be 50% of the materials required for the following month's production.

Materials are paid for in the month following purchase. Labour and direct expenses are paid for in the month in which they occur. Overheads for production, administration and distribution will be £34,000 per month, including depreciation of £12,000 per month. These overheads are payable in the month in which they occur. Acred Ltd has a £750,000 bank loan at 8% per annum on which it pays interest twice per year, in March and September.

The cash balance at the end of June 20X4 is expected to be £50,000.

**Required:**

(a)    Prepare the following budgets for Acred Ltd on a month by month basis for the six month period from July to December 20X4:

    (i)    production budget (units)

    (ii)    cash budget.                              **(13 marks)**

(b)    Critically discuss the relative merits of periodic budgeting and continuous budgeting.

                                                   **(7 marks)**

(c)    Discuss the consequences of budget bias (budgetary slack) for cost control.  **(5 marks)**

                                                **(Total: 25 marks)**

## 52    SYCHWEDD PLC

Sychwedd plc manufacture and sell three products R, S, and T which make use of two machine groups, 1 and 2. The budget for period 1, the first quarter of their next accounting year, includes the following information:

| | *Machine Group* | |
| --- | --- | --- |
| **Fixed overhead absorption rates:** | *1* | *2* |
| Rate per machine hour | £10.00 | £11.20 |

| | *Product R* | *Product S* | *Product T* |
| --- | --- | --- | --- |
| Sales (kilos) | 12,000 | 25,000 | 40,000 |
| | £ | £ | £ |
| Sales | 120,000 | 250,000 | 360,000 |
| Variable costs | 73,560 | 164,250 | 284,400 |
| Fixed overheads | 19,752 | 38,300 | 42,400 |
| Budgeted net profit | 26,688 | 47,450 | 33,200 |

For the second quarter (period 2), it is estimated that the budgeted machine hours and direct labour hours needed to produce 1,000 kilos of each of the products are:

| | *Machine Group* | |
| --- | --- | --- |
| **Machine hours** | 1 | 2 |
| Product | | |
|   R | 75 | 80 |
|   S | 30 | 110 |
|   T | 50 | 50 |
| **Direct labour hours** | | |
| Product | | |
|   R | 30 | 40 |
|   S | 10 | 50 |
|   T | 20 | 20 |
| **Budgeted fixed overheads** (to be absorbed using a machine hour rate) | £40,800 | £68,365 |
| **Budgeted variable labour and overheads,** rate per direct labour hour | £7.50 | £8.50 |

|  | Product R | Product S | Product T |
|---|---|---|---|
| **Budgeted material costs** per 1,000 kilos | £4,508 | £5,096 | £6,125 |
| **Expected sales** (kilos) | 10,000 | 25,000 | 50,000 |
| Planned price changes: |  |  |  |
| Compared with period 1 | 10% increase | No change | No change |

A sales commission of 4% of the sales value will be paid.

There are no budgeted opening or closing stocks i.e., all production is expected to be sold.

**Required:**

(a)    Compute the machine hour rate for each machine group for period 2.    **(4 marks)**

(b)    Calculate the budgeted contribution and net profit for each of the three products for period 2.    **(12 marks)**

(c)    Assuming that the sales trend shown over the two periods is forecast to continue, comment briefly on the figures and advise management accordingly.    **(9 marks)**

**(Total: 25 marks)**

## 53    PRIVATE HOSPITAL

A private hospital is organised into separate medical units which offer specialised nursing care (e.g. maternity unit, paediatric unit). Figures for the paediatric unit for the year to 31 May 20X3 have just become available. For the year in question the paediatric unit charged patients £200 per patient day for nursing care and £4.4m in revenue was earned.

Costs of running the unit consist of variable costs, direct staffing costs and allocated fixed costs. The charges for variable costs such as catering and laundry are based on the number of patient days spent in hospital. Staffing costs are established from the personnel requirements applicable to particular levels of patient days. Charges for fixed costs such as security administration etc, are based on bed capacity, currently 80 beds.

The number of beds available to be occupied is regarded as bed capacity and this is agreed and held constant for the whole year. There was an agreement that a bed capacity of 80 beds would apply to the paediatric unit for the 365 days of the year to 31 May 20X3.

The tables below show the variable, staffing and fixed costs applicable to the paediatric unit for the year to 31 May 20X3.

**Variable costs** (based on patient days)

|  | £ |
|---|---|
| Catering | 450,000 |
| Laundry | 150,000 |
| Pharmacy | 500,000 |
|  | 1,100,000 |

**Staffing costs**

Each speciality recruits its own supervisors and assistants. The staffing requirements for the paediatric unit are based on the actual patient day, see the following table:

| Patient days per annum | Supervisors | Nurses | Assistants |
|---|---|---|---|
| Up to 20,500 | 4 | 10 | 20 |
| 20,500 to 23,000 | 4 | 13 | 24 |
| Over 23,000 | 4 | 15 | 28 |

The annual costs of employment are: supervisors £22,000 each, nurses £16,000 each and assistants £12,000 each.

**Fixed costs** (based on bed capacity)

|  | £ |
|---|---|
| Administration | 850,000 |
| Security | 80,000 |
| Rent and property | 720,000 |
|  | 1,650,000 |

During the year to 31 May 20X3 the paediatric unit operated at 100% occupancy (i.e. all 80 beds occupied) for 100 days of the year. In fact the demand on these days was for at least 20 beds more.

As a consequence of this, in the budget for the following year to 31 May 20X4, an increase in the bed capacity has been agreed. 20 extra beds will be contracted for the whole of the year. It is assumed that the 100 beds will be fully occupied for 100 days, rather than being restricted to 80 beds on those days. An increase of 10% in employment costs for the year to 31 May 20X4, due to wage rate rises, will occur for all personnel. The revenue per patient day, all other cost factors and the remaining occupancy will be the same as the year to 31 May 20X3.

**Required:**

(a) Determine for the year to 31 May 20X3, the actual number of patient-days, the bed occupancy percentage, the net profit/loss and the break-even number(s) of patient days for the paediatric unit. **(6 marks)**

(b) Determine the budget for the year to 31 May 20X4 showing the revised number of patient-days, the bed occupancy percentage, the net profit/loss and the number of patient-days required to achieve the same profit/loss as computed in (a) above. **(5 marks)**

(c) Comment on your findings from (a) and (b) offering advice to the management of the unit. **(6 marks)**

(d) A business or operating unit can have both financial and social objectives and at times these can be in conflict. Briefly explain and give an example. **(3 marks)**

**(Total: 20 marks)**

## 54 PUBLIC SECTOR ORGANISATION

A public sector organisation is extending its budgetary control and responsibility accounting system to all departments. One such department concerned with public health and welfare is called 'Homecare'. The department consists of staff who visit elderly 'clients' in their homes to support them with their basic medical and welfare needs.

A monthly cost control report is to be sent to the department manager, a copy of which is also passed to a Director who controls a number of departments. In the system, which is still being refined, the budget was set by the Director and the manager had not been consulted over the budget or the use of the monthly control report.

Shown below is the first month's cost control report for the Homecare department

**Cost Control Report - Homecare Department**
**Month ending May 20X0**

|  | Budget | Actual | (Overspend)/ Underspend |
|---|---|---|---|
| Visits | 10,000 | 12,000 | (2,000) |
|  | £ | £ | £ |
| Department expenses: |  |  |  |
| Supervisory salary | 2,000 | 2,125 | (125) |
| Wages (Permanent staff) | 2,700 | 2,400 | 300 |
| Wages (Casual staff) | 1,500 | 2,500 | (1,000) |
| Office equipment depreciation | 500 | 750 | (250) |
| Repairs to equipment | 200 | 20 | 180 |
| Travel expenses | 1,500 | 1,800 | (300) |
| Consumables | 4,000 | 6,000 | (2,000) |
| Administration and telephone | 1,000 | 1,200 | (200) |
| Allocated administrative costs | 2,000 | 3,000 | (1,000) |
|  | 15,400 | 19,795 | (4,395) |

In addition to the manager and permanent members of staff, appropriately qualified casual staff are appointed on a week to week basis to cope with fluctuations in demand. Staff use their own transport, and travel expenses are reimbursed. There is a central administration overhead charge over all departments. Consumables consist of materials which are used by staff to care for clients. Administration and telephone are costs of keeping in touch with the staff who often operate from their own homes.

As a result of the report, the Director sent a memo to the manager of the Homecare department pointing out that the department must spend within its funding allocation and that any spending more than 5% above budget on any item would not be tolerated. The Director requested an immediate explanation for the serious overspend.

You work as the assistant to the Directorate Management Accountant. On seeing the way the budget system was developing, he made a note of points he would wish to discuss and develop further, but was called away before these could be completed.

**Required:**

(a)  Develop and explain the issues concerning the budgetary control and responsibility accounting system which are likely to be raised by the management accountant. You should refer to the way the budget was prepared, the implications of a 20% increase in the number of visits, the extent of controllability of costs, the implications of the funding allocation, social aspects and any other points you think appropriate. You may include numerical illustrations and comment on specific costs, but you are not required to reproduce the cost control report.  **(14 marks)**

(b)  Briefly explain Zero-Based Budgeting (ZBB), describe how (in a situation such as that above) it might be implemented, and how as a result it could improve the budget setting procedure.  **(6 marks)**

**(Total: 20 marks)**

## 55 ZERO BASED BUDGETING

(a) Explain why Zero Based Budgeting might be a useful tool to employ to ensure that budgetary requirements are kept up to date. **(4 marks)**

(b) Describe the steps needed to be undertaken in order to implement a Zero Based Budgeting system in respect of:

– the questioning of why expenditure needs to be incurred

– how a decision is made as to which activities should be provided with a budget, and

– what questions should be asked when budgeted activities need to be ranked to allocate scarce resources. **(8 marks)**

(c) Critically assess the use of Zero Based Budgeting as a tool that might be used to motivate employees. **(6 marks)**

(d) Explain the advantages of encouraging employee participation in budget setting. **(7 marks)**

**(Total: 25 marks)**

## 56 ROLLING BUDGETS

A company operates a system of quarterly rolling budgets. Budgets for the next three quarters have been prepared. The figures below reflect the likely cost behaviour of each element of cost. Quarter four is being developed based on these budgets and other information available.

**Budget Quarters 1 to 3**

|  | Q1 (000) | Q2 (000) | Q3 (000) |
|---|---|---|---|
| Activity: | | | |
| Sales (units) | 18 | 34 | 30 |
| Production (units) | 20 | 40 | 30 |
| | | | |
| Costs: | £000 | £000 | £000 |
| Direct materials | 50 | 100 | 75 |
| Production labour | 180 | 280 | 230 |
| Factory overheads (excluding indirect labour) | 170 | 200 | 185 |
| Administration | 30 | 30 | 30 |
| Selling and distribution | 29 | 37 | 35 |

In the current planning stage for quarter four, flexible budgets are to be developed for low, most likely and high sales volumes (38,000, 44,000 and 50,000 units respectively). The company wishes to have a closing stock (end of quarter four) equal to the opening stock for quarter one. Management will therefore adjust the production levels to fall in line with this policy.

Cost structures as for quarters one to three will apply to quarter four except that:

(i) raw material prices are expected to rise by 10%

(ii) production labour rates will increase by 2.5%. However, management have declared that all labour rate increases must be matched by increased efficiency so that labour costs (both total fixed and variable per unit) are unaltered.

(iii) a quarterly bonus payment, of 50% of the variable labour cost per unit, will apply for all production above 40,000 units.

(iv) fixed factory overheads and fixed selling and distribution expenses will rise by 5%.

The expected selling price per unit is £18. Stock is valued at full factory cost of £13 per unit. This has been established using absorption principles and based on long run cost and capacity predictions. Small fluctuations in cost prices or volumes will not cause this unit cost to be amended.

**Required:**

(a)   Explain what is meant by a 'rolling budget' and what additional benefit may be claimed for this compared to the annual style of budget.   **(4 marks)**

(b)   Summarise the variable cost per unit and the total fixed cost, for each cost heading, that will apply to quarter four, for production below 40,000 units.   **(6 marks)**

(c)   Prepare detailed flexed budget profit statements for quarter four under the separate assumptions of low, most likely and high levels of sales and corresponding production volumes.   **(8 marks)**

(d)   Produce in *summary form only* a statement of the likely change in profit for quarter four if management change their policy on stock levels so as to manufacture the same volume as the forecast sales for the quarter. Comment on the reason for the profit change and how this might motivate management regarding production levels in the future.   **(7 marks)**

**(Total: 25 marks)**

## 57   STORRS PLC

It is mid-June and the new managing director of Storrs plc is reviewing sales forecasts for Quarter 3 of 20X3, which begins on 1 July, and for Quarter 4. The company manufactures garden furniture and experiences seasonal variations in sales, which has made forecasting difficult in the past. Sales for the last two calendar years were as follows:

| Year | Quarter 1 | Quarter 2 | Quarter 3 | Quarter 4 |
|------|-----------|-----------|-----------|-----------|
| 20X1 | £2,700,000 | £3,500,000 | £3,400,000 | £3,000,000 |
| 20X2 | £3,100,000 | £3,900,000 | £3,600,000 | £3,400,000 |

Sales in Quarter 1 of 20X3 were £3,600,000. There is two weeks to go until the end of Quarter 2 and the managing director of Storrs plc is confident that it will achieve sales of £4,400,000 in this quarter.

The existing sales forecasts for the two remaining quarters of the year were made by the sales director (who has been with the company for several years) during last year's budget-setting process. These forecasts are £3,800,000 for Quarter 3 and £3,600,000 for Quarter 4. Budgets within Storrs plc have traditionally been prepared and agreed by the directors of the company before being implemented by junior managers.

As a basis for revising the sales forecasts for the two remaining quarters of 20X3, the management accountant of Storrs plc has begun to apply time series analysis in order to identify the seasonal variations in sales. He has so far calculated the following centred moving averages, using a base period of four quarters.

| Year | Quarter 1 | Quarter 2 | Quarter 3 | Quarter 4 |
|------|-----------|-----------|-----------|-----------|
| 20X1 | | | £3,200,000 | £3,300,000 |
| 20X2 | £3,375,000 | £3,450,000 | £3,562,500 | £3,687,500 |

**Required:**

(a)   Using the sales information and centred moving averages provided, and assuming an additive model, forecast the sales of Storrs plc for Quarter 3 and Quarter 4 of 20X3, and comment on the sales forecasts made by the sales director.

(Note that you are NOT required to use regression analysis)   **(8 marks)**

(b)    Discuss the limitations of the sales forecasting method used in part (a).    **(5 marks)**

(c)    Discuss the relative merits of top-down and bottom-up approaches to budget setting.

**(12 marks)**

**(Total: 25 marks)**

## 58    BUDGET BEHAVIOUR

For many organisations in both the private and public sectors the annual budget is the basis of much internal management information. When preparing and using budgets, however, management and the accountant must be aware of their behavioural implications.

**Required:**

(a)    Briefly discuss four purposes of budgets.    **(8 marks)**

(b)    Explain the behavioural factors which should be borne in mind and the difficulties of applying them in the process of budgeting and budgetary control.    **(12 marks)**

**(Total: 20 marks)**

## 59    NOT-FOR-PROFIT ORGANISATIONS

**Required:**

(a)    Discuss how costing information and principles may be applied in a not-for-profit organisation in the following areas:

(i)     the selection of cost units;

(ii)    the use of performance measures to measure output and quality;

(iii)   the comparison of planned and actual performance.    **(10 marks)**

(b)    Discuss the key features of zero-based budgeting and explain how it may be applied in a not-for-profit organisation.    **(8 marks)**

(c)    Briefly discuss how activity-based budgeting might be introduced into a manufacturing organisation and the advantages that might arise from the use of activity-based budgeting in such an organisation.    **(7 marks)**

**(Total: 25 marks)**

# PERFORMANCE MEASUREMENT

## 60    INDEX

(a)    Explain the term 'weighted index'.    **(4 marks)**

(b)    A company manufactures and sells three products, A, B and C. Sales data for the three products over the last four periods is set out below:

|  | *Product A* | | *Product B* | | *Product C* | |
|---|---|---|---|---|---|---|
|  | *Sales volume units* | *Sales value £* | *Sales volume units* | *Sales value £* | *Sales volume units* | *Sales value £* |
| Period 1 | 20,200 | 15,352 | 51,320 | 61,584 | 10,400 | 16,848 |
| Period 2 | 16,360 | 13,088 | 52,100 | 66,688 | 12,080 | 20,536 |
| Period 3 | 15,100 | 12,382 | 57,300 | 76,209 | 15,960 | 27,930 |
| Period 4 | 16,200 | 13,770 | 57,530 | 80,542 | 22,725 | 40,905 |

**Required:**

(i)    Calculate the base weighted (Laspeyre) sales price index for Period 4 based on Period 1.    **(3 marks)**

(ii)   Calculate the current weighted (Paasche) sales quantity index for Period 4 based on Period 3.    **(3 marks)**

**(Total: 10 marks)**

## 61    WINDERMERE

Windermere operates a divisional organisation structure. The performance of each division is assessed on the basis of the Return on Capital Employed (ROCE) that it generates.

For this purpose the ROCE of a division is calculated by dividing its 'trading profit' for the year by the 'book value of net assets' that it is using at the end of the year. Trading profit is the profit earned excluding non-recurring items. Book value of net assets excludes any cash, bank account balance or overdraft because Windermere plc uses a common bank account (under the control of its head office) for all divisions.

At the start of every year each division is given a target ROCE. If the target is achieved or exceeded than the divisional executives are given a large salary bonus at the end of the year.

In 20X1, Windermere plc's division A was given a target ROCE of 15%. On 15 December 20X1 A's divisional manager receives a forecast that trading profit for 20X1 would be £120,000 and net assets employed at the end of 20X1 would be £820,000. This would give an ROCE of 14.6% which is slightly below A's target.

The divisional manager immediately circulates a memorandum to his fellow executives inviting proposals to deal with the problem. By the end of the day he has received the following proposals from those executives (all of whom will lose their salary bonus if the ROCE target is not achieved):

(1)   from the Works Manager: that £100,000 should be invested in new equipment resulting in cost savings of £18,000 per year over the next fifteen years;

(2)   from the Chief Accountant: that payment of a £42,000 trade debt owed to a supplier due on 16 December 20X1 be deferred until 1 January 20X2. This would result in a £1,000 default penalty becoming immediately due;

(3)   from the Sales Manager: that £1,500 additional production expenses be incurred and paid in order to bring completion of an order forward to 29 December 20X1 from its previous scheduled date of 3 January 20X2. This would allow the customer to be invoiced in December, thereby boosting 20X1 profits by £6,000, but would not accelerate customer payment due on 1 February 20X2.

(4)   From the Head of Internal Audit: That a regional plant producing a particular product be closed allowing immediate sale for £120,000 of premises having a book value of £90,000. This would result in £50,000 immediate redundancy payments and a reduction in profit of £12,600 per year over the next fifteen years.

(a)   **You are required** to assess each of the above four proposals having regard to:

(i)    their effect on divisional performance in 20X1 and 20X2 as measured by Windermere plc's existing criteria,

(ii)   their intrinsic commercial merits,

(iii)  any ethical matters that you consider relevant.

You should ignore taxation and inflation.    **(20 marks)**

(b)     **You are required** to discuss what action Windermere plc's Finance Director should take when the situation at division A and the above four proposals are brought to his attention.

**(5 marks)**

**(Total: 25 marks)**

## 62     KDS LTD

KDS Ltd is an engineering company which is organised for management purposes in the form of several autonomous divisions. The performance of each division is currently measured by calculation of its return on capital employed (ROCE). KDS Ltd's existing accounting policy is to calculate ROCE by dividing the net assets of each division at the end of the year into the operating profit generated by the division during the year. Cash is excluded from net assets since all divisions share a bank account controlled by KDS Ltd's head office. Depreciation is on a straight-line basis.

The divisional management teams are paid a performance-related bonus conditional upon achievement of a 15% ROCE target. On 20 December 20X5 the divisional managers were provided with performance forecasts for 20X5 which included the following:

| Forecast | Net assets at 31 December 20X5 | 20X5 operating profit | ROCE |
|---|---|---|---|
| | £ | £ | |
| Division K | 4,400,000 | 649,000 | 14.75% |
| Division D | 480,000 | 120,000 | 25.00% |

Subsequently, the manager of Division K invited members of her management team to offer advice.  The responses she received included the following:

From the divisional administrator:

'We can achieve our 20X5 target by deferring payment of a £90,000 trade debt payable on 20 December until 1 January. I should add that we will thereby immediately incur a £2,000 late payment penalty.'

From the works manager:

'We should replace a number of our oldest machine tools (which have nil book value) at a cost of £320,000.  The new equipment will have a life of eight years and generate cost savings of £76,000 per year. The new equipment can be on site and operational by 31 December 20X5.'

From the financial controller:

'The existing method of performance appraisal is unfair. We should ask head office to adopt residual income (RI) as the key performance indicator, using the company's average 12% cost of money for a finance charge.'

### Required:

(a)     Compare and appraise the proposals of the divisional administrator and the works manager, having regard to the achievement of the ROCE performance target in 20X5 and to any longer term factors you think relevant.     **(9 marks)**

(b)     Explain the extent to which you agree or disagree with the financial controller's proposal.     **(7 marks)**

(c)     Explain the value and use of non-financial performance measures.

**(4 marks)**

**(Total: 20 marks)**

Demand for July 20X3 onwards is expected to be the same as June 20X3. The probability of each level of demand occurring each month is as follows:

High 0.05;                          Medium 0.85;                          Low 0.10.

It is expected that 10% of the total sales value will be cash sales, mainly being retail customers making small purchases. The remaining 90% of sales will be made on two months' credit. A 2.5% discount will, however, be offered to credit customers settling within one month. It is estimated that customers, representing half of credit sales by value, will take advantage of the discount while the remainder will take the full two months to pay.

Variable production costs (excluding costs of rejects) per £1,000 of sales are as follows:

|  | £ |
|---|---|
| Labour | 300 |
| Materials | 200 |
| Variable overhead | 100 |

Labour is paid in the month in which labour costs are incurred. Materials are paid one month in arrears and variable overheads are paid two months in arrears. Fixed production and administration overheads, excluding depreciation, are £7,000 per month and are payable in the same month as the expenditure is incurred.

Jack employed a firm of consultants to give him initial business advice. Their fee of £12,000 will be paid in February 20X3. Smelting machinery will be purchased on 1 January 20X3 for £200,000 payable in February 20X3. Further machinery will be purchased for £50,000 in March 20X3 payable in April 20X3. This machinery is highly specialized and will have a low net realisable value after purchase.

Jack has redundancy money from his previous employment and savings totalling £150,000, which he intends to pay into his bank account on 1 January 20X3 as the initial capital of the business. He realises that this will be insufficient for his business plans, so he is intending to approach his bank for finance in the form of both a fixed term loan and an overdraft. The only asset Jack has is his house that is valued at £200,000, but he has an outstanding mortgage of £80,000 on this property.

The consultants advising Jack have recommended that rather than accumulating sufficient stock to satisfy the following month's demand he should not maintain any stock levels but merely produce sufficient in each month to meet the expected demand for that month.

Jack's production manager objected: 'I need to set up my production schedule based on the expected average demand for the month. I will reduce production in the month if it seems demand is low. However, there is no way production can be increased during the month to accommodate demand if it happens to be at the higher level that month. As a result, under this new system, there would be no stocks to fall back on and the extra sales, when monthly demand is high, would be lost, as customers require immediate delivery.' In respect of this, an assessment of the impact of the introduction of just-in-time stock management on cash flows has been made that showed the following:

|  | January | February | March | April | May | June |
|---|---|---|---|---|---|---|
| Net cash flow (£) | 143,000 | (223,279) | (7,587) | (50,667) | 1,843 | 1,704 |
| Month-end balance (£) | 143,000 | (80,279) | (87,866) | (138,533) | (136,690) | (134,986) |

**Required:**

(a)  Prepare a monthly cash budget for Jack Geep's business for the six month period ending 30 June 20X3. Calculations should be made on the basis of the expected values of sales. The cash budget should show the net cash inflow or outflow in each month and the cumulative cash surplus or deficit at the end of each month.

For this purpose ignore bank finance and the suggested use of just-in-time stock management. **(17 marks)**

(b)  Assume now that just-in-time stock management is used in accordance with the recommendations of the consultants. Calculate for EACH of the six months ending 30 June 20X3:

(i)  receipts from sales

(ii)  payments to labour. **(6 marks)**

(c)  Evaluate the impact for Jack Geep of introducing just-in-time stock management. This should include an assessment of the wider implications of just-in-time stock management in the particular circumstances of Jack Geep's business. **(10 marks)**

(d)  Write a report to Jack Geep which identifies the financing needs of the company. It should consider the following:

(i)  the extent of financing required

(ii)  the factors that should be considered in determining the most appropriate mix of short-term financing (e.g. overdraft) and long-term financing (e.g. fixed term bank loan)

(iii)  the extent to which improved working capital management (other than just-in-time stock management) might reduce the company's financing needs and describe how this might be achieved.

Where appropriate, show supporting calculations. **(17 marks)**

**(Total: 50 marks)**

## 3  DOE LIMITED

Assume that 'now' is December 20X3.

At a recent meeting of the Board of Doe Ltd, a supplier of industrial and commercial clothing, it was suggested that the company might be suffering liquidity problems as a result of overtrading, despite encouraging growth in turnover. The Finance Director was instructed to report to the next Board meeting on this matter.

Extracts from the financial statements of Doe Ltd for 20X2, and from the forecast financial statements for 20X3, are given below.

*Profit and Loss Account extracts for years ending 31 December*

|  | 20X3 £000 | 20X2 £000 |
|---|---|---|
| Turnover | 8,300 | 6,638 |
| Cost of sales | 4,900 | 3,720 |
| Gross profit | 3,400 | 2,918 |
| Administration and distribution expenses | 2,700 | 2,318 |
| Operating profit | 700 | 600 |
| Interest | 125 | 100 |
| Profit before tax | 575 | 500 |

### Additional information

(1)    The nominal value of ordinary share capital is 50 pence per share.

(2)    Costs are classified as fixed or variable as follows:

Cost of sales: 100% variable

Selling and distribution: £100,000 per annum fixed, balance variable

Administration costs: £7 million per annum fixed, balance variable.

(3)    The current rate of corporation tax is 30%.

(4)    Current liabilities as at 31 December 20X0 includes a £2 million overdraft, and a £450,000 VAT bill.

(5)    The current market price of ordinary shares in Spender plc is £6.50.

(6)    Working capital needs are expected to rise in line with sales.

(7)    The dividend forecast for year ending 31 December 20X1 is 25 pence per share.

(8)    Bank interest charges for the year to 31 December 20X1 are forecast to be £280,000. Interest is charged at 12.5% per annum.

(9)    Depreciation charges on fixed assets for the year to 31 December 20X0 are £435,000.

(10)   Assume that payments totalling £2.5 million were made during 20X0 in respect of creditors outstanding at the end of the previous year.

(11)   Working capital requirements for 20X0 were the same as those for the previous year.

### Required:

(a)    Explain and illustrate, using the above data, each of the following terms and comment upon the implications of these two forms of gearing for the equity investors in Spender Construction plc:

(i)     operational gearing

(ii)    financial gearing.                                                            **(14 marks)**

(b)    Calculate how much external finance Spender must raise in order to finance the planned sales growth and the investment in the new HQ and IT centre. Assume that both additional working capital and the capital funds are required in full immediately, i.e. on 1 January 20X1.                                              **(8 marks)**

(c)    Given that it currently has an overdraft of £2 million, under what circumstances would it be prudent for Spender plc to replace this short-term funding with long-term debt finance?                                                          **(5 marks)**

(d)    Evaluate (by comparison of shareholder risks and returns, including EPS) the relative merits of raising the £7 million required for the capital investment via a 1 for 6 rights issue priced at £5.25, or a 10% debenture issue redeemable in 20 years time. Ignore issue costs.                                                        **(10 marks)**

(e)    Explain the meaning of the term dividend cover and, using the forecast figures for the year ending 31 December 20X1, calculate the dividend cover for Spender plc assuming the debenture issue is made.                                      **(3 marks)**

**(Total: 40 marks)**

## 6   STADIUM EATS

Stadium Eats is a themed football (soccer) restaurant, seating 150 people, which was set up four years ago by a partnership of two graduate caterers. The restaurant has proved very popular, and sales are now (20X8) averaging £8,500 per week for the 50 weeks of the year that the restaurant is open. The average spend per customer is £15 per head on Saturdays and Sundays, and £12 per head on weekdays. The gross profit margin is 20% and the operating profit margin is 11%.

Stadium Eats is now facing the problem of having to turn customers away on Saturdays and Sundays, as demand is starting to exceed the capacity. Customers are finding that they are needing to place bookings around eight weeks ahead in order to be certain of getting a table at the required time on these days.

In order to overcome the capacity problem, and expand the business further, Stadium Eats are planning to open a second restaurant. They have already identified a suitable site, and drawn up a simple forecast profit and loss account for the new outlet for the first year of trading and an end of year balance sheet. The forecasts are *loosely* based on the revenues and costs of the existing outlet, and are detailed below.

### Forecast profit and loss account for the year ended 30 June 20X9

|                     | £000 |
|---------------------|-----:|
| Sales               | 600  |
| Operating profit    | 135  |
| Interest payable    | 18   |
| Profit before tax   | 117  |
| Taxation            | 35   |
| Profit after tax    | 82   |

*Notes*

(1)   In calculating operating profit, the two owners have not allowed for any salary costs for themselves, as they already draw a salary of £22,000 each from the existing business.

(2)   The new restaurant will be able to seat 180 people, and will be open 50 weeks of the year.

(3)   The tax rate is assumed to be 30%.

(4)   After tax profit is shared equally between the two partners, but will be wholly re-invested in the business. To date, the partners have made no drawings other than the salaries indicated above.

(5)   The current cash balance in the existing business amounts to £45,000, and it is expected that £25,000 of this will be required for refurbishment of the premises for the new restaurant.

(6)   The two partners will own equal shares in the new concern.

### Forecast balance sheet as at 30 June 20X9

|                          | £000 | £000 |
|--------------------------|-----:|-----:|
| *Assets employed:*       |      |      |
| *Fixed (net)*            |      |      |
| Premises                 |      | 280  |
| Fixtures and fittings    |      | 75   |
|                          |      | 355  |

| Current assets | | |
|---|---|---|
| Food stocks | 3 | |
| Debtors | 7 | |
| Cash | 18 | |
| | — | |
| | | 28 |
| *Current liabilities* | | |
| Creditors | 12 | |
| | — | |
| Net current assets | | 16 |
| | | — |
| Total assets less current liabilities | | 371 |
| Long-term creditors | | 195 |
| | | — |
| Net assets | | 176 |
| | | — |
| *Financed by:* | | |
| Ordinary shares (25p nominal) | | 94 |
| Profit & loss account | | 82 |
| | | — |
| | | 176 |
| | | — |

**Notes**

(1) The long-term creditors would be made up of bank loans and a mortgage against the premises. The mortgage outstanding at 30 June 20X9 would be £184,000 and the balance of the long-term creditors represents a bank loan at 10% interest (fixed rate). The loan would be repaid in monthly instalments, and the balance cleared after five years.

(2) Stadium Eats is currently run as a partnership, but it is intended that the new restaurant will be operated as a private limited company.

(3) In order to raise the cash for their equity investment in the new venture, the two partners would need to raise loans totalling £75,000 against their own homes. They have been assured that the loans will be available but are a little concerned at the risk that they may be taking in borrowing so much to invest in a new business.

**Required:**

(a) State and explain any reservations that you may have regarding the figures in the forecast profit and loss account, and draft a revised version, adjusted to take account of your criticisms. **(10 marks)**

(b) A bank may be concerned about the level of gearing in a business which has applied for additional loan finance. Explain the meaning of the term capital gearing, and why a lender/investor should be wary of further borrowing when gearing is already high.

**(10 marks)**

(c) Calculate and comment on the level of gearing based on the 20X9 forecast balance sheet. (Note that this excludes the proposed £75,000 personal loans for the new restaurant). **(4 marks)**

(d) Given that Stadium Eats are already operating successfully, what other sources of long-term finance might be available to the new business? **(8 marks)**

(e)   An accountant has advised the partners that it might be best for them to combine the two restaurants under the umbrella of a single company, and seek a flotation on AIM in five years' time.

Explain the role of AIM within the financial markets, and identify the factors to be considered in seeking a stock market quotation.                        **(8 marks)**

**(Total: 40 marks)**

## 7    WATER SUPPLY SERVICES PLC

Water Supply Services plc is a small regional supplier of water to domestic premises. The company has been operating for a number of years. Its sole customer is the Regional Water Authority (RWA), which allows the company to charge a 25% mark up of agreed costs. The agreed costs that can be incorporated into any calculation of mark up are only labour costs, materials costs, variable overheads, fixed overheads and machine rentals.

Water Supply Services has been approached by RWA with a proposal to increase output to meet a further domestic customer base not previously supplied with water. The company would have to increase its capacity to meet this demand and increased demand from existing customers. Water output is measured in units, with each unit being 1,000 litres. Water Supply Services is currently operating at capacity which is 80,000 units per annum as determined by processing capability.

Increasing processing capability would require the rental of further machines that are involved in the chemical cleaning of water. There is an overall maximum capacity of 200,000 units beyond which the company cannot produce water because of physical limitations of its production site. Each water-cleaning machine has the following rental and unit capacity details.

| *Water cleaning machine* | |
|---|---|
| Annual rental (£) | 22,000 |
| Maximum annual capacity (units) | 45,000 |

Water Supply Services has an existing budgeted direct cost structure based on its current level of output of 80,000 units, as follows:

| | £/unit |
|---|---|
| Labour grade 1 | 45.00 |
| Labour grade 2 | 64.00 |
| Material A costs | 23.85 |
| Material B costs | 62.25 |

Variable overheads (electricity, maintenance etc.) are absorbed at the rate of £2 per kg of material B used. 5kg of material B is used in the manufacture of 1,000 litres of water. Fixed overheads are based on an existing output of 80,000 units and are absorbed at the rate of £10.20 per unit. Above 160,000 units, fixed overheads would be expected to increase at the rate of £50,000 per annum for every additional 40,000 units produced, or part thereof.

The existing agreement that Water Supply Services will charge a 25% mark up of agreed costs will apply for this proposal. The acceptance of this proposal would not affect any charges relating to the existing supply of 80,000 units.

Domestic demand for water in the next year, if the customer base is expanded, is estimated to total 110,000 units rising by 15% per annum thereafter. This level of demand growth is expected to continue for the foreseeable future.

Working capital requirements are estimated at 15% of sales value and are required to be in place at the start of the period to which the sales relate. Capital investment of £7·5m would be required in order to provide the necessary support facilities to expand capacity to 200,000 units per annum. Thereafter, updating costs of £30,000 would be required at the end of every four years. The cost of capital used in appraising projects is 20% per annum.

All sales and costs should be assumed to arise at the end of the year unless otherwise identified. Ignore the impact of taxation in your answer.

**Required:**

(a) Evaluate the proposal to expand capacity using present value methods. Make your evaluation on the basis of a five-year period only.

Express all calculations in this part of the question to the nearest £1,000. You are advised to state any assumptions made. **(20 marks)**

(b) In your capacity as Senior Accountant, draft a report to the Board of Directors that considers the following:

(i) the limitations of the five year period of analysis

(ii) the problems and difficulties associated with forecasting

(iii) the choice of an appropriate discount rate, and

(iv) any non-quantifiable factors you feel might influence the decision to accept the proposal. **(20 marks)**

(c) The sales director believes that quarterly forecasts of demand would provide better information for planning purposes. He has asked you, in your capacity as senior company accountant, to forecast demand for the 1st quarter of year 6. In forecasting quarterly demand the following quarterly seasonal adjustments should be made to the basic trend:

| Quarter | 1 | 2 | 3 | 4 |
|---|---|---|---|---|
| Percentage adjustment | - 8 | + 2 | + 15 | - 9 |

**Required:**

On the assumption that capacity is expanded to 200,000 units per annum and that growth in demand continues at 15% per annum, estimate output for the 1st quarter of year 6. Briefly comment on your results. **(5 marks)**

(d) The production director has heard that regression analysis is an alternative to seasonal forecasting by time series and wondered if it might be useful in forecasting costs faced by the company. She has had one of her team look at this and has produced the following linear equation:

Total costs (£) = 816,000 + 205·1x

**Required:**

(i) Describe what is meant by each of the following components of the linear equation:

- 816,000

- 205.1

- x **(2 marks)**

(ii) Comment on your interpretation of the figure 816,000 and whether it is likely to be relevant for year 6. **(3 marks)**

**(Total: 50 marks)**

## 8    TOWER RAILWAYS PLC

Assume that 'now' is December 20X3.

Tower Railways plc, which has a financial year-end of 31 December, operates a rail passenger service between the major cities in England. It is currently negotiating with the regulatory authorities about a five-year extension and enhancement of its existing contract. Tower Railways has forecast passenger use over the next five-year period to 31 December 20X8 and, based on its proposed carriage capacity, has calculated the following figures:

*Five year projections:*

| | |
|---|---|
| Number of carriages used on the line: | 8 |
| Maximum passengers per carriage: | 55 |
| Average occupancy rate: | 60% |
| Average number of return journeys per day: | 10 |
| Average price per return trip: | £12 |
| Number of days operating per year: | 340 |

Contribution per unit (sales price less variable costs) is expected to remain at a constant 35% of price over the period. Additional fixed costs of £1m per annum will be incurred on the new project. The management accountant has suggested that, in addition, the existing fixed overhead apportionment be increased by £200,000 per annum to reflect the increased activities relating to this part of the business. If the contract is renewed, other services offered by Tower Railways will be reduced to enable capacity expansion on the new contract. This will involve the loss of a long-standing contract, which was expected to continue indefinitely, worth £250,000 in pre-tax cash inflows per annum.

One of the conditions of a successful new bid is that a minimum investment of £5m, in support equipment to enhance the existing service, is required at the start of the new contract on 31 December 20X3. This equipment will no longer be needed to support the contract after four years and will be disposed of for £0.5m on 31 December 20X7. Capital allowances are available for these transactions. A balancing charge or allowance would arise on disposal of the asset. The investment in this asset should be treated separately from any other asset investment for tax purposes (ignore any pooling requirements). Assume all tax payments and allowances arise at the end of the year in which the taxable transactions arise (in other words, not delayed). Assume that all operating cash inflows arise at the relevant year-end.

*Other relevant information:*

| | |
|---|---|
| After tax discount rate per annum: | 10% |
| Corporation tax rate: | 30% |
| Writing down allowance: | 25% per annum, reducing balance |

**Required:**

(a)    Calculate separately the present value of the net operating cash flows (after payment of corporation tax and using annuities and perpetuities where appropriate), and the capital flows (investment, disposal and related tax flows). Assess if it is beneficial for Tower Railways to begin the new contract on 31 December 20X3.

Express all calculations in this and other parts of the question to the nearest £1,000. State any assumptions you make.    **(18 marks)**

(b)    The Chairman of Tower Railways is concerned about the risk of the project, particularly with respect to the average price charged.

Calculate the sensitivity of the project in relation to the average price charged.
    **(4 marks)**

Assume, in your answer that all other factors are as per your analysis in part (a).

(c)    On reviewing the initial proposal from your answer to part (a), the regulatory authorities are now insisting that further investment of £7m be made to ensure carriage availability to meet targets for the level of proposed service provision. This would not involve the purchase of additional carriages. Assume that by incorporating the additional £7m investment on top of the existing £5m, a total NPV at 31 December 20X3 of £9.220m (negative) for the capital cash flows only will arise.

**Required:**

(i) Calculate the occupancy rate required to break even (that is, to produce a zero NPV). **(4 marks)**

(ii) Calculate the length of the contract required to break even (that is, to produce a zero NPV). **(4 marks)**

Assume, in your answers to each case, that all other factors are as per your analysis in part (a).

(d) Write a report to the Chairman of Tower Railways, in your capacity as an external consultant, explaining:

(i) what is meant by business risk

(ii) the methods of estimating business risk in the context of NPV, and

(iii) the methods of reducing business risk. **(20 marks)**

**(Total: 50 marks)**

## 9    AMBER PLC

Amber plc operates a daily return high-speed train service between the UK and mainland Europe, via the Channel Tunnel. In an attempt to reduce overheads, the company is considering using an outside supplier to take over responsibility for all on-train catering services. Amber invited tenders for a five-year contract, and at the same time the senior management accountant drafted a schedule of costs for in-house provision of an equivalent service. This cost schedule, together with the details of the lowest price tender which was received, are given below. (See Table 1 and additional information).

**Table 1: In-house provision of train catering services**

**Schedule of costs, Amber plc**

|  | Pence per £ sales |
|---|---|
| *Variable costs* | |
| Direct material | 55 |
| Variable overhead | 12 |
| | |
| *Fixed costs (allocated to products)* | |
| Labour (Year 1) | 10 |
| Purchase/storage management | 3 |
| Depreciation (catering equipment) | 4 |
| Insurance | 2 |
| Total cost | 86 |

The train service operates 360 days per year and a single restaurant carriage is adequate to service the catering needs of a train carrying up to 600 passengers. The tendered contract (and the in-house schedule of costs) is for the provision of one catering carriage per train. Past sales data indicates that 45% of passengers will use the catering service, spending an average of £4.50 each per single journey or £9.00 per return journey. This is expected to remain unchanged over the next five years, unless Amber invests in quality improvements.

Statistical forecasts of the level of demand for the train service, under differing average weather conditions and average exchange rates over the next five years, are shown in Table 2.

**Table 2: Forecast passenger figures (per single journey)**

| Exchange rate: € per £1 | UK weather conditions | | |
|---|---|---|---|
| | *Poor* | *Reasonable* | *Good* |
| 1.52 | 500 | 460 | 420 |
| 1.54 | 550 | 520 | 450 |
| 1.65 | 600 | 580 | 500 |

The differing weather conditions are all assumed to be equally likely.

Based on historical trends, the probability of each different exchange rate occurring is estimated as follows:

| Exchange rate €per £1 | Probability |
|---|---|
| 1.52 | 0.2 |
| 1.54 | 0.5 |
| 1.65 | 0.3 |

**Additional information**

(1) Labour costs are expected to rise at a rate of 5% per year over the next five years.

(2) Variable costs per £ sales are expected to remain unchanged over the next five years.

(3) Some catering equipment will need to be replaced at the end of Year 2 at a cost of £500,000. This would increase the depreciation charge on catering equipment to 5 pence per £ sales. The equipment value at the end of Year 5 is estimated to be £280,000.

(4) The outside supplier (lowest price tender) has agreed to purchase immediately (for cash) the existing catering equipment owned by Amber plc at a price equal to the current book value i.e. £650,000. The supplier would charge Amber a flat fee of £250 per day for the provision of this catering service, and Amber would receive 5% of gross catering receipts where these exceeded an average of £2,200 per day in each 360 day period. The quality of the catering service is expected to be unaffected by the contracting out.

(5) In the event of Amber deciding to contract out the catering, the following fixed costs will be saved:

| | |
|---|---|
| Depreciation | £35,000 per year |
| Purchasing/storage costs | £18,000 per year |
| Insurance | £3,000 per year |
| Labour costs | £74,844 (Year 1) |

(6) The cost of capital for Amber plc is 12%.

Assume that all cash flows occur at the end of each year. Taxation may be ignored in answering this question.

**Required:**

(a) Calculate the expected number of passengers per single journey for the train service.

**(5 marks)**

(b) Draft a table of annual cash flows and, using discounted cash flow analysis, determine which of the two alternatives (in-house provision or contracting out) is preferred.

**(16 marks)**

(c)   Calculate and comment upon the financial effect on the decision of a forecast ten per cent increase in the number of passengers purchasing food and beverages on each train if the in-house catering service were to be improved. Any such improvement would require Amber investing £10,000 per year over five years on staff training.   **(7 marks)**

(d)   Comment on the limitations of using demand forecasts, such as that given in Table 2, for the purposes of the decision in question.   **(5 marks)**

(e)   Identify and critically comment upon three non-financial factors which need to be taken into account when a business is considering this type of decision.   **(7 marks)**

**(Total: 40 marks)**

## 10   SPRINGBANK PLC

Springbank plc is a medium-sized manufacturing company that plans to increase capacity by purchasing new machinery at an initial cost of £3 million. The following are the most recent financial statements of the company:

### Profit and loss accounts for years ending 31 December

|  | 20X2 £000 | 20X1 £000 |
|---|---|---|
| Sales | 5,000 | 5,000 |
| Cost of sales | 3,100 | 3,000 |
| Gross profit | 1,900 | 2,000 |
| Administration and distribution expenses | 400 | 250 |
| Profit before interest and tax | 1,500 | 1,750 |
| Interest | 400 | 380 |
| Profit before tax | 1,100 | 1,370 |
| Tax | 330 | 400 |
| Profit after tax | 770 | 970 |
| Dividends | 390 | 390 |
| Retained earnings | 380 | 580 |

### Balance Sheets as at 31 December

|  | 20X2 £000 | 20X2 £000 | 20X1 £000 | 20X1 £000 |
|---|---|---|---|---|
| Fixed assets |  | 6,500 |  | 6,400 |
| Current assets |  |  |  |  |
| Stock | 1,170 |  | 1,000 |  |
| Debtors | 850 |  | 900 |  |
| Cash | 130 |  | 100 |  |
|  | 2,150 |  | 2,000 |  |
| Current liabilities | 1,150 |  | 1,280 |  |
|  |  | 1,000 |  | 720 |
|  |  | 7,500 |  | 7,120 |
| 10% Debentures 20X7 |  | 3,500 |  | 3,500 |
|  |  | 4,000 |  | 3,620 |
| Capital and reserves |  | 4,000 |  | 3,620 |

The investment is expected to increase annual sales by 5,500 units. Investment in replacement machinery would be needed after five years. Financial data on the additional units to be sold is as follows:

|  | £ |
|---|---|
| Selling price per unit | 500 |
| Production costs per unit | 200 |

Variable administration and distribution expenses are expected to increase by £220,000 per year as a result of the increase in capacity. In addition to the initial investment in new machinery, £400,000 would need to be invested in working capital. The full amount of the initial investment in new machinery of £3 million will give rise to capital allowances on a 25% per year reducing balance basis. The scrap value of the machinery after five years is expected to be negligible. Tax liabilities are paid in the year in which they arise and Springbank plc pays tax at 30% of annual profits.

The Finance Director of Springbank plc has proposed that the £3.4 million investment should be financed by an issue of debentures at a fixed rate of 8% per year.

Springbank plc uses an after tax discount rate of 12% to evaluate investment proposals. In preparing its financial statements, Springbank plc uses straight-line depreciation over the expected life of fixed assets.

Average data for the business sector in which Springbank operates is as follows:

| Gearing (book value of debt/book value of equity) | 100% |
|---|---|
| Interest cover | 4 times |
| Current ratio | 2:1 |
| Stock days | 90 days |
| Return before interest and tax/Capital employed | 25% |

**Required:**

(a)   Calculate the net present value of the proposed investment in increased capacity of Springbank plc, clearly stating any assumptions that you make in your calculations.
**(11 marks)**

(b)   Calculate the increase in sales (in units) that would produce a zero net present value for the proposed investment. **(4 marks)**

(c)   (i)   Calculate the effect on the gearing and interest cover of Springbank plc of financing the proposed investment with an issue of debentures and compare your results with the sector averages. **(6 marks)**

(ii)   Analyse and comment on the recent financial performance of the company. **(13 marks)**

(iii)   On the basis of your previous calculations and analysis, comment on the acceptability of the proposed investment and discuss whether the proposed method of financing can be recommended. **(10 marks)**

(d)   Briefly discuss the possible advantages to Springbank plc of using an issue of ordinary shares to finance the investment. **(6 marks)**

**(Total: 50 marks)**

## 11   THE INDEPENDENT FILM COMPANY

The Independent Film Company plc is a film distribution company which purchases distribution rights on films from small independent producers, and sells the films on to cinema chains for national and international screening. In recent years the company has found it difficult to source sufficient films to maintain profitability. In response to the problem, the Independent Film Company has decided to invest in commissioning and producing films in its own right. In order to gain the expertise for this venture, the Independent Film Company is considering purchasing an existing filmmaking concern, at a cost of £400,000. The main difficulty that is anticipated for the business is the increasing uncertainty as to the potential success/failure rate of independently produced films. Many cinema chains are adopting a policy of only buying films from large international film companies, as they believe that the market for independent films is very limited and specialist in nature. The Independent Film Company is prepared for the fact that they are likely to have more films that fail than that succeed, but believe that the proposed film production business will nonetheless be profitable.

Using data collected from the existing distribution business and discussions with industry experts, they have produced cost and revenue forecasts for the five years of operation of the proposed investment. The company aims to complete the production of three films per year. The after tax cost of capital for the company is estimated to be 14%.

Year 1 sales for the new business are uncertain, but expected to be in the range of £4 million – £10 million. Probability estimates for different forecast values in Year 1 are as follows:

| Sales (£ million) | Probability |
|---|---|
| 4 | 0.2 |
| 5 | 0.4 |
| 7 | 0.3 |
| 10 | 0.1 |

Sales are expected to grow at an annual rate of 5%.

Anticipated costs related to the new business in Year 1 are as follows:

| Cost type | £000 |
|---|---|
| Purchase of film-making company | 400 |
| Annual legal and professional costs | 20 |
| Annual lease rental (office equipment) | 12 |
| Studio and set hire (per film) | 180 |
| Camera/specialist equipment hire (per film) | 40 |
| Technical staff wages (per film) | 520 |
| Screenplay (per film) | 50 |
| Actors' salaries (per film) | 700 |
| Costumes and wardrobe hire (per film) | 60 |
| Set design and painting (per film) | 150 |
| Annual non-production staff wages | 60 |

**Additional information**

(1)  No capital allowances are available.

(2)  Tax is payable one year in arrears, at a rate of 33%, and full use can be made of tax refunds as they fall due.

(3)  Staff wages (technical and non-production staff) and actors' salaries, are expected to rise by 10% per annum.

(4)  Studio hire costs will be subject to an increase of 30% in Year 3.

(5)  Screenplay costs per film are expected to rise by 15% per annum due to a shortage of skilled writers.

(6)  The new business will occupy office accommodation which has to date been let out for an annual rent of £20,000. Demand for such accommodation is buoyant and the company anticipates no problems in finding future tenants at the same annual rent.

(7)  A market research survey into the potential for the film production business cost £25,000.

**Required:**

(a) Using DCF analysis, calculate the expected Net Present Value of the proposed investment. (Workings should be rounded to the nearest £000.) **(15 marks)**

(b) Outline the main limitations of using expected values when making investment decisions. **(6 marks)**

(c) In addition to the possible purchase of the filmmaking business, the company has two other investment opportunities, the details of which are given below:

**Post-tax cash flows, £000**

|  | Year 0 | Year 1 | Year 2 | Year 3 | Year 4 | Year 5 | Year 6 |
|---|---|---|---|---|---|---|---|
| Investment X | (200) | 200 | 200 | 150 | 100 | 100 | 100 |
| Investment Y | (100) | 80 | 80 | 40 | 40 | 40 | 40 |

The Independent Film Company has a total of £400,000 available for capital investment in the current year. No project can be invested in more than once.

**Required:**

(i) Define the term 'profitability index', and briefly explain how it may be used when a company faces a problem of capital rationing in any single accounting period. **(4 marks)**

(ii) Calculate the profitability index for each of the investment projects available to the Independent Film Company, i.e. purchase of the film production company, Investment X and Investment Y, and outline the optimal investment strategy. Assume that all of the projects are indivisible. **(6 marks)**

(iii) Explain the limitations of using a profitability index in a situation where there is capital rationing. **(4 marks)**

(d) Briefly explain how the tax treatment of capital purchases can affect an investment decision. **(5 marks)**

**(Total: 40 marks)**

## 12    SASSONE PLC

Sassone plc is a medium-sized profitable company that manufactures engineering products. Its stated objectives are to maximise shareholder wealth and to maintain an ethical approach to the production and distribution of engineering products. It has in issue two million ordinary shares, held as follows:

|  | *Number of shares* |
|---|---|
| Pension funds | 550,000 |
| Insurance companies | 250,000 |
| Investment trusts | 200,000 |
| Unit trusts | 100,000 |
| Directors of Sassone | 350,000 |
| Other shareholders | 550,000 |
|  | ————— |
|  | 2,000,000 |
|  | ————— |

# Section 3

# ANSWERS TO PRACTICE QUESTIONS

## FINANCIAL MANAGEMENT OBJECTIVES AND ENVIRONMENT

### 1    TAGNA

(a)    Market efficiency is commonly discussed in terms of pricing efficiency.

A stock market is described as efficient when share prices fully and fairly reflect relevant information.

**Weak form efficiency** occurs when share prices fully and fairly reflect all past information, such as share price movements in preceding periods. If a stock market is weak-form efficient, investors cannot make abnormal gains by studying and acting upon past information.

**Semi-strong form efficiency** occurs when share prices fully and fairly reflect not only past information, but all publicly available information as well, such as the information provided by the published financial statements of companies or by reports in the financial press. If a stock market is semi-strong-form efficient, investors cannot make abnormal gains by studying and acting upon publicly available information.

**Strong form efficiency** occurs when share prices fully and fairly reflect not only all past and publicly available information, but all relevant private information as well, such as confidential minutes of board meetings. If a stock market is strong-form efficient, investors cannot make abnormal gains by acting upon any information, whether publicly available or not. There is no empirical evidence supporting the proposition that stock markets are strong form efficient and so the bank is incorrect in suggesting that in six months the stock market will be strong-form efficient. However, there is a great deal of evidence suggesting that stock markets are semi-strong-form efficient and so Tagna's share are unlikely to be under-priced.

(b)    A **substantial interest rate increase** may have several consequences for Tagna in the areas indicated.

(i)    As a manufacturer and supplier of luxury goods, it is likely that Tagna will experience a **sharp decrease in sales** as a result of the increase in interest rates. One reason for this is that sales of luxury goods will be more sensitive to changes in disposable income than sales of basic necessities, and disposable income is likely to fall as a result of the interest rate increase. Another reason is the likely effect of the interest rate increase on consumer demand. If the increase in demand has been supported, even in part, by the increase in consumer credit, the substantial interest rate increase will have a negative effect on demand as the cost of consumer credit increases. It is also likely that many chain store customers will buy Tagna's goods by using credit.

(ii) Tagna may experience an **increase in operating costs** as a result of the substantial interest rate increase, although this is likely to be a smaller effect and one that occurs more slowly than a decrease in sales. As the higher cost of borrowing moves through the various supply chains in the economy, producer prices may increase and the cost of materials and other inputs Tagna may rise by more than the current rate of inflation. Labour costs may also increase sharply if the recent sharp rise in inflation leads to high inflationary expectations being built into wage demands. Acting against this will be the deflationary effect on consumer demand of the interest rate increase. If the Central Bank has made an accurate assessment of the economic situation when determining the interest rate increase, both the growth in consumer demand and the rate of inflation may fall to more acceptable levels, leading to a lower increase in operating costs.

(iii) The **earnings (profit after tax)** of Tagna are likely to fall as a result of the interest rate increase. In addition to the decrease in sales and the possible increase in operating costs discussed above, Tagna will experience an increase in interest costs arising from its overdraft. The combination of these effects is likely to result in a sharp fall in earnings. The level of reported profits has been low in recent years and so Tagna may be faced with insufficient profits to maintain its dividend, or even a reported loss.

(c) The objectives of public sector organisations are often difficult to define. Even though the cost of resources used can be measured, the benefits gained from the consumption of those resources can be difficult, if not impossible, to quantify. Because of this difficulty, public sector organisations often have financial targets imposed on them, such as a target rate of return on capital employed. Furthermore, they will tend to focus on maximising the return on resources consumed by producing the best possible combination of services for the lowest possible cost. This is the meaning of **'value for money'**, often referred to as the pursuit of economy, efficiency and effectiveness.

**Economy** refers to seeking the lowest level of input costs for a given level of output. **Efficiency** refers to seeking the highest level of output for a given level of input resources. **Effectiveness** refers to the extent to which output produced meets the specified objectives, for example in terms of provision of a required range of services.

In contrast, private sector organisations have to compete for funds in the capital markets and must offer an adequate return to investors. The objective of **maximisation of shareholder wealth** equates to the view that the primary financial objective of companies is to reward their owners. If this objective is not followed, the directors may be replaced or a company may find it difficult to obtain funds in the market, since investors will prefer companies that increase their wealth. However, shareholder wealth cannot be maximised if companies do not seek both economy and efficiency in their business operations.

| ACCA marking scheme | | Marks |
|---|---|---|
| (a) | Pricing efficiency | 1 |
| | Meaning and significance of weak form | 2 |
| | Meaning and significance of semi strong form | 2 |
| | Meaning and significance of strong form | 2 |
| | Comments on banks recommendation | 2 |
| | | 9 |
| (b) | Up to 2 marks for each detailed consequence | 10 |
| (c) | Value for money | 3 |
| | Maximization of shareholder wealth | 3 |
| | | 6 |
| Total | | 25 |

size will offer the opportunity to take advantage of possible economies of scale via bulk ordering. In this way, margins could be widened and the overall business made more profitable.

- With a larger number of stores covering a wider geographic area, News For You will be able to broaden the nature of their business base, so that it will be less vulnerable to regional economic trends.

**Arguments against any expansion include the following:**

- The potential to increase sales substantially via food sales is very limited. The majority of people purchase most of their food from larger stores, and will only use a local shop for small low cost items, for which it is not worthwhile making a special car journey to the supermarket. It is unlikely a profitable business can be created based on this type of sale.

- The widespread ownership of televisions and access to differing forms of mass media communications is likely to mean that fewer people will purchase newspapers on a daily basis. This is particularly true of those papers that are also published in electronic form. Many newsagents are dependent for the bulk of their sales on customers who come into the shop to buy a newspaper and then purchase additional items at the same time. If customers do not come in for a newspaper, then the associated sales income will also be lost. Expanding a business where there is such a risk of demand falling away may be regarded as very risky.

- The information in the question suggests that the competitive environment for News For You is becoming much tougher on a number of different fronts simultaneously, with rising excise duties, powerful food retailers and a reduction in tobacco and newspaper purchases. Expansion usually occurs because a business is very confident of the future, but in this case it is questionable whether News For You has much about which to be confident.

It would therefore seem advisable for News For You to postpone its expansion plans, and perhaps look at ways of using its existing outlets to sell very different products, thereby 're-inventing' their business, perhaps by moving completely away from confectionery and into, for example, video rental.

## 5 DISCOURAGING MONOPOLY AND AVAILABILITY OF FINANCE

### Key answer tips

To answer part (a), a knowledge of basic economics would be helpful, but common sense and an awareness of the business environment could help you to provide a reasonable answer. Don't let part (a) put you off the question. Part (b) and part (c) are both relatively straightforward. The answer provided here discusses obtaining a listing to issue shares on a main stock market, as well as private sources of equity finance. It would also be reasonable to make the point that companies whose shares are traded on a junior market, such as AIM in the UK, are not 'listed' companies, and an unlisted company could therefore raise equity by issuing shares on the junior market.

(a) Many governments consider it necessary to prevent or control monopolies.

A **pure monopoly** exists when one organisation controls the production or supply of a good that has no close substitute. In practice, legislation may consider a monopoly situation to occur when there is limited competition in a particular market. For example, UK legislation considers a monopoly to occur if an organisation controls 25% or more of a particular market.

Governments consider it necessary to act against an existing or potential monopoly because of the economic problems that can arise through the abuse of a dominant market position. Monopoly can lead to *economic inefficiency in the use of resources*, so that output is at a higher cost than necessary. Further inefficiency can arise as a monopoly *may lack the incentive to innovate*, to research technological improvements, or to eliminate unnecessary managers, since it can always be sure of passing on the cost of its inefficiencies to its customers. Inefficiencies such as these have been seen as major problems in state-owned monopolies and have fuelled the movement towards privatisation in recent years. It has been expected that the competition arising following privatisation will lead to the elimination of these kinds of inefficiency.

Monopoly can also result in *high prices* being charged for output, so that the cost to customers is higher than would be the case if significant competition existed, allowing monopolies to generate monopoly profits.

The government can prevent monopolies occurring by *monitoring proposed takeovers and mergers*, and acting when it decides that a monopoly situation may occur. This monitoring is carried out in the UK by the Office of Fair Trading, which can refer takeovers and mergers that are potentially against the public interest to the Competition Commission for detailed investigation.

The Competition Commission has the power to prevent a proposed takeover or merger, or to allow it to proceed with conditions attached, such as disposal of a portion of the business in order to preserve competition.

### Tutorial note

Your answer might refer to legislation or regulations in a country other than the UK.

(b)    In the UK, a company is required by law to offer an issue of new shares to raise cash on a pro-rata basis to its existing shareholders. This ensures that the existing pattern of ownership and control will not be affected if all shareholders take up the new shares offered. Because this right of existing shareholders to be offered new equity is a legal one, such an issue is called a **rights issue**. (However, shareholders can vote to waive their rights, such as when the company wishes to obtain a stock market quotation for the shares.)

If an unlisted company decides that it needs to raise a large amount of equity finance and provided existing shareholders have agreed, it can decide to obtain a listing for its shares, and offer ordinary shares to new investors (the public at large) via an **offer for sale**. Such an offer is usually part of the process of seeking a stock exchange quotation, and it leads to the wider spread of ownership that is needed to meet the requirements of the listing regulations and the stock exchange concerned. An offer for sale may be either at a fixed price, where the offer price is set in advance by the issuing company, or by tender, where investors are invited to submit bids for shares. (*Tutorial note*: Offers for sale by tender are uncommon.) An offer for sale will result in a significant change to the shareholder structure of the company, for example by bringing in institutional investors. In order to ensure that the required amount of finance is raised, offers for sale are underwritten by institutional investors who guarantee to buy any unwanted shares.

A **placing** is cheaper than an offer for sale. In a placing, large blocks of shares are placed with institutional investors, so that the spread of new ownership is not as wide as with an offer for sale. While a placing may be part of seeking a listing and a stock exchange quotation (for example, it is very popular with companies wanting to float on markets for smaller companies such as the Alternative Investment Market in the UK), it can also provide equity finance for a company that wishes to remain unlisted.

New shares can also be sold by an unlisted company by **private negotiation,** to individual investors or a venture capital organisation. While the amount of equity finance raised by this method is small, it has been supported in the UK in recent years by government initiatives such as the Enterprise Investment Scheme and Venture Capital Trusts schemes in the UK.

(c) The factors that should be considered by a company when choosing between an issue of debt and issue of equity finance could include the following:

**Risk and return**

Raising debt finance will increase the gearing and the financial risk of the company, while raising equity finance will lower gearing and financial risk.

Financial risk arises since raising debt brings a commitment to meet regular interest payments, whether fixed or variable. Failure to meet these interest payments gives debt holders the right to appoint a receiver to recover their investment. In contrast, there is no right to receive dividends on ordinary shares, only a right to participate in any dividend (share of profit) declared by the directors of a company. If profits are low, then dividends can be passed, but interest must be paid regardless of the level of profits. Furthermore, increasing the level of interest payments will increase the volatility of returns to shareholders, since only returns in excess of the cost of debt accrue to shareholders.

**Cost**

Debt is cheaper than equity because debt is less risky from an investor point of view. This is because it is often secured by either a fixed or floating charge on company assets and ranks above equity on liquidation, and because of the statutory requirement to pay interest. Debt is also cheaper than equity because interest is an allowable deduction in calculating taxable profit. This is referred to as the tax efficiency of debt.

**Ownership and control**

Issuing equity can have ownership implications for a company, particularly if the finance is raised by means of a placing or offer for sale. Shareholders also have the right to appoint directors and auditors, and the right to attend general meetings of the company. While issuing debt has no such ownership implications, an issue of debt can place restrictions on the activities of a company by means of restrictive covenants included in the issue documents. For example, a restrictive covenant may specify a maximum level of gearing or a minimum level of interest cover which the borrowing company must not exceed, or a covenant may forbid the securing of further debt on particular assets.

**Redemption**

Equity finance is permanent capital that does not need to be redeemed, while debt finance will need to be redeemed at some future date. Redeeming a large amount of debt can place a severe strain on the cash flow of a company, although this can be addressed by refinancing or by using convertible debt.

**Flexibility**

Debt finance is more flexible than equity, in that various amounts can be borrowed, at a fixed or floating interest rate and for a range of maturities, to suit the financing need of a company. If debt finance is no longer required, it can more easily be repaid (depending on the issue terms).

**Availability**

A new issue of equity finance may not be readily available to a listed company or may be available on terms that are unacceptable with regards to issue price or issue quantity, if the stock market is depressed (a bear market). Current shareholders may be unwilling to subscribe to a rights issue, for example if they have made other investment plans or if they have urgent calls on their existing finances. A new issue of debt finance may not be available to a listed company, or available at a cost considered to be unacceptable, if it has a poor credit rating, or if it faces trading difficulties.

| ACCA marking scheme | | Marks |
|---|---|---|
| (a) | Meaning of monopoly | 1 |
| | Discussion of economic problems of monopoly | 5 |
| | Discussion of role of government | 3 |
| | | 9 |
| (b) | Rights issue | 2 |
| | Offer for sale | 2 |
| | Placing | 2 |
| | Private sale to individuals or institutions | 2 |
| | | 8 |
| (c) | Up to 2 marks for each well discussed factor | 8 |
| Total | | 25 |

## 6 PLANKERS LTD

(a) (i)

| | £m |
|---|---|
| Cash brought forward at 1 June 20X5: | 8.48 |
| Building programme investment | (12.00) |
| Minimum cash balance requirement | 1.00 |
| Additional loan required at 1 June 20X5: | 4.52 |

The cash balance needed for 31 May 20X6 will be added to by cash retentions during the year. This can be found from the P&L account for 31 May 20X6.

**Projected P&L for the year to 31 May 20X6**

| | £m |
|---|---|
| PBIT before depreciation | 1.980 |
| (£1.71m × 1.05 × 1.05 × 1.05) | |
| Extra depreciation (15% of (50% of £12m) | (0.900) |
| Interest charges (see note) | (1.037) |
| Profit before tax | 0.043 |
| Tax (30%) | 0.013 |
| Profit after tax | 0.030 |

**Cash available in profit after tax:**

| | |
|---|---|
| Profit after tax | 0.030 |
| Add back depreciation (non-cash expense) | 0.900 |
| | 0.930 |

*Note on interest charges*:
Total loans = £7m + £4.52m = £11.52m
Interest rate = 9%
Interest = £11.52m × 0.09 = £1.037m.

(ii)  **Check on cash balances at 31 May 20X6**

| Cash ledger | DR £m | CR £m |
|---|---|---|
| Brought forward 1 June 20X5 | 8.48 | |
| Cash retentions | 0.93 | |
| Additional loan financing | 4.52 | |
| Building programme expenditure | | 12.00 |
| Carried forward balance 31 May 20X6 | | 1.93 |

The conditions of the loan and the other targets can then be checked:

Interest cover: $= (1.98 - 0.9)/1.037: = 1.041$ times

EPS: (Profit after tax/number of shares = £0.03m/4m shares): 0.75p

The minimum cash balance target is met. However, the target minimum interest cover (3 times) and the target minimum EPS (20 pence) are not met.

(iii)  **Options**

1  Delay the building programme until sufficient funds are available from cash retentions

2  Re-negotiate the terms of the long-term loan

3  Pay out less in dividends

4  Leasing assets rather than buying them

5  Raise further equity capital

6  Sell assets

7  Reduce working capital investments

8  Combinations of the above

(iv)  The only condition satisfied is that relating to the minimum cash balance. Both the interest cover and the EPS conditions are breached. The scale of the building programme suggests that options 1, 3, 4, 6 and 7 are very unlikely to provide sufficient additional capital. Extending the loan facilities in option 2 would likely make worse the interest cover and EPS figures. The only viable option appears to be an equity issue.

(b)  (i)  **Responding to various stakeholder groups**

If a company has a single objective in terms of maximising profitability then it is only responding to one stakeholder group, namely shareholders. However, companies can no longer fail to respond to the interests and concerns of a wider range of groups, particularly with respect to those who may have a non-financial interest in the organisation. Stakeholder groups with a non-financial interest can therefore generate for companies non-financial objectives and place constraints on their operations to the extent that the company is prepared to respond to such groups.

Various stakeholder groupings can emerge. The following represents examples of likely groups, their non-financial objectives and/or the constraints they may place on a business:

| Stakeholder | Objective | Constraints |
|---|---|---|
| Employees | Employee welfare | Maximum hours worked |
| Community | Responding to community concerns | Limits on activities |
| Customers | Product or service levels | Minimum quality standards |

| Stakeholder | Objective | Constraints |
|---|---|---|
| Suppliers | Good trading relationships | |
| Government | Protecting the consumer | Minimum standards on products or services |
| Trade bodies | Protecting professional reputation | Minimum standards on products or services |

(ii) **The difficulties associated with managing organisations with multiple objectives**

To the extent that an organisation faces a range of stakeholders, then they also face multiple objectives. This would not particularly be a problem if the multiple objectives were congruent, but they normally are not. There are a number of difficulties:

- Multiple stakeholders imply multiple objectives. To the extent that they conflict then compromises must be made. This will lead potentially to opportunity costs in that maximisation of profitability will potentially be reduced.

- Responding to stakeholders other than shareholders involves costs, either in management time or in directly responding to their needs.

- Some objectives are not clearly defined, for example what is actually meant by 'protecting the consumer'? It will therefore not always be clear to the organisation that they have met the needs of all of their stakeholders.

- Some of the objectives may actually be conflicting where compromise is not possible. Prioritisation and ranking will then have to take place. Questions then arise as to who is the most important stakeholder or what ranking should be assigned?

- New stakeholder groups often emerge. This can create a problem of longer-term strategic management in that plans can be diverted if new pressures arise. For example, environmental issues were not so important 20 years ago.

- Management of the organisation becomes complex when multiple objectives have to be satisfied. Each managerial decision is likely to face many constraints.

| ACCA marking scheme | | | | |
|---|---|---|---|---|
| | | | | *Marks* |
| (a) | (i) | Additional loan required | | 2 |
| | | Projected P&L | | 1 |
| | | Cash retention | | 2 |
| | (ii) | Cash carried forward | | 1 |
| | | Assessment of constraints | | 2 |
| | (iii) | 1 mark each for five realistic options | | 5 |
| | (iv) | Relevant comments | up to | 3 |
| | | | | 16 |
| (b) | (i) | 1 mark each for identified constraint | up to | 4 |
| | (ii) | 2 marks for each detailed point on multiple objectives | up to | 5 |
| Total | | | | 25 |

## 7    RZP CO

(a)    Analysis of data provided

| Year | 20X4 | 20X3 | 20X2 | 20X1 | 20X0 |
|---|---|---|---|---|---|
| Dividend per share | 2.8p | 2.3p | 2.2p | 2.2p | 1.7p |
| Annual dividend growth | 21.7% | 4.5% | Nil | 29.4% | |
| Earnings per share | 19.04p | 14.95p | 11.22p | 15.84p | 13.43 |
| Annual earnings growth | 27.3% | 33.2% | -29.2% | 17.9% | |
| Price/earnings ratio | 22.0 | 33.5 | 25.5 | 17.2 | 15.2 |
| Share price | 418.9p | 500.8p | 286.1p | 272.4p | 204.1p |
| Annual share price growth | -16.3% | 75.0% | 5.0% | 33.5% | |
| Dividend per share | 2.8p | 2.3p | 2.2p | 2.2p | 1.7p |
| General price index | 117 | 113 | 110 | 105 | 100 |
| Real dividend per share | 2.4p | 2.0p | 2.0p | 2.1p | 1.7p |
| Annual dividend growth | 20.0% | Nil | -4.8% | 23.5% | |

Average dividend growth:

Arithmetic mean = (21.7 + 4.5 + 0 + 29.4)/4 = 55.6/4 = 13.9%
Equivalent annual growth rate = [(2.8/1.7)0.25 – 1] × 100 = 13.3%

Average earnings per share growth:

Arithmetic mean = (27.3 + 33.2 – 29.2 + 17.9)/4 = 49.2/4 = 12.3%
Equivalent annual growth rate = [(19.04/13.43)0.25 – 1] × 100 = 9.1%

Average share price growth:

Arithmetic mean = (–16.3 + 75.0 + 5.0 + 33.5)/4 = 97.2/4 = 24.3%
Equivalent annual growth rate = [(418.9/204.1)0.25 – 1] × 100 = 19.7%

Average real dividend growth:

Arithmetic mean = (20.0 + 0 – 4.8 + 23.5)/4 = 38.7/4 = 9.7%
Equivalent annual growth rate = [(2.4/1.7)0.25 – 1] × 100 = 9.0%

**Discussion of analysis and views expressed by chairman**

The chairman's statement claims that RZP Co has delivered growth in every year in dividends, earnings and ordinary share price, apart from 20X2. Analysis shows that the chairman is correct in excluding 20X2, when no growth occurred in dividends, earnings fell by 29.2%, and real dividends fell by 4.8%. Analysis also shows that no growth in real dividends occurred in 20X3 and that the company's share price fell by 16.3% in 20X4. It is possible the chairman may not have been referring to real dividend growth, in which case his statement could be amended. However, shareholders will be aware of the decline in share price in 20X4 or could calculate the decline from the information provided, so the chairman cannot claim that RZP Co has delivered share price growth in 20X4. In fact, the statement could explain the reasons for the decline in share price in order to reassure shareholders. It also possible for the five-year summary to be extended to include annual share price data, such as maximum, minimum and average share price, so that shareholders have this information readily available.

The chairman's statement claims that RZP Co has consistently delivered above-average performance. The company may have delivered above- or below-average performance in individual years but without further information in the form of sector averages for individual years, it is not possible to reach a conclusion on this point. The average growth rates for the sector cannot therefore be used to comment on the performance of RZP Co in individual years. If the company has consistently delivered above-average performance, however, the company's average annual growth rates should be greater than the sector averages.

The growth rates can be compared as follows:

|  | Arithmetic mean | Equivalent annual rate | Sector |
|---|---|---|---|
| Nominal dividends | 13.9% | 13.3% | 10% |
| Real dividends | 9.7% | 9.0% | 9% |
| Earnings per share | 12.3% | 9.1% | 10% |
| Share price | 24.3% | 19.7% | 20% |

It can be seen that if the sector average growth rates are arithmetic mean growth rates, the chairman's statement is correct. If the sector average growth rates are equivalent annual growth rates, however, only the nominal dividend growth rate is greater than the sector average. The basis on which the sector average growth rates have been prepared should therefore be clarified in order to determine whether the chairman's statement is correct.

(b)     The dividend yield and capital growth for 20X4 must be calculated with reference to the 20X3 end-of-year share price. The dividend yield is 0.56% (100 × 2.8/500.8) and the capital growth is –16.35% (100 × (418.9 – 500.8)/500.8), so the total shareholder return is –15.79% or –15.8% (0.56 – 16.35). A negative return of 15.8% looks even worse when it is noted that annual inflation for 20X4 was 3.5% (117/113).

While the negative total shareholder return is at odds with the chairman's claim to have delivered growth in dividends and share price in 20X4, a different view might have emerged if average share prices had been used, since the return calculation ignores share price volatility. The chairman should also be aware that share prices may be affected by other factors than corporate activity, so a good performance in share price terms may not be due to managerial excellence. It also possible that the negative return may represent a good performance when compared to the sector as a whole in 20X4: further information is needed to assess this.

Note that total shareholder return can also be found as (100 × (2.8 + 418.9 – 500.8)/500.8).

(c)     The objectives of managers may conflict with the objectives of shareholders, particularly with the objective of maximisation of shareholder wealth. Management remuneration package are one way in which goal congruence between managers and shareholders may be increased. Such packages should motivate managers while supporting the achievement of shareholder wealth maximisation. The following factors should be considered when deciding on a remuneration package intended to encourage directors to act in ways that maximise shareholder wealth.

**Clarity and transparency**

The terms of the remuneration package should be clear and transparent so that directors and shareholders are in no doubt as to when rewards have been earned or the basis on which rewards have been calculated.

**Appropriate performance measure**

The managerial performance measure selected for use in the remuneration package should support the achievement of shareholder wealth maximisation. It is therefore likely that the performance measure could be linked to share price changes.

**Quantitative performance measure**

The managerial performance measure should be quantitative and the manner in which it is to be calculated should be specified. The managerial performance measure should ideally be linked to a benchmark comparing the company's performance with that of its peers. The managerial performance measure should not be open to manipulation by management.

**Time horizon**

The remuneration package should have a time horizon that is linked to that of shareholders. If shareholders desire long-term capital growth, for example, the remuneration package should discourage decisions whose objective is to maximise short-term profits at the expense of long-term growth.

**Impartiality**

In recent years there has been an increased emphasis on decisions about managerial remuneration packages being removed from the control of managers who benefit from them. The use of remuneration committees in listed companies is an example of this. The impartial decisions of non-executive directors, it is believed, will eliminate or reduce managerial self-interest and encourage remuneration packages that support the achievement of shareholder rather than managerial goals.

**Appropriate management remuneration packages for RZP Co**

Remuneration packages may be based on a performance measure linked to values in the profit and loss account. A bonus could be awarded, for example, based on growth in turnover, profit before tax, or earnings (earnings per share). Such performance measures could lead to maximisation of profit in the short-term rather than in the long-term, for example by deferring capital expenditure required to reduce environmental pollution, and may encourage managers to manipulate reported financial information in order to achieve bonus targets. They could also lead to sub-optimal managerial performance if managers do enough to earn their bonus, but then reduce their efforts once their target has been achieved.

RZP Co has achieved earnings growth of more than 20% in both 20X3 and 20X4, but this is likely to reflect in part a recovery from the negative earnings growth in 20X1, since over the five-year period its earnings growth is not very different from its sector's (it may be worse). If annual earnings growth were to be part of a remuneration package for RZP Co, earnings growth could perhaps be compared to the sector and any bonus made conditional upon ongoing performance in order to discourage a short-term focus.

Remuneration packages may be based on a performance measure linked to relative stock market performance, e.g. share price growth over the year compared to average share price growth for the company's sector, or compared to growth in a stock market index, such as the FTSE 100. This would have the advantage that managers would be encouraged to make decisions that had a positive effect on the company's share price and hence are likely to be consistent with shareholder wealth maximisation. However, as noted earlier, other factors than managerial decisions can have a continuing effect on share prices and so managers may fail to be rewarded for good performance due to general economic changes or market conditions.

RZP Co recorded negative share price growth in 20X4 and the reasons for this should be investigated. In the circumstances, a remuneration package linked to benchmarked share price growth could focus the attention of RZP managers on decisions likely to increase shareholder wealth. The effect of such a remuneration package could be enhanced if the reward received by managers were partly or wholly in the form of shares or share options. Apart from emphasising the focus on share price growth, such a reward scheme would encourage goal congruence between shareholders and managers by turning managers into shareholders.

| ACCA marking scheme | | |
|---|---|---|
| | | *Marks* |
| (a) Growth in dividends per share: analysis/discussion | | 4-5 |
| Share price growth: analysis/discussion | | 4-5 |
| Growth in earnings per share: analysis/discussion | | 4-5 |
| | Maximum | 13 |
| (b) Calculation of total shareholder return | | 2 |
| Comment | | 1 |
| | Maximum | 3 |
| (c) Discussion of factors | | 5-6 |
| Examples of appropriate remuneration packages | | 4-5 |
| | Maximum | 9 |
| Total | | 25 |

# MANAGEMENT OF WORKING CAPITAL

## 8   HEXICON PLC

### Key answer tips

Part (a) is standard textbook material. For five marks, you should give at least five reasons, and don't forget a brief explanation: 'it uses cash flows' will not get the full marks available. As the question mentions other approaches, you should structure your answer around direct comparisons with alternative methods of investment appraisal.

In part (b) you are applying the familiar EOQ model in the context of a change to a just-in-time system. To answer both parts, you need to assess the 'before' and 'after' positions, evaluating the changes between the two. Note that the question includes information on tax and discount rates, so you are clearly intended to take account of both of these in your evaluation (particularly in the light of part (a)). You should be prepared for the examiner to include various syllabus areas and techniques within one question.

Part (c) first requires an explanation of JIT agreements ('the nature of') and then a discussion as to the reasons for such agreements ('the objectives of').

(a)   The following reasons may be cited for using the net present value (NPV) method of investment appraisal:

   (i)   Compared to accounting rate of return (ARR), it discounts real cash flows as opposed to accounting profits which are affected by non-cash items.

   (ii)   Compared to measuring internal rate of return (IRR), the NPV method only gives one solution. In some circumstances, (when there are a number of outflows occurring at different times), multiple IRR solutions are possible.

   (iii)   Compared to the payback method, NPV considers all of the cash flows of a project.

   (iv)   By using a discount rate it measures the opportunity cost of the money invested by a person in a project.

   (v)   The interest rate used can be increased/decreased depending upon the level of perceived risk in the investment.

   (vi)   The NPV of a project can be shown to be equal to the increase in the value of shareholder's equity in the company. Thus the method is consistent with the objective of shareholder wealth maximisation.

(b)  (i)  The **present EOQ** is $\sqrt{\dfrac{2 \times £100 \times 40,000}{20\% \times £2.50}}$ = 4,000 units/order

The **revised EOQ** = $\sqrt{\dfrac{2 \times £25 \times 40,000}{20\% \times £2.50}}$ = 2,000 units/order

From this it can be seen that the EOQ is halved.

(ii)  The number of orders has increased from (40,000/4,000) 10 orders to (40,000/2,000) 20 orders. However, ordering costs are reduced by:

(10 × £100) - (20 × £25) = £500 per annum

Average stocks have also reduced from $\dfrac{4,000}{2}$ (2,000 units) to $\dfrac{2,000}{2}$ (1,000 units). Consequently carrying costs have reduced by 20% × £2.50 × 1,000 = £500 per annum.

Total inventory costs are thereby reduced by £1,000 per annum (before tax).

Assuming that Hexicon plc pays tax in the same year as it earns profits, the present value of the proposal is found by comparing the outflow cost with the discounted after-tax savings over the eight-year life of the proposal (using a 12% discount rate). The after-tax savings are £1,000 × 67% = £670.

*Discounted savings:*

| *Year* | *Item* | *Cash flow* £ | *Discount factor at 12%* | *Present value* £ |
|--------|--------|------|-----------|-------|
| 1 - 8 | After-tax savings | 670 | 4.968 | 3,329 |
| 0 | Cost of reorganisation | (4,000) | 1.000 | (4,000) |
| 0 | Tax saving (assume same year: 33% × £4,000) | 1,320 | 1.000 | 1,320 |
| | Net benefit | | | 649 |

As the present value of the proposal is positive, it is worthwhile.

(c)  The **main objective of Just In Time (JIT) purchasing** is to match the delivery of components from suppliers to their usage in production. If this is achieved there are significant benefits to be gained by both the supplier and the customer.

The customer is likely to use only one supplier for each component and to build up a relationship with the supplier which encourages communication thus enabling the supplier to benefit from advanced production planning and economies of scale. To enhance this relationship, the customer makes a long-term commitment to future orders.

The supplier guarantees to deliver goods of an appropriate quality in accordance with an agreed delivery schedule. The benefit to the customer is thereby a reduction (or elimination) of stockholding and significant cost savings. These arise in both holding costs and also in materials handling, because goods are transferred directly from goods inwards to production.

## 9 BLIN

### Key answer tips

Parts (a) and (c) of this question should be fairly straightforward. For part (a), your answer should give some emphasis to the yield curve. Part (b) is probably more difficult, because it is not necessarily easy to see what the examiner had in mind with 'approaches'. Thinking about the question logically might help you to construct an answer. You are asked to comment on approaches to the mix of long-term and short-term funding to finance working capital. Logically, the approaches are (1) to have mainly long-term capital and not much short-term capital, (2) to have mainly short-term capital and not much long-term capital, and (3) to have a more balanced mixture of short-term and long-term capital. These are the approaches in the solution.

However, the distinction between 'permanent' levels of current assets and 'fluctuating' levels of current assets is a useful distinction, which the solution in part (b) uses as a basis for analysis. A company's current assets are continually changing in total amount, up and down, but there is usually a 'permanent' amount below which the total of current assets does not fall. Fluctuating current assets are current assets in excess of the minimum level.

(a)     The following factors will influence the rate of interest charged on the new bank loan.

**General level of interest rates**

Interest rates charged on loans will depend on the general level of interest rates. Typically, interest rates on a bank loan are set at a margin above a 'base rate' or 'prime rate' or at a margin above a money market benchmark rate such as LIBOR. Similarly, longer-term fixed interest rates are at a margin above either a government bond rate or the swap rate. When the general level of interest rates goes up, rates on new lending will also rise.

**Risk of default**

The bank providing the loan to Blin will make an assessment of the risk that the company might default on its loan commitments and charge an interest rate that reflects this risk. Since Blin is listed on a stock exchange it will be seen as less risky than an unlisted company and will pay a lower interest rate as a result. The period of time that the company has been listed may also be an influential factor.

Since Blin has expanded sales significantly and relies heavily on overdraft finance, it may be overtrading. This could increase the risk of default and so increase the rate of interest charged on the loan. The bank would need to be convinced through financial information supporting the loan application, such as cash flow forecasts, that Blin would be able to meet future interest payments and repayments of principal.

**Security offered**

The rate of interest charged on the loan will be lower if the debt is secured against an asset or assets of the company. It is likely in Blin's case that the loan will carry a fixed charge on particular assets, such as land or buildings. In the event of default by the company, the bank can recover its loan by selling the secured assets.

**Duration of loan**

The longer the period of the loan taken out by Blin, the higher the interest rate that will be charged. This reflects the shape of the normal yield curve.

**Yield curve**

The normal yield curve shows that the yield required on debt increases in line with the term to maturity. One reason for this is that loan providers require compensation for deferring their use of the cash they have lent, and the longer the period for which they are deprived of their cash, the more compensation they require. This is described as the liquidity preference explanation for the shape of the normal yield curve.

Other explanations for the shape of the normal yield curve are expectations theory and market segmentation theory. Expectations theory suggests that interest rates rise with maturity because rates of interest are expected to rise in the future, for example due to an expected increase in inflation. Market segmentation theory suggests that the market for long-term debt differs from the market for short-term debt.

**Amount borrowed**

The rate of interest charged on the new loan could be lower if the amount borrowed is not a small sum. It is more convenient from an administrative point of view for a bank to lend a large sum rather than several small amounts.

(b)   The approaches that Blin could adopt regarding the relative proportions of long- and short-term finance to meet its working capital needs could be described as conservative, moderate and aggressive.

The assets of a business are categorised into current assets and fixed assets. Current assets are used up on a regular basis within a single accounting period and fixed assets benefit a business for several accounting periods. Current assets can be further categorised into permanent current assets and fluctuating current assets. Permanent current assets represent the core level or minimum level of investment in current assets needed for a given level of business activity, and arise from the need for businesses to carry stock and to extend credit. Fluctuating current assets represent a variable need for investment in current assets, arising from either seasonal or unpredictable variations in business activity.

With a *conservative* **approach** to the financing mix, long-term finance is the main source of working capital funds. Long-term finance is used to finance fixed assets, permanent current assets and some fluctuating current assets.

Long-term debt finance is less risky to a company than short-term debt finance, since once in place it is not subjected to the dangers of renewal or immediate repayment. However, it is more expensive in that the rate of interest charged normally increases with maturity. A conservative approach would therefore increase the amount of lower-risk long-term debt finance used by the company, but would also incur higher total interest payments than an approach emphasizing the use of short-term debt. This approach will therefore lead to relatively lower profitability. A similar argument can be made when equity finance is used as long-term finance; equity requires an even higher return than long-term debt finance.

With an *aggressive* **approach** to the financing mix, short-term finance is the main source of working capital funds. This approach, which is currently being used by Blin, uses short-term finance for fluctuating current assets and some permanent current assets, with long-term finance being used for the balance of permanent current assets and fixed assets. This increases the relative amount of higher-risk short-term finance used by the company, but will also incur lower total interest payments than the conservative approach discussed above, leading to relatively higher profitability.

Between these two approaches lies a **moderate or matching approach**. This approach applies the matching principle, whereby the maturity of the funding is matched with life of the assets financed. Here, long-term finance is used for permanent current assets and fixed assets, while short-term finance is used for fluctuating current assets.

The repayment of the overdraft will result in Blin adopting a conservative approach to the mix of long- and short-term finance. This will resolve an overtrading situation, if it exists. However, it may reduce profitability more than necessary. If Blin continues to expand sales, or reintroduces overdraft finance, the conservative position will only be temporary and a moderate position may arise in the future. The speed with which this happens will depend on the size of the loan taken out, and whether a moderate position is desirable will depend on the company's attitude to risk and return. It may be preferable to reduce the overdraft to a lower level rather than repaying it completely. A clearer picture would emerge if we knew the intended use for, and the amount of, the balance of the loan not being used to repay the overdraft.

(c)   The **cash operating cycle** is the length of time between paying trade creditors and receiving cash from debtors. It can be calculated by adding together the average stock holding period and the average time for debtors to pay, and then subtracting the average time taken to pay trade creditors. The stock holding period may be subdivided into the holding periods for raw materials, work-in-progress and finished goods. Using accounting ratios, the cash operating cycle can be approximated by adding together stock days and debtor days (debtors' ratio) and subtracting creditor days (creditors' ratio). If creditors are paid before cash is received from debtors, the cash operating cycle is positive; if debtors pay before trade creditors are paid, the cycle is negative.

The significance of the cash operating cycle in determining the level of investment in working capital is that the longer the cash operating cycle, the higher the investment in working capital.

The length of the cash operating cycle varies between industries: for example, a service organization may have no stock holding period, a retail organization will have a stock holding period based almost entirely on finished goods and a very low level of debtors, and a manufacturing organization will have a stock holding period based on raw materials, work-in-progress and finished goods. The level of investment in working capital will therefore depend on the nature of business operations.

The cash operating cycle and the resulting level of investment in working capital does not depend only on the nature of the business, however. Companies within the same business sector may have different levels of investment in working capital, measured for example by the accounting ratio of sales/net working capital, as a result of adopting different working capital policies. A relatively aggressive policy on the level of investment in working capital is characterised by lower levels of stock and debtors: this lower level of investment increases profitability but also increases the risk of running out of stock, or of losing potential customers due to better credit terms being offered by competitors. A relatively conservative policy on the level of investment in working capital has higher levels of investment in stock and debtors: profitability is therefore reduced, but the risk of stock-outs is lower and new credit customers may be attracted by more generous terms.

It is also possible to reduce the level of investment in working capital by reducing the length of the cash operating cycle. This is achieved by reducing the stock holding period (for example by using JIT methods), by reducing the average time taken by debtors to pay (for example by improving debtor management), or by increasing the length of credit period taken from suppliers (for example by settling invoices as late as possible). In this way an understanding of the cash operating cycle can assist in taking steps to improve working capital management and profitability.

| ACCA marking scheme | | Marks |
|---|---|---|
| (a) | Risk of default | 2 |
| | Security | 2 |
| | Duration | 1 |
| | Yield curve | 3 |
| | Amount borrowed | 1 |
| | | 9 |

| (b) | Relative risk of long- and short-term finance | 1 |
| | Discussion of aggressive approach | 2 |
| | Discussion of conservative approach | 2 |
| | Discussion of moderate/matching approach | 2 |
| | Comment on repayment of overdraft | 2 |
| | | 9 |
| (c) | Meaning of cash operating cycle | 2 |
| | Significance re level of working capital investment | 5 |
| | | 7 |
| Total | | 25 |

## 10 VELM PLC

(a) The benefits of the proposed policy change are as follows.

Trade terms are 40 days, but debtors are taking $365 \times 550,000/4$ million = 50 days.

Current level of debtors = £550,000.

Cost of 1% discount = $0.01 \times 4m \times 2/3$ = £26,667.

Proposed level of debtors = $(4,000,000 - 26,667) \times (26/365)$ = £283,000.

Reduction in debtors = $550,000 - 283,000$ = £267,000.

Debtors appear to be financed by the overdraft at an annual rate of 9%.

| | | £ |
|---|---|---|
| Reduction in financing cost | £267,000 × 9% | 24,030 |
| Reduction of 0.6% in bad debts | 0.6% × £4 million | 24,000 |
| Salary saving from early retirement | | 12,000 |
| Total benefits | | 60,030 |
| Cost of 1% discount (see above) | | (26,667) |
| Net benefit of discount | | 33,363 |

A discount for early payment of one per cent will therefore lead to an increase in profitability for Velm plc.

(b) **Short-term sources of debt finance** include overdrafts and short-term loans. An **overdraft** offers flexibility but it is technically repayable on demand. Consequently it is a relatively risky source of finance. A company could experience liquidity problems if an overdraft were called in, until an alternative source of finance were found. The danger with a **short-term loan** as a source of finance is that it may be renewed at maturity on less favourable terms if economic circumstances have deteriorated and short-term interest rats are higher.

Short-term finance should be cheaper than long-term finance, based on the assumption of a normal shape to the yield curve. Economic circumstances could invert the yield curve, for example if short-term interest rates have been increased in order to curb economic growth or to dampen inflationary pressures.

**Long-term sources of debt finance** include loan stock, debentures and long-term loans. These are relatively secure forms of finance. For example if a company meets its contractual obligations on debentures in terms of interest payments and loan covenants, it will not have to repay the finance until maturity. The risk for the company is therefore lower if it finances working capital from a long-term source.

However, long-term finance is usually more expensive than short-term finance. The shape of the normal yield curve indicates that providers of debt finance will expect compensation for deferred consumption and default risk, as well as protection against expected inflation.

The choice between short-term and long-term debt for the financing of working capital is hence a choice between cheaper but riskier short-term finance and more expensive but less risky long-term debt.

(c) Working capital policies on the method of financing working capital can be characterised as conservative, moderate and aggressive. A **conservative financing policy** would involve financing working capital needs predominantly from long-term sources of finance. If current assets are analysed into permanent and fluctuating current assets, a conservative policy would use long-term finance for permanent current assets and some of the fluctuating current assets. Such a policy would increase the amount of lower-risk finance used by the company, at the expense of increased interest payments and lower profitability.

Velm plc is clearly not pursuing a conservative financing policy, since long-term debt only accounts for 2.75% (40/1,450) of non-cash current assets. Rather, it seems to be following an **aggressive financing policy**, characterised by short-term finance being used for all of fluctuating current assets and most of the permanent current assets as well. Such a policy will decrease interest costs and increase profitability, but at the expense of an increase in the amount of higher-risk finance used by the company.

Between these two extremes in policy terms lies a **moderate or matching approach**, where short-term finance is used for fluctuating current assets and long-term finance is used for permanent current assets. This is an expression of the matching principle, which holds that the maturity of the finance should match the maturity of the assets.

(d) The objectives of working capital management are often stated to be profitability and liquidity. These objectives are often in conflict, since liquid assets earn the lowest return and so liquidity is achieved at the expense of profitability. However, liquidity is needed in the sense that a company must meet its liabilities as they fall due if it is to remain in business. For this reason cash is often called the lifeblood of the company, since without cash a company would quickly fail. Good working capital management is therefore necessary if the company is to survive and remain profitable.

The fundamental objective of the company is to maximise the wealth of its shareholders and good working capital management helps to achieve this by **minimising the cost of investing in current assets**. **Good credit management**, for example, aims to minimise the risk of bad debts and expedite the prompt payment of money due from debtors in accordance with agreed terms of trade. Taking steps to optimise the level and age of debtors will minimise the cost of financing them, leading to an increase in the returns available to shareholders.

A similar case can be made for the **management of stock**. It is likely that Velm plc will need to have a good range of stationery and office supplies on its premises if customers' needs are to be quickly met and their custom retained. Good stock management, for example using techniques such as the economic order quantity model, ABC analysis, stock rotation and buffer stock management can minimise the costs of holding and ordering stock. The application of just-in-time methods of stock procurement and manufacture can reduce the cost of investing in stock. Taking steps to improve stock management can therefore reduce costs and increase shareholder wealth.

**Cash budgets** can help to determine the transactions need for cash in each budget control period, although the optimum cash position will also depend on the precautionary and speculative need for cash. Cash management models such as the Baumol model and the Miller-Orr model can help to maintain cash balances close to optimum levels.

The different elements of good working capital management therefore combine to help the company to achieve its primary financial objective.

| ACCA marking scheme | | Marks |
|---|---|---|
| (a) | Reduction in debtors | 1 |
| | Cost of discount | 1 |
| | Reduction in financing costs | 1 |
| | Reduction in bad debts | 1 |
| | Calculation of net benefit and conclusion | 1 |
| | | 5 |
| (b) | Risks of short-term finance | 2 |
| | Cost of short-term finance | 1 |
| | Risks of long-term finance | 1 |
| | Cost of long-term finance | 1 |
| | Discussion and conclusion | 1 |
| | | 6 |
| (c) | Permanent and fluctuating current assets | 2 |
| | Explanation of financing policies | 4 |
| | Discussion and link to Velm plc | 1 |
| | | 7 |
| (d) | Objectives of working capital management | 2 |
| | Credit management | 2 |
| | Stock management | 2 |
| | Discussion and link to Velm plc | 1 |
| | | 7 |
| Total | | 25 |

## 11    SPECIAL GIFT SUPPLIES PLC

(a)    The funding requirements for working capital is the sum of:

|  | Months |
|---|---|
| Stock holding period | 3.5 |
| Debtors collection period | 2.5 |
| Creditors payment period | (2.0) |
| Working capital funding period | 4.0 |

Diagrammatically, the funding requirement may be represented as follows.

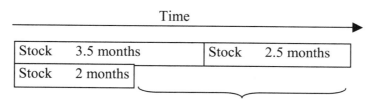

Funding requirement = 4 months

(b)    Annual sales:    £2.5m

Credit sales:    £2.5m × 90% = £2.25m

Commission charges payable to the sales force are ignored in the following calculations since they are common to both. The allocated overheads are also irrelevant for the evaluation. The factor's better record with bad debts is not part of the evaluation of the proposal in terms of the benefits to Special Gift Supplies, because the factor's service will be provided without recourse (i.e. the factor will take on the bad debt risk).

| **Existing position** | £ |
|---|---|
| Credit control salary | 12,500 |
| Bad debts 3% × £2.25m = | 67,500 |
| Annual funding costs for debtors £468,750 × 12% (see note below) | 56,250 |
| | ——— |
| Total costs | 136,250 |
| | ——— |

*Note:*

Average debtors are currently (2.5/12) × £2.25 million = £468,750.

The annual cost of financing these debtors at 12% per annum is:

12% × £468,750 = £56,250.

| **Factor's offer:** | £ |
|---|---|
| Factor finance charge (see note 1 below) | 22,500 |
| Unfactored funding costs (see note 2 below) | 4,500 |
| Factor service charge: 4% × £2.25m | 90,000 |
| One-off payment funding costs: £25,000 × 12% (note 3 below) | 3,000 |
| | ——— |
| | 120,000 |
| | ——— |

**Conclusion**

It is worthwhile to factor the debts because it will be less costly.

*Notes*

(1)     The debtors for which the factor will provide finance at 15% = 80% of £2.25 million = £1.8 million.

The average debt collection period will be 1 month, so the average amount of debtors for which the factor will provide finance is (1/12 × £1.8 million) = £150,000.

The cost of the finance at 15% per annum is £22,500 (15% × £150,000).

(2)     The unfactored debts will be 20% of £2.25 million = £450,000 each year. The debt collection period will be 1 month, so the average amount of unfactored debts for which finance will be required is (1/12 × £450,000) £37,500. These will be financed by the company itself at 12%, so the annual interest cost will be £4,500.

(3)     *Tutorial note*: The one-off payment of £25,000 to the factor has to be converted into an annual cost, for comparison purposes (i.e. comparing costs with the existing position). Here the cost has been established using the assumption that the annual cost is the interest cost on the £25,000 using the company's overdraft rate (12%) as the cost of capital. You might prefer to make a different assumption. The assumption used here is the one preferred by the examiner when this question was set in the examination.

(c)     **Report on the credit control, factoring of debtors and the financing of working capital**

| | |
|---|---|
| **To:** | Financial Controller, Special Gift Supplies plc |
| **From:** | A Student |
| **Date:** | xx/xx/xx |
| **Subject:** | **Credit control** |

A good credit control department would exhibit a number of characteristics, some of which are included in the list below:

1   Preferably have a cash business relationship with customers to begin with

2   Obtain references for new customers and possibly visit their premises

3   Access the services of a credit rating agency

4   Only incrementally raise credit limits to that preferred by the customer

5   Maintain a history of transactions with each customer

6   Have documented procedures that explain to credit control employees credit limits and duration with clear action plans when these limits are breached

7   Create good reporting controls, such as aged list of debtors, and ensure the line of reporting is clear so that senior management are aware of problem cases

8   Ensure the credit control reports form part of the monitoring of the working capital cycle as a whole so that imbalances do not arise

9   Access published information on customers, particularly through financial statements or through information services via credit or other agencies

10   Ensure all customers' credit limits are periodically reviewed

**The benefits of factoring**

A list of the benefits of factoring might include:

1   Access to flexible sources of finance. This is important for small businesses that experience rapid growth since the facility would normally grow with the business.

2   Sales ledger expertise. Factors can often bring a level of expertise to debtor management that small businesses may not have, either in skills or resources, thus making them more effective.

3   Factors can bring economies of scale to debtor management thus making them more efficient than a single small company could be.

4   The business can pay its own debts more promptly, thus ensuring continued supply of goods, for example and also in being able to access early payment discounts which may be substantial.

5   Stock levels may be optimally managed since they will be unencumbered by restrictions relating to payment difficulties. For example, it may be optimal for stock management purposes to reorder stock at lower, more expensive levels so that the whole of the stock related costs are minimised.

6   Debt factoring is a source of funds that ensure adequate financing for growing businesses. By facilitating this, one of the key issues involved in over trading is addressed.

7   Costs of sales ledger administration are avoided.

### Financing of working capital

The financing of the components of working capital is not always undertaken on a completely maturity-matched basis. That is, whilst working capital is regarded as net current assets that arguably should be funded by short-term sources of finance, this is not always the case for two reasons. First, by construction, net current assets are funded by long-term sources of finance to the extent that all short-term sources of finance have been exhausted. This can be demonstrated from a characterisation of a typical balance sheet.

Fixed assets + net current assets – long term loans = capital and reserves

By simply re-arranging we see that:

Net current assets = capital and reserves + long term loans – fixed assets

That is, net current assets are funded by long-term sources of finance not otherwise tied up in fixed assets. This amount will vary day to day because the components of working capital vary from day to day. However, to the extent that there exists positive net current assets, then adequate long term financing needs have to be considered.

Second, the liabilities components of working capital (trade creditors and bank overdrafts) represent sources of finance. As such, they are normally regarded as short-term sources of finance. In reality for many businesses, there is likely to be a core of current assets that will always need funding: whilst the components of current assets will change on a day to day basis, their level – to an extent – will remain predictable. It is this predictable component that enables managers to utilise longer term sources of finance in the knowledge that the finance will always be required. The distinction is often made between **fluctuating current assets** and **permanent current assets**. To the extent that current assets are permanent, they are more efficiently financed by longer-term sources (because these are usually cheaper). This will help avoid the higher interest costs (implicit or explicit) in shorter term sources of finance. The distinction between fluctuating and permanent current assets is illustrated in the following diagram that indicates the relationship between asset variability and funding maturity.

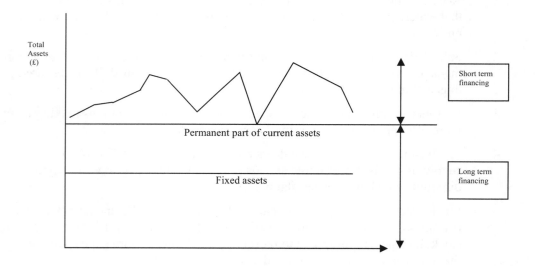

| | ACCA marking scheme | | |
|---|---|---|---|
| | | | *Marks* |
| (a) | Calculation of funding requirements in months | | 2 |
| (b) | Evaluation of existing position | 2 | |
| | Evaluation of factor's offer | 4 | |
| | Omission of overheads from evaluation | 1 | |
| | Omission of factor's bad debt record | 1 | |
| | | | 8 |
| (c) | 1 mark for each item characterising good credit control | 5 | |
| | 1 mark for each benefit of factoring | 5 | |
| | Up to 2 marks for each detailed point on financing | 6 | |
| | Presentation and quality of argument | 2 | |
| | Maximum marks available | 18 | |
| | Maximum marks awarded | | 15 |
| Total | | | 25 |

## 12 TNG

(a) TNG has a current order size of 50,000 units

Average number of orders per year = demand/order size = 255,380/50,000 = 5.11 orders
Annual ordering cost = 5.11 × 25 = £127.75

Buffer stock held = 255,380 × 28/365 = 19,591 units
Average stock held = 19,591 + (50,000/2) = 44,591 units
Annual holding cost = 44,591 × 0.1 = £4,459.10

Annual cost of current ordering policy = 4,459.10 + 127.75 = £4,587

(b) We need to calculate the economic order quantity:
EOQ = ((2 × 255,380 × 25)/0.1)0.5 = 11,300 units

Average number of orders per year = 255,380/11,300 = 22.6 orders
Annual ordering cost = 22.6 × 25 = £565.00

Average stock held = 19,591 + (11,300/2) = 25,241 units
Annual holding cost = 25,241 × 0.1 = £2,524.10

Annual cost of EOQ ordering policy = 2,524.10 + 565.00 = £3,089

Saving compared to current policy = 4,587 – 3,089 = £1,498

(c) Annual credit purchases = 255,380 × 11 = £2,809,180
Current creditors = 2,809,180 × 60/365 = £461,783
Creditors if discount is taken = 2,809,180 × 20/365 = £153,928
Reduction in creditors = 461,783 – 153,928 = £307,855
Finance cost increase = 307,855 × 0.08 = £24,628

Discount gained = 2,809,180 × 0.01 = £28,091
Net benefit of taking discount = 28,091 – 24,628 = £3,463
The discount is financially acceptable.

An alternative approach is to calculate the annual percentage benefit of the discount. This can be done on a simple interest basis:

(1/(100 – 1)) × (365/40) = 9.2%

Alternatively, the equivalent annual rate can be calculated:

(100/(100 – 1))365/40 – 1 = 9.6%

Both methods indicate that the annual percentage benefit is greater than the current cost of short-term debt (8%) of TNG and hence can be recommended on financial grounds.

(d)     The economic order quantity (EOQ) model is based on a cost function for holding stock which has two terms: holding costs and ordering costs. With the EOQ, the total cost of having stock is minimised when holding cost is equal to ordering cost. The EOQ model assumes certain knowledge of the variables on which it depends and for this reason is called a deterministic model. Demand for stock, holding cost per unit per year and order cost are assumed to be certain and constant for the period under consideration. In practice, demand is likely to be variable or irregular and costs will not remain constant. The EOQ model also ignores the cost of running out of stock (stockouts). This has caused some to suggest that the EOQ model has little to recommend it as a practical model for the management of stock.

The model was developed on the basis of zero lead time and no buffer stock, but these are not difficulties that prevent the practical application of the EOQ model. As our earlier analysis has shown, the EOQ model can be used in circumstances where buffer stock exists and provided that lead time is known with certainty it can be ignored.

The EOQ model also serves a useful purpose in directing attention towards the costs that arise from holding stock. If these costs can be reduced, working capital tied up in stock can be reduced and overall profitability can be increased.

If uncertainty exists in terms of demand or lead time, a more complex stock management model using probabilities (a stochastic model) such as the Miller-Orr model can be used. This model calculates control limits that give guidance as to when an order should be placed.

(e)     Just-in-time (JIT) stock management methods seek to eliminate any waste that arises in the manufacturing process as a result of using stock. JIT purchasing methods apply the JIT principle to deliveries of material from suppliers. With JIT production methods, stock levels of raw materials, work-in-progress and finished goods are reduced to a minimum or eliminated altogether by improved work-flow planning and closer relationships with suppliers.

**Advantages**

JIT stock management methods seek to eliminate waste at all stages of the manufacturing process by minimising or eliminating stock, defects, breakdowns and production delays[3]. This is achieved by improved workflow planning, an emphasis on quality control and firm contracts between buyer and supplier.

One advantage of JIT stock management methods is a stronger relationship between buyer and supplier. This offers security to the supplier, who benefits from regular orders, continuing future business and more certain production planning. The buyer benefits from lower stock holding costs, lower investment in stock and work in progress, and the transfer of stock management problems to the supplier. The buyer may also benefit from bulk purchase discounts or lower purchase costs.

The emphasis on quality control in the production process reduces scrap, reworking and set-up costs, while improved production design can reduce or even eliminate unnecessary material movements. The result is a smooth flow of material and work through the production system, with no queues or idle time.

**Disadvantages**

A JIT stock management system may not run as smoothly in practice as theory may predict, since there may be little room for manoeuvre in the event of unforeseen delays. There is little room for error, for example, on delivery times.

The buyer is also dependent on the supplier for maintaining the quality of delivered materials and components. If delivered quality is not up to the required standard, expensive downtime or a production standstill may arise, although the buyer can protect against this eventuality by including guarantees and penalties in to the supplier's contract. If the supplier increases prices, the buyer may find that it is not easy to find an alternative supplier who is able, at short notice, to meet his needs.

| ACCA marking scheme | | |
|---|---|---|
| | | *Marks* |
| (a) Annual ordering cost | | 1 |
| Annual holding cost | | 2 |
| Annual cost of current policy | | 1 |
| | | 4 |
| (b) Calculation of economic order quantity | | 1 |
| Annual ordering cost | | 1 |
| Annual holding cost | | 1 |
| Annual cost of EOQ policy | | 1 |
| Saving from using EOQ policy or discussion | | 1 |
| | | 5 |
| (c) Analysis | | 2–3 |
| Discussion | | 1–2 |
| | Maximum | 4 |
| (d) Discussion of limitations of EOQ model | | 4 |
| (e) Advantages of JIT stock management methods | | 4–5 |
| Disadvantages of stock management methods | | 4–5 |
| | Maximum | 8 |
| TOTAL | | 25 |

# SOURCES OF FINANCE

## 13 ASSOCIATED INTERNATIONAL SUPPLIES LTD

(a) **Analysis of company position**

**Associated International Supplies Ltd**

Circulation: Associated International Supplies Ltd (AIS Ltd)

Author:

Date: xx/xx/xx

**General appraisal**

The first point to note is that, by most standards, the company would be regarded as small, and is therefore likely to exhibit many of the problems typical of the small company sector. Generally, small companies which are characterised by strong growth also usually exhibit substantial borrowings in relation to equity funds. It is likely, therefore, that the appropriate mix of financing for the business becomes a critical issue in the appraisal of AIS Ltd.

**Growth and liquidity**

In the five year period from 20X4 to 20X9 sales for AIS have grown by 150%. In terms of supporting the business with adequate working capital, the pressures of such growth can be substantial. Thus, in the same period we see that current assets have expanded by 54% and current liabilities by 91%. Whilst this aspect of the business will be dealt-with in more detail below, it is worthwhile questioning at this stage whether sufficient funding for working capital is available to support the growth in sales.

Whilst there has been significant growth in sales during the period, profit before tax (PBT) as a percentage of sales has actually declined from 8% to about 5%. This must call into question either the management of costs (operational or financial) or whether the company is unable to force price increases on to customers. Given the information available, the most likely source of this problem appears to relate to interest costs. Both current and long term liabilities have increased substantially (91% and 276%, respectively) against a background of barely increased equity funding. Debt funding (both long and short term) looks to have increased (see detail below) and this will have an associated interest burden. This has an importance in relation to the sustainability of the business.

**Earnings retentions do not appear sufficient** to fund business growth, and hence it is clear that **borrowings have been increased** to deal with this problem. However, a balance must be kept in the business between its earnings capability and its capacity to service its debt commitments. Whilst PBT has increased by 53% over the period, retentions have declined by about 74%. This may be partly explained by an increased tax burden, but is obviously due mainly to excessive distributions. In other words, not enough funds are being retained in the business to support its growth or funded from increased equity issues.

The impact of excessive growth in relation to its funding base might have a severe impact on liquidity. **Net current assets** are not seriously out of line if a ratio of current assets to current liabilities of 1.0 (unity) is considered acceptable. However, when current assets are looked at in relation to sales a different picture emerges. The ratio was 54% in 20X4 and only 33% in 20X9. This suggests, in combination with the other information, that stocks, debtors and cash resources might be insufficient to support the volume of sales. It might be argued that this reflects greater efficiency in current asset management. This is indeed the case when debtor days are compared over the period (they declined from 99 to 61), but it is not in relation to creditor days which also declined (from 88 to 67 during the period). When working capital is measured as a proportion of sales, we observe a decline from 11.4% in 20X4 to 0.5% in 20X9. This appears to be a reflection of reduced current asset investment and overdraft increases.

Because it is debt rather than equity funding that has grown, the business faces a potentially critical situation. We know that current assets consist mainly of stock and debtors (because the business has substantial borrowings, it is unlikely to simultaneously have large cash balances) and that this is being funded by borrowing rather than retained earnings. The reason why this is the case is because the business is **not generating adequate profits** and it is distributing too much of post tax earnings. The outlook is for greater borrowing. The poor profit figures suggest that **a critical point has been reached in terms of liquidity and solvency**. This is reflected in debt/equity ratios which have increased from 2.19 in 20X4 to 4.22 in 20X9 (current and long term liabilities used as debt and capital and reserves used as equity). Unless a capital reorganisation can take place quickly, either through injected funds or conversion of debt into equity, the business is likely to become insolvent.

**Company capacity to continue trading**

Given the points made above, it is unlikely that the business can continue in its current form. The trading performance is obviously very strong when measured in terms of its sales capacity and growth. This indicates a good customer base and the ability to service customer needs. The markets the company serves suggest a long-term future for its product or service.

However, it is likely that the company's cost base will be overwhelmed by interest charges, which is resulting in reduced PBT/Sales ratios over the period in spite of significant sales growth. If that is the case, it may well be that the underlying trading profitability is good. If it is not found to be good after further investigation then additional action may need to be taken. For example if low profitability is due to aggressive pricing, an investigation into alternative marketing strategies may be appropriate. In addition, given the significant growth, it may now be an appropriate time to look at the customer base and withdraw service from those customers who are either unprofitable or otherwise difficult (late payers, for example). Product mix might be usefully assessed to focus on higher-margin sales activities and to decrease effort on lower-margin activities. A business plan describing the customer base and the strategy for greater profitability will underpin any bid for a reorganisation of AIS Ltd's finances.

**Bank support** is crucial to long term survival if the debt is in the form of bank related lending. Alternative sources of finance should also be considered, particularly in the form of equity which is required to re-balance the business.

**Other factors**

(i)     Venture capitalists might be interested in the business because of its significant growth but poorly structured finance. An equity injection would stabilise the business' finances.

(ii)    Future projections of growth might provide a clearer picture of how to respond to the situation the business is now in.

(iii)   The maturity of the debt obligations would indicate any critical repayments that may be due.

(iv)    Comparisons with other businesses in the sector may provide some assurance as to the debt levels if high debt is a characteristic of the sector.

(v)     Investigation of possible renegotiation of the debt to ease the interest burden.

(vi)    Investigation of potential sale of the business or merger with a large partner with a view to securing a realistic equity base.

(vii)   Information on detailed trading results would enable an accurate assessment of the profitability of AIS Ltd.

(viii)  Working capital management needs to be investigated to assess if it is being efficiently organised.

**Appendix to report: Ratio calculations**

Sales growth:                    $(3,010 - 1,200)/1,200 = 150\%$
Current asset growth:            $(1,000 - 650)/650 = 54\%$
Current liability growth:        $(982 - 513)/513 = 91\%$
Long term liabilities growth:    $(158 - 42)/42 = 276\%$
PBT growth:                      $(150 - 98)/98 = 53\%$
Retained earnings decline:       $(65 - 17)/65 = 74\%$

|  | 20X4 | 20X9 |
|---|---|---|
| PBT/Sales | $98/1,200 = 8\%$ | $150/3,010 = 5\%$ |
| Current assets/ Current liabilities | $650/513 = 1.3$ | $1,000/982 = 1.0$ |
| Current assets / Sales | $650/1,200 = 54\%$ | $1,000/3,010 = 33\%$ |
| Working capital/Sales | $(650–513)/1,200 = 11.4\%$ | $(1,000–982)/3,010 = 0.5\%$ |
| Debt/Equity | $(513 + 42)/210 = 2.64$ | $(982 + 158)/270 = 4.22$ |
| Debtors at 50% of current assets | £325,000 | £500,000 |
| Sales per day (365 days) | £3,288 | £8,247 |
| Debtor days | $325,000/3,288 = 99$ | $500,000/8,247 = 61$ |
| Creditors at 25% of current liabilities | £128,000 | £245,500 |
| Cost of sales per day (365 days) | £1,452 | £3,643 |
| Creditor days | $128,000/1,452 = 88$ | $245,500/3,643 = 67$ |

(b)   **General**

Funds for fixed assets would normally be **long term in nature** in order to match asset use with funding maturity. Moreover, if the asset is a building or other major asset which has a secondary market value, then secured lending may be arranged where lower rates of interest are accessible. In particular, **specific asset financing** may be available (such as for fleet cars) which may represent an efficient source of funds. In general, the **finance leasing** option is available and represents a significant source of flexibility to the business. Fixed assets with secondary market values may also be subject to **sale and leaseback** arrangements.

Long-term sources of finance would typically be either **equity funds** (either injections or dividend retentions), **bank debt** or **possibly venture capital** equity interests for small businesses. What would not be appropriate are debentures, convertibles, warrants, equity public issues, and listings (with the potential exception of a small company stock market like AIM).

The most significant barrier to secure external equity funding for small firms is the lack of liquidity, or the inability to either find a market or buyer for the shares when the time arrives when the investor wishes to sell. There is evidence that small companies tend to have low gearing ratios when long-term debt finance to long-term finance plus equity is used as the measure of gearing. Moreover, a large proportion of the debt finance, in general, comes from overdrafts and short-term loans.

**Sources of finance**

No details are given concerning the nature of a business to comment on, and hence only general recommendations can be made. Given that fixed asset finance is required, long-term finance that is likely to be the most appropriate. Below are listed some ideas of what might be most suitable:

(i)    If the fixed asset is substantial, such as a new building, or tooling for a new product, then the Alternative Investment Market may be suitable. AIM is directed largely at small and growing companies who do not qualify for the main stock market. The restrictions for admission are not that binding and may suit a company such as AIS Ltd. In particular, there are no eligibility criteria for new entrants in terms of size, profitability or existence. By listing on AIM, a company would address the market liquidity issue of equity investments for small firms.

(ii)   Venture capital may also be suitable. This would be desirable from the point of view that, whilst venture capitalists may take an equity participation, they are likely to liquidate their shareholders to the owners of the business and hence ownership dilution would not occur.

(iii)  Cash or dividend retentions. This would clearly take time for major asset purchases and may not be suitable for companies that face a funding shortfall in any case (the costs required in asset purchase may simply be too big for any realistic retention timescale).

(iv)   Entering a merger or partnership, or accessing 'Business Angel' funding.

(v)    Leasing the asset or arranging secured loans at lower interest rates.

(vi)   Possible mortgages for buildings, or specialist financing for cars (for example hire purchase, leasing).

(vii)  Availability of government grants, European funding or other agency assistance.

| ACCA marking scheme | | |
|---|---|---|
| | | *Marks* |
| (a) | 1 mark each for relevant ratio, up to a maximum of: | 6 |
| | Analysis of company position | 6 |
| | Comments on the capacity to continue trading | 2 |
| | Other relevant factors | 2 |
| | Quality of presentation of report | 1 |
| | | 17 |
| (b) | 2 marks for each identified appropriate sources of finance, up to max of | 8 |
| Total | | 25 |

## 14 ARWIN

### Key answer tips

Part (a) should be straightforward, except that you need to be careful with the calculation of the fixed costs in the cost of sales. These are not expected to rise next year, and so should be calculated using the current year figures. For part (b), the question does not state how financial gearing or operational gearing should be measured: there are different methods of calculation. Make clear the method of calculation you are using. (The solution here gives two methods of measuring financial gearing and three methods of measuring operational gearing, but your answer only needs one of each.) For part (c), you need to discuss the problems of high gearing, and you need to spot that 'gearing' in this question refers to both financial gearing and operational gearing. The question hints at this strongly, by referring to both business risk and financial risk. Unfortunately, an unwary student will overlook operational gearing and business risk entirely.

(a)     The forecast profit and loss accounts are as follows:

| | *Debt finance* | *Equity finance* |
|---|---|---|
| | *£000* | *£000* |
| Sales (50,000 × 1.12) | 56,000 | 56,000 |
| Variable cost of sales (85% × sales) | 28,560 | 28,560 |
| Fixed cost of sales (15% × 30,000) | 4,500 | 4,500 |
| | | |
| Gross profit | 22,940 | 22,940 |
| Administration costs (14,000 × 1.05) | 14,700 | 14,700 |
| | | |
| Profit before interest and tax | 8,240 | 8,240 |
| Interest (see working) | 800 | 300 |
| | | |
| Profit before tax | 7,440 | 7,940 |
| Taxation at 30% | 2,232 | 2,382 |
| | | |
| Profit after tax | 5,208 | 5,558 |
| Dividends paid (60%) | 3,125 | 3,335 |
| | | |
| Retained earnings | 2,083 | 2,223 |

*Working:*

Interest under debt financing = £300,000 + (£5,000,000 × 0.10) = £800,000.

(b) **Financial gearing**

If financial gearing is measured as the debt: equity ratio:

| Using debt/equity ratio: | Current | Debt finance | Equity finance |
| --- | --- | --- | --- |
| Debt | 2,500 | 7,500 | 2,500 |
| Share capital and reserves | 22,560 | 24,643 | 29,783 |
| Debt/equity ratio (%) | 11.1 | 30.4 | 8.4 |

*Workings:*

Share capital and reserves (debt finance) = 22,560 + 2,083 = £24,643

Share capital and reserves (equity finance) = 22,560 + 5,000 + 2,223 = £29,783.

If financial gearing is measured as the ratio of debt capital to total capital:

| Using capital (total) gearing: | Current | Debt finance | Equity finance |
| --- | --- | --- | --- |
| Debt | 2,500 | 7,500 | 2,500 |
| Total long-term capital | 25,060 | 32,143 | 32,283 |
| Capital (total) gearing (%) | 10.0 | 23.3 | 7.7 |

**Operational gearing:**

If operational gearing is measured as the ratio of fixed costs to total costs:

| Using fixed costs/total costs: | Current | Debt finance | Equity finance |
| --- | --- | --- | --- |
| Fixed costs | 18,500 | 19,200 | 19,200 |
| Total costs | 44,000 | 47,760 | 47,760 |
| Operational gearing (%) | 42.0% | 40.2% | 40.2% |

Total costs are assumed to consist of cost of sales plus administration costs.

If operational gearing is measured as the ratio of fixed costs to variable costs:

| Using fixed costs/variable costs: | Current | Debt finance | Equity finance |
| --- | --- | --- | --- |
| Fixed costs | 18,500 | 19,200 | 19,200 |
| Variable costs | 25,500 | 29,560 | 28,560 |
| Operational gearing (%) | 0.73 | 3.3 | 3.3 |

If operational gearing is measured as the ratio of contribution to profit before interest and tax (PBIT):

| Using contribution/PBIT | Current | Debt finance | Equity finance |
| --- | --- | --- | --- |
| Contribution | 24,500 | 27,440 | 27,440 |
| PBIT | 6,000 | 8,240 | 8,240 |
| Operational gearing | 4.1 | 3.3 | 3.3 |

Contribution is sales revenue minus the variable cost of sales.

**Interest cover:**

| | Current | Debt finance | Equity finance |
| --- | --- | --- | --- |
| Profit before interest and tax | 6,000 | 8,240 | 8,240 |
| Debt interest | 300 | 800 | 300 |
| Interest cover | 20 | 10.3 | 27.5 |

**Earnings per share:**

| | Current | Debt finance | Equity finance |
| --- | --- | --- | --- |
| Profit after tax | 3,990 | 5,208 | 5,558 |
| Number of shares | 10,000 | 10,000 | 11,250 |
| Earnings per share (pence) | 39.9 | 52.1 | 49.4 |

**Comment:**

The debt finance proposal leads to the largest increase in earnings per share, but results in an increase in financial gearing and a decrease in interest cover. Whether these changes in financial gearing and interest cover are acceptable depends on the attitude of both investors and managers to the new level of financial risk; a comparison with sector averages would be helpful in this context. The equity finance proposal leads to a decrease in financial gearing and an increase in interest cover. The expansion leads to a decrease in operational gearing, whichever measure of operational gearing is used, indicating that fixed costs have decreased as a proportion of total costs.

(c) **Business risk** could be described as the possibility of a company experiencing changes in the level of its profit before interest as a result of changes in turnover or operating costs. For this reason it is also referred to as operating risk. Business risk relates to the nature of the business operations undertaken by a company. For example, we would expect profit before interest to be more volatile for a luxury goods manufacturer than for a food retailer, since sales of luxury goods will be more closely linked to varying economic activity than sales of a necessity good such as food.

The nature of business operations influences the proportion of fixed costs to total costs. Capital intensive business operations, for example, will have a high proportion of fixed costs to total costs. From this perspective, operational gearing is a measure of business risk. As operational gearing increases, a business becomes more sensitive to changes in turnover and the general level of economic activity, and profit before interest becomes more volatile. A rise in operational gearing may therefore lead to a business experiencing difficulty in meeting interest payments. Managers of businesses with high operational risk will therefore be keen to keep fixed costs under control.

**Financial risk** in the context of this question can be described as the possibility of a company experiencing changes in the level of its distributable earnings as a result of the need to make interest payments on debt finance. The earnings volatility of companies in the same business will therefore depend not only on business risk, but also on the proportion of debt finance each company has in its capital structure. Since the relative amount of debt finance employed by a company is measured by gearing, financial risk is also referred to as gearing risk.

As financial gearing increases, the burden of interest payments increases and earnings become more volatile. Since interest payments must be met, shareholders may be faced with a reduction in dividends; at very high levels of gearing, a company may cease to pay dividends altogether as it struggles to find the cash to meet interest payments.

The pressure to meet interest payments at high levels of gearing can lead to a liquidity crisis, where the company experiences difficulty in meeting operating liabilities as they fall due. In severe cases, liquidation may occur.

The focus on meeting interest payments at high levels of financial gearing can cause managers to lose sight of the primary objective of maximizing shareholder wealth. Their main objective becomes survival and their decisions become focused on this, rather than on the longer-term prosperity of the company. Necessary investment in fixed asset renewal may be deferred or neglected.

A further danger of high financial gearing is that a company may move into a loss-making position as a result of high interest payments. It will therefore become difficult to raise additional finance, whether debt or equity, and the company may need to undertake a capital reconstruction.

It is likely that a business with high operational gearing will have low financial gearing, and a business with high financial gearing will have low operational gearing.

This is because managers will be concerned to avoid excessive levels of total risk, i.e. the sum of business risk and financial risk. A business with a combination of high operational gearing and high financial gearing clearly runs an increased risk of experiencing liquidity problems, making losses and becoming insolvent.

| ACCA marking scheme | | |
|---|---|---|
| | | *Marks* |
| (a) | Sales and administration cost | 1 |
| | Cost of sales | 1 |
| | Interest | 1 |
| | Profit after tax | 1 |
| | Retained earnings | 1 |
| | | 5 |
| (b) | Revised share capital and reserves | 1 |
| | Financial gearing | 2 |
| | Operational gearing | 2 |
| | Interest cover | 2 |
| | Earnings per share | 2 |
| | Calculation of current values | 1 |
| | Discussion | 2 |
| | | 12 |
| (c) | Explanation of business risk | 1 |
| | Explanation of financial risk | 1 |
| | Up to 2 marks for each danger of high gearing | 6 |
| | | 8 |
| Total | | 25 |

## 15   JERONIMO PLC

### Key answer tips

In part (a) note there are three parts to this requirement - (1) the difference between the two types of issue, (2) why companies make rights issues and (3) the effect on private investors. Marks are allocated for each part - don't throw them away by overlooking any of them.

Part (b)(i) hinges around the computation of the theoretical ex-rights price, a fairly standard formula with which you should be familiar. The price at which the investor will sell the rights should be that which leaves him no worse off than if he had taken them up. Taking them up will give him a share worth £1.55, at a cost of £1.30, a net gain of £0.25. This is therefore the compensation he needs for selling the rights instead.

Part (c) – the dividend growth model is central to equity value theory, and you must be confident in using it. Here, growth is estimated from past dividends, and applied to the current dividend to estimate next year's.

Part (d) really tests your understanding of the *implications* of market efficiency, rather than simply the ability to regurgitate definitions.

(a)   A **rights issue** is a way of raising finance via the issue of shares to existing equity shareholders. In order to make such an issue, a company must have an authorised share capital which exceeds the share capital that would be in issue after the rights issue. (The shareholders could be asked to vote for an increase in the authorised share capital if necessary.) Companies choose to make rights issues because they need to raise long-term finance, and choose to do so by raising new equity finance. A rights issue might well be the most cost effective or desirable method of raising finance. The finance raised may be used to fund any type of long-term investment such as an acquisition, expansion of production facilities, or overseas investment.

A **scrip issue** (also called a bonus issue or capitalisation issue) is an issue of shares to existing shareholders, in proportion to their existing shareholdings, for which no charge is made. In other words, the shares are issued free to existing shareholders.

The advantage of a rights issue to existing shareholders, as opposed to an issue via public subscription, is that existing shareholders are assumed to have some level of commitment to the company already. As such, it may prove relatively easy to persuade them to buy new shares, and certainly easier and less costly than making a public offering. It is, however, important for the company to explain the reason behind the share issue – what it is going to do with the cash raised. If an investor is to be persuaded to pay cash for additional shares, then it must be demonstrated that their newly-invested cash will be used to earn returns at least equal to those they are currently receiving from their investment. If the return on capital is expected to decline in the company after the rights issue, then the issue is unlikely to be successful. As with any new share issue, it is common practice for a rights issue to be underwritten.

In the UK, it is a legal requirement that, unless existing shareholders have voted to waive their pre-emption rights, a new issue of shares for cash must be in the form of a rights issue.

The individual investor in a company which is making a rights issue will be invited to take up or sell his/her rights. If the rights are taken up, then the investor will have to make a payment to the company equal to the price of the rights purchased. Alternatively, the investor may choose not to increase his investment, and instead can sell the rights on the open market. In an efficient market, the investor is no better nor no worse off by choosing to sell his/her rights.

Scrip issues are often justified on the basis that there is a need to increase the number of shares in issue in order to bring down the price per share. It is often argued that the market 'dislikes' shares which individually have a very high price, and by increasing the number of shares in issue, the unit share price can be diluted. This can be beneficial to shareholders, because research evidence suggests that the drop in the unit share price is not as great as the proportionate change in the number of shares in issue. For example, if 10 million shares are in issue, and the current market price is £10 each, the market value of the equity is £100 million. If 10 million shares are now distributed via a scrip issue, one would expect the share price to drop to £5, leaving the overall equity value at £100 million. In practice, the lowering of the share price may make the shares more marketable, such that the post issue price settles at, say, £6. This results in an increase in the value of individual shareholdings, together with a rise in the total value of the equity. Individual investors may therefore experience some capital gain from a scrip issue.

When making a scrip issue, a company is converting some of the reserves into share capital, and the number of shares (fully paid up) to which an investor is entitled, will be expressed in relation to the current holding, e.g. a 2 for 5 issue means that two new shares will be given to shareholders for every five shares they currently hold. As already suggested, although the private investor gains no theoretical advantage from this conversion of reserves, there may be a benefit in practice, because the shares are now likely to be more marketable.

(b) (i) **Theoretical ex-rights price/value**

$$\frac{(\text{No. shares in issue} \times \text{market value}) + (\text{No. rights shares} \times \text{rights share price})}{\text{Total shares in issue post rights}}$$

$$= \frac{(5\text{m} \times £1.60) + (1\text{m} \times £1.30)}{6\text{m}}$$

$$= £1.55 \text{ per share}$$

After taking up the rights issue, James Brown will hold $10,000 + (0.2 \times 10,000)$ = 12,000 shares. The theoretical value of the holding, at £1.55 per share is thus £18,600.

**Alternative method of calculation**

|  | £ |
|---|---|
| Current value of 5 existing shares ($\times$ £1.60) | 8.00 |
| Value of 1 new share in rights issue | 1.30 |
| Theoretical value of 6 shares | 9.30 |

Theoretical ex-rights price per share = £9.30/6 = £1.55 per share.

(ii) **The value of the rights per share**

= Theoretical ex-rights price – Cost of taking up the rights

The value of the rights per share = £1.55 – £1.30

The value of the rights per share = £0.25 per share

If James Brown sells all of his rights to 2,000 shares, he can expect to receive: $2,000 \times £0.25 = £500$.

**Alternative method of calculation**

|  | £ |
|---|---|
| Current value of shares | 1.60 |
| Theoretical ex-rights price | 1.55 |
| Theoretical value of rights per existing share | 0.05 |

Theoretical value of each new share that can be purchased = $5 \times 5p = £0.25$. The value of the rights per share is therefore £0.25.

(c) **Using the dividend growth formula:**

$$R = \left( \frac{D_1}{MV} + g \right) \times 100$$

Where:

| $D_1$ | = Next year's dividend |
|---|---|
| $g$ | = Dividend growth rate |
| MV | = Market price of share |
| R | = Percentage required return |

It is assumed that the average growth rate in dividends between 20X5 and 20X9 will be a reliable guide to the future annual growth rate in dividends. Between 20X5 and 20X9 (4 years) dividends per share have grown by a factor of 12/8 = 1.5 times. The average annual growth rate over this period is calculated as the fourth root of 1.5, minus 1.

$$g = \sqrt[4]{\frac{12}{8}} - 1$$

$$= 0.1067 \text{ or } 11\%$$

$$D1 = 1.11 \times 12 \text{ pence}$$

$$= 13.32 \text{ pence, say 13 pence.}$$

$$R = \left( \frac{13}{160} + 0.11 \right) \times 100$$

$$R = 19.125\%$$

(d)     In a strongly efficient market, finance directors will be alert to the fact that market prices are an accurate reflection of their company's financial prospects, and that if they behave in a manner which results in bad financial decisions, the share price will quickly fall to compensate for the worsening prospects.

This means that the effect of an efficient market on financial management is that it keeps managers alert to the consequences of their decisions. In an inefficient world, prices may take a while to adjust to reflect poor planning or control, but in a semi-strong or strong market environment this will not be true. It can thus be said that a strong-form efficient market encourages higher quality financial management. In a similar vein, it also serves to discourage the artificial manipulation of accounting information, as the truth will quickly be realised, and prices adjusted accordingly.

## 16     TECHFOOLS

(a)     **Why convertibles might be an attractive source of finance for companies**

(i)      Convertibles can provide immediate finance at lower cost since the conversion option effectively reduces the interest rates payable.

(ii)     They represent attractive investments to investors since they are effectively debt risks for future equity benefits. Hence, finance is relatively easily raised.

(iii)    Should the company's assumption regarding the likelihood of conversion prove true then there is no problem of establishing a large sinking fund for the redemption of the debentures.

(iv)    Convertibles allow for higher gearing levels than would otherwise be the case with straight debt (interest costs are potentially lower with convertibles).

### Tutorial note

This solution assumes that a company has sufficient creditworthiness to be able to issue convertibles in the bond market. By no means all companies can do this.

(b)     (i)

Calculate **PV of cash flows per £100 (nominal value) of debentures** (assuming conversion at end of year 5)

| Year | Cash flow | Discount factor at 15% | PV at 15% |
|---|---|---|---|
| 1 (Annual interest at 8%) | 8 | 0.870 | 6.96 |
| 2 (Annual interest at 8%) | 8 | 0.756 | 6.05 |
| 3 (Annual interest at 8%) | 8 | 0.658 | 5.26 |
| 4 (Annual interest at 8%) | 8 | 0.572 | 4.58 |
| 5 (Annual interest at 8%) | 8 | 0.497 | 3.98 |
| 5 (Conversion): = 4 × 45 | 180 | 0.497 | 89.46 |
| Estimated market value per £100 of debentures | | | 116.29 |

The value of 45 shares in 5 years' time is expected to be £4 × 45 = £180. The value of debenture redemption will be £110. Hence **it is likely that conversion will take place**, because the conversion value of the bonds will be higher than their redemption value.

(ii)     Arguably, the most important reservation concerns the future value of the share since it is likely to be the most uncertain aspect of the calculation. Other factors that may be relevant, but which are less uncertain, are issue price, and the cost of capital used.

(c)   The conversion premium for convertible bonds is the amount by which the value of the convertible as a bond exceeds the current market value of the shares into which they will be convertible in the future.

By maximising the conversion premium the greatest amount of funds are raised for the fewest number of new shares issued.

Companies can issue convertibles with a high conversion premium because, firstly, the calculation in part (a)(i) produces a positive NPV against issue costs and, secondly, because there is high growth potential in share value.

(d)   Financial intermediation refers to the role of a bank or other financial institution that serves to bring together lenders and borrowers. Investors are seeking avenues to place surplus funds whilst companies are seeking sources of finance. Because of the disparate nature of both investors and companies it is difficult to match investors to a company where the requirements of the investor are met and the needs of the company are satisfied. Thus, banks (as an example) act as a conduit through which investors can place funds and companies can borrow funds. In return, investors obtain interest on their deposits and the banks obtain interest on their loans. Clearly, the interest charged by the bank to the company is higher than it pays out to investors.

The role that financial intermediaries perform is to pool together investor funds to facilitate easy access by companies. Without financial intermediaries, companies would almost certainly face capital shortages.

The **benefits of financial intermediation** are as follows:

Investors can pool their funds in a bank deposit account to facilitate access by companies to larger resources than would otherwise be the case. This enables companies to:

(i)    Exploit investment opportunities that would otherwise be untapped.

(ii)   Become larger than would otherwise be the case and thus take advantage of economies of scale.

(iii)  Find capital readily and easily thus reducing the costs associated with raising funds.

(iv)   Reduce the cost of finance since:

(1)   Banks can, with their greater financial expertise, more accurately assess the risk of corporate investments.

(2)   Banks can diversify their risk across many companies thus lowering their required rate of return, which in turn reduces the cost base on which interest charges to companies will be referenced.

(3)   Banks can reduce interest costs because of their size. They are able to borrow on the wholesale market at rates that are not accessible to small banks or individual investors.

(v)    Bridge the maturity gap. Banks can lend longer term than individual investors desire since banks will have access to a level of funds that is largely constant irrespective of a high turnover of constituent investors.

(vi)   Access finance for high-risk projects that banks may find acceptable because of their capacity to diversify.

**Investors benefit substantially from financial intermediation** because:

(i)    By investing in a market or bank, investors can get access to diversified portfolios which might otherwise be difficult. Since their funds are pooled, investors benefit from the banks' abilities to aggregate funds and allocate them efficiently.

(ii) Investors can access bank expertise in assessing corporate risk, thus obtaining the best return for a particular level of risk.

(iii) Investor risk is reduced because of the banks' diversifying activities. Minimised risk, subject to a required rate of return, is passed onto investors in a competitive banking market.

(iv) Legislation that provides for investor protection should a bank fail (in terms of either central bank support or investor guarantee schemes by other banks), further reduces the risk investors face.

(v) Investors can choose their exposure to a particular level of risk subject to depositing money in appropriate funds. For example, mutual funds offer a range of risk profiles from which the investor can choose.

| ACCA marking scheme | | | |
|---|---|---|---|
| | | | *Marks* |
| (a) | | Up to 2 marks for each detailed point on convertibles as a source of finance | 4 |
| (b) | (i) | Cash flows | 2 |
| | | NPV calculation | 1 |
| | | Assessment | 2 |
| | (ii) | Identification and justification of major reservation | 2 |
| (c) | | Explanation of maximising conversion premium | 2 |
| | | Explanation of ability to obtain high premium | 2 |
| (d) | | 2 marks for each detailed advantage for companies | up to 7 |
| | | 2 marks for each detailed advantage for investors | up to 7 |
| | | Maximum marks available | 10 |
| Total | | | 25 |

## 17 TIRWEN PLC

(a) Rights issue price = 4.00 × 0.85 = £3.40

(i) Theoretical ex rights price = ((5 × 4.00) + 3.40)/6 = £3.90

(ii) Value of rights per existing share = (3.90 − 3.40)/5 = 10p

(b) Value of 1,200 shares after rights issue = 1,200 × 3.90 = £4,680

Value of 1,000 shares before rights issue = 1,000 × 4.00 = £4,000

Value of 1,000 shares after rights issue = 1,000 × 3.90 = £3,900

Cash subscribed for new shares = 200 × 3.40 = £680

Cash raised from sale of rights = 1,000 × 0.1 = £100

The investor could do nothing, take up the offered rights, sell the rights into the rights market, or any combination of these actions. The effect of the rights issue on the wealth of the investor depends on which action is taken.

The rights issue has a neutral effect if the rights attached to the 1,000 shares are exercised to purchase an additional 200 shares, since the value of 1,200 shares after the rights issue (£4,680) is equal to the sum of the value of 1,000 shares before the rights issue (£4,000) and the cash subscribed for new shares (£680). Part of the investor's wealth has changed from cash into shares, but no wealth has been gained or lost. The theoretical ex rights per share therefore acts as a benchmark following the rights issue against which other ex rights share prices can be compared.

The rights issue also has a neutral effect on the wealth of the investor if the rights attached to existing shares are sold. The value of 1,000 shares after the rights issue (£3,900) plus the cash received from the sale of rights (£100) is equal to the value of

1,000 shares before the rights issue (£4,000). In this case, part of the investor's wealth has changed from share into cash.

If the investor neither subscribes for the new shares offered nor sells the rights attached to the shares already held, a loss of wealth of £100 will occur, due to the difference between the value of 1,000 shares before the rights issue (£4,000) and the value of 1,000 shares after the rights issue (£3,900).

The theoretical ex rights price is simply a weighted average of the cum rights price and the rights issue price, ignoring any use made of the funds raised. The actual ex rights price will depend on the use made of the funds raised by the rights issue, as well as the expectations of investors and the stock market.

(c)    Current share price = £4.00

Earnings per share = $100 \times (4.00/15.24) = 26.25p$

Number of ordinary shares = 2m/0.5 = 4m shares

Earnings of Tirwen = $4m \times 0.2625 = £1.05m$

Funds raised from rights issue = $800,000 \times £4.00 \times 0.85 = £2,720,000$

Funds raised less issue costs = 2,720,000 − 220,000 = £2,500,000

Debenture interest saved = $2,500,000 \times 0.12 = £300,000$

Profit before tax of Tirwen = 1,050,000/(1 − 0.3) = £1,500,000

Current debenture interest paid = $4,500,000 \times 0.12 = £540,000$

Current overdraft interest = $1,250,000 \times 0.07 = £87,500$

Total interest = 540,000 + 87,500 = £627,500

Current profit before interest and tax = 1,500,000 + 627,500 = £2,127,500

Revised total interest = 627,500 − 300,000 = £327,500

Revised profit after tax = $(2,127,500 − 327,500) \times 0.7 = £1,260,000$

(Or revised profit after tax = $1,050,000 + (300,000 \times 0.7) = £1,260,000$)

New shares issued = 4m/5 = 800,000

Shares in issue = 4,000,000 + 800,000 = 4,800,000

Revised earnings per share = $100 \times (1,260,000/4,800,000) = 26.25p$

(d)    As the price/earnings ratio is constant, the share price expected after redeeming part of the debentures will remain unchanged at £4.00 per share ($26.25 \times 15.24$). Since this is greater than the theoretical ex rights share price of £3.90, using the funds raised by the rights issue to redeem part of the debentures results in a capital gain of 10p per share. The proposal to use the rights issue funds to redeem part of the debentures therefore results in an increase in shareholder wealth.

(e)    A rights issue will be an attractive source of finance to Tirwen plc as it will reduce the gearing of the company. The current debt/equity ratio using book values is:

Debt/equity ratio = $100 \times 4,500/3,500 = 129\%$

Including the overdraft, debt/equity ratio = $100 \times 5,750/3,500 = 164\%$

Both values are above the sector average of 100% and issuing new debt will not be attractive in this situation. A substantial reduction in gearing will occur, however, if the rights issue is used to redeem £2.5m of debentures:

Debt/equity ratio = $100 \times 2,000/6,000 = 33\%$

Including the overdraft, debt/equity ratio = $100 \times 3{,}250/6{,}000 = 54\%$

If the rights issue is not used to redeem the debenture issue, the decrease in gearing is less dramatic:

Debt/equity ratio = $100 \times 4{,}500/6{,}000 = 75\%$

Including the overdraft, debt/equity ratio = $100 \times 5{,}750/6{,}000 = 96\%$

In both cases, the debt/equity ratio falls to less than the sector average, signalling a decrease in financial risk. The debt/equity ratio would fall further if increased retained profits were included in the calculation, but the absence of information on Tirwen's dividend policy makes retained profits uncertain.

If the rights issue is used to redeem £2.5m of debentures, there will be an improvement in interest cover from 3.4 times (2,127,500/627,500), which is below the sector average of 6 times, to 6.5 times (2,127,500/327,500), which is marginally better than the sector average. Interest cover might also increase if the funds raised are invested in profitable projects.

A rights issue will also be attractive to Tirwen plc since it will make it more likely that the company can raise further debt finance in the future, possibly at a lower interest rate due to its lower financial risk.

It should be noted that a decrease in gearing is likely to increase the average cost of the finance used by Tirwen plc, since a greater proportion of relatively more expensive equity finance will be used compared to relatively cheaper debt. This will increase the discount rate used by the company and decrease the net present value of any expected future cash flows.

| ACCA marking scheme | | Marks |
|---|---|---|
| (a) | Theoretical ex rights price per share | 2 |
| | Value of rights per existing share | 1 |
| | | 3 |
| (b) | Effect on wealth of exercising rights | 2 |
| | Effect on wealth of sale of rights | 2 |
| | Discussion of right issue and shareholder wealth | 2 |
| | | 6 |
| (c) | Current earnings per share | 1 |
| | Current earnings | 1 |
| | Funds raised via rights issue | 1 |
| | Interest saved by redeeming debentures | 1 |
| | Revised earnings | 1 |
| | Revised earnings per share | 1 |
| | | 6 |
| (d) | Expected share price after redeeming debentures | 1 |
| | Comparison with theoretical ex rights price | 1 |
| | Discussion and conclusion | 1 |
| | | 3 |
| (e) | Effect of rights issue on debt/equity ratio | 2 |
| | Effects of rights issue on interest cover | 2 |
| | Discussion and link to Tirwen plc | 3 |
| | | 7 |
| Total | | 25 |

# CAPITAL INVESTMENT APPRAISAL

## 18    INVESTMENT APPRAISAL

(a)    **Accounting rate of return (ARR)** is a measure of the return on an investment where the annual profit before interest and tax is expressed as a percentage of the capital sum invested. There are a number of alternative formulae which can be used to calculate ARR, which differ in the way in which they define capital cost. The more common alternative measures available are:

- average annual profit to initial capital invested, and

- average annual profit to average capital invested.

The method selected will affect the resulting ARR figure, and for this reason it is important to recognise that the measure might be subject to manipulation by managers seeking approval for their investment proposals. The value for average annual profit is calculated after allowances for depreciation, as shown in the example below:

Suppose ARR is defined as: $\dfrac{\text{Average profit (after depreciation)}}{\text{Initial capital invested}} \times 100$

A project costing £5 million, and yielding average profits of £1,250,000 per year after depreciation charges of £500,000 per year, would give an ARR of:

$1{,}250{,}000/5{,}000{,}000 \times 100 = 25\%$

If the depreciation charged were to be increased to £750,000 per year, for example as a result of technological changes reducing the expected life of an asset, the ARR becomes:

$1{,}000{,}000/5{,}000{,}000 \times 100 = 20\%$

The attraction of using ARR as a method of investment appraisal lies in its simplicity and the ease with which it can be used to specify the impact of a project on a company's profit and loss account. The measure is easily understood and can be directly linked to the use of ROCE as a performance measure. Nonetheless, ARR has been criticised for a number of major drawbacks, perhaps the most important of which is that it uses accounting profits after depreciation rather than cash flows in order to measure return. This means that the capital cost is over-stated in the calculation, via both the numerator and the denominator. In the numerator, the capital cost is taken into account via the depreciation charges used to derive accounting profit, but capital cost is also the denominator. The practical effect of this is to reduce the ARR and thus make projects appear less profitable. This might in turn result in some worthwhile projects being rejected. Note, however, that this problem does not arise where ARR is calculated as average annual profit as a percentage of average capital invested.

The most important criticism of ARR is that it takes no account of the time value of money. A second limitation of ARR, already suggested, is that its value is dependent on accounting policies and this can make comparison of ARR figures across different investments very difficult. A further difficulty with the use of ARR is that it does not give a clear decision rule. The ARR on any particular investment needs to be compared with the current returns being earned within a business, and so unlike NPV for example, it is impossible to say 'all investments with an ARR of X or below will always be rejected.

The **payback method** of investment appraisal is used widely in industry - generally in addition to other measures. Like ARR, it is easily calculated and understood. The payback approach simply measures the time required for cumulative cash flows from an investment to sum to the original capital invested.

*Example*

Original investment £100,000

> Cash flow profile: Years 1–3 £25,000 p.a.
>
> Years 4 – 5 £50,000 p.a.
>
> Year 6 £5,000

The cumulative cash flows are therefore:

| | |
|---|---|
| End Year 1 | £25,000 |
| End Year 2 | £50,000 |
| End Year 3 | £75,000 |
| End Year 4 | £125,000 |
| End Year 5 | £175,000 |
| End Year 6 | £180,000 |

The original sum invested is returned via cash flows some time during the course of Year 4. If cash flows are assumed to be even throughout the year, the cumulative cash flow of £100,000 will have been earned halfway through year 4. The payback period for the investment is thus 3 years and 6 months.

The payback approach to investment appraisal is useful for companies which are seeking to claw back cash from investments as quickly as possible. At the same time, the concept is intuitively appealing as many businessmen will be concerned about how long they may have to wait to get their money back, because they believe that rapid repayment reduces risks. This means that the payback approach is commonly used for initial screening of investment alternatives.

The disadvantages of the payback approach are as follows:

(i)     Payback ignores the overall profitability of a project by ignoring cash flows after payback is reached. In the example above, the cash flows between 3–5 years and the end of the project total £80,000. To ignore such substantial cash flows would be naïve. As a consequence, the payback method is biased in favour of fast-return investments. This can result in rejecting investments that generate cash flows more slowly in the early years, but which are overall more profitable.

(ii)    As with ARR, the payback method ignores the time value of money.

(iii)   The payback method, in the same way as ARR, offers no objective measure of what is the desirable return, as measured by the length of the payback period.

(b)   (i)    **Discounted cash flow analysis** is a technique whereby the value of future cash flows is discounted back to a present value, so that the monetary values of all cash flows are equivalent, regardless of their timing. The logic for discounting is that the value of money declines over time because of individual time preferences and the impact of inflation in eroding spending power. People value money received sooner rather than later because as soon as cash is received they can increase consumption, or re-invest the capital.

**NPV** uses discounting to calculate the present value of all cash flows associated with a project. The present value of cash outflows is then compared with the present value of cash inflows, to obtain a net present value (NPV). If the present value (PV) of cash outflows exceeds the PV of cash inflows, then the NPV will be negative. If the present value (PV) of cash inflows exceeds the PV of cash outflows, then the NPV will be positive. The size of the NPV is dependent on the cash flow pattern and the rate of discount that is applied. The general rule is that a company will discount the forecast cash flows at a rate equal to its cost of capital. The reason for this is that if a company has an overall cost of capital of, for example, 12%, it is essential that the rate of return exceeds 12% or the funding costs will not be covered. Hence if the cash flows are discounted at the cost of capital and the project yields a positive NPV, this implies that the return exceeds the cost of capital. When using NPV for investment appraisal then a simple rule is applied: invest if NPV is positive, and do not invest if it is negative.

**IRR** uses discounting in a slightly different way to determine the profitability of an investment. The Internal Rate of Return is defined as the discount rate at which the net present value equals zero. For example, an investment may yield a forecast NPV of £15,000 when the cash flows are discounted at 10%. If the rate of discount is increased, the net present value will fall, and the IRR represents the effective, break-even discount rate for the investment. Suppose, for example, that the IRR is 15%, this figure can then be used to establish a decision rule for investments. An IRR of 15% means that if the cost of capital exceeds 15% then the investment would generate a negative NPV. If the company is currently having to pay 12% on its investment funds, then it knows that it can afford to see its cost of capital rise by 3% before the investment will become financially non-viable. As long as the IRR exceeds the cost of capital, then the company should invest and so, as a general rule, the higher the IRR the better.

NPV and IRR measures may sometimes contradict one another when used in relation to **mutually exclusive investments**. An example of the ambiguity which can occur when choosing between mutually exclusive decisions is when one of the investments has a higher NPV than the other, and so is preferable on that basis, but at the same time it has a lower IRR. When IRR and NPV give conflicting results, the preferred alternative is the project with the highest NPV

In conclusion, although both NPV and IRR use discounted cash flows as a method of arriving at an investment decision, the results that they generate need to be interpreted with care, and they do not always yield the same investment decisions. NPV is the preferred criterion for selecting between two or more mutually exclusive investments, where the two approaches give differing recommendations.

(ii)  If the laptops are replaced every year:

**NPV of one year replacement cycle**

| Year | Cash flow | Discount factor at 14% | PV |
|---|---|---|---|
| | £ | | £ |
| 0 | (2,400) | 1.000 | (2,400.0) |
| 1 | 1,200 | 0.877 | 1,052.4 |
| | | | (1,347.6) |

*Equivalent annual cost* = PV of cost of one replacement cycle/Cumulative discount factor

= £1,347.6/0.877

= **£1,536.6**

**NPV of two-year replacement cycle**

| Year | Cash flow | Discount factor at 14% | PV |
|---|---|---|---|
| | £ | | £ |
| 0 | (2,400) | 1.000 | (2,400.0) |
| 1 | (75) | 0.877 | (65.8) |
| 2 | 800 | 0.769 | 615.2 |
| | | | (1,850.6) |

*Equivalent annual cost* = PV of cost of one replacement cycle/Cumulative discount factor

= £1,850.6/1.647

= **£1,123.6**

**NPV of three-year replacement cycle**

| Year | Cash flow | Discount factor at 14% | PV |
|------|-----------|------------------------|------|
|      | £         |                        | £ |
| 0 | (2,400) | 1.000 | (2,400.0) |
| 1 | (75) | 0.877 | (65.8) |
| 2 | (150) | 0.769 | (115.4) |
| 3 | 300 | 0.675 | 202.5 |
|   |     |       | (2,378.7) |

*Equivalent annual cost* = PV of cost of one replacement cycle/Cumulative discount factor

= £2,378.7/2.322

= **£1,024.4**

**Conclusion**

The **optimal cycle for replacement is every three years**, because this has the lowest equivalent annual cost. Other factors which need to be taken into account are the non-financial aspects of the alternative cycle choices. For example, computer technology and the associated software is changing very rapidly and this could mean that failure to replace annually would leave the salesmen unable to utilise the most up to date systems for recording, monitoring and implementing their sales. This could have an impact on the company's competitive position. The company needs to consider also the compatibility of the software used by the laptops with that used by the in-house computers and mainframe. If system upgrades are made within the main business which render the two computers incompatible, then rapid replacement of the laptops to regain compatibility is essential.

## 19    BREAD PRODUCTS LTD

**Tutorial note**

This question tests your ability to carry out a DCF asset replacement analysis. The solution below demonstrates both the lowest common multiple technique and the equivalent annual cost technique.

(a)    There are a number of methods to answering this question and two are presented. The first problem is in deciding which broad approach to use. The broad approach which seems best is to inflate the cash flows at their different inflation rates and to discount them at the money discount rate.

1    **Lowest common multiple method**

The lowest common multiple is $2 \times 3 = 6$ years. Hence the cash flows for each of the alternatives will be presented in these terms.

**Two-year cycle for replacement**: (Cash flows are inflated according to their individual inflation rates, original cost and resale values at 5% each year and maintenance costs at 10%.)

| Year | 0 | 1 | 2 | 3 | 4 | 5 | 6 |
|---|---|---|---|---|---|---|---|
| Original cost | 24,500 | | 27,011 | | 29,780 | | |
| Maintenance | | 550 | 968 | 666 | 1,170 | 805 | 1,417 |
| Resale values | | | (17,199) | | (18,962) | | (20,905) |
| Total net cost | 24,500 | 550 | 10,780 | 666 | 11,989 | 805 | (19,488) |
| Discount factor at 15% | 1.000 | 0.870 | 0.756 | 0.658 | 0.572 | 0.497 | 0.432 |
| Present values | 24,500 | 479 | 8,150 | 438 | 6,858 | 400 | (8,419) |
| NPV of cost | **32,406** | | | | | | |

**Three-year cycle for replacement**: (Cash flows are inflated according to their individual inflation rates)

| Year | 0 | 1 | 2 | 3 | 4 | 5 | 6 |
|---|---|---|---|---|---|---|---|
| Original cost | 24,500 | | | 28,362 | | | |
| Maintenance | | 550 | 968 | 1,997 | 732 | 1,288 | 2,657 |
| Resale values | | | | (12,965) | | | (15,009) |
| Total net cost | 24,500 | 550 | 968 | 17,394 | 732 | 1,288 | (12,352) |
| Discount factor at 15% | 1.000 | 0.870 | 0.756 | 0.658 | 0.572 | 0.497 | 0.432 |
| Present values | 24,500 | 478 | 732 | 11,445 | 419 | 640 | (5,336) |
| NPV of cost | **32,878** | | | | | | |

Hence, a **two-year replacement cycle is preferable** since it represents (slightly) the lower cost over a six-year cycle.

2  **Equivalent annual cost method**

Alternatively, an equivalent annual cost approach could be used:

**Two-year cycle for replacement**: (Cash flows are inflated according to their individual inflation rates)

| | 0 | 1 | 2 |
|---|---|---|---|
| Original cost | 24,500 | | |
| Maintenance | | 550 | 968 |
| Resale values | | | (17,199) |
| Net total cost | 24,500 | 550 | (16,231) |
| Discount factor | 1.000 | 0.870 | 0.756 |
| Present values | 24,500 | 479 | (12,271) |
| Net present value of costs | **12,708** | | |

**Equivalent annual cost** = 12,708/(annuity factor at 15% for two years) = 12,708/1.626 = **7,815**.

**Three-year cycle for replacement**: (Cash flows are inflated according to their individual inflation rates)

| | 0 | 1 | 2 | 3 |
|---|---|---|---|---|
| Original cost | 24,500 | | | |
| Maintenance | | 550 | 968 | 1,997 |
| Resale values | | | | (12,965) |
| Net total cost | 24,500 | 550 | 968 | (10,968) |
| Discount factor at 15% | 1.000 | 0.870 | 0.756 | 0.658 |
| Present values | 24,500 | 479 | 732 | (7,217) |
| Net present value of costs | **18,494** | | | |

**Equivalent annual cost** = 18,494/(annuity factor at 15% for three years) = 18,494/2.283 = **8,101**.

Again, the conclusion is that a two-year replacement cycle is preferable.

(b) **General limitations of Net Present Value when applied to investment appraisal**

NPV is a commonly used technique employed in investment appraisal, but it is subject to a number of restrictive assumptions and limitations which call into question its general relevance. Nonetheless, if the assumptions and limitations are understood then its application is less likely to be undertaken in error.

Some of the difficulties with NPV are listed below:

(i) NPV assumes that firms pursue an objective of maximising the wealth of their shareholders. This is questionable given the wider range of stakeholders who might have conflicting interests to those of the shareholders.

(ii) NPV is largely redundant if organisations are not wealth maximising. For example, public sector organisations may wish to invest in capital assets but will use non-profit objectives as part of their assessment.

(iii) NPV is potentially a difficult method to apply in the context of having to estimate what is the correct discount rate to use. This is particularly so when questions arise as to the incorporation of risk premia in the discount rate, since an evaluation of the riskiness of the business, or of the project in particular, will have to be made but may be difficult to discern. Alternative approaches to risk analysis, such as sensitivity and decision trees are, themselves, subject to fairly severe limitations.

(iv) NPV assumes that cash surpluses can be reinvested at the discount rate. This is subject to other projects being available which produce at least a zero NPV at the chosen discount rate.

(v) NPV can most easily cope with cash flows arising at period ends and is not a technique that is used easily when complicated, mid-period cash flows are present.

(vi) NPV is not universally employed, especially in a small business environment. The available evidence suggests that businesses assess projects in a variety of ways (payback, IRR, accounting rate of return). The fact that such methods are used which are theoretically inferior to NPV calls into question the practical benefits of NPV, and therefore hints at certain practical limitations.

(vii) The conclusion from NPV analysis is the present value of the surplus cash generated from a project. If reported profits are important to businesses, then it is possible that there may be a conflict between undertaking a positive NPV project and potentially adverse consequences on reported profits. This will particularly be the case for projects with long time horizons, large initial investment and very delayed cash inflows. In such circumstances, businesses may prefer to use accounting measures of investment appraisal.

(viii) Managerial incentive schemes may not be consistent with NPV, particularly when long time horizons are involved. Thus managers may be rewarded on the basis of accounting profits in the short term and may be incentivised to act in accordance with these objectives, and thus ignore positive NPV projects. This may be a problem of the incentive schemes and not of NPV; nonetheless, a potential conflict exists and represents a difficulty for NPV.

(ix) NPV treats all time periods equally, with the exception of discounting far cash flows more than near cash flows. In other words, NPV only accounts for the time value of money. To many businesses, distant horizons are less important than near horizons, if only because that is the environment in which they work. Other factors besides applying higher discount rates may work to reduce the impact of distant years. For example, in the long term, nearly all aspects of the business may change and hence a too-narrow focus on discounting means that NPV is of limited value and more so the further the time horizon considered.

(x)     NPV is of limited use in the face of non-quantifiable benefits or costs. NPV does not take account of non-financial information which may even be relevant to shareholders who want their wealth maximised. For example, issues of strategic benefit may arise against which it is difficult to immediately quantify the benefits but for which there are immediate costs. NPV would treat such a situation as an additional cost since it could not incorporate the indiscernible benefit.

| ACCA marking scheme | | |
|---|---|---|
| | | *Marks* |
| (a) | Identification of appropriate cash flows for each alternative | 4 |
| | Identification of appropriate cash flows for each alternative | 2 |
| | Calculation of discounted cash flows | 2 |
| | Calculation of optimal policies | 4 |
| | | 12 |
| (b) | Up to 2 marks for each detailed limitations of NPV (1 mark each for limited responses). Up to a maximum of: | 13 |
| Total | | 25 |

## 20   HOWDEN PLC

### Key answer tips

In part (a) the answer implies that it is possible to determine a 'real' rate of return which can then be adjusted in the light of estimated future rates of inflation. The most likely method of calculating a company's required rate of return will actually produce a 'money cost of capital'. To produce a 'real' cost of capital requires some tinkering with this initial calculation.

In part (b) a clear lay out will greatly assist both you and the marker. With projects of short time span, up to, say, five years, a horizontal tabulation is generally best. Where various annuities in real terms are inflating at different rates the best approach is to split them into single year flows and inflate each separately.

Note that in (c), the consideration is not limited to investment decisions – take care to read the requirements carefully.

(a)     Investors invest capital in companies expecting a reward for both the delay in waiting for their returns (time value of money) and also for the risks to which they expose their capital (risk premium). In addition, if prices in general are rising, shareholders require compensation for the erosion due to inflation in the real value of their capital.

For example, suppose that in the absence of inflation, shareholders require a company to offer a return of 10%. The need to cover price inflation of, say, 5% will raise the overall required return to about 15%. If people in general expect a particular rate of inflation, the structure of interest rates in the capital market will adjust to incorporate these inflationary expectations. This is known as the **'Fisher effect'**.

More precisely, the relationship between the **real required return (r)** and the nominal or **money rate of return (m)**, i.e. the rate which includes an allowance for inflation, is given by:

$(1 + r) \times (1 + p) = (1 + m)$, where p is the expected rate of price inflation.

It is essential when evaluating an investment project under inflation that future expected price level changes are treated in a consistent way. Companies may correctly allow for inflation in two ways each of which computes the real value of an investment project:

(i)     Inflate the future expected cash flows at the expected rate of inflation (allowing for inflation rates specific to the project), and discount these cash flows at a discount rate of at m. This is the fully-inflated rate or 'money terms' approach.

(ii)    Strip out the inflation element from the market-determined rate and apply the resulting real rate of return, r, to the stream of project cash flows expressed in today's or constant prices. This is the 'real terms' approach.

(b)    First, the **relevant set-up cost** needs identification. The **offer of £2m for the building**, if rejected, represents an opportunity lost, although this appears to be compensated by its predicted eventual resale value of £3m.

The **cost of the market research study** has to be met irrespective of the decision to proceed with the project or not and is thus **not relevant**.

Secondly, **incremental costs and revenues** are identified. All other items are avoidable except the element of apportioned overhead, leaving the incremental overhead alone to include in the evaluation.

Thirdly, all items of incremental cash flow, including this additional overhead, must be **adjusted for their respective rates of inflation**. Because (with the exception of labour and variable overhead) the inflation rates differ, a disaggregated approach is required.

The appropriate discount rate is given by:

$$(1 + p) \times (1 + r) - 1 = m$$

$$= (1.06) \times (1.085) - 1$$

$$= 15\%$$

Assuming that the inflated costs and prices apply from and including the first year of operation, the cash-flow profile is as follows.

*Cash flow profile*

| Item | 0 | 1 | 2 | 3 | 4 | 5 |
|------|------|------|------|------|------|------|
| | £m | £m | £m | £m | £m | £m |
| Equipment | (10.50) | | | | | 2.00 |
| Forgone sale of buildings | (2.00) | | | | | |
| Residual value of building | | | | | | 3.00 |
| Working capital* | (0.50) | | | | | 0.50 |
| Revenue | | 5.04 | 5.29 | 5.56 | 5.83 | 6.13 |
| Materials | | (0.62) | (0.64) | (0.66) | (0.68) | (0.70) |
| Labour and variable overhead | | (0.43) | (0.46) | (0.49) | (0.52) | (0.56) |
| Relevant fixed overhead | - | (0.53) | (0.55) | (0.58) | (0.61) | (0.64) |
| Net cash flows | (13.00) | 3.46 | 3.64 | 3.83 | 4.02 | 9.73 |
| | | | | | | |
| Discount factor at 15% | 1.000 | 0.870 | 0.756 | 0.658 | 0.572 | 0.497 |
| Present value | (13.00) | 3.01 | 2.75 | 2.52 | 2.30 | 4.84 |

**NPV = +£2.42m**

NPV = +£2.42m, i.e. positive, therefore, the project appears to be acceptable.

However, the financial viability of the project depends quite heavily on the estimate of the residual value of the building and equipment.

*Note:* The working capital cash recovery towards the end of the project is approximately equal to the initial investment in stocks, because the rate of material cost inflation tends to cancel out the JIT-induced reduction in volume, leading to roughly constant stock-holding in value terms throughout most of the project life-span.

(c)     Inflation adds an extra element of uncertainty into forecasting future cash flows, because it becomes more difficult to estimate what future prices and costs will be. This extra uncertainty means that financial evaluations will be less reliable.

In addition to the problems offered for investment appraisal such as forecasting the various rates of inflation relevant to the project, inflation poses a wider range of difficulties in a variety of business decision areas.

Inflation may pose a problem for businesses if it distorts the signals transmitted by the market. In the absence of inflation, the price system should translate the shifting patterns of consumer demand into price signals to which producers respond in order to plan current and future output levels. If demand for a product rises, the higher price indicates the desirability of switching existing production capacity to producing the goods or of laying down new capacity.

Under inflation, however, the producer may lose confidence that the correct signals are being transmitted, especially if the prices of goods and services inflate at different rates. He may thus be inclined to delay undertaking new investment. This applies particularly if price rises are unexpected and erratic.

Equally, it becomes more difficult to evaluate the performance of whole businesses and individual segments when prices are inflating. A poor operating performance may be masked by price inflation, especially if the price of the product sold is increasing at a rate faster than prices in general or if operating costs are inflating more slowly. The rate of return on capital achieved by a business is most usefully expressed in real terms by removing the effect on profits of generally rising prices (or better still, the effect of company-specific inflation). The capital base of the company should also be expressed in meaningful terms. A poor profit result may translate into a high ROI if the capital base is measured in historic terms. Unless these sorts of adjustment are made, inflation hinders the attempt to measure company performance on a consistent basis and thus can cloud the judgement of providers of capital in seeking out the most profitable areas for investment.

## 21    FILTREX PLC

### Key answer tips

The first parts of (a) are textbook definitions, leading into a discussion as to the circumstances under which soft capital rationing may arise. To get maximum marks, clearly split your response to this into separate points (reasons).

The sentence that dictates the approach to (b)(i) is 'Project A and C are mutually exclusive and no project can be sub-divided.' This rules out the pure NPV/£ invested key factor analysis approach, and some trial and error is needed. Take care not to overrun here – even if you don't arrive at the actual optimal solution, a well-argued, logical approach will gain most of the marks.

Part (c) requires some imaginative thinking; whilst raising further finance is an obvious possibility (and you should be specific about the various methods to get good marks) the examiner will reward any alternatives solutions, such as that given in the answer.

(a)     **Hard capital rationing** applies when a firm is restricted, due to a shortage of capital, from undertaking all apparently worthwhile investment opportunities, and the reasons for the capital shortage are factors external to the company, over which it has no control. These factors might include government monetary restrictions and the general economic and financial climate, for example, a depressed stock market, precluding a rights issue of ordinary shares.

**Soft capital rationing** applies when a company decides to limit the amount of capital expenditure that it is prepared to authorise. The capital budget becomes a control variable, which the company may relax if it chooses. Segments of divisionalised companies often have their capital budgets imposed on them by the main board of directors, and have to make their investment decisions within this imposed capital constraint.

A company may purposely curtail its capital expenditure for a number of reasons:

(i) It may consider that it has **insufficient depth of management expertise** to exploit all available opportunities without jeopardising the success of both new and ongoing operations.

(ii) It may be deliberate board policy to restrict the capital budget, **to concentrate managerial attention** on generating the very best and most carefully thought out and analysed proposals. In this regard, self-imposed capital rationing may be an exercise in quality control.

(iii) Many companies adopt the policy of **restricting capital expenditure to the amounts which can be generated by internal resources,** i.e. retained earnings and depreciation provisions (or in reality, internally-generated cash flow). This reluctance to use the external capital markets may be due to a risk-averse attitude to financial gearing, possibly because of the operating characteristics of the industry e.g. high operating gearing in a cyclical industry. Alternatively, it may be due to reluctance to issue equity in the form of a rights issue, for fear of diluting earnings, or in the case of an unlisted company, reluctance to seek a quotation owing to the time and expense involved and the dilution of ownership.

(b)  (i)  Assuming Filtrex wishes to maximise the wealth of its shareholders, it will seek the set of investment projects with the highest combined NPVs.

As a first approximation, it may examine the projects ranked according to their estimated NPVs, and select the projects with the highest NPVs, consistent with the budget limitation. However, this approach would confine the programme to project E alone, which apart from losing any benefits of diversification, is a solution which can be improved upon. This is because it overlooks the relationship between the NPV itself and the amount of capital required to yield the estimated NPV. Under capital rationing, it is often considered desirable to examine the productivity of each pound of scarce capital invested in the various projects. This information is given by the **profitability index (PI)**, which is the ratio of the NPV to the capital outplay in the year of capital rationing. The ranking of the five projects according to their PIs is:

| | | | |
|---|---|---|---|
| A | 65/150 | = | 0.43 |
| B | 50/120 | = | 0.42 |
| C | 80/200 | = | 0.40 |
| D | 30/80 | = | 0.38 |
| E | 120/400 | = | 0.30 |

Moving down the ranking, Filtrex would select projects A and B, but then, due to the **indivisibility problem**, and also the fact that projects A and C are mutually exclusive, it would have to depart from the rankings and move down as far as D, where after the remaining project E is too demanding of capital. The selected programme of ABD would require an outlay of £350,000 and generate an NPV of £145,000. £50,000 of scarce capital would remain unspent and according to the stated policy, would be invested in short-term assets. Although of low risk, these offer a return less than the 18% required by shareholders. Consequently, it might be preferable to return this unspent capital to shareholders in the form of a dividend or share repurchase, if shareholders are able to invest for higher returns in alternative activities. Perhaps, closer liaison with major shareholders is required to determine their preferences.

It is possible to improve on both of the previous selections by **trial and error**, in an attempt to utilise the whole of the capital budget. The optimal selection is BCD which offers a joint NPV of £160,000. However, even this result is suspect, as it relies on evaluating the projects at the rate of return required in the absence of rationing, in this case, 18% post-tax. This neglects the impact of capital rationing on the cost of capital – if apparently worthwhile projects are rejected, there is an opportunity cost in the form of the returns otherwise obtainable on the rejected projects. Projects should be evaluated at the discount rate reflecting the rate of return on the best of the rejected projects. Unfortunately, until the evaluation and selection is made, this remains an unknown! Unless project indivisibility is a problem, ranking and selection using the internal rate of return (IRR) will yield the same solution – it would therefore be helpful to find the IRR for each project.

(ii) In addition to IRRs, other information which may aid the decision-maker might include the following.

(1) Whether the rationing is likely to apply **over the long-term**, in which case its cost of capital (i.e. its opportunity cost of capital) should be raised.

(2) The degree of **postponability of projects** should be more closely assessed, i.e. whether a project can be postponed and what would be the impact of postponement on its profitability. If projects can be postponed, it may be desirable for Filtrex to select projects in the base period offering a rapid return flow of cash in order to provide funds to enable investment to be made in the postponed projects in the next time period. In other words, it would be helpful to examine the cash flow profiles of these projects and hence their **speed of payback**.

(3) The **respective degrees of risk** of these projects. It is implied in the analysis above that all projects have a similar degree of risk, but this is unlikely in practice, especially for the types of new product development planned by Filtrex. A capital-constrained company may use its limited access to finance to justify rejecting a high risk activity, especially if it is reliant on subsequent cash flows to finance postponed projects.

(4) The likelihood of obtaining marginal supplies of finance and on what terms.

(c) There are two basic ways in which a company in Filtrex's position might still manage to exploit more projects. On one hand, it can involve other parties in the project, and on the other, it can resolve to seek outside capital.

**Sharing the projects**

(i) To the extent that some part of the project(s) still require further development, for example design and market research, some of this work can be sub-contracted to specialist agencies. These might be able to perform the work at lower cost, and might even agree to take a deferred payment out of the project cash flows.

(ii) The production and/or sale of the products can be **licensed or franchised** to another party, with Filtrex arranging to receive a royalty or a percentage of sales. This is particularly appropriate for overseas activities.

(iii) A **joint venture** could be mounted with a competitor, although for commercial reasons, it is often safer to arrange such alliances with companies outside the industry, or with overseas companies wishing to penetrate the UK market. Clearly, such an agreement would have to be carefully negotiated.

(iv)  The **patent rights to one or more products could be sold** and the purchaser allowed to develop the projects.

**Raising external finance**

(i)  A certain amount of marginal finance could be squeezed out of more intensive use of working capital, although this could be counter-productive, for example reducing credit periods for customers may lose sales.

(ii)  Some equipment could be leased, reducing the requirement for investment capital to buy assets.

(iii)  If Filtrex has assets of sufficient quality, it may be possible to raise a mortgage or issue debentures secured on these assets.

(iv)  Alternatively, good quality property assets could be sold to a financial institution and their continued use secured via a leaseback arrangement.

(v)  Filtrex might approach official sources of aid such as a regional development agency, if relevant, or perhaps the European Investment Bank.

(vi)  Filtrex might approach a venture capitalist which specialises in extending development capital to small-to-medium-sized firms. However, the venture capitalist will probably require a substantial equity stake, and possibly insist on placing an appointee on the Board to monitor their interests.

(vii)  Filtrex may decide to seek a Stock Exchange quotation, either on the main London market or AIM. However, this would be time-consuming and costly, and involve releasing a substantial part of the equity (less for AIM) to a wider body of shareholders.

## 22  ARMCLIFF LTD

### Key answer tips

In part (a) the first part of the data in the question relates to current operations - try to think why the examiner has given you this. The requirement is to determine whether the proposed project is attractive to *Armcliff* - not the parent company. Presumably what will make a project attractive to a division's management is one that will improve their current performance measure. Thus it is useful to know what the current level of ARR being achieved. This can then be compared with the project ARR.

Remember that the ARR is a financial accounting based measure - returns are in terms of accounting profits, and investments valued at balance sheet amounts - you must try to put all 'relevant cost' principles to the back of your mind. Whilst there are various possible definitions of the ARR (a point that can be raised in (b)) here you are given precise directions, so make sure you follow them. Both average profits and average investment need to be ascertained.

Don't forget to conclude by comparison with both current and required rates of return.

In part (b) the question requires you to show both theoretical and practical knowledge about investment appraisal methods. Your points must be made in sufficient depth to convince the examiner you actually understand the relevance of what you are saying. *Why* is the use of accounting profits potentially a problem?

In part (c), even though this is a examining a general area of credit management, try wherever you can to relate your points to the business in the question - it is stated that Armcliff intends to extend its credit to improve sales. Again make sure that you explain points enough to get the marks available, whilst still offering sufficient variety. Note that it is not enough simply to say that the advantages of APR is its simplicity. With spreadsheets, this is hardly going to be a consideration. Show instead that you appreciate that mangers are influenced by the methods used for their performance measurement - both internally and externally.

(a)   **Current return on capital employed**

= Operating profit/capital employed

= £20m/(£75m + £25m)

= £20m/£100m = 20%.

**Analysis of the project**

Project capital requirements are £14 million fixed capital plus £0.5 million stocks. The annual depreciation charge (straight line) is:

(£14m – expected residual value of £2m)/4 = £3 million per annum.

**Profit profile (£m)**

| Year | 1 | 2 | 3 | 4 |
|---|---|---|---|---|
| Sales | (5.00 × 2m) = 10.00 | (4.50 × 1.8m) = 8.10 | (4.00 × 1.6m) = 6.40 | (3.50 × 1.6m) = 5.60 |
| Operating costs | (2.00) | (1.80) | (1.60) | (1.60) |
| Fixed costs | (1.50) | (1.35) | (1.20) | (1.20) |
| Depreciation | (3.00) | (3.00) | (3.00) | (3.00) |
| Profit | 3.50 | 1.95 | 0.60 | (0.20) |

Total profit over four years = £5.85 million.

**Capital employed (start-of-year):**

| | | | | |
|---|---|---|---|---|
| Fixed | 14.00 | 11.00 | 8.00 | 5.00 |
| Stocks | 0.50 | 0.50 | 0.50 | 0.50 |
| Total capital employed | 14.50 | 11.50 | 8.50 | 5.50 |

Average capital employed = (14.50 + 11.50 + 8.50 + 5.50)/4 = £10 million.

$$\text{Average rate of return} = \frac{\text{Average profit}}{\text{Average capital employed}} = \frac{£5.85m/4}{£10.0m} = \frac{£1.46m}{£10.0m}$$

= 14.6%

*Note:* If debtors were to be included in the definition of capital employed, this would reduce the calculated rate of return, while the inclusion of creditors would have an offsetting effect. However, using the ARR criterion as defined, the proposal has an expected return above the minimum stipulated by Shevin plc. It is unlikely that the managers of Armcliff will propose projects which offer a rate of return below the present 20% even where the expected return exceeds the minimum of 10%. To undertake projects with returns in this range will depress the overall divisional return and cast managerial performance in a weaker light.

However, it is unlikely that the senior managers of the Armcliff subsidiary would want to undertake the project.

(b)   (i)   The **ARR can be expressed in a variety of ways**, and is therefore susceptible to manipulation. Although the question specifies average profit to average capital employed, many other variants are possible, such as average profit to initial capital, which would raise the computed rate of return.

It is also **susceptible to variation in accounting policy** by the same firm over time, or as between different firms at a point in time. For example, different methods of depreciation produce different profit figures and hence different rates of return.

Perhaps, most fundamentally, it is **based on accounting profits expressed net of deduction for depreciation provisions, rather than cash flows.** This effectively results in double-counting for the initial outlay i.e. the capital cost is allowed for twice over, both in the numerator of the ARR calculation and also in the denominator. This is likely to depress the measured profitability of a project and result in rejection of some worthwhile investment.

Finally, because it simply averages the profits, it **makes no allowance for the timing of the returns** from the project.

(ii) The continuing use of the ARR method can by explained largely by its utilisation of balance sheet and profit-and-loss-account magnitudes familiar to managers, namely 'profit' and 'capital employed'. In addition, the impact of the project on a company's financial statements can also be specified. Return on capital employed is still the commonest way in which business unit performance is measured and evaluated, and is certainly the most visible to shareholders. It is thus not surprising that some managers may be happiest in expressing project attractiveness in the same terms in which their performance will be reported to shareholders, and according to which they will be evaluated and rewarded.

(c) Armcliff intends to achieve a sales increase by extending its debtor collection period. This policy carries several dangers. It implies that credit will be extended to customers for whom credit is an important determinant of supplier selection, hinting at financial instability on their part. Consequently, the risk of later than expected, or even no payment, is likely to increase. Although losses due to default are limited to the incremental costs of making these sales rather than the invoiced value, Armcliff should recognise that there is an opportunity cost involved in tying up capital for lengthy periods. In addition, companies which are slow payers often attempt to claim discounts to which they are not entitled. Armcliff may then face the difficult choice between acquiescence to such demands versus rejection, in which case, it may lose repeat sales.

The **creditworthiness of customers can be assessed** in several ways as follows.

**Analysis of accounting statements**

In the case of companies which publish their annual accounts, or file them at Companies House, key financial ratios can be examined to assess their financial stability. However, these almost certainly will be provided in arrears and may not give a true indication of the companies' current situation. Some customers may be prepared to supply more up-to-date accounts directly to the seller, although these are unlikely to have been audited.

**Analysis of credit reports**

It may be possible to obtain detailed assessment of the creditworthiness of customers from other sources, such as their bankers, specialist credit assessment agencies such as Dun & Bradstreet, and from trade sources such as other companies who supply them. These assessments are likely to be more up-to-date than company accounts, but will inevitably be more subjective.

**Previous experience**

If the firm has supplied the customer in the past, its previous payment record will be available.

**Cash-only trial period**

If accounting and other data is sparse, and there is no previous trading record with the customer, the seller may offer a trial period over which cash is required, but if the payment record is acceptable (e.g. if the customer's cheques always clear quickly), further transactions may be conducted on credit.

**Background information**

General background information on the industry in which the customer operates will generate insights into the financial health of companies in that sector, and by implication, that of the customer. Many agencies supply such information, although it should only be used as a back-up to other assessments.

## 23    SLUDGEWATER PLC

(a)    The expected present value of the fines is equal to:

$$EV = (0.3 \times £1.0m) + (0.5 \times £1.8m) + (0.2 \times £2.6m)$$

$$= £0.3m + £0.9m + £0.52m$$

$$= £1.72 \text{ million.}$$

Calculation of the net present value of the investment requires computation of the capital cost plus incremental production costs as set out in the following table:

| Year | 0 | 1 | 2 | 3 | 4 |
|---|---|---|---|---|---|
| | £m | £m | £m | £m | £m |
| Equipment purchase | (4.0) | | | | |
| European Union grant (25% of cost) | | 1.000 | | | |
| Increased production costs | | (0.315) | (0.331) | (0.347) | |
| Tax saving at 30% | | | 0.095 | 0.099 | 0.104 |
| Tax saving on WDA (see note 3 below) | | 0.300 | 0.225 | 0.169 | 0.506 |
| Net cash flow | (4.0) | 0.985 | (0.011) | (0.079) | 0.610 |
| Discount factor at 10% | 1.000 | 0.909 | 0.826 | 0.751 | 0.683 |
| Present value of cash flow | (4.0) | 0.895 | (0.009) | (0.059) | 0.417 |

**Net Present Value = (£2.756m)**

*Notes:*

1    The consultant's charge has already been incurred and (as a committed cost) is therefore irrelevant to the current decision. The consultant's charge has already been incurred, and as a committed or sunk cost, it is not relevant to the current decision.

2    *Increased production costs*

| Year | Sales | Extra production costs (2%) |
|---|---|---|
| | £m | £m |
| 1 | 15.750 | 0.315 |
| 2 | 16.538 | 0.331 |
| 3 | 17.364 | 0.347 |

3    *Writing down allowances*:

| Year | Written down value | Writing down allowance (25%) | Tax saved (one year in arrears, at 30%) |
|---|---|---|---|
| 0 | 4.00 | 1.000 | 0.300 |
| 1 | 3.00 | 0.750 | 0.225 |
| 2 | 2.25 | 0.563 | 0.169 |
| 3 | 1.687 (balance) | | 0.506 |

The negative NPV on the investment in spray painting equipment exceeds the present value of the fines which Sludgewater might expect to pay. It therefore seems that the project is not viable in financial terms, and it would be cheaper to risk payment of the fines. However, the company must accept that to do so might risk incurring the wrath of both shareholders and the environmental lobby.

(b) **MEMORANDUM**

**To:** Sludgewater Board

**From:** Accountant

**Subject: Air pollution**

On purely non-financial criteria, it can be argued that our company has a moral and community responsibility to install anti-pollution equipment as long as the cost of installation does not jeopardise the long-term survival of the company.

However, the figures attached suggest that **the project is not wealth-creating** for Sludgewater's shareholders, because the value of the expected saving in fines (£1.72 million) is below the expected cost of the project (£2.756 million). The difficulty is that this conclusion is dependent on the current size of the fines payable, and if they were to rise substantially, then the optimal choice (in financial terms) might change. The difference between the expected value of the fines and the cost of the project is currently just over £1 million. This means that the fines would need to rise by nearly 60% (1/1.72 x 100) before the project becomes financially worthwhile. Changes in the size of the fines would be very difficult to predict as it is a political issue. However, since the company is a persistent offender, and the green lobby is becoming more influential, it is not unreasonable to anticipate that the fines will rise in the future as a result of political pressure.

It would be advisable, from a **public relations perspective**, for the Board to consider alternative and perhaps less expensive anti-pollution measures. It is also possible that the market for this company's products might increase if it is perceived to be more environmentally friendly, and if customers are sensitive to this. It is even possible that the company's share price might benefit from managers of 'ethical' investment funds deciding to include Sludgewater shares in their portfolio.

In addition, the company needs to think about its **long-term strategic objectives**, and its stance on anti-pollution systems in relation to these objectives. The market positioning of the company over the longer term is likely to be affected by decisions made in the short term, and so even if not investing in the project makes short-term financial sense, it may be more attractive from a long-term viewpoint. It is also possible that technological and legal circumstances will change over time, and such changes need to be anticipated in current decisions.

| ACCA marking scheme | | Marks |
|---|---|---|
| (a) | Omission of consultants fee | 1 |
| | EV fines | 2 |
| | Production costs | 1 |
| | Tax saving on higher costs | 1 |
| | Writing down allowance | 1 |
| | Tax on WDA | 1 |
| | Net cash flow | 1 |
| | Discount factor | 1 |
| | Net present value | 1 |
| | Discussion | 2 |
| | | 12 |

| (b) | Memo format | 1 |
| | Community responsibility | 2 |
| | Significance of fine size | 2 |
| | Possible changes in fines | 1 |
| | Market effect of pollution avoidance | 2 |
| | | 8 |
| Total | | 20 |

## 24  LEAMINGER PLC

### (a)  Purchase outright

| | 20X2 £ | 20X3 £ | 20X4 £ | 20X5 £ | 20X6 £ | 20X7 £ |
|---|---|---|---|---|---|---|
| Outlay/residual value | (360,000) | | | | 20,000 | |
| Maintenance | | (15,000) | (15,000) | (15,000) | (15,000) | |
| Resulting reduction in tax | | | 4,500 | 4,500 | 4,500 | 4,500 |
| Tax effect of WDAs (W1) | | 27,000 | 20,250 | 15,188 | 11,391 | |
| Tax effect of balancing allowance (W2) | | | | | | 28,172 |
| Cash flow | (360,000) | 12,000 | 9,750 | 4,688 | 20,891 | 32,672 |
| Discount factor at 10% | 1.000 | 0.909 | 0.826 | 0.751 | 0.683 | 0.621 |
| Present value | (360,000) | 10,908 | 8,054 | 3,251 | 14,269 | 20,289 |

**NPV of cost = £(302,959)**

(W1) *Writing down allowances*

| Year | Tax written down value b/d £ | Writing down allowance (WDA) 25% £ | Tax effect at 30% - tax reduction £ |
|---|---|---|---|
| 20X2 | 360,000 | 90,000 | 27,000 |
| 20X3 | 270,000 | 67,500 | 20,250 |
| 20X4 | 202,500 | 50,625 | 15,188 |
| 20X5 | 151,875 | 37,969 | 11,391 |
| 20X6 | 113,906 | | |

The tax effect is one year in arrears, so the reduction relating to 20X2 affects cash flows in 20X3, and so on.

(W2) *Balancing allowance/charge and its tax effect*

| | £ |
|---|---|
| Tax written down value at start of year of sale | 113,906 |
| Sale proceeds | 20,000 |
| Balancing allowance | 93,906 |
| Effect on tax: reduction in tax at 30% | £28,172 |

The cash flow effect is one year in arrears.

### Finance lease

| | £ |
|---|---|
| Annual lease rental | 135,000 |
| Maintenance | 15,000 |
| Annual expenditure | 150,000 |

The tax saving on this annual cash flow is 30% × £150,000 = £45,000, one year in arrears.

| Discount factor at 10%, years 1 - 5 | 3.791 |
|---|---|
| Discount factor at 10%, year 1 | 0.909 |
| Discount factor at 10%, years 2 - 5 | 2.882 |

| Years | | Cash flow | Discount factor at 10% | Present value |
|---|---|---|---|---|
| | | £ | | £ |
| 1 – 4 | Annual expenditure | (150,000) | 3.170 | (475,500) |
| 2 - 5 | Annual reduction in tax | 45,000 | 2.882 | 129,690 |
| | **Net PV of cost** | | | **(345,810)** |

**Operating lease**

The present value of cost is calculated on the assumption that the agreement will last for four years, with annual renewals.

The tax saving on the annual rental cost is 30% × £140,000 = £42,000, one year in arrears.

| Years | | Cash flow | Discount factor at 10% | Present value |
|---|---|---|---|---|
| | | £ | | £ |
| 0 - 3 | Annual expenditure | (140,000) | 3.487 | (475,500) |
| 1 - 4 | Annual reduction in tax | 42,000 | 3.170 | 129,690 |
| | **Net PV of cost** | | | **(345,810)** |

On the basis of net present value, purchasing outright appears to be the least cost method.

(b) Each £1 of outlay before 31 December 20X3 would mean a loss in NPV on the alternative project of £0.20. There is thus an opportunity cost of using funds in 20X2.

**Purchasing**

| | £ |
|---|---|
| Net present value of cost | (302,959) |
| Opportunity cost (0.2 × 360,000) | (72,000) |
| Net PV of cost | **(374,959)** |

**Finance lease**

Net present cost =             £(345,818)

There is no cash flow before 31 December 20X3 in this case, and thus no opportunity cost.

**Operating lease**

| | £ |
|---|---|
| Net present value of cost | (355,040) |
| Opportunity cost (0.2 × 140,000) | (28,000) |
| Net PV of cost | **(383,040)** |

Thus the finance lease is now the lowest cost option.

All the above assume that the alternative project cannot be delayed.

(c)

# REPORT

**To:** The Directors of Leaminger plc

**From:** A business advisor

**Date:** xx/xx/xx

**Subject:** Acquiring the turbine machine

**Introduction**

In financial terms, and without capital rationing, outright purchase is the preferred method of financing as it has the lowest NPV of cost. With capital rationing, a finance lease arrangement becomes the least-cost method. There are, however, a number of other factors to be considered before a final decision is taken.

(1) If capital rationing persists into further periods, the value of cash used in leasing becomes more significant and so purchasing would become relatively more attractive.

(2) Even without capital rationing, leasing has a short-term cash flow advantage over purchasing, which may be significant for liquidity.

(3) The use of a 10% cost of capital may be inappropriate as these are financing issues and are unlikely to be subject to the average business risk. Also they may alter the capital structure and thus the financial risk of the business and thus the cost of capital itself. This may alter the optimal decision in the face of capital rationing.

(4) The actual cash inflows generated by the turbine are constant for all options, except that under an operating lease the lessor may refuse to lease the turbine at the end of any annual contract thus making it unavailable from this particular source. On top of capital rationing, we need to consider the continuing availability of finance under the operating lease.

(5) Conversely, however, with the operating lease Leaminger plc can cancel if business conditions change (e.g. a technologically improved asset may become available). This is not the case with the other financing options. On the other hand, if the market is buoyant then the lessor may raise lease rentals, whereas the cost is fixed under the other options and hence capital rationing might be more severe.

(6) On the issue of maintenance costs of £15,000 per annum, this is included in the operating lease if the machine becomes unreliable, but there is greater risk beyond any warranty period under the other two options.

(7) It is worth investigating if some interim measure can be put in place which would assist in lengthening the turbine's life such as sub-contracting work outside or overhauling the machine.

| ACCA marking scheme | | Marks |
|---|---|---|
| (a) **Purchase** | | |
| | Capital allowances | 3 |
| | Maintenance | 1 |
| | Taxation | 1 |
| | NPV | 1 |
| | **Finance lease** | |
| | PV outflows | 1 |
| | PV tax relief | 1 |
| | NPV | 1 |

|     | **Operating lease**                          |      |
| --- | -------------------------------------------- | ---- |
|     | PV outflows                                  | 1    |
|     | PV tax relief                                | 1    |
|     | NPV                                          | 1    |
|     | Recommendation                              | 1    |
| (b) | Opportunity cost                             | 1    |
|     | Revised NPV for each option (1 mark each)    | 3    |
|     | Evaluation                                   | 1    |
| (c) | 2 marks for each explained point             | 8    |
| Total |                                            | 25   |

## 25   PRIME PRINTING PLC

### Key answer tips

In part (a) take care not to be too general - you are being asked to explain the cash flow characteristics of the three options, so go through each saying what cash flows will arise, and when. The tax aspect of each can be included as you go through, or it can be discussed at the end.

Part (b) is a fairly standard lease or buy problem, also incorporating the investment decision. The most important principle here is the separation of the two decisions. The investment decision uses operating cash flows (cash savings) and capital cash flows (purchase cost/scrap proceeds of machine), with related tax effects (additional tax arising from savings and tax savings from capital allowances). These are discounted at the company's cost of capital. The finance decision concentrates on the cash flows you have discussed in (a), which are discounted at the post-tax cost of borrowing. Note that you can either include the tax savings from capital allowances as a direct benefit of the buy option, or as an opportunity cost of the lease option (but not both!). Don't forget to summarise your results and recommendations in words at the end. There are a number of different ways of calculating the comparative cost of the lease versus purchase, but all methods yield the same result. You will not be disadvantaged by the use of a specific method of approach.

(a)   A **finance lease** is usually arranged with a finance house, with the intention of providing the business (lessee) with the funding to acquire an asset. The time scale of a finance lease is set such that at the end of the initial leasing period, the lessor has more than recovered the cost of the asset. The lessee is then given the choice of either continuing to lease the asset at a small ('nominal') rental, or selling the item on behalf of the lessor and retaining the bulk of the proceeds.

The cash flow pattern of a finance lease is such that cash flow is evenly spaced throughout the leasing period, and the company acquiring an asset is not therefore required to pay out a large sum of cash in one go in order to obtain the use of that asset. The interest rate charged for the finance is usually fixed for the duration of the lease, and the predictability of the outgoing cash flow in such circumstances can be very useful in helping smaller companies to plan their finances. One possible area of uncertainty about expenditure is that under such an agreement, the lessee is responsible for maintenance costs of the equipment/machinery. These costs might not be easily predictable, and be related to level of usage.

A cash flow advantage may arise because of the tax treatment of finance leases. Some businesses may be earning insufficient profits to allow them to take advantage of all the capital allowances that may be available to them if they choose to purchase machinery and equipment outright. Where a finance lease is used, no capital allowances can be claimed by the lessee, but instead the lessee can claim tax relief against the full leasing cost. The lower annual cost could mean that the company is able to maximise its use of tax relief, and so reduce the effective cost of the leased equipment.

An alternative source of medium-term finance is a **bank loan**. In terms of cash flow, the loan agreement will define the level of regular repayments, which will be a mix of capital repayment plus an interest component. The loan may be subject to either a fixed or a variable rate of interest. In the latter case, the repayments may change over the life of the loan, if interest rates alter. Under such circumstances the cash flow pattern is clearly less certain than under a finance lease based on a fixed finance charge.

The company can claim capital allowances on the purchase, and so obtain tax relief to reduce its corporation tax liability. As indicated above, such tax relief is only of value if the company has profits against which the relief can be offset. This means that the tax paying position of a company plays a critical role in determining the comparative advantage of leasing versus borrowing to pay for a business asset.

A third source of finance to pay for acquisition of a business asset is the **use of existing cash holdings/funds on deposit**. Where funds are withdrawn from deposit, there will be a cash-flow impact in terms of the loss of regular interest receivable. Furthermore, the conversion of the current asset of cash into a fixed asset (piece of equipment) alters the structure of the company's balance sheet. The outflow of a single large cash payment will reduce the liquidity of the business (at least temporarily). If cash flows from operations are adequate to meet regular cash outgoings, this will not matter. If, however, there is a potential cash shortfall, this is not a sensible source of funding for asset purchases. As with loan finance, the purchase of the asset for cash means that capital allowances can be claimed, and the same considerations on the usefulness of those allowances need to be taken into account.

(b)   *Tutorial note:* The first decision to consider is the acquisition decision, i.e. is it worthwhile acquiring the machine, assuming that it is purchased? For this assessment we use the company's cost of capital. If the acquisition appears to be financially justified, the second decision is the financing decision, i.e. should the machine be purchased with money from a loan or should it be leased? For this assessment, we use the after-tax cost of borrowing as the cost of capital.

*Workings*

(W1)

|  | Written down value of asset | Writing down allowance (WDA) (25%) | Tax saving due to WDA (30%) |
|---|---|---|---|
|  | £ | £ | £ |
| Year 1 | 120,000 | 30,000 | 9,000 |
| Year 2 | 90,000 | 22,500 | 6,750 |
| Year 3 | 67,500 | 16,875 | 5,063 |
| Year 4 | 50,625 | 12,656 | 3,797 |
| Year 5 | 37,969 |  |  |
| Year 5 | Balancing allowance (see above) | 37,969 | 11,391 |

(W2) **Taxable profits and tax liability**

| Year | Cash savings £000 | Capital allowance £ | Taxable profits £ | Tax at 30% £000 |
|---|---|---|---|---|
| 1 | 50 | 30,000 | 20,000 | 6.00 |
| 2 | 50 | 22,500 | 27,500 | 8.25 |
| 3 | 50 | 16,875 | 33,125 | 9.94 |
| 4 | 50 | 12,656 | 37,344 | 11.20 |
| 5 | 50 | 37,969 | 12,031 | 3.61 |

## Acquisition decision

| Year | Equipment | Cash savings | Tax | Net cash flow | Discount factor at 15% | Present value |
|---|---|---|---|---|---|---|
| | £000 | £000 | £000 | £000 | | £000 |
| 0 | (120.0) | | | (120.00) | 1.000 | (120.00) |
| 1 | | 50 | | 50.00 | 0.870 | 43.50 |
| 2 | | 50 | (6.00) | 44.00 | 0.756 | 33.26 |
| 3 | | 50 | (8.25) | 41.75 | 0.658 | 27.47 |
| 4 | | 50 | (9.94) | 40.06 | 0.572 | 22.91 |
| 5 | | 50 | (11.20) | 38.80 | 0.497 | 19.28 |
| 6 | | | (3.61) | (3.61) | 0.432 | (1.56) |
| | | | | | **NPV** | 24.86 |

The **NPV is positive** and so the company should acquire the machine.

**Present value of purchase**

Discounting cash flows at the after tax cost of borrowing, i.e. at:

$13\% \times 0.7 = 9.1\%$, say 9%.

*Note*: This is approximate, as tax relief is lagged by one year.

| Year | Item | Cash flow | Discount factor at 9% | Present value |
|---|---|---|---|---|
| | | £ | | £ |
| 0 | Purchase cost | (120,000) | 1.000 | (120,000) |
| 2 | Tax savings from allowances | 9,000 | 0.842 | 17,578 |
| 3 | Tax savings from allowances | 6,750 | 0.772 | 15,211 |
| 4 | Tax savings from allowances | 5,063 | 0.708 | 13,585 |
| 5 | Tax savings from allowances | 3,797 | 0.650 | 12,468 |
| 6 | Tax savings from allowances | 11,391 | 0.596 | 16,789 |
| | **NPV of cost** | | | (94,369) |

## Present value of leasing

The lease payments would be made annually in advance.

| Year | Lease payment | Tax savings | Discount factor at 9% | Present value |
|---|---|---|---|---|
| | | £ | | £ |
| 0 – 4 | (28,000) p.a. | | 4.239 | (118,692) |
| 1 – 5 | | 8,400 p.a. | 3.890 | 32,676 |
| | **NPV of cost** | | | (86,016) |

This means that it is **cheaper to lease the machine** than to purchase it via the bank loan.

## 26    CAPITAL RATIONING

### Key answer points

You need to start your answer in part (a) by calculating the NPV of each project. Having calculated the NPVs, you can (1) work out an NPV per unit of limiting factor (per £1 invested) to answer the question assuming that projects are divisible, and (2) compare the feasible combinations of projects if they are not divisible, within the constraints imposed by limited capital to invest.

Unless you are aware of 'hard' and 'soft' capital rationing, you might struggle to provide a complete answer to part (c).

It is worth noting that although parts (b) and (d) should be straightforward, you need to make your points clearly and briefly.

(a)    (i)

**Analysis of projects assuming they are divisible**

|  | Discount factor at 12% | Project 1 Cash flow | PV | Project 3 Cash flow | PV |
|---|---|---|---|---|---|
|  |  | £ | £ | £ | £ |
| Initial investment | 1.000 | (300,000) | (300,000) | (400,000) | (400,000) |
| Year 1 | 0.893 | 85,000 | 75,905 | 124,320 | 111,018 |
| Year 2 | 0.797 | 90,000 | 71,730 | 128,795 | 102,650 |
| Year 3 | 0.712 | 95,000 | 67,640 | 133,432 | 95,004 |
| Year 4 | 0.636 | 100,000 | 63,600 | 138,236 | 87,918 |
| Year 5 | 0.567 | 95,000 | 53,865 | 143,212 | 81,201 |
| PV of savings |  |  | 332,740 |  | 477,791 |
| NPV |  |  | 32,740 |  | 77,791 |
| Profitability index |  |  | 332,740/300,000 = 1.11 |  | 477,791/400,000 = 1.19 |

|  | Discount factor at 12% | Project 2 Cash flow | PV |
|---|---|---|---|
|  |  | £ | £ |
| Initial investment | 1.000 | (450,000) | (450,000) |
| Annual cash flows, years 1 - 5 | 3.605 | 140,800 | 507,584 |
| Net present value |  |  | 57,584 |
| Profitability index | 507,584/450,000 |  | = 1.13 |

Order of preference (in order of profitability index) = Project 3 then Project 2 then Project 1.

| Project | Profitability index | Ranking | Investment | NPV |
|---|---|---|---|---|
|  |  |  | £ | £ |
| 3 | 1.19 | 1st | 400,000 | 77,791 |
| 2 | 1.13 | 2nd | 400,000 | 51,186  (= 57,584 × 400/450) |
|  |  |  | 800,000 | 128,977 |

(ii) **Analysis of projects assuming they are indivisible**

If the projects are assumed to be indivisible, the total NPV of combinations of projects must be considered.

| Projects | Investment £ | NPV £ | |
|---|---|---|---|
| 1 and 2 | 750,000 | 90,324 | £(32,740 + 57,584) |
| 1 and 3 | 700,000 | 110,531 | £(32,740 + 77,791) |
| 2 and 3 | 850,000 | not feasible, too much investment | |

The optimum combination is now projects 1 and 3.

(b) The NPV decision rule requires that a company invest in all projects that have a positive net present value. This assumes that sufficient funds are available for all incremental projects, which is only true in a perfect capital market. When insufficient funds are available, that is when capital is rationed, projects cannot be selected by ranking by absolute NPV. Choosing a project with a large NPV may mean not choosing smaller projects that, in combination, give a higher NPV. Instead, if projects are divisible, they can be ranked using the profitability index in order make the optimum selection. If projects are not divisible, different combinations of available projects must be evaluated to select the combination with the highest NPV.

(c) The NPV decision rule, to accept all projects with a positive net present value, requires the existence of a perfect capital market where access to funds for capital investment is not restricted. In practice, companies are likely to find that funds available for capital investment are restricted or rationed.

**Hard capital rationing** is the term applied when the restrictions on raising funds are due to causes external to the company. For example, potential providers of debt finance may refuse to provide further funding because they regard a company as too risky. This may be in terms of financial risk, for example if the company's gearing is too high or its interest cover is too low, or in terms of business risk if they see the company's business prospects as poor or its operating cash flows as too variable. In practice, large established companies seeking long-term finance for capital investment are usually able to find it, but small and medium-sized enterprises will find raising such funds more difficult.

**Soft capital rationing** refers to restrictions on the availability of funds that arise within a company and are imposed by managers. There are several reasons why managers might restrict available funds for capital investment. Managers may prefer slower organic growth to a sudden increase in size arising from accepting several large investment projects. This reason might apply in a family-owned business that wishes to avoid hiring new managers. Managers may wish to avoid raising further equity finance if this will dilute the control of existing shareholders. Managers may wish to avoid issuing new debt if their expectations of future economic conditions are such as to suggest that an increased commitment to fixed interest payments would be unwise.

One of the main reasons suggested for soft capital rationing is that managers wish to create an internal market for investment funds. It is suggested that requiring investment projects to compete for funds means that weaker or marginal projects, with only a small chance of success, are avoided. This allows a company to focus on more robust investment projects where the chance of success is higher (*Tutorial note*: Watson, D. and Head, A. (2001) *Corporate Finance: Principles and Practice*, 2nd edition, FT Prentice Hall, p.73.) This cause of soft capital rationing can be seen as a way of reducing the risk and uncertainty associated with investment projects, as it leads to accepting projects with greater margins of safety.

(d) When undertaking the appraisal of an investment project, it is essential that **only relevant cash flows** are included in the analysis. If non-relevant cash flows are included, the result of the appraisal will be misleading and incorrect decisions will be made. A relevant cash flow is a differential (incremental) cash flow, one that changes as a direct result of an investment decision.

If current fixed production overheads are expected to increase, for example, the additional fixed production overheads are a relevant cost and should be included in the investment appraisal. Existing fixed production overheads should not be included.

A new cash flow arising as the result of an investment decision is a relevant cash flow. For example, the purchase of raw materials for a new production process and the net cash flows arising from the production process are both relevant cash flows.

The incremental tax effects arising from an investment decision are also relevant cash flows, providing that a company is in a tax-paying position. Direct labour costs, for example, are an allowable deduction in calculating taxable profit and so give rise to tax benefits: tax liabilities arising on incremental taxable profits are also a relevant cash flow.

One area where caution is required is interest payments on new debt used to finance an investment project. They are a differential cash flow and hence relevant, but the effect of the cost of the debt is incorporated into the discount rate used to determine the net present value. Interest payments should not therefore be included as a cash flow in an investment appraisal.

Market research undertaken to determine whether a new product will sell is often undertaken prior to the investment decision on whether to proceed with production of the new product. This is an example of a **sunk cost**. These are costs already incurred as a result of past decisions, and so are not relevant cash flows.

| ACCA marking scheme | | | Marks |
|---|---|---|---|
| (a) | (i) | NPV of project 1 | 1 |
| | | NPV of project 2 | 1 |
| | | NPV of project 3 | 2 |
| | | Calculation of profitability indices | 2 |
| | | Optimum investment schedule | 2 |
| | (ii) | Selection of optimum combination | 2 |
| | | | 10 |
| (b) | | NPV decision rule | 1 |
| | | Link to perfect capital markets | 1 |
| | | Explanation of ranking problem and solution | 1 |
| | | | 3 |
| (c) | | Hard capital rationing | 3 |
| | | Soft capital rationing | 4 |
| | | | 7 |
| (d) | | Explanation of relevant cash flows | 2 |
| | | Examples of relevant cash flows | 3 |
| | | | 5 |
| Total | | | 25 |

## 27    UMUNAT PLC

(a)    The investment appraisal process is concerned with assessing the value of future cash flows compared to the cost of investment.

Since future cash flows cannot be predicted with certainty, managers must consider how much confidence can be placed in the results of the investment appraisal process. They must therefore be concerned with the risk and uncertainty of a project. Uncertainty refers to the situation where probabilities cannot be assigned to future cash flows. Uncertainty cannot therefore be quantified and increases with project life: it is usually true to say that the more distant is a cash flow, the more uncertain is its value. Risk refers to the situation where probabilities can be assigned to future cash flows, for example as a result of managerial experience and judgement or scenario analysis. Where such probabilities can be assigned, it is possible to quantify the risk associated with project variables and hence of the project as a whole.

If risk and uncertainty were not considered in the investment appraisal process, managers might make the mistake of placing too much confidence in the results of investment appraisal, or they may fail to monitor investment projects in order to ensure that expected results are in fact being achieved. Assessment of project risk can also indicate projects that might be rejected as being too risky compared with existing business operations, or projects that might be worthy of reconsideration if ways of reducing project risk could be found in order to make project outcomes more acceptable.

(b)    Contribution per unit = 3.00 – 1.65 = £1.35 per unit

Total annual contribution = 20,000 × 1.35 = £27,000 per year

Annual cash flow after fixed costs = 27,000 – 10,000 = £17,000 per year

Payback period = 50,000/17,000 = 2.9 years

(assuming that cash flows occur evenly throughout the year)

The payback period calculated is greater than the maximum payback period used by Umunat plc of two years and on this basis should be rejected. Use of payback period as an investment appraisal method cannot be recommended, however, because payback period does not consider all the cash flows arising from an investment project, as it ignores cash flows outside of the payback period. Furthermore, payback period ignores the time value of money.

The fact that the payback period is 2.9 years should not therefore be a reason for rejecting the project. The project should be assessed using a discounted cash flow method such as net present value or internal rate of return, since the project as a whole may generate an acceptable return on investment.

(c)    Calculation of project net present value

Annual cash flow = ((20,000 × (3 – 1.65)) – 10,000 = £17,000 per year

Net present value = (17,000 × 3.605) – 50,000 = 61,285 – 50,000 = £11,285

| | PV (£) |
|---|---|
| Alternatively: | |
| Sales revenue: 20,000 × 3.00 × 3.605 = | 216,300 |
| Variable costs: 20,000 × 1.65 × 3.605 = | (118,965) |
| Contribution | 97,335 |
| Initial investment | (50,000) |
| Fixed costs: 10,000 × 3.605 = | (36,050) |
| Net present value: | 11,285 |

Sensitivity of NPV to sales volume

Sales volume giving zero NPV = ((50,000/3.605) + 10,000)/1.35 = 17,681 units

This is a decrease of 2,319 units or 11.6%

Alternatively, sales volume decrease = 100 × 11,285/97,335= 11.6%

Sensitivity of NPV to sales price

Sales price for zero NPV = (((50,000/3.605) + 10,000)/20,000) + 1.65 = £2.843

This is a decrease of 15.7p or 5.2%

Alternatively, sales price decrease = 100 × 11,285/216,300 = 5.2%

Sensitivity of NPV to variable cost

Variable cost must increase by 15.7p or 9.5% to make the NPV zero.

Alternatively, variable cost increase = 100 × 11,285/118,965 = 9.5%

Sensitivity analysis evaluates the effect on project net present value of changes in project variables. The objective is to determine the key or critical project variables, which are those where the smallest change produces the biggest change in project NPV. It is limited in that only one project variable at a time may be changed, whereas in reality several project variables may change simultaneously. For example, an increase in inflation could result in increases in sales price, variable costs and fixed costs. Sensitivity analysis is not a way of evaluating project risk, since although it may identify the key or critical variables, it cannot assess the likelihood of a change in these variables. In other words, sensitivity analysis does not assign probabilities to project variables. Where sensitivity analysis is useful is in drawing the attention of management to project variables that need careful monitoring if a particular investment project is to meet expectations. Sensitivity analysis can also highlight the need to check the assumptions underlying the key or critical variables.

(d)    Expected value of sales volume:

(17,500 × 0.3) + (20,000 × 0.6) + (22,500 × 0.1) = 19,500 units

Expected NPV = (((19,500 × 1.35) – 10,000) × 3.605) – 50,000 = £8,852

Since the expected net present value is positive, the project appears to be acceptable. From earlier analysis we know that the NPV is positive at 20,000 per year, and the NPV will therefore also be positive at 22,500 units per year. The NPV of the worst case is:

(((17,500 × 1.35) – 10,000) × 3.605) – 50,000 = (£882)

The NPV of the best case is:

(((22,500 × 1.35) – 10,000) × 3.605) – 50,000 = £23,452

There is thus a 30% chance that the project will produce a negative NPV, a fact not revealed by considering the expected net present value alone.

The expected net present value is not a value that is likely to occur in practice: it is perhaps more useful to know that there is a 30% chance that the project will produce a negative NPV (or a 70% chance of a positive NPV), since this may represent an unacceptable level of risk as far as the managers of Umunat plc are concerned. It can therefore be argued that assigning probabilities to expected economic states or sales volumes has produced useful information that can help the managers of Umunat to make better investment decisions. The difficulty with this approach is that probability estimates of project variables or future economic states are likely to carry a high degree of uncertainty and subjectivity.

| ACCA marking scheme | | |
|---|---|---:|
| | | *Marks* |
| (a) | Discussion of risk | 2 |
| | Discussion of uncertainty | 1 |
| | Value of considering risk and uncertainty | 2 |
| | | 5 |
| (b) | Calculation of payback period | 2 |
| | Discussion of payback period | 2 |
| | | 4 |
| (c) | Calculation net present value | 2 |
| | Sensitivity of NPV to sales volume | 2 |
| | Sensitivity of NPV to sales price | 2 |
| | Sensitivity of NPV to variable cost | 1 |
| | Discussion of sensitivity analysis | 3 |
| | | 10 |
| (d) | Calculation of expected value of sales | 1 |
| | Calculation of expected net present value | 1 |
| | Discussion of expected net present value | 4 |
| | | 3 |
| Total | | 25 |

# COSTING SYSTEMS AND TECHNIQUES

## 28 BUD PLC

(a) **Preliminary workings:**

*Budgeted sales (units and value)*

| Product | Units | Price | Value (£) |
|---|---|---|---|
| F1 | 34,000 | £50.00 | 1,700,000 |
| F2 | 58,000 | £30.00 | 1,740,000 |
| | | | 3,440,000 |

*Budgeted production (units)*

| Product | Sales units | Stock increment units | Production units |
|---|---|---|---|
| F1 | 34,000 | 1,000 | 35,000 |
| F2 | 58,000 | 2,000 | 60,000 |

(i) **Component purchase and usage budget (units and value)**

| Product | | Component C3 units | | Component C4 units | Total |
|---|---|---|---|---|---|
| F1 | (35,000 × 8) | 280,000 | (35,000 × 4) | 140,000 | |
| F2 | (60,000 × 4) | 240,000 | (60,000 × 3) | 180,000 | |
| | | 520,000 | | 320,000 | |
| | | £ | | £ | |
| Value | (× £1.25) | 650,000 | (× £1.80) | 576,000 | £1,226,000 |

(ii)   **Direct labour budget (hours and value)**

| Product | | Assembly hours | | Finishing hours | Total |
|---|---|---|---|---|---|
| F1 | (35,000 × 30 mins) | 17,500 | (35,000 × 12 mins) | 7,000 | |
| F2 | (60,000 × 15 mins) | 15,000 | (60,000 × 10 mins) | 10,000 | |
| | | 32,500 | | 17,000 | |
| | | £ | | £ | |
| Value | (× £5) | 162,500 | (× £6) | 102,000 | £264,500 |

(iii)   **Departmental manufacturing overhead recovery rates**

| | Assembly | Finishing |
|---|---|---|
| Total overhead cost per month | £617,500 | £204,000 |
| Total direct labour hours | 32,500 | 17,000 |
| Overhead recovery rate (per direct labour hour) | £19.00 | £12.00 |

(iv)   **Selling overhead recovery rate**

| | |
|---|---|
| Total overhead cost per month | £344,000 |
| Total sales value (Month 9) | £3,440,000 |
| Selling overhead recovery rate | 10% |

| *Unit manufacturing costs* | | | F1 | | F2 |
|---|---|---|---|---|---|
| | | | £ | | £ |
| Materials | C3 | 8 × £1.25 | 10.00 | 4 × £1.25 | 5.00 |
| | C4 | 4 × £1.80 | 7.20 | 3 × £1.80 | 5.40 |
| Labour | Assembly | 30/60 × £5 | 2.50 | 15/60 × £5 | 1.25 |
| | Finishing | 12/60 × £6 | 1.20 | 10/60 × £6 | 1.00 |
| M'fg. overhead | Assembly | 30/60 × £19 | 9.50 | 15/60 × £19 | 4.75 |
| | Finishing | 12/60 × £12 | 2.40 | 10/60 × £12 | 2.00 |
| Manufacturing cost | | | 32.80 | | 19.40 |

(v)   **Closing stock budget**

| Product | Units | Cost £ | Value £ |
|---|---|---|---|
| F1 | 1,000 | 32.80 | 32,800 |
| F2 | 2,000 | 19.40 | 38,800 |
| | | | 7,1600 |

(b)   **Standard unit cost (Month 9)**

| | | F1 £/unit | F2 £/unit |
|---|---|---|---|
| Material | C3 | 10.00 | 5.00 |
| | C4 | 7.20 | 5.40 |
| Labour | Assembly | 2.50 | 1.25 |
| | Finishing | 1.20 | 1.00 |
| M'fg. overhead | Assembly | 9.50 | 4.75 |
| | Finishing | 2.40 | 2.00 |

|  | F1 £/unit | F2 £/unit |
|---|---|---|
| Manufacturing cost | 32.80 | 19.40 |
| Selling overhead (10% of price) | 5.00 | 3.00 |
| Total cost | 37.80 | 22.40 |
| Selling price | 50.00 | 30.00 |
| Profit | 12.20 | 7.60 |

(c) **Budgeted profit and loss account (Month 9)**

| *Cost element* | £ |
|---|---|
| Direct materials (see note) | 1,226,000 |
| Direct labour (see note) | 264,500 |
| Manufacturing overhead (617,500 + 204,000) | 821,500 |
|  | 2,312,000 |
| Less closing stock | 71,600 |
| Manufacturing cost of sales | 2,240,400 |
| Selling overhead | 344,000 |
| Total cost of sales | 2,584,400 |
| Sales | 3,440,000 |
| Net profit | 855,600 |

*Note: Direct materials cost*

$(35,000 \times £17.20) + (60,000 \times £10.40) = £1,226,000.$

*Direct labour cost*

$(35,000 \times £3.70) + (60,000 \times £2.25) = £264,500$

(d)   Under a system of absorption costing, an overhead rate is used to apply overheads to each unit produced. At present, the company applies manufacturing overhead to products based on the budgeted labour hours and the budgeted expenditure in each month. Such figures are used to establish a **separate predetermined rate for each month**. As a result, **unit overhead costs fluctuate** from one month to the next if production levels fluctuate, because any fixed element of overheads is spread over the fluctuating volumes.

It can be disconcerting and misleading for production and sales staff to be dealing with product costs which fluctuate on a monthly basis. This is especially so when the fluctuation has not been caused by changes in production efficiency and it bears no relation to changes in the general market price.

One way to overcome this is to compute an overhead rate based on a longer time period, for example quarterly or a predetermined annual rate as mentioned in the question. This enables large fluctuations in, and extreme values of, product costs to be avoided. This would mean that management would be able to monitor the business volume and overhead costs on which the calculations were based, to ensure that over the longer term the average product costs which were predicted are in fact achieved.

## 29 ABC

(a) Activity Based Costing (ABC) has been implemented across a range of organisations to enhance management information systems. The introduction of ABC changed the focus of cost accumulation from processes to activities. In this way, decision-relevant costs could be identified since management could, in principle, alter the activities undertaken. Traditional methods of product costing were often volume related (e.g. hours of labour used) but this did not develop with the growth in activities that had no relation to volume, or in multi-product businesses where there are complex production processes.

There are general conditions under which ABC are most likely to operate and these relate to the following factors:

(i) Where there is a requirement to apportion costs (e.g. in a multi-product business).

(ii) Where there are significant overheads to apportion.

(iii) Where the availability of sophisticated information retrieval systems allows management to track product costs as they pass through a production system.

### Multi-product businesses

The main issue is that there have to be at least two products in the business otherwise there are no costs to apportion between products. For a single product company, all the costs of the business are identifiable with the product.

However, ABC might still be useful in single product businesses when management decisions are required to determine the level of production. In such cases, optimum levels of output can be defined once costs can be split between fixed and variable elements. ABC will help identify variable costs as those that vary with the level of activities that incur costs. In principle, fixed costs are then those costs that do not vary with activity, and hence it becomes possible to undertake profitability analysis in relation to activity levels.

Other advantages of ABC in multiproduct business relate to the accurate valuation of stock and facilitating the effective management of stock levels with multiple products. There is also reduced cross-subsidisation of products: with costs accurately identified with products, it becomes easier for management to distinguish which products are profitable from those that are not.

### The significance of overheads and the ABC method of charging costs

Since ABC is a cost apportionment system then it is principally beneficial when there is a high proportion of overhead costs to apportion to products. If a business incurs only direct costs, there is no issue for ABC to resolve.

ABC is based on the premise that activities lead to costs being incurred and that costs should therefore be apportioned on the basis of the activities that different products consume. In this way, management can better understand the behaviour of overheads as they relate to decisions.

ABC apportions costs by first identifying the activities that generate costs. Cost drivers are then chosen that reflect the events that create costs when the activities are undertaken. The costs associated with each activity are then collected into cost pools where there are common cost drivers. Finally, costs are allocated to products on the basis of the activities they use. In sum, if product overheads can be seen in terms of activities, and activities have costs associated with them, then the use of activities by a product can be costed.

**Retrieval systems**

A basic requirement for any cost allocation system is information availability. This is particularly so for ABC systems which rely heavily on activity information. Moreover, production systems are far more complex than in the days when traditional absorption costing was most effective. For example, manufacturing processes rely far more on quality control monitoring, inspection and set-up processes than they ever did and are not necessarily related to the volume of activity. With many products, and variants on products, the monitoring of costs itself becomes a large and complex process. With complexity inevitably follows greater support services, of which a major category would be computer support services.

In addition, ABC requires the monitoring of activities that have not involved monitoring previously. This raises issues of information capture and it is in new technology that answers to this are most likely to be found.

(b)   One of the key problems in assessing manager performance is in ensuring that costs on which managers' performance is judged are **controllable** and **hence traceable to manager decisions.** Manager performance will be unfairly assessed if non-controllable costs are incorrectly taken into account, and the manager is made accountable for them. ABC is often claimed to rest on a more accurate information base than absorption costing, and hence the impact of management decisions is potentially more easily seen under ABC than it is under traditional volume-related absorption methods. Thus, it becomes possible to more closely align management decisions with their consequences and improve performance appraisal.

For example, in allocating and apportioning overheads, the re-apportionment of service department costs is reduced or eliminated under ABC. This is because ABC establishes separate cost pools for support activities and the costs of these activities are assigned to products directly on the basis of the appropriate driver. The accuracy of ABC in this context rests on the accurate identification of cost pools and cost drivers.

Also, ABC absorbs costs into products in a wider variety of ways than traditional absorption methods, which rely mostly on labour and/or machine hours. In extending the range of absorption bases, ABC is able to more closely track costs to the causes of the costs which then links to management decisions.

The foregoing does not rule out accurate costing using traditional absorption methods, especially when a business has most of its costs varying with production volume. However, when overheads do not vary with output, other means of determining absorption rates are preferable, such as those based on cost drivers. Thus, the scope for arbitrariness in manager performance appraisal is reduced.

| ACCA marking scheme | | |
|---|---|---|
| | | *Marks* |
| (a) Comments on general conditions for ABC | | 1 |
| 2 marks each for detailed comments on overheads and the methods ABC uses to allocate costs. Up to a maximum of: | | 7 |
| Comments on the impact of ABC for multi-product businesses | | 3 |
| Comments on information retrieval systems | | 4 |
| Quality and presentation of report | | 2 |
| | | 17 |
| (b) General comments on performance evaluation | | 2 |
| 2 marks each for detailed comments on ABC and absorption costing. Up to a maximum of: | | 6 |
| | | 8 |
| Total | | 25 |

## 30  ABKABER PLC

(a)  (i)  **Absorption costing using labour hour absorption rate**

| | | |
|---|---|---|
| Total overhead cost | = | £2,400,000 + £6,000,000 + £3,600,000 |
| | = | £12,000,000 |
| Total labour hours | = | 200,000 + 220,000 + 80,000 |
| | = | 500,000 |
| Overhead absorption rate/labour hour | = | £12,000,000/500,000 = £24 |

| | Sunshine | Roadster | Fireball |
|---|---|---|---|
| Units of production and sale | 2,000 | 1,600 | 400 |
| Direct labour hours | 200,000 | 220,000 | 80,000 |
| | £ | £ | £ |
| Direct labour (£5/hour) | 1,000,000 | 1,100,000 | 400,000 |
| Materials (at £400/600/900) | 800,000 | 960,000 | 360,000 |
| Overheads (£24/direct labour hour) | 4,800,000 | 5,280,000 | 1,920,000 |
| Total costs | 6,600,000 | 7,340,000 | 2,680,000 |
| | £ | £ | £ |
| Cost per unit | 3,300 | 4,587.5 | 6,700 |
| Selling price | 4,000 | 6,000.0 | 8,000 |
| Profit/(loss) per unit | 700 | 1,412.5 | 1,300 |
| Total profit/(loss) per product | £1,400,000 | £2,260,000 | £520,000 |

**Total profit = £4,180,000**

(ii)  **Activity Based Costing**

| | | | |
|---|---|---|---|
| Number of deliveries to retailers | 100 + 80 + 70 | = | 250 |
| Charge rate for deliveries | £2,400,000/250 | = | £9,600 |
| Number of set-ups | 35 + 40 + 25 | = | 100 |
| Charge rate for set-ups | £6,000,000/100 | = | £60,000 |
| Number of purchase orders | 400 + 300 + 100 | = | 800 |
| Charge rate for deliveries inwards | £3,600,000/800 | = | £4,500 |

| | Sunshine | Roadster | Fireball |
|---|---|---|---|
| Units of production and sale | 2,000 | 1,600 | 400 |
| | £ | £ | £ |
| Direct labour (as above) | 1,000,000 | 1,100,000 | 400,000 |
| Materials (as above) | 800,000 | 960,000 | 360,000 |
| Overheads: | | | |
| Deliveries at £9,600 (100:80:70) | 960,000 | 768,000 | 672,000 |
| Set-ups at £60,000 (35:40:25) | 2,100,000 | 2,400,000 | 1,500,000 |
| Purchase orders at £4,500 (400:300:100) | 1,800,000 | 1,350,000 | 450,000 |
| Total costs | 6,660,000 | 6,578,000 | 3,382,000 |
| | £ | £ | £ |
| Cost per unit | 3,330 | 4,111.25 | 8,455 |
| Selling price | 4,000 | 6,000.00 | 8,000 |
| Profit/(loss) per unit | 670 | 1,888.75 | (455) |
| Total profit/(loss) per product | £1,340,000 | £3,022,000 | £(182,000) |

**Total profit = £4,180,000**

(b)

## REPORT – ABKABER PLC

**To:** Directors of Abkaber plc

**From:** Management Accountant

**Date:** xx/xx/xx

**Subject:** **The Introduction of Activity Based Costing**

(i) **Direct costs**

The direct costs of labour and materials are unaffected by the use of ABC as they are directly attributable to units of output.

Notwithstanding the fact that labour is a relatively minor cost, however, the use of labour hours to allocate overheads magnifies its importance.

**The labour hours allocation basis**

As labour appears to be paid at a constant rate, an allocation using labour cost or labour hours gives the same result.

The central concern is, however, whether there is a cause and effect relationship between overheads and labour hours. Moreover for this allocation base to be correct overheads would need to be directly variable with labour hours. This seems unlikely on the basis of the information available.

**ABC and labour hours cost allocation**

ABC attempts to allocate overheads using a number of cost drivers rather than just one (such as direct labour hours). It therefore attempts to identify a series of cause-and-effect relationships. Moreover, those in favour of ABC argue that it is activities that generate costs, not direct labour hours – at least in the longer term if not the shorter term.

While costs are likely to be caused by multiple factors, the accuracy of any ABC system will depend on both the number of factors selected and the appropriateness of each of these activities as a driver for costs. Each cost driver should be appropriate to the pool of overheads to which it relates. As noted already, there should ideally be a direct cause-and-effect relationship between the cost driver and the relevant overhead cost pool (whereby costs increase proportionately with the number of activities operated).

The contrast between the labour hours costing system and ABC can be seen in requirement (a). These differences can be brought out by reviewing the comments of the directors.

(ii) **The Finance Director**

Using the labour hours method of allocation, the Fireball makes an overall profit of £520,000 but using ABC it makes a loss of £182,000. There is a significant difference in the levels of cost allocated, and so in profitability, between the two methods.

The major reason for the difference appears to be that while labour hours are not all that significant for Fireball production, the low volumes of Fireball sales cause a relatively high amount of set-ups, deliveries and purchase processes, and this is recognised by ABC.

If the Fireball model is to continue, a review of the assembly and distribution systems may be needed in order to reduce costs.

There may, however, be other non-financial reasons to maintain the Fireball, e.g. maintaining a wide product range and raising the reputation of the motorcycles, which may increase sales of other models.

### The Marketing Director

The marketing director suggests that ABC may have a number of problems and its conclusions should not be believed unquestioningly. These problems include:

(1)     For decisions such as the closure of Fireball production or the pricing of the new motorbike rental contract, what is really needed is the incremental cost to determine a break-even position. While ABC may be closer to this concept than a labour hours allocation basis, its accuracy depends upon identifying appropriate cost drivers.

(2)     The use of ABC for one-off decisions can be distinguished from its use in normal, ongoing costing procedures. It is perfectly possible that while labour hours may have been used for normal costing, an incremental costing analysis would be undertaken for important one-off decisions such as the closure of Fireball production or the pricing of the new motorbike rental contract. In these circumstances, the introduction of ABC in normal costing procedures may have restricted benefits.

(3)     There may be interdependencies between both costs and revenues that ABC is unlikely to capture. Where costs are truly common to more than one product then this may be difficult to capture by any given single activity.

(4)     As with labour hours allocations it is the future that matters. Any relationship between costs and activities based upon historic experience and observation may be unreliable as a guide to the future.

### The Managing Director

(1)     ABC normally assumes that the cost per activity is constant as the number of times the activity is repeated increases. In practice there may be a learning curve, such that costs per activity are non-linear. As a result, the marginal cost of increasing the number of activities is not the same as the average.

(2)     Also in this case, fixed costs are included which would also mean that the marginal cost does not equal the average cost.

(3)     The MD is correct in stating that some costs do not vary with either labour hours or any cost driver, and thus do not fall easily under ABC as a method of cost attribution as there is no cause and effect relationship. Depreciation on the factory building might be one example.

### The Chairman

From a narrow perspective of reporting profit, it is true that the two methods give the same overall profit of £4,180,000, as is illustrated in answer (a). There are, however, a number of qualifications to this statement:

(1)     If the company carried stock then the method of cost allocation would, in the short term at least, affect stock values and thus would influence profit.

(2)     If the ABC information can be relied on as a method of identifying overhead costs that vary with activity, a decision might be taken to cease Fireball production, as it generates a negative profit of £182,000. This 'loss' was not apparent using traditional absorption costing and a direct labour hour absorption rate. Although we do not know the extent to which overheads would be reduced by ceasing production of fireball, ABC suggests that there is a possibility that closure would improve profitability, by up to £182,000 each year.

**Further issues**

The following should also be considered in evaluating ABC:

- The need to develop new data capture systems, and the relevant costs of doing so

- Increased and on-going analysis work

- Continued evaluation of cause and effect relationships between cost drivers and cost pools.

| ACCA marking scheme | | |
|---|---|---|
| | | *Marks* |
| (a) | **Absorption costing using labour hours** | |
| | Overhead per labour hour | 1 |
| | Labour costs for each product | 1 |
| | Materials | 1 |
| | Total profit | 1 |
| | **ABC** | |
| | Costs per activity | 3 |
| | Labour | 1 |
| | Materials | 1 |
| | Overheads | 3 |
| | Total profit | 1 |
| (b) | Report format | 1 |
| | 2 marks for each detailed point | 12 |
| Total | | 25 |

## 31   ADMER

### Key answer tips

Part (a) of the question might seem straightforward, but you must beware of writing an over-simplified answer. Activity-based costing should be based on a close analysis of activities, the costs of activities and the drivers of those costs. The question does not provide this depth of analysis, and part (a) of the question expects you to recognise this. If your answer explains how useful ABC can be for management, you have missed much of the point of the question, because it is very doubtful whether ABC can be applied here usefully with the information available. The risk is that ABC becomes nothing more than an alternative approach to absorption costing, which would be of little information value to management.

Part (b) of the question asks for an ABC analysis, but leaves it to you to decide what the cost drivers might be. This is not necessarily clear, and your answer should state the assumptions that you make. Part (c) requires you to compare the original profit figures with ABC profit figures, and to discuss a possible decision to close the bathrooms department. It is essential to remember that for decision-making purposes, relevant costs and benefits should be considered - not absorption costing information. In part (c), you should also consider the many other factors that will influence a decision about whether to shut the department or not. There are a lot of points that can be made!

Part (d) of the question is challenging because it takes the basic issue of the usefulness of activity-based costing, and asks you to apply it to a specific case study – here, a chain of home furnishing stores. Your answer should refer specifically to the case study.

(a) Activity-based costing is based on identifying the activities that give rise to costs. This identification process does not seem to have been undertaken in this case. Simply collecting information on different activities is not enough. A detailed analysis of business operations is needed in order to identify relationships between costs and cost drivers. There should ideally be a one-to-one relationship between cost and cost driver. To the extent that this is not so, activity-based costing provides less useful information on product costs and for the purpose of cost control.

The management accountant believes that he can use the information provided to review the store's performance from an activity-based costing perspective. However, the relationship between 'other costs' for the three-month period and the proposed cost drivers (number of items sold, purchase orders, etc) is unclear.

If sales staff, warehouse staff, consultation staff and administration staff are on fixed salaries, their wage costs will not be linked to items sold, purchase orders or consultations. If wage costs are apportioned to product costs using the proposed cost drivers, it is likely that better product cost information will arise, simply because the apportionment bases being used are likely to be more appropriate to retailing than floor area. However at what point does a more sophisticated absorption costing system become an activity-based costing system?

The information provided can be used in an activity-based costing analysis if wage costs do depend to some extent on the proposed cost drivers, for example if sales staff wages include a commission for each purchase order raised. The management accountant needs to eliminate confusion by undertaking an investigation to establish and clarify the links between costs and activities if he wishes to use activity-based costing.

(b)     **Proposed cost drivers:**

Total number of items sold = 1,000 + 1,500 + 4,000 = 6,500

Total number of purchase orders = 1,000 + 900 + 2,500 = 4,400

Total floor area = 16,000 + 10,000 + 14,000 = 40,000

Total number of consultations = 798 + 200 + 250 = 1,248

*Sales staff wages*

Are sales staff wages linked to items sold or to purchase orders?

(1)     If sales staff wages are linked to items sold:

Sales staff wages recovery rate = £64,800/6,500 = £9.97/item sold

(2)     If sales staff wages are linked to purchase orders:

Sales staff wages recovery rate = £64,800/4,400 = £14.727/purchase order

*Consultation staff wages*

It seems reasonable to link consultation staff wages to the number of consultations:
Consultation staff wages recovery rate = £24,960/1,248 = £20.00/consultation

*Warehouse staff wages*

Warehouse staff wages could be linked to either purchase orders fulfilled or to items sold:

(1)     If each item needs to be handled, items sold might be preferred;

Warehouse staff wages recovery rate = £30,240/6,500 = £4.652/ item sold

(2)     If warehouse staff wages are linked to purchase orders fulfilled:

Warehouse staff wages recovery rate = £30,240/4,400 = £6.873/purchase order

*Administration staff wages*

Administration staff process purchase orders and organise consultations, but no indication is given as to whether these tasks are equally weighted. If they are, the total number of tasks = 4,400 + 1,248 = 5,648 and:

Administration staff wages recovery rate = £30,624/5,648 = £5.422/task

*General overheads*

General overheads appear to be related to floor space, but there will be other overheads that are not space costs; these will need to be apportioned on a different basis, or even not apportioned at all. Using the information provided:

General overheads absorption rate = £175,000/40,000 = £4.375/square metre

**Possible activity-based costing profit statement**:

| Department | Kitchens £ | Bathrooms £ | Dining Rooms £ | Total £ |
|---|---|---|---|---|
| Sales | 210,000 | 112,500 | 440,000 | 762,500 |
| Cost of goods sold | (63,000) | (37,500) | (176,000) | (276,500) |
| Variable contribution | 147,000 | 75,000 | 264,000 | 486,000 |
| Sales staff wages | (14,727) | (13,255) | (36,818) | (64,800) |
| Consultation staff wages | (15,960) | (4,000) | (5,000) | (24,960) |
| Warehouse staff wages | (4,652) | (6,978) | (18,610) | (30,240) |
| Admin staff wages | (9,749) | (5,964) | (14,911) | (30,624) |
| General overheads | (70,000) | (43,750) | (61,250) | (175,000) |
| Profit | 31,912 | 1,053 | 127,411 | 160,376 |

*Notes:*

1    Sales staff wages are apportioned using purchase orders.

2    Warehouse staff wages are apportioned using items sold.

Other choices are possible.

(c)    The absorption costing system currently used by the company indicates that the bathrooms department makes a loss.

From an activity-based costing perspective, however, the bathrooms department might make a small profit. The department makes a contribution towards other costs and overheads of £75,000 and a profit before general overheads of £44,803. Therefore financial grounds for closure do not appear to be compelling, although there may be a need to investigate the department with a view to improving profitability.

A more detailed profitability analysis of bathroom sales might lead to a greater understanding of which products were relatively profitable, which products were slow-moving and which products might be removed from sale without adversely affecting sales of other lines. Less drastic alternatives than closure might be suggested by such an analysis.

If the department were closed, it could be argued that general overheads would still need to be met and so overall profit would fall by about £45,000 in each three-month period. Overall profit could fall by more than this if some of the other costs allocated to the bathroom department remained after the closure. For example, the number of staff laid off would not correspond exactly to allocated wage costs.

However, it is unlikely the space vacated by the bathrooms department would remain unused. The remaining departments might be expanded to fill it, or it might be used for a new venture (selling carpets, for example). The key question is whether a better use exists for the space. If an alternative use is found, staff redundancies might be reduced or eliminated entirely.

A further problem is that closure of the bathrooms department could affect sales of the other departments. The store might be seen as no longer offering an adequate range of products and potential customers might prefer other stores with a greater range of home furnishings. The potential for satisfied customers to return with further business would also be reduced if the store offered a more limited range of products.

It is also unlikely that the closure decision would be made at the level of an individual store, since it carries consequences for the company as a whole. The image of the company might suffer if it were seen to be changing its product range, or if it were seen as being unable to compete with other stores selling bathrooms.

(d)   Activity-based costing could help Admer understand more clearly the factors that 'drive' its costs. The nature of Admer's business means that only a small number of cost drivers is likely to exist, but even given the limited information provided, the revised profit statement is likely to be more useful than treating all overhead costs as being related to floor area.

Activity-based costing can help Admer to control costs by highlighting the activities that generate them. For example, consultation staff wages are high compared to sales staff wages in the kitchen department in this store. Perhaps sales staff could be trained to provide in-store consultations and the number of home visits reduced; this could lower administration costs and reduce the cost of consultations.

It is clear that general overheads are the most significant cost other than cost of sales and existing information does not suggest ways of reducing these. However, a more detailed analysis of overheads might reveal activity-based costs that are currently aggregated. Once disaggregated, they become more amenable to understanding and control.

It is argued that activity-based costing leads to more accurate product costs, and in order to achieve this Admer needs a more detailed analysis of sales revenue and cost, based on the nature of the products sold. For example, the company might be able to classify kitchens as basic, intermediate and deluxe, and collect sales and cost data accordingly.

A key advantage claimed for activity-based costing is that it can provide better information to aid decision-making. In this case, it could provide more appropriate information to aid managers in reaching a decision on whether to close the bathrooms department. With better or more detailed information on product cost, managers are likely to make better decisions in key areas such as product pricing and cost control.

Even after introducing activity-based costing, however, Admer will still face the problem that some arbitrary apportionment of costs may still be required when pooling costs. The general overheads of light, heat and rates, for example, are likely to need to be treated in this way, along with the wages of administration staff. A related problem is that not all costs are generated by activities that can be measured in quantitative terms.

The management accountant of Admer should also be aware that the costs of introducing and maintaining an activity-based costing system may exceed the benefits that such a costing system may provide. Appropriate cost drivers will need to be determined and the required information may not be available. The existing management accounting information system may therefore need to be modified to generate the required information, and perhaps new accounting software purchased or developed.

| ACCA marking scheme | | Marks |
|---|---|---|
| (a) | Costs and cost drivers | 2 |
| | Limitations of information provided | 2 |
| | | 4 |

| | | |
|---|---|---|
| (b) | Analysis and discussion | 4 |
| | Activity-based profit statement | 5 |
| | | 8 |
| (c) | Evaluation and discussion of closure proposal | 6 |
| (d) | Up to 2 marks for each detailed advantage | 6 |
| | Up to 2 marks for each detailed disadvantage | 4 |
| Total | | 25 |

## 32 BML

(a) **Existing costing system:**

Calculation of overhead recovery rate:

Labour cost $= (£4 \times 7,500) + (£8 \times 12,500) + (£6.40 \times 4,000)$

$= £155,600$

Overhead rate $= \dfrac{\text{Overhead cost}}{\text{Labour cost}} \times 100\%$

$= \dfrac{£718,688}{£155,600} \times 100\%$

$= 462\%$ of labour cost.

| | P1 £ | P2 £ | P3 £ |
|---|---|---|---|
| Direct materials | 18.00 | 25.00 | 16.00 |
| Direct labour cost | 4.00 | 8.00 | 6.40 |
| Overhead cost (462% of labour) | 18.48 | 36.96 | 29.57 |
| Unit cost | 40.48 | 69.96 | 51.97 |

(b) **Activity-based costing**

ABC workings:

*Receiving and handling materials cost*

Total cost = £150,000

Cost driver = Number of materials movements

Number of materials movements = 4 + 25 + 50 = 79 movements

Cost per material movement = £150,000/79 = £1,898.73.

Cost per unit of P1 = (£1,898.73 × 4)/7,500 = £1.01 per product unit

Cost per unit of P2 = (£1,898.73 × 25)/12,500 = £3.80 per product unit

Cost per unit of P3 = (£1,898.73 × 50)/4,000 = £23.73 per product unit.

*Maintenance and depreciation cost*

Total cost = £390,000

Cost driver = Number of machine hours

Number of machine hours = (0.5 × 7,500) + (0.5 × 12,500) + (0.2 × 4.000) = 10,800

Cost per machine hour = £390,000/10,800 = £36.11 per machine hour

Cost per unit of P1 = £36.11 × 0.5 = £18.06 per product unit

Cost per unit of P2 = £36.11 × 0.5 = £18.06 per product unit

Cost per unit of P3 = £36.11 × 0.2 = £7.22 per product unit.

*Set-up labour cost*

Total cost = £18,688

Cost driver = Number of set-ups

Number of set-ups 1 + 5 + 10 = 16

Cost per set-up = 18,688/16= £1,168 per set-up

Cost per unit of P1 = (£1,168 × 1)/7,500 = £0.16 per product unit

Cost per unit of P2 = (£1,168 × 5)/12,500 = £0.47 per product unit

Cost per unit of P3 = £(1,168 × 10)/4,000 = £2.92 per product unit.

*Engineering cost*

Total cost = £100,000

Cost driver: Based on proportion of engineering work.

Cost per unit of P1 = (£100,000 × 30%)/7,500 = £4.00 per product unit

Cost per unit of P2 = (£100,000 × 20%)/12,500 = £1.60 per product unit

Cost per unit of P3 = (£100,000 × 50%)/4,000 = £12.50 per product unit.

*Packing cost*

Total cost = £60,000

Cost driver = Number of orders packed

Number of orders packed = 1 + 7 + 22 = 30

Cost per order = £60,000/30 = £2,000

Cost per unit of P1 = (£2,000 × 1)/7,500 = £0.27 per product unit

Cost per unit of P2 = (£2,000 × 7)/12,500 = £1.12 per product unit

Cost per unit of P3 = £(2,000 × 22)/4,000 = £11.00 per product unit

| **Unit costs** | *P1* | *P2* | *P3* |
| --- | --- | --- | --- |
| | £ | £ | £ |
| Direct materials | 18.00 | 25.00 | 16.00 |
| Direct labour | 4.00 | 8.00 | 6.40 |
| Overhead costs: | | | |
|   Receiving/materials handling | 1.01 | 3.80 | 23.73 |
|   Maintenance and depreciation | 18.06 | 18.06 | 7.22 |
|   Set-up labour | 0.16 | 0.47 | 2.92 |
|   Engineering | 4.00 | 1.60 | 12.50 |
|   Packing | 0.27 | 1.12 | 11.00 |
| Sub total overhead costs | 23.50 | 25.05 | 57.37 |
| | | | |
| Total unit cost | 45.50 | 58.05 | 79.77 |

**Examiner's note**

An alternative approach to the ABC calculations would be to allocate the total overhead costs to each product line using the cost drivers identified above, finally dividing by the number of units to arrive at the unit cost, as follows:

| | *Total* | *P1* | *P2* | *P3* |
| --- | --- | --- | --- | --- |
| | £ | £ | £ | £ |
| Receiving and handling | 150,000 | 7,595 | 47,468 | 94,937 |
| Maintenance/depreciation | 390,000 | 135,417 | 225,694 | 28,889 |
| Set-up labour | 18,688 | 1,168 | 5,840 | 11,680 |

|  | Total | P1 | P2 | P3 |
|---|---|---|---|---|
|  | £ | £ | £ | £ |
| Engineering | 100,000 | 30,000 | 20,000 | 50,000 |
| Packing | 60,000 | 2,000 | 14,000 | 44,000 |
| Sub-total overhead costs | 718,688 | 176,180 | 313,002 | 229,506 |
| Number of units |  | 7,500 | 12,500 | 4,000 |
| Unit overhead cost (£) |  | £23.49 | £25.04 | £57.38 |

Any difference between the figures for unit overhead costs derived by the two methods is due to rounding differences.

(c)   P1 is shown to have lower unit costs under the original ('traditional') absorption costing system than on the ABC basis. This is caused by its relatively higher machine hour usage and smaller proportion of labour cost, compared to the other products, and the effect this has on the overhead cost allocation. Using ABC, P1 has a very small profit margin. This must therefore raise questions about its viability at its current selling price of £47.

It is a relatively simple product to make. For example, it seems to consist of just one production run and one packing order for the whole output, which means it does not use much of these supporting resources. However it does use a considerable proportion of machine hours, which is what gives rise to much of its allocated overhead cost.

In comparison to P1, Product P3 seems to be a complex product to administer, made in small batches with small orders. In the original system, P3 was being under-costed, being subsidised by P2. It appears to offer a good margin based on its original cost, but the ABC analysis shows that at a selling price of £68, it does not manage to cover all of the direct and overhead costs assigned to it.

There is therefore little surprise that this new product line is attracting additional business, because it is priced below the cost of making it if all of the activities the company undertakes are needed. The company cannot afford to continue business at this price and needs to find some way of managing up the price of this product to make it viable in the future. An alternative may be to re-examine the way it is manufactured, and the ABC system may offer some help in this by assisting with an analysis of what is involved in its manufacture. Presently, it is the high proportion of overhead costs for material movement, engineering and packing which make it expensive. If it is seen to have a future, BML may need to re-engineer their manufacturing methods in relation to this product which makes quite modest use of machining resources.

P2 has the highest volume of the three products, though we are told it is suffering a loss of market share. It is the most labour intensive product and this resulted in serious over-costing under the original system, because overhead was apportioned on a labour cost basis. To put it another way, the ABC cost is lower because the product makes less use of engineering machine hours etc, than the other products. It would seem competitors discovered that they could manufacture this and sell it for a lower price and still make a profit. BML should realise that its major cost is in the use of machinery, and for the volume produced it makes little use of other support costs. It is therefore quite economical to make, though the original system does not reveal this. BML still make a good volume of this product and although we do not know much about the market for it a lower price might stimulate demand, and offer higher sales volumes recovering some of the market share.

**Examiner's note**

The above comments are based on the information as presented in the question. We know nothing about any other overhead costs relating, for example, to administration and selling. No information about the market for the three products is supplied, e.g. market shares or competitors' prices. Such information as this would place the company in a better position to judge the adequacy of the results of its costing system.

## 33    BRUNTI PLC

**Key answer tips**

In part (a) you have already been given the traditional absorption rates, so the main work in (i) is simply converting unit revenues and costs to totals for each product. For (ii) new activity based absorption rates for the individual categories of overheads need to be computed from the cost driver information supplied. These are then applied to products according to their relative use of the cost drivers.

In part (b) the best answers to this part will be those that draw on information given/derived in (a) to illustrate the points being made. The tendency otherwise may be to talk in vague terms about 'more representative cost allocation without specifically explaining why that is the case.

(a)   (i)   **Absorption costing profit statement**

|  | | Product XYI | | | Product YZT | | | Product ABW |
|---|---|---|---|---|---|---|---|---|
| Sales/production (units) | | 50,000 | | | 40,000 | | | 30,000 |
|  | £000 | £000 | £000 | £000 | £000 | £000 | £000 | £000 |
| Sales | | 2,250.00 | | | 3,800.00 | | | 2,190.00 |
| Less: | | | | | | | | |
| Prime cost | 1,600.00 | | | 3,360.00 | | | 1,950.00 | |
| Overheads | | | | | | | | |
| Machine dept | 120.00 | | | 240.00 | | | 144.00 | |
| Assembly dept | 288.75 | | | 99.00 | | | 49.50 | |
| | | 2,008.75 | | | 3,699.00 | | | 2,143.50 |
| Profit (loss) | | 241.25 | | | 101.00 | | | 46.50 |

**Total profit = £388,750**

(ii)

| | | | **Cost pools** | | |
|---|---|---|---|---|---|
| *Machining services* | *Assembly services* | *Assembly* | *Order processing* | *Purchasing* |
| £357,000 | £318,000 | £26,000 | £156,000 | £84,000 |
| 420,000 machine hours | 530,000 direct labour hours | 520 set-ups | 32,000 customer orders | 11,200 supplier orders |
| *Cost:* | | | | |
| £0.85 per machine hour | £0.60 per direct labour hour | £50 per set-up | £4.875 per customer order | £7.50 per supplier order |

**Activity-based costing profit statement**

|  | | Product XYI | | Product YZT | | Product ABW |
|---|---|---|---|---|---|---|
| Sales/production (units) | | 50,000 | | 40,000 | | 30,000 |
| | £000 | £000 | £000 | £000 | £000 | £000 |
| Sales | | 2,250.0 | | 3,800.0 | | 2,190.0 |
| Less: | | | | | | |
| Prime cost | 1,600.0 | | 3,360.0 | | 1,950.0 | |
| Cost pools | | | | | | |
| Machine dept at £0.85 | 85.0 | | 170.0 | | 102.0 | |

| | Product XYI | | Product YZT | | Product ABW | |
|---|---|---|---|---|---|---|
| Assembly dept at £0.60 | 210.0 | | 72.0 | | 36.0 | |
| Set-up costs at £50 | 6.0 | | 10.0 | | 10.0 | |
| Order processing at £4.875 | 39.0 | | 39.0 | | 78.0 | |
| Purchasing at £7.50 | 22.5 | | 30.0 | | 31.0 | |
| Total cost | | 1,962.5 | | 3,681.0 | | 2,207.5 |
| *Total cost £389,000* | | | | | | |
| Profit/loss | | 287.5 | | 119.0 | | (17.5) |

(b)   Activity-based costing (ABC) is considered to present a fairer valuation of the product cost per unit for the following reasons:

- It overcomes some of the problems that are associated with conventional absorption costing. In answer (a) (i), all the production overheads and some other overheads had to be allocated or apportioned to the two cost centres, machine department, assembly department and to service cost centres. Those overheads which could not be identified with a particular cost centre would have had to be shared between cost centres on some arbitrary basis, such as floor area or the number of employees. In addition, the service department costs would have been apportioned to production cost centres using some arbitrary basis or technical estimates. The total overheads for each production cost centre would then be divided by the estimated number of machine hours or direct labour hours, as appropriate. This means that costs which could have been more accurately related to the product were not, for example set up costs vary more with the number of set-ups than with the number of machine hours or direct labour hours.

- In answer (a) (ii), it can be seen that by having a number of 'cost pools' and dividing them by their 'cost driver', i.e. the activity which causes the cost, a more accurate and realistic assessment can be produced. The information so produced using ABC can be significantly different to that which is generated by traditional absorption costing. The differing levels of activity incurred on behalf of each product in terms of the 'cost drivers', for example the number of set-ups, customer orders and so on, can have quite a significant impact on the product cost per unit.

# 34   ABC PLC

## Key answer tips

For Part (a), (i) the computations will only account for 1-2 marks, so don't waste time by repeating detail from the question - start with the operating profit figures given, and deduct the allocated overhead costs as a total figure for each store. Explanation of the term 'cost driver' should be reasonably straightforward from a rudimentary knowledge of ABC; for what is required for 'volume' and 'complexity' in both explanation and comment, you must focus on the area of cost allocation and think how these issues can affect it.

Part (a), (ii) the apportionment of individual overhead costs between cost centres on different bases is a procedure that should be familiar to you. The relevant bases are fairly obvious from the cost driver information given in the question, with the exception of warehouse costs (depreciation and part of HO costs). Don't waste time worrying about the 'right' basis to use, make a rational decision, jot it down, and carry on. Again, the computations account for a minority of the allocated marks - ensure you allow enough time to consider what the figures show. Try not to be too categorical – 'this method now produces the correct allocation of costs and shows that store C is unprofitable and must be closed' - as any method of allocating true central shared costs between units will have some arbitrary element and needs to be used with care in decision making. Remember fixed costs are fixed whatever fancy methods are used to split them.

In the computations, time could be saved by working in £000s and using a total column.

In part (b), do not waste any of the few marks allocated to this part by explaining the mechanics of the techniques themselves; think how they can be applied in this particular context. Discuss both regression and correlation

(a)   (i)                                        **Report**

> **To:**       Group management
>
> **From:**     Accountant
>
> **Date:**     xx/xx/xx
>
> **Subject:**  **Reporting store's profits**

This report presents the budgeted profits for 20X8 of stores A, B and C based on the method of sharing central costs that was originally employed by the group - sales value. As a result of discussions with management at various levels, alternative 'drivers' of these costs have been revealed. This is explained and then applied to the results budgeted for 20X8, finally drawing some conclusions.

|  | A £ | B £ | C £ |
|---|---|---|---|
| Operating profit | 840,000 | 370,000 | 290,000 |
| Central costs (apportion 5:4:3) | 416,667 | 333,333 | 250,000 |
| Net profit | 423,333 | 36,667 | 40,000 |

**Cost drivers** are events or activities which result in costs being incurred. They are commonly used to allocate costs to cost objectives, or reported and 'managed' in order to 'manage' the costs they influence. It is argued that in many traditional costing systems, the cost drivers or allocation bases which were used have 'volume' implications, for example the number of units produced or sold, the machine hours worked or, in our case, sales value. It is clear that there are many other factors which give rise to costs being incurred or resources consumed. It is not only the volume of business but the way that business is done which causes costs. Dealing with a small volume of business in a **complex product** or for a **difficult customer** is sometimes more costly than a large volume in a familiar situation. It is important that cost reports reveal this issue of complexity, so that management can take steps to deal with any business issues which arise. In the original allocation it is implied that store A, which makes the most sales, consumes the greatest proportion of the central resources. This need not be the case, because it depends on what and how it sells and how it is served by the central resource.

Our company has used sales value to allocate all central costs. It is unlikely that this accurately reflects the way central resources have been consumed by the three stores. The basis seems to be one which is conveniently available and one which is related more to what each store can 'bear' of the central costs, rather than any cost causality. It has a tendency to penalise a store if its sales are high, and this can be seen in the case of store A. It is therefore a discouragement to a better-performing store. Additionally, it may influence the accuracy of the budgets, in that stores might deliberately under-state their budgets in order to attract a lower overhead charge.

(ii)    A revised profit for each store is shown below which uses the information obtained from recent discussions with staff at all locations.

|  | Total | Warehouse operations | Store A | Store B | Store C |
|---|---|---|---|---|---|
| **Head office** | £ | £ | £ | £ | £ |
| Salaries | 200,000 | 20,000 | 60,000 | 60,000 | 60,000 |
| Advertising (5:4:3) | 80,000 | - | 33,333 | 26,667 | 20,000 |
| Establishment (10:30:30:30) | 120,000 | 12,000 | 36,000 | 36,000 | 36,000 |
|  |  | 32,000 |  |  |  |
| **Warehouse** |  |  |  |  |  |
| Depreciation (40:30:30) *(note 1)* | 100,000 |  | 40,000 | 30,000 | 30,000 |
| Storage (40:30:30) *(note 1)* | 80,000 |  | 32,000 | 24,000 | 24,000 |
| Operating and despatch | 120,000 + 32,000 | *(note 2)* | 55,000 | 45,000 | 52,000 |
| Delivery *(note 3)* | 300,000 |  | 100,000 | 71,429 | 128,571 |
| **Store costs** |  |  | 356,333 | 293,096 | 350,571 |
| Operating profit |  |  | 840,000 | 370,000 | 290,000 |
| Net profit/(loss) |  |  | 483,667 | 76,904 | (60,571) |

*Notes:*

1    Apportion on the basis of storage space occupied.

2    Apportion on the basis of the number of despatches (550:450:520).

3    Apportion on the basis of delivery distances (70:50:90).

The revised calculations show that the costs identified with store C exceed the current level of operating profit, and an overall loss is disclosed. Stores A and B show improved results based on these allocations. The bases selected are believed to bear a closer relationship to how the resources are consumed in providing service to the three stores. The allocation reflects the benefit they receive rather than their 'ability to bear' the cost. There are, however, still some costs which will always prove difficult to identify, and these inevitably result in an arbitrary allocation (if management requires them to be allocated). Advertising costs are one such example. It is useful for management to be aware of this analysis, though they should use it with care, since it does not directly make decisions for them. It does not give any information about the efficiency with which store C is managed, nor does it indicate that the company would make more profit by closing store C.

It would be useful to see a trend of this information over a period of years. It would also be important to know the extent of competition in the area and the market being served.

In the current situation, it may be uneconomic to service store C at its present volume. Having made this point, store C has the smallest gross margin percentage (37%), compared with store A (44%). It has a different sales mix or different pricing structure. From the further statistics, it is also a difficult store to support. It requires proportionately more despatches and greater delivery distances to be travelled. This information suggests there is scope to rationalise delivery to reduce costs, consider direct delivery from some suppliers, examine vehicle routing schedules, and so on.

Further investigation and discussion is required before taking any firm decisions but the information presented above has highlighted issues which would not have been disclosed by the allocation method previously adopted.

(b) **Regression analysis** and the use of r² would demonstrate the association between some of the central costs and allocation bases proposed. In the case of delivery miles, it would be necessary to accumulate cost of delivery for a number of periods, say quarterly for three years, and set these against the miles travelled. The value would require adjusting for accruals and inflation over the three year periods. A **regression equation** would identify the variable and fixed elements of the cost. The **coefficient of determination** (r²) would express the degree of association between the variable cost and the delivery miles. A close association between these would produce a value for r² of close to 1.

## 35 PARSER LTD

(a) Opportunity costs represent the value of the loss or sacrifice when choosing between scarce alternatives. It is the benefit forgone by choosing one course of action instead of the next most profitable option. Lack of scarcity implies zero opportunity cost.

(b) Revised costs for special order = **relevant costs**:

|  | Notes | £ |
|---|---|---|
| Sub-contractor costs | 1 | 31,300 |
| Supervisor costs | 2 | 1,000 |
| General overheads | 3 | 1,000 |
| Machine maintenance | 4 | 500 |
| Machine overheads | 5 | 22,000 |
| Materials | 6 | 31,500 |
| Interest costs | 7 | 900 |
| Total relevant costs |  | 88,200 |

*Notes*

1 The choice lies between the two alternative sub-contractors that have to be employed because of the shortage of existing labour. The relevant cost is the least-cost alternative, which is to employ the subcontractor who is skilled in the special process.

2 Only the difference between the bonus and the incentive payment represents an additional cost that arises due to the special order. Fixed salary costs do not change. The relevant cost is the extra bonus payable (£3,500) minus the normal incentive payments that will be saved (£2,500).

3 Only incremental costs are relevant. Apportioned fixed overhead costs are not an incremental cost and so are not relevant.

4 Depreciation is both a period fixed cost, not related to the special order, and also a non-cash item of expenditure. It is therefore not relevant. Additional maintenance costs, however, are relevant because they represent extra cash spending.

5 The relevant costs are the extra variable overheads (£3 × 6,000 hours) that will be incurred, plus the displacement costs (loss of contribution) of £2 × 2,000 hours making a total of £22,000.

6 Since the materials are no longer used, the replacement cost is irrelevant (because if the existing stock is used, it will not be replaced). The historical cost of £34,000 is a sunk cost (past cost) and so is also irrelevant. The relevant cost is the lost sale value if the stock used in the special order. This is 7,500 kg × £4.20 per kg = £31,500.

7 Full opportunity costing will also allow for imputed interest costs on the incremental loan. The correct interest rate is the overdraft rate since this represents the incremental cost (i.e. the actual cash payment) the company will pay. Simple interest charged for three months is therefore: 3/12 × £20,000 × 18% = £900.

(c)     **Introduction**

SMEs contribute in a significant way to many economies in the world. Besides generating income, in often large proportions in relation to GNP across the world, they are frequently major employers and the sector which is most identified with new ideas and entrepreneurial spirit. It is these latter factors that help sustain and support growth rates in many economies.

Despite this background of potential, SMEs often experience difficulties in accessing appropriate sources of finance. There are three main issues involved: uncertainty concerning the business, lack of assets available to offer as collateral or security, and the sources of finance for business start-ups or very new businesses.

### Uncertainty concerning the business

It has been recognised in various studies that the problem of adequately financing SMEs is a problem of uncertainty. A defining characteristic of SMEs is the uncertainty surrounding their activities. However much owners or managers inform their banks of what they are doing, there is always an element of uncertainly remaining that is not a feature of larger businesses. Larger businesses have grown from smaller businesses and have a track record – especially in terms of a long-term relationship with their bankers. Bankers can observe over a period of time that the business is well-run, and that managers can manage its affairs and can therefore be trusted with handling bank loans in a proper way. New businesses, typically SMEs, obviously don't have this track record. The problem is even broader. Large businesses conduct most of their activities in public (e.g. subject to more external scrutiny) than do SMEs. Thus, if information is public, there is less uncertainty. For example, a larger business might be quoted on a stock exchange and therefore be subject to press scrutiny, the stock exchange rules regarding the certain of its activities, and would have to publish audited accounts. Many SMEs do not have to have audits, certainly don't publish their accounts to a wide audience and the press are not really interested in them.

### Lack of assets available to offer as collateral security

If SMEs wish to access bank finance, for example, then banks will wish to address the information problem referred to above. First, banks will screen loan applications to assess the underlying product or service, the management team, the market addressed and, importantly, any collateral or security that can be offered. It is this last point which is of interest here. Besides investigating business plans, banks will look to see what security is available for any loan provided. This phase is likely to involve an audit of the firm's assets and detailed explanation of any personal security offered by the directors and owner managers. Collateral is important because it can reduce the level of credit risk a bank is exposed to in granting a loan to a new business. In assessing a business plan and security, a bank would make assessment of the risk of the business and any loan interest rate will reflect that risk. A key feature for accessing bank finance is therefore in the assessment of risk from the information gathered and the security offered.

### Potential sources of finance for very new businesses

Initial owner finance is nearly always the first source of finance for a business, whether from the owner or from family connections. At this stage, many of the assets may be intangible and thus external financing is an unrealistic prospect at this stage or at least has been in the past. This is often referred to as the equity gap.

With no organised market for 'Business Angel' finance, there are only limited means by which SMEs can find equity investors. Trade credit finance is important at this stage too, although it is nearly always very expensive if viewed in terms of lost early payment discounts. Also, it is inevitably very short-term and very limited in duration (except that always taking 60 days to pay a creditor will obviously roll-over and become medium term financing. 'Business Angel' financing might be important. This refers to 'high net worth' individuals or groups of individuals who invest directly in small businesses. It is possible, when a new business or its owner can offer adequate security, that a bank loan may be arranged. Another form of security that may underpin a bank loan is in the form of a guarantee from a reliable individual or other business with a banking track record.

| ACCA marking scheme | | Marks |
|---|---|---|
| (a) | Definition of opportunity cost, up to | 2 |
| (b) | Subcontractor costs | 2 |
| | Supervisor costs | 1 |
| | General overheads | 1 |
| | Machine depreciation | 1 |
| | Machine variable overheads | 2 |
| | Materials | 2 |
| | Interest costs | 2 |
| | | 11 |
| (c) | Up to 2 marks each for detailed points relating to uncertainty | 5 |
| | Up to 2 marks each for detailed points relating to collateral | 5 |
| | Up to 2 marks each for detailed points relating sources of finance | 5 |
| | Presentation and quality of argument | 2 |
| | Maximum available | 17 |
| | Maximum awarded | 12 |
| Total | | 25 |

## 36 ALBION PLC

(a) The optimum production schedule is found using **limiting factor analysis**.

| | AR2 | £ | GL3 | £ | HT4 | £ |
|---|---|---|---|---|---|---|
| Material R2 (£2.50/kg) | 2kg | 5.00 | 3kg | 7.50 | 3kg | 7.50 |
| Material R3 (£2/kg) | 2kg | 4.00 | 2.2kg | 4.40 | 1.6kg | 3.20 |
| Labour (£4/hour) | 0.6hrs | 2.40 | 1.2hrs | 4.80 | 1.5hrs | 6.00 |
| Variable o/hd (£/unit) | | 1.10 | | 1.30 | | 1.10 |
| Variable cost/unit | | 12.50 | | 18.00 | | 17.80 |
| Selling price (£/unit) | | 21.00 | | 28.50 | | 27.30 |
| Contribution (£/unit) | | 8.50 | | 10.50 | | 9.50 |
| Material R2 (kg/unit) | | 2 | | 3 | | 3 |
| Contribution/kg of R2 (£) | | 4.25 | | 3.50 | | 3.17 |
| Ranking | | 1st | | 2nd | | 3rd |

| Product | Demand units | R2 used kg | Production units | | Contribution £ |
|---|---|---|---|---|---|
| AR2 | 950 | 1,900 | 950 | (× £8.50) | 8,075 |
| GL3 | 1,000 | 3,000 | 1,000 | (× £10.50) | 10,500 |
| | | 4,900 | | | |
| HT4 | 900 | 600 | 200 | (× £9.50) | 1,900 |
| | | 5,500 | | | 20,475 |

The optimum production schedule is 950 units of Product AR2, 1,000 units of GL3 and 200 units of HT4, giving a total contribution of £20,475. The fixed production overheads are ignored in this analysis because they are assumed not to vary with changes in the level of production.

(b)    Further supplies of Material R2 will be used to produce additional units of Product HT4. The contribution per kg of Material R2 of Product HT4 is £3.17. The normal price of R2 is £2.50/kg, and so if Albion pays £3.17 + £2.50 = £5.67 per kg for Material R2, the additional units of Product HT4 produced will make a zero contribution towards fixed costs. Therefore **£5.67 is the maximum price** that the company should be prepared to pay.

(c)    The variable cost of Product XY5:

|  | £/unit |
|---|---|
| Material R3: 3kg x £2 | 6.00 |
| Labour: 1.7 hours x £4 | 6.80 |
| Variable overhead | 1.40 |
|  | 14.20 |

The substitute offered by Folam gives a saving of £4 per unit. However, Albion plc would also pay an annual fee of £50,000 for the right to use the substitute. The company would need to manufacture more than 50,000/4 = 12,500 units per year of Product XY5, or 1,042 units per month, in order for the offered substitute to be financially acceptable. If it needed less than 12,500 units of Product XY5 per year, it would be cheaper to manufacture the product in-house.

This evaluation is from a short-term perspective: in the longer term, buying in may lead to fixed cost savings and lower investment, increasing the benefits of buying in and lowering the break-even point.

Albion plc would also need to assure itself that the **quality of the substitute** was acceptable and that this quality could be maintained: the lower price offered by Folam might be associated with poorer quality than that deemed necessary by Albion plc. Orders for the substitute product would also **need to be delivered promptly** in order to avoid production hold-ups. Albion plc could also become **dependent on Folam Limited for supplies** of the substitute product and might be vulnerable to future price increases by the supplier. Such price increases might reduce or even eliminate the cost saving of buying in.

(d)    Marginal costing (variable costing) treats fixed costs as a period cost, on the assumption that fixed costs do not change in the short term. The difference between selling price and variable costs is the variable contribution made by units sold towards meeting fixed costs and generating profit.

Marginal costing has traditionally been used for short-term decisions such as whether to cease production of a product, whether to make a product or buy it from a supplier, and how to allocate scarce resources in order to maximise contribution.

A major limitation with using marginal costing as the basis for making short-term decisions is the assumption that fixed costs are irrelevant to short-term decisions. In the longer term, fixed costs will change: for example, rent is usually regarded as a fixed cost and in the longer term rent might be expected to increase due to inflation. However, a change in fixed costs may be the result of a short-term decision: for example, if a product is discontinued and as a result the work of the marketing department decreases, in the longer term marketing costs would be expected to decrease.

This points to the danger of relying on a simplistic analysis of costs into fixed costs and variable costs, and of assuming that only variable costs are relevant for decision-making purposes. It is possible for a fixed cost to be a relevant cost. It is also possible for a variable cost to be irrelevant, for example in the case where a variable cost is common to two decision alternatives. If fuel costs are incurred whether a machine is leased or bought, for example, these costs are not relevant to the decision on whether to lease or buy.

Reliance on marginal costing as a basis for making short-term decisions may therefore lead to sub-optimal decisions overall for a company, as the analysis may fail to consider all relevant costs. A **relevant cost** is an incremental or differential cost at the whole company level. If a cost changes or is incurred, now or in the future, as a result of a decision, it is a relevant cost and should be considered when making a decision. When making short-term decisions, therefore, it is essential to adopt a whole company perspective in determining relevant costs.

When making short-term decisions, a **detailed analysis of cost behaviour** is therefore needed in order to determine not only variable costs and fixed costs, but all other relevant costs as well.

| ACCA marking scheme | | Marks |
|---|---|---|
| (a) | Calculation of contribution per unit | 2 |
| | Calculation of contribution per kg of R2 | 2 |
| | Optimum production schedule | 4 |
| | | 8 |
| (b) | Calculation of maximum price | 1 |
| | Discussion | 2 |
| | | 3 |
| (c) | Calculation of cost saving | 1 |
| | Calculation of breakeven point | 1 |
| | Discussion of relevant issues | 5 |
| | | 7 |
| (d) | Up to 2 marks for each detailed point made | 7 |
| Total | | 25 |

## 37 THROUGHPUT

(a) Identification of the bottleneck resource.

*Machine X:* Maximum output per week

= 180 frame panels/4 panels per TRL

= 45 TRLs/week

On average 17.5 hours per month or 4.375 hours per week can be lost, reducing the maximum capacity by 10.9375% $\left(\frac{4.375}{40}\times100\%\right)$. This reduces Machine X's capacity to 40 TRLs, on average, per week (45 × (1 - 0.109375)).

*Machine Y:* Maximum output = 52 TRLs/week

*Machine Z:* Maximum output = 30 TRLs/week

**Machine Z is therefore the key, or bottleneck resource.**

**Calculation of return per factory hour**

Time on key resource (machine Z) $= \dfrac{40\text{ hours}}{30\text{ TRLs}} = 1.3333$ hours/TRL

Sale price – material cost $= £2,000 - £600$

$= £1,400$

$$\therefore \text{ Return per factory hour} = \frac{£1,400}{1.3333} = £1050/\text{hour}$$

**Calculation of cost per factory hour**

Fixed costs are £450,000/48 = £9,375/week.

$$\text{Cost per factory hour} = \frac{£5,500 + £8,000 + £9,375}{40} = £571.875/\text{hour}$$

**Throughput accounting ratio** $\quad = \dfrac{£1,050}{£571.875}$

$$= \mathbf{1.836}$$

(b) Throughput accounting is an approach advocated as a means of applying the 'Theory of Constraints' first developed by Goldratt and Cox in the early 1980s. The basic concept of throughput accounting is the notion of throughput itself. This can be defined as:

*'The rate of production of a defined process over a stated period of time'*

*CIMA Official Terminology*

Throughput is calculated as sales revenue minus the cost of materials, which is regarded as the only variable cost in the short term.

Underpinning this basic concept are three further concepts, which can be stated as follows:

(1) In the short-term all manufacturing costs, with the exception of material costs, are largely pre-determined and can, therefore, be regarded as fixed. 'Contribution' is therefore sales minus material costs.

(2) Holding and producing inventory is not a value-added activity. Profitability is seen as being inversely proportional to the time taken for production to respond to demand, i.e. throughput time. In other words, the longer it takes to produce output, the lower the profitability. Since holding inventory lengthens throughput time, profitability can be seen as being inversely proportional to the level of inventory in the system. This supports the advocacy of a 'Just-in-Time' system of inventory management.

(3) Overall product profitability is determined by two factors:

(i) The rate at which it contributes money – this is a measure of the product's *relative* profitability, and

(ii) The rate at which the factory spends money.

Comparing the rate at which a product contributes money to the rate at which the factory spends it determines absolute profitability.

The objective is to maximise the 'throughput' in any given time period and this automatically focuses attention on any bottleneck resource(s). If profit is to be maximised (in the short-term) then the optimal utilisation of any bottleneck resources needs to be determined and, if possible, the bottleneck resource removed.

(c) The throughput accounting ratio, as defined, measures the rate at which the business generates money compared with the rate at which the business spends money. This ratio needs to exceed one if the business is to maintain itself as a going concern. The definition of throughput, explained in part (a), is similar to the existing concept of 'value added'.

In effect, MN Ltd needs to add value to the business at a greater rate than it is expending conversion costs to add that value. The ratio implies that only products with a throughput accounting ratio greater than one should be produced and that these products can be ranked in terms of profitability by their throughput accounting ratio. To maximise this throughput in the short-term, the product(s) with the highest throughput accounting ratio should be produced.

However, this short-term approach may conflict with longer-term measures of profitability. For instance, MN Ltd is proposing to replace machine Z with machine G and possibly overhaul machine X. This proposal may cause the throughput accounting ratio for the TRLs to decline in the short-term.

(d)     Whilst throughput accounting and marginal costing have many similarities, the main difference arises from the definition of contribution or, more specifically, what can be regarded as a variable cost. The traditional marginal costing approach assumes that direct labour is a variable cost. Whilst this may have been true 30 or 40 years ago when labour was typically paid a piece rate, this is no longer the case – in the short-term, throughput accounting treats labour as a fixed cost. Marginal costing also tends to emphasise cost behaviour, especially overheads, and usually attempts to separate these into fixed and variable components. As with labour costs, throughput accounting treats all production overhead costs as fixed in the short-term and aggregates these with labour into what is referred to as 'total factory cost'. Consequently, in throughput accounting the only cost that is treated as variable in the short-term is the direct material cost.

Furthermore, marginal costing does not provide a direct disincentive to produce for, or carry stock. Throughput accounting discourages this by using the *total* cost of direct materials *purchased* in the period in the calculation of throughput, rather than the cost of material actually used, as is the case with marginal costing.

(e)     If machine G is purchased and machine X is overhauled, then the capacity of each machine will be as follows:

Machine X = 45 TRLs per week

Machine G = 45 TRLs per week

Machine Y = 52 TRLs per week

This means that both machine X and machine G will become potential bottleneck resources. However, demand is not forecast to exceed 45 TRLs per month until July so the emphasis, initially, will be on ensuring that the new machine is installed and machine X is overhauled by the end of June at the latest, and preferably by the end of May. Once these machines are fully operational they will both need to be monitored to ensure they are fully utilised, especially in periods where demand exceeds maximum available capacity. Calculation of the return per factory hour for each machine and the associated throughput accounting ratio will assist this process, as will monitoring the level of reworks and rejects that use the bottleneck resources.

## 38    SPRING PLC

(a)     Activity-based costing is based on the insight that activities create costs, while products consume activities. It is claimed that activity-based costing attaches overheads to product cost in a more meaningful way than traditional absorption costing.

A key feature of activity-based costing is that overhead costs are collected in cost pools, which correspond to a particular activity or group of activities that generate costs. A classic example of a cost pool is set-up costs for a production line. The cost of each set-up is included in the cost pool reflecting the recognition that it is set-ups that incur costs, rather than the volume of production on the production line. Set-up costs are an example of an indirect cost, and both traditional absorption costing and activity-based costing are concerned with the allocation of indirect costs onto product cost. Traditional absorption costing assigns indirect costs or overheads to production departments and service departments and then reallocates service department overheads to production centres. Activity-based costing is likely to use, or has the potential to use, considerably more cost pools than traditional absorption costing uses production centres. In activity-based costing, the link between cost pools and product cost is called a cost driver. A cost driver represents the extent to which a particular activity has been used by a particular product in its production. Continuing our example, an appropriate cost driver would be number of set-ups. A product which is produced in frequent short production runs would therefore incur a greater share of set-up costs than a product produced in a single production run. In traditional absorption costing, overheads are linked to product cost through overhead absorption rates such as cost per machine hour or cost per labour hour. Activity-based costing is likely to use considerably more cost drivers than traditional absorption costing uses overhead absorption rates.

The key steps in introducing an activity-based costing system are as follows:

1    Identify the main activities that generate costs through activity analysis

2    Assign costs to cost pools

3    Select appropriate cost drivers for assigning cost pool costs to products

4    Calculate activity-based charge rates to assign the cost of activities to products

The following benefits have been claimed for an activity-based costing:

1    Product costs are more accurate due to the more sophisticated analysis and assignment of overhead costs. Overhead costs are assigned on a cause-and-effect basis rather than on an ad hoc or subjective basis.

2    Cost behaviour is better understood due to the analysis of activities.

3    Cost control is facilitated through the identification and management of cost-generating activities. For example, in order to reduce set-up costs, production planning could be used to eliminate short production runs and hence reduce the number of set-ups.

4    Poor decisions due to inadequate cost information are less likely to occur.

As for disadvantages, identifying the main activities that generate costs in an organisation is expensive. Careful thought must also be given to the ability of existing management accounting information systems to provide the detailed activity and cost information required by an activity-based costing system: upgrading or replacement may be needed. A further expense is the cost of training staff to use the new costing system. Once introduced, an activity-based costing system can be significantly more expensive than a traditional absorption costing system. It is possible, therefore, that in some organisations the cost of introducing and maintaining an activity-based costing system may exceed the benefits gained.

Activity-based costing may be most appropriate in an organisation where indirect costs are a significant proportion of total cost, or where a wide product range is maintained with a variety of different activity consumption patterns. Spring plc should consider the significance of indirect costs to its product costs and undertake a cost-benefit analysis before making a decision to implement an activity-based costing system. Spring plc should also consider that further developments can flow from the introduction of an activity-based costing system, for example in budgeting (activity-based budgeting) and management philosophy (activity-based management).

(b)  Managerial performance and organisational performance are inextricably linked, since managers are the key decision makers in an organisation and their decisions therefore determine organisational performance.

Managerial and organisational performance needs to be measured as part of the control process within an organisation. The three elements of the control process are recording or measuring actual performance or output, comparing performance with planned performance or some benchmark, and taking action to correct or modify continuing performance in order to achieve planned performance. Managerial and organisational performance can be measured in a wide variety of ways, depending on which aspect of performance, financial or non-financial, is the object of interest.

A wide variety of financial (or money) performance measures can be used to assess managerial and organisational performance. Financial performance is of interest to internal and external stakeholders who are concerned to monitor the progress and risk of their investment, the security of their employment, and so on. Examples of financial performance measures include:

**Profit**

Profit before interest and tax or profit after tax are usually expected to increase on an annual basis and the financial media often refer to profit when discussing managerial and organisational performance. Managers are expected to deliver increasing profits and organisations are expected to produce profit increases equal to or greater than their competitors.

**Earnings per share**

Earnings per share is a profit measure of interest to shareholders and the financial market, since it represents the maximum dividend per share that a company could pay. Managerial rewards could be linked in part to meeting performance targets based on earnings per share.

**Cash flow**

Because profit may be affected by arbitrary adjustments linked to accounting policies and because profit does not measure directly the ability to generate returns for investors, many shareholders and providers of debt finance prefer to concentrate on changes in cash flow as a means of assessing managerial and organisational performance.

**Costs**

A focus on managerial and organisational performance in terms of cost control or cost reduction may be especially appropriate for organisations in the public sector. Here, profitability is an inappropriate performance measure and a key objective is value for money, in terms of the drive for economy, efficiency and effectiveness.

**Share price**

Since one of the ways in which shareholders receive a return from their investment in a company is through capital growth, they will be interested in assessing managerial and organisational performance in terms of share price growth. If managers invest in projects with a positive net present value then, theoretically, the share price should increase to reflect the rise in corporate net present value. Conversely, organisations in which managers are believed to be poor performers will experience a share price decrease.

Measuring financial performance alone is not sufficient, since financial performance results from a range of organisational activities which must also therefore be monitored. Non-financial performance measures may be quantitative or qualitative. An example of a quantitative performance measure is the number of complaints received from customers. An example of a qualitative performance measure is feedback from a sales representative to the effect that most customers are very happy with the after-sales service provided by the organisation.

An attempt is usually made to replace qualitative performance measures with a substitute measure that can be quantified. For example, the number of customer complaints can be used as a substitute measure of product quality or customer satisfaction. Similarly, the number of warranty claims can be used as a substitute measure of product reliability.

Modern organisations compete in terms of product quality, flexibility and reliability, customer satisfaction, and product dimensions such as after-sales care and customer loyalty. These features are captured by non-financial indicators such as number of customer complaints, number of warranty claims, and quality ratings (such as the star ratings of hotels or restaurants, or the position of an organisation in a league table).

A more balanced assessment of organisational and managerial performance will consider both financial and non-financial performance. For example, Kaplan and Norton's Balanced Scorecard considers the customer perspective, the innovation perspective, the internal process perspective and the financial perspective, and requires the identification of quantitative and non-quantitative goals and performance measures.

| ACCA marking scheme | | Marks |
|---|---|---|
| (a) | Key features of activity-based costing | 5-6 |
| | Advantages of activity-based costing | 5-6 |
| | Disadvantages of activity-based costing | 4-5 |
| | | 14 |
| (b) | Need for measurement of performance | 3-4 |
| | Examples of financial performance measures | 4-5 |
| | Examples of non-financial performance measures | 4-5 |
| | | 11 |
| Total | | 25 |

# STANDARD COSTING AND VARIANCE ANALYSIS

## 39 STANDARD COSTING

(a) Standard costing has been employed for many years in situations where there is a **significant degree of repetition** in the production process or the service supplied. Repetition is a condition, since standards presuppose that averages, as expected values, are accurate to a fair degree.

The main uses of standard costing relate to:

1 **Valuation of stocks** and costs of production for reporting purposes, either internally or for statutory reasons.

2 Providing an excellent device which enables costs to be monitored, reviewed and controlled by management.

3 Enabling **exception reporting** through the use of variance analysis. Exception reporting allows management to exercise control with a lower degree of effort and less time than otherwise would be the case.

4 Assisting in the **budgeting** process. Standards, once established in a business, become the common language by which performance is discussed and measured.

5    **Evaluating managerial performance.**

6    **Motivation** of staff by setting standards at levels to which staff feel able to respond. In this respect, standards have been characterised as 'ideal', 'attainable', 'current' and 'basic' as a way of categorising the different ways standards may be viewed in terms of their motivational impact.

7    **Improving efficiency.** Standard setting is often viewed as a way of understanding the detail of a process through monitoring its important components. If standards are an accurate reflection of a process, then they can be used to highlight ways of improving efficiency and act as signals when the process becomes inefficient.

Once standards have been set, they cannot be assumed to be accurate over long periods of time. **Standards have to be reviewed** to enable the benefits of standard costing to continue. In this respect, standards must change with the changing practices of an organisation. For example, in environments which continuously seek greater efficiency and reduced costs of production, standards have to change to reflect such improvements. In fact, under such circumstances, standards can very quickly become out of date. In order to review standards, they must be continually assessed to ensure that the basis of their calculation still applies. Moreover, other purposes of standards are undermined, if they are not continually reviewed. Thus, for example:

1    The motivational impact of standards may no longer be effective if standards are out of date.

2    Assessment of managerial performance becomes inaccurate.

3    Reporting procedures are undermined.

4    The credibility of standards in their role in assisting with the budget setting process is called into question.

5    The fate of standard costing as a management tool is put at risk if management do not trust the standards. Alternative mechanisms for management control inevitably emerge which may be undesirable, untested and lack organisational approval.

(b)    Financial statements of any sort are only an expression of organisational activities that can be measured. Many of the activities of an organisation cannot be easily measured, nor can its relations with various stakeholder groups who may have a non-financial interest in the organisation.

**Non-finance objectives** that may be difficult to measure or express in financial terms include:

1    Welfare of employees and management

- Health

- Safety

- Leisure and other services

2    Welfare in the broader community

- Minimisation of intrusion into the community (e.g. traffic)

3    The provision of a service for which no charge is made, for example:

- Public hospitals

- Local or regional government services

- Housing

- Education

4       The effective supply of goods or services (in addition to costs/efficiency issued) such as:

- Product or service quality

- Ensuring product or service supply (e.g. vital services)

- Timeliness

- After-sales support

- Customer/user satisfaction

5       Fulfilment of product or services responsibilities: this is a very broad area and would cover many of the core activities of a business such as:

- Leadership in research and development

- Product development

- Maintenance of standards in goods or service provision

- Maintenance of good business and community relationships

- Employee training and support.

6       Support for community activities

7       Minimisation of externalities (e.g. pollution and other socially responsible objectives)

8       Fulfilment of statutory or regulatory responsibilities

Whilst it may be argued that many of the objectives expressed have an impact on profitability or costs, they only do so in an indirect manner. Moreover, as with most organisational activities, non-financial objectives crystallises into financial issues given enough time. Thus, for example, poor service provision will ultimately lead to loss of customers in a competitive environment.

The range of stakeholders that may have an interest in an organisation's activities are wide and, because organisations have to respond to stakeholder interests, the non-financial responsibilities and hence range of objectives, is extended. In this respect, stakeholders create for organisations a range of non-financial issues that have to be addressed. If organisations are responsive then these issues become part of the culture of an organisation and hence part of its broader purposes. Interest in the organisation's activities from a non-financial perspective can arise even if the stake holder has a financial relationship with the organisation. Thus, the stakeholders who may have an interest might include the following:

1       shareholders

2       suppliers and trade creditors

3       debt holders

4       customers

5       employees

6       pensioners and ex-employees

7       competitors

8       local community

9       broader national and international interests

10      government

11    regulatory authorities

12    tax authorities

13    special interest groups concerned with pollution, for example

Moreover, many of the stakeholders have common interests and hence stakeholders groupings can emerge.

| ACCA marking scheme | | | |
|---|---|---|---|
| | | *Marks* | |
| (a) | 1 mark for each item referring to the use of standard costing | 8 | |
| | 2 marks for each detailed item on why standards need reviewing | 8 | |
| | Maximum available | 16 | |
| | Maximum awarded | | 13 |
| (b) | Up to 2 marks for each detailed item on describing non-financial objectives | 12 | |
| | Up to 2 marks on role of stakeholders in shaping objectives | 2 | |
| | 1 mark for identification of stakeholder | 1 | |
| | Maximum available | 15 | |
| | Maximum awarded | | 12 |
| Total | | | 25 |

## 40    MATERIAL VARIANCES

(a)    **Standard cost per tonne of input**

| | | | £ |
|---|---|---|---|
| Material X: | 60% | at £30 per tonne | 18 |
| Material Y: | 40% | at £45 per tonne | 18 |
| | 100% | | 36 |
| Standard loss | 10% | | |
| Standard yield | 90% | | |

**Standard cost per standard tonne of output** = £36/90% = £40.

**Material price variance**

| | January £ | February £ | March £ |
|---|---|---|---|
| *Material Y*: | | | |
| Actual price of £45 = standard price. So | | | |
| material price variance = | Nil | Nil | Nil |
| | | | |
| *Material X*: | | | |
| Total cost of all materials | 32,400 | 31,560 | 38,600 |
| Less cost of material Y (360 × £45) | 16,200 | 16,200 | 16,200 |
| Actual cost of material X | 16,200 | 15,360 | 22,400 |
| Standard price of material X used | | | |
| January: 540 tonnes should cost (× £30) | 16,200 | | |
| February: 480 tonnes should cost (× £30) | | 14,400 | |
| March: 700 tonnes should cost (× £30) | | | 21,000 |
| Material X price variance | Nil | 960 (A) | 1,400 (A) |

**Mix variances**

**January**

| | Actual mix tonnes | | Standard mix tonnes | Mix variance tonnes |
|---|---|---|---|---|
| Material X | 540 | (60%) | 540 | 0 |
| Material Y | 360 | (40%) | 360 | 0 |
| | 900 | | 900 | 0 |

**February**

| | Actual mix tonnes | | Standard mix tonnes | Mix variance tonnes | Standard price £ | Mix variance £ |
|---|---|---|---|---|---|---|
| Material X | 480 | (60%) | 504 | 24 (F) | 30 | 720 (F) |
| Material Y | 360 | (40%) | 336 | 24 (A) | 45 | 1,080 (A) |
| | 840 | | 840 | | | 360 (A) |

**March**

| | Actual mix tonnes | | Standard mix tonnes | Mix variance tonnes | Standard price £ | Mix variance £ |
|---|---|---|---|---|---|---|
| Material X | 700 | (60%) | 636 | 64 (A) | 30 | 1,920 (A) |
| Material Y | 360 | (40%) | 424 | 64 (F) | 45 | 2,880 (F) |
| | 1,060 | | 1,060 | | | 960 (F) |

**Yield variances**

**January**

| 810 tonnes of output | should use (× 10/9) | 900 | tonnes |
|---|---|---|---|
| | did use (540 + 360) | 900 | tonnes |
| Yield variance | | 0 | tonnes |

**February**

| 765 tonnes of output | should use (× 10/9) | 850 | tonnes |
|---|---|---|---|
| | did use (480 + 360) | 840 | tonnes |
| Yield variance | | 10 | tonnes (F) |
| Standard price per tonne of input | | £36 | |
| Yield variance in £ | | £360 (F) | |

**March**

| 900 tonnes of output | should use (× 10/9) | 1,000 | tonnes |
|---|---|---|---|
| | did use (700 + 360) | 1,060 | tonnes |
| Yield variance | | 60 | tonnes (A) |
| Standard price per tonne of input | | £36 | |
| Yield variance in £ | | £2,160 (A) | |

**Summary**

| | January £ | £ | February £ | £ | March £ | £ |
|---|---|---|---|---|---|---|
| Material price variance | | | | | | |
| Material X | | 0 | 960 (A) | | 1,400 (A) | |
| Material Y | | 0 | 0 | | 0 | |
| Materials mix variance | 0 | | 360 (A) | | 960 (F) | |
| Materials yield variance | 0 | | 360 (F) | | 2,160 (A) | |
| Materials usage variance | | 0 | | 0 | 1,200 (A) | |
| Total materials variances | | 0 | | 960 (A) | | 2,600 (A) |

***Tutorial note:*** In the time available, it should be permissible to calculate the usage variance as the sum of the mix and yield variances. If you wanted to calculate the usage variances from first principles, you could use the following method.

| **January** | | Material X | | | Material Y |
|---|---|---|---|---|---|
| | | *tonnes* | | | *tonnes* |
| **810 units of output:** | | | | | |
| should use | (60% of 900) | 540 | (40% of 900) | | 360 |
| did use | | 540 | | | 360 |
| Usage variance in tonnes | | 0 | | | 0 |

| **February** | | Material X | | | Material Y |
|---|---|---|---|---|---|
| | | *tonnes* | | | *tonnes* |
| **765 units of output:** | | | | | |
| should use | (60% of 850) | 510 | (40% of 850) | | 340 |
| did use | | 480 | | | 360 |
| Usage variance in tonnes | | 30 (F) | | | 20 (A) |
| Standard price per tonne | | £30 | | | £45 |
| Usage variance in £ | | £900 (F) | | | £900 (A) |

**Total usage variance = £0**

| **March** | | Material X | | | Material Y |
|---|---|---|---|---|---|
| | | *tonnes* | | | *tonnes* |
| **900 units:** | | | | | |
| should use | (60% of 1,000) | 600 | (40% of 1,000) | | 400 |
| did use | | 700 | | | 360 |
| Usage variance in tonnes | | 100 (A) | | | 40 (F) |
| Standard price per tonne | | £30 | | | £45 |
| Usage variance in £ | | £3,000 (A) | | | £1,800 (F) |

**Total usage variance = £1,200 (A)**

(b)  Production in January is exactly according to standard. The price of Y has remained at standard for the whole period. The price of X is £2 (£960/480) in excess of standard in February and £2 (£1,400/700) in excess of standard in March. If this continues, the standard price of X will need to be increased. The proportion of X in the mix changed to 57% (480/840) and 66% (700/1,060) in February and March respectively. The cost increase in February, shown as an adverse mix variance of £360, is caused by dearer Y being used instead of cheaper X. There is an improvement in yield in February. The increased yield could be viewed as an abnormal gain of 9 tonnes [(840 × 90% − 765)] with a standard value of (× £40 =) £360. There is also a reduction in volume produced in February.

In March, the significant increase in the usage proportion of X (which is cheaper) has caused a favourable mix variance but may also have contributed to the large adverse yield variance. Production in March is considerably higher than for January and February - this may be a reason for the adverse yield variance.

Overall, there appears to be a link between mix and yield. If the proportion of Y is increased, causing an adverse mix variance since Y is more expensive, the yield is improved - as occurred in February. The opposite took place in March.

There could also be a link between yield and the volume of production - in February production is low and yield is high, whereas in March production is high and yield is low.

(c)  This information helps to explain the increased proportion of Y used in February. If not used. Y would be wasted, and this could involve disposal costs. It could therefore be argued that the adverse mix variance on Y of £1,080 in February is a sunk cost, i.e. using a greater proportion of Y has not increased the purchase quantity. Using more of Y has improved yield.

In March, the restriction on Y has resulted in adverse yield arising from the increased proportion of X needed to increase production volume. This has resulted in an overall adverse usage variance of £1,200. This excess cost should be included in the evaluation of decisions to try to obtain more of Y by, for example, paying a premium price.

It would be necessary to ascertain whether and how the quality of the final product is affected by changes in mix, and whether the quality is then acceptable to customers.

## 41 PERSEUS CO LTD

### Key answer tips

This is a straightforward variances question, and provided you are well-prepared on this topic is quite manageable in the time allowed. Note in the answer to (a), the two statements have been combined in columnar form, which saves time. Whilst the answer interprets "standard costing profit statement" as a flexed budget, it would be equally acceptable to base this statement on the budgeted activity level.

Whether you include a sales volume variance in part (b) depends upon the approach taken in (a); note that mix and yield variances are not generally required unless specifically requested or the working of the question indicates they would be useful/relevant.

(a) *Workings*

| Standard variable cost per unit | | £ |
|---|---|---|
| Materials: | | |
| 007 | 6 kilos at £12.25 per kilo | 73.50 |
| XL90 | 3 kilos at £3.20 per kilo | 9.60 |
| | | 83.10 |
| Labour | 4.5 hours at £8.40 per hour | 37.80 |
| | | 120.90 |

**Standard usages and time:**

| Material 007 | 15,400 units should use (× 6) | 92,400 kilos |
|---|---|---|
| Material XL90 | 15,400 units should use (× 3) | 46,200 kilos |
| Labour | 15,400 units should take (× 4.5) | 69,300 hours |

**15,400 units of production and sale**

| | Actual | | Standard | |
|---|---|---|---|---|
| | £ | £ | £ | £ |
| Sales | (at £138.25) | 2,129,050 | (at £140) | 2,156,000 |
| Costs | | | | |
| Materials | | | | |
| 007 | | 1,256,640 | (15,400 × £73.50) | 1,131,900 |
| XL90 | | 132,979 | (15,400 × £9.60) | 147,840 |
| Labour | | 612,766 | (15,400 × £37.80) | 582,120 |
| Fixed overheads | | 96,840 | | 86,400 |
| Total costs | | 2,099,225 | | 1,948,260 |
| Profit | | 29,825 | | 207,740 |

(b) **Reconciliation**

*Workings*

| *Sales price* | £ |
|---|---|
| 15,400 units should sell for | 2,156,000 |
| They did sell for | 2,129,050 |
| Sales price variance | 26,950 (A) |

| *Materials 007* | kg | |
|---|---|---|
| 15,400 units should use | 92,400 | |
| They did use | 98,560 | |
| Material 007 usage variance (kg) | 6,160 | (A) |

| | | |
|---|---|---|
| Standard price/kg | £12.25 | |
| Usage variance in £ | £75,460 | (A) |

| *Materials 007* | £ | |
|---|---|---|
| 98,560 kg should cost (× £12.25) | 1,207,360 | |
| They did cost | 1,256,640 | |
| Material price variance | 49,280 | (A) |

| *Materials XL90* | kg | |
|---|---|---|
| 15,400 units should use | 46,200 | |
| They did use | 42,350 | |
| Material 007 usage variance (kg) | 3,850 | (F) |

| | | |
|---|---|---|
| Standard price/kg | £3.20 | |
| Usage variance in £ | £12,320 | (F) |

| *Materials XL90* | £ | |
|---|---|---|
| 42,350 kg should cost (× £3.20) | 135,520 | |
| They did cost | 132,979 | |
| Material price variance | 2,541 | (F) |

$$\text{Actual hours worked} = \frac{£612,766}{£8.65} = 70,840 \text{ hours}$$

| *Labour efficiency* | Hours | |
|---|---|---|
| 15,400 units should take | 69,300 | |
| They did take | 70,840 | |
| Labour efficiency variance (hrs) | 1,540 | (A) |
| Standard rate/hour | £8.40 | |
| Efficiency variance in £ | £12,396 | (A) |

| *Labour rate* | £ | |
|---|---|---|
| 70,840 hours should cost (× £8.40) | 595,056 | |
| They did cost | 612,766 | |
| Material price variance | 17,710 | (A) |

| *Fixed overhead expenditure* | £ | |
|---|---|---|
| Budgeted fixed overhead costs | 86,400 | |
| Actual fixed overhead costs | 96,840 | |
| Expenditure variance | 10,440 | (A) |

**Reconciliation**

| | | £ |
|---|---|---|
| **Standard profit** on 15,400 units of sale, as above | | 207,740 |

| | Fav | Adverse |
|---|---|---|
| | £ | £ | £ |
| **Variances:** | | | |
| Sales price | | | 26,950 |
| Materials 007 usage | | | 75,460 |

| | | |
|---|---:|---:|
| Materials XL90 usage | 12,320 | |
| Materials 007 price | | 49,280 |
| Materials XL90 price | 2,541 | |
| Labour efficiency | | 12,936 |
| Labour rate | | 17,710 |
| Fixed overhead expenditure variance | | 10,440 |
| | 14,861 | 192,776 |
| Total variances | | 177,915 A |
| **Actual profit** | | 29,825 |

(c)     The causes of variances might be inter-related, and the reason why one variance is favourable could also help explain why another variance is adverse.

Using poor quality materials could result in a favourable price variance because of paying a lower price. The poor quality material could be the cause of both an adverse material usage variance and an adverse labour efficiency variance, because cheaper materials might be more difficult to work with, resulting in more rejects/spoilt work, or more waste.

If a higher grade of labour was used, compared with that which was planned, there would most certainly be an adverse labour rate variance. The higher skill level employed could well be the reason for a favourable labour efficiency variance and a favourable material usage variance, for example due to a lower number of rejects and less waste of materials.

## 42     WOODEEZER LTD

(a)     *Workings*

| | Units | |
|---|---:|---|
| Budgeted sales | 4,000 | |
| Actual sales | 3,200 | |
| Sales volume variance | 800 | (A) |
| | | |
| Standard profit/unit | £28 | |
| Sales volume profit variance | £22,400 | (A) |

| | £ | |
|---|---:|---|
| 3,200 units of sales should sell for (× £220) | 704,000 | |
| but did sell for | 720,000 | |
| Sales price variance | 16,000 | (F) |

| | £ | |
|---|---:|---|
| 80,000 kg of wood should cost (× £3.20) | 256,000 | |
| but did cost | 280,000 | |
| Materials price variance | 24,000 | (A) |

| | kg | |
|---|---:|---|
| 3,600 units produced should use (× 25 kg) | 90,000 | |
| but did use | 80,000 | |
| Materials usage variance in kg | 10,000 | (F) |

| | | |
|---|---:|---|
| Standard price/kg of wood | £3.20 | |
| Sales volume profit variance | £32,000 | (F) |

| *Labour rate* | £ | |
|---|---|---|
| 16,000 hours should cost (× £8) | 128,000 | |
|   but did cost | 112,000 | |
| Labour rate variance | 16,000 | (F) |

| | Hours | |
|---|---|---|
| 3,600 units produced should take (× 4 hrs) | 14,400 | |
|   but did take | 16,000 | |
| Efficiency variance in hours | 1,600 | (A) |

| | | |
|---|---|---|
| Standard rate/hour for labour | £8 | |
| Labour efficiency variance | £12,800 | (A) |

| | | |
|---|---|---|
| Standard rate/hour for variable overhead | £4 | |
| Variable overhead efficiency variance | £6,400 | (A) |

| | | |
|---|---|---|
| Standard rate/hour for fixed overhead | £16 | |
| Fixed overhead efficiency variance | £25,600 | (A) |

| *Variable overhead expenditure* | £ | |
|---|---|---|
| 16,000 hours should cost (× £4) | 64,000 | |
|   but did cost | 60,000 | |
| Variable overhead expenditure variance | 4,000 | (F) |

| *Fixed overhead expenditure* | £ | |
|---|---|---|
| Budgeted fixed costs (4,000 units × £64) | 256,000 | |
| Actual fixed costs | 196,000 | |
| Fixed overhead expenditure variance | 60,000 | (F) |

| | Hours | |
|---|---|---|
| Budgeted hours of work (4,000 × 4 hrs) | 16,000 | |
| Actual hours of work | 16,000 | |
| Capacity variance in hours (and £) | 0 | |

**Operating statement**

| | £ | |
|---|---|---|
| Budgeted profit (4,000 × £28) | 112,000 | |
| Sales volume profit variance | (22,400) | (A) |
| Standard profit on actual sales | 89,600 | |
| Sales price variance | 16,000 | (F) |
| | 105,600 | |

| Cost variances | Fav £ | Adv £ | | |
|---|---|---|---|---|
| Material price | | 24,000 | | |
| Material usage | 32,000 | | | |
| Labour rate | 16,000 | | | |
| Labour efficiency | | 12,800 | | |
| Variable overhead expenditure | 4,000 | | | |
| Variable overhead efficiency | | 6,400 | | |
| Fixed overhead expenditure | 60,000 | | | |
| Fixed overhead efficiency | | 25,600 | | |
| | 112,000 | 68,800 | 43,200 | (F) |
| Actual profit | | | 148,800 | |

(b)   **Motivation and budget setting**

Absorption costing profit has increased by £53,600, from £95,200 (28 × 3,400) to £148,800.

It would apear that in the past an expectations budget has been set whereby the target output was set at the level that employees were expected to achieve.

Mr Beech appears to have considered the evidence that suggests that the best budget for motivating employees to maximize achievement (in this case output) is one which is difficult but credible (an aspirations budget). In maximising actual performance, however, it is normally expected that production will fall short of the budget target. This means that there is an expectation of adverse planning variances.

**Explanations of variances**

The sales volume variance and the sales price variance may be inter-related as an increase in price is likely to reduce demand, thus an adverse sales volume variance is consistent with a favourable sales price variance given the price increase.

Better quality materials are being purchased by Mr Beech and, given this was not foreseen at the time of the budget, then it may explain a higher price resulting in an adverse materials price variance. Conversely, however, with better materials there may be less waste and thus it may have contributed to the favourable materials usage variance.

The lower skilled labour may account for the favourable labour rate variance but may also account for the adverse labour efficiency variance as less skilled labour may take longer to complete a given task. Also if new labour is introduced there may be an initial learning effect.

The impact of the efficiency variance is magnified by the variable and fixed overhead efficiency variances as they are directly related to the labour efficiency variance. The meaning of the fixed overhead efficiency variance is questionable however. By definition fixed overheads do not vary with labour hours and this variance merely 'balances the books' in an absorption costing system.

The fixed overhead expenditure variance is significant and requires further consideration. This is particularly the case if it involves discretionary expenditure which has been reduced but which may have a long-term impact on the business.

(c)   **Marginal costing**

Standard contribution/unit = £(220 − 80 − 32 − 16) = £92.

**Marginal cost statement** (this could be in summarised form)

|  |  | £ |  |
|---|---|---|---|
| Budgeted contribution (4,000 × £92) |  | 368,000 |  |
| Sales volume contribution variance |  | 73,600 | (A) |
| (800 units × £92) |  |  |  |
| Standard contribution on actual sales |  | 294,400 |  |
| Sales price variance |  | 16,000 | (F) |
|  |  | 310,400 |  |

| Cost variances | Fav | Adv |
|---|---|---|
|  | £ | £ |
| Material price |  | 24,000 |
| Material usage | 32,000 |  |
| Labour rate | 16,000 |  |
| Labour efficiency |  | 12,800 |

| | | | |
|---|---|---|---|
| Variable overhead expenditure | 4,000 | | |
| Variable overhead efficiency | | 6,400 | |
| | 52,000 | 43,200 | 8,800 (F) |
| Actual contribution | | | 319,200 |
| Budgeted fixed overhead | | 256,000 | |
| Fixed overhead expenditure variance (favourable) | | 60,000 | |
| Actual fixed overheads | | | 196,000 |
| Actual profit | | | 123,200 |

| Reconciliation | £ |
|---|---|
| Absorption costing profit | 148,800 |
| Fixed costs in additional closing stocks (400 units × £64) | (25,600) |
| Marginal costing profit | 123,200 |

### Tutorial note

The absorption costing profit is higher than the marginal costing profit because closing stocks are higher than opening stocks of finished goods. Consequently, with absorption some fixed overhead costs are carried forward in the stock value whereas in marginal costing all fixed overhead costs are charged against profit in the current period.

Thus some of the 'success' of Mr. Beech in increasing profit arises from the fact that fixed overheads of £25,600 are not being written off in the current month but are being carried forward as part of closing stock, notwithstanding that they are period costs and are thus sunk costs. Unless sales can be increased this position is unsustainable.

Nevertheless, some improvement has been made as the previous contribution was £312,800 [3,400 × (£220 – 128)], taking the budget as the historic norm. This is lower than the £319,200 achieved by Mr. Beech. The difference is, however, much lower than would be implied by the absorption costing statement.

| ACCA marking scheme | | |
|---|---|---|
| | | Marks |
| (a) | 1 mark for each variance (including Fixed overhead capacity nil variance) Budgeted profit Standard profit Reconciliation to actual profit | 14 |
| (b) | Effect on profitability Comments on motivation (1 mark for each explained profit) Comments on explaining variances (1 mark for each explained point) | 6 |
| (c) | 1 mark for each of correct calculations relating to budgeted contribution, standard contribution on actual sales, actual contribution, appropriate inclusion of fixed overheads (maximum 3) Reconciliation Comments on marginal costing (2 marks for each explained point) | 5 |
| Total | | 25 |

## 43   BICYCLES

(a)   (i)

$$\text{Break-even point} = \frac{\text{Fixed costs}}{\text{Contribution per unit}}$$

Fixed costs = £1,200,000 + £340,000 = £1,540,000

Variable costs per unit (from Table 1) = (£45 + £15 + £15) = £75.

Contribution per unit = £190 - £75 = £115.

$$\text{Break-even point} = \frac{£1,540,000}{£115 \text{ per unit}} = 13,391 \text{ units}$$

(ii)   It is assumed that the Sales Manager, given his interest in break even, will calculate the profit using marginal costing principles.

|  |  | £000 |
|---|---|---:|
| Sales | 11,800 units × £190 | 2,242 |
| Variable costs | 11,800 units × £75 | 885 |
| Contribution |  | 1,357 |
| Fixed costs |  | 1,540 |
| Loss |  | (183) |

(b)   (i)

**Manufacturing fixed overhead volume variance**:

| | |
|---|---:|
| Budgeted production volume | 20,000 units |
| Actual production volume | 16,800 units |
| Volume variance in units | 3,200 units   (A) |

Manufacturing fixed overhead recovery rate (from Table 1)

$$\frac{£1,200,000}{20,000} = £1,200,000 = £60 \text{ per unit}$$

**Volume variance in £** = 3,200 units (A) × £60 = **£192,000 (A).**

The volume variance is caused by the actual production level for the period falling below the production volume that was used to compute the fixed overhead recovery rate, in this case the budgeted volume. It is an under-recovery of fixed overhead, which the company must charge against the profits for the period. It occurs because a standard absorption costing system charges fixed overhead costs to products on a unit rate. It does not specifically represent an extra cost or a 'real' loss to the company, as these fixed costs would be incurred anyway. However, since fixed overheads incurred have not been fully recovered, because of the shortfall in production volume, the un-recovered amount is written off against profits for the period.

(ii)   *Tutorial note*: It is most unusual to absorb fixed sales overhead into the cost of sales. It is much more usual to treat fixed sales and administration overheads as period costs, and write them off against profits in the period they arise. The only variances are therefore expenditure variances.

| *Variable selling overhead:* | £000 | |
|---|---:|---|
| 11,800 units of sale | | |
| Overhead expenditure should be (11,800 × £15 per unit) | 177 | |
| Actual variable selling overhead expenditure | 138 | |
| Variable selling overhead expenditure variance | 39 | (F) |

| *Fixed selling overhead:* | £000 | |
|---|---:|---|
| Budgeted expenditure | 340 | |
| Actual expenditure | 376 | |
| Fixed selling overhead expenditure variance | 36 | (A) |

> ***Tutorial note:*** Should you wish to calculate a fixed sales overhead volume variance, it would be the difference between actual and budgeted sales volume (= 20,000 – 11,800 units) multiplied by the budgeted fixed sales overhead cost per unit (= 340/20 = £17). The fixed sales overhead volume variance would then be 8,200 units (A) × £17 = £139,400 (A). However, it must be stressed that this would be an unusual variance to come across in practice.

(c) ***Tutorial note:*** The reconciliation must allow for the fact that the profit of £72,000 is based on absorption costing principles, and the loss of £183,000 is based on marginal costing principles. The absorption costing profit is higher because some fixed overheads are carried forward in closing stock values, and are not charged against the profit of the current period.

|  | | £000 |
|---|---|---|
| Predicted loss, Sales Manager | | (183) |
| Expenditure variances: | | |
| Manufacturing | 48 (A) | |
| Variable sales | 39 (F) | |
| Fixed sales | 36 (A) | |
| | | 45 (A) |
| | | (228) |
| Fixed overhead carried forward in closing stock value (5,000 units at £60) | | 300 (F) |
| Actual profit recorded, absorption costing | | 72 |

An explanation of why an actual profit is revealed when a loss was anticipated by the sales manager is contained within the reconciliation above. The reconciliation is achieved when all the differences between the two statements are accounted for. This involves expenditure variances, which were not in the sales manager's budgeted statement but which are in the actual profit statement.

Finally, and most significantly, a variable costing statement applies only variable manufacturing costs to stock values. An absorption costing statement, which the company uses for reporting actual results, values stock at full manufacturing costs. The production and sales levels for the period imply 5,000 units were added to stock, therefore a difference between the two stock values accounts for a difference in profit. The absorption costing statement is adjusted (relieved of cost) by fixed overhead carried forward in the increased stock value. That is 5,000 units at £60 per unit fixed overhead rate, £300,000. Thus the loss anticipated by the sales manager becomes a profit in the actual results reported.

| ACCA marking scheme | | | Marks |
|---|---|---|---|
| (a) | (i) | Break even point calculation | 2 |
| | (ii) | Budgeted loss | 2 |
| | | | 4 |
| (b) | (i) | Variance calculation | 2 |
| | | Explanation | 3 |
| | (ii) | 1 mark for each variance, including mention or calculation of sales overhead volume variance | 3 |
| | | | 8 |
| (c) | | Expenditure variances | 2 |
| | | Overheads in stock | 2 |
| | | Achieving correct reconciliation | 2 |
| | | Explanation | 2 |
| | | | 8 |
| Total | | | 20 |

## 44    PAN-OCEAN CHEMICALS

(a)    (i)    **Direct materials mix variance:**

*Method 1 of calculation*

| Standard cost per batch: | | | £ |
|---|---|---|---|
| S1: | 8 kg × £0.3 | = | 2.4 |
| S2: | 5 kg × £0.5 | = | 2.5 |
| S3: | 3 kg × £0.4 | = | 1.2 |
| | 16 kg: | | 6.1 |

| | *Actual usage* | *Standard price* | *Actual usage at standard price* |
|---|---|---|---|
| | kg | £ | £ |
| S1 | 8,284 | 0.3 | 2,485.2 |
| S2 | 7,535 | 0.5 | 3,767.5 |
| S3 | 3,334 | 0.4 | 1,333.6 |
| | 19,153 | | 7,586.3 |

***Actual usage in standard mix*:**

| | *Actual usage* | *Standard mix* | *Actual usage in standard mix* |
|---|---|---|---|
| | | | kg |
| S1 | | (8) | 9,576.5 |
| S2 | | (5) | 5,985.3 |
| S3 | | (3) | 3,591.3 |
| Total | 19,153 | | 19,153.0 |

Standard cost of input per kg: £6.1/16 kg = £0.38125

Input in standard mix = 19,153 kg × £0.31825 = £7,302.1

| | £ |
|---|---|
| Actual usage/mix at standard price | 7,586.3 |
| Standard mix at standard price | 7,302.1 |
| Mix variance | 284.2    (A) |

*Method 2 of calculation*

| | *Actual usage* | | *Actual usage in standard mix* | *Mix variance* | *Standard cost per kg* | *Mix variance* |
|---|---|---|---|---|---|---|
| | kg | | kg | kg | £ | £ |
| S1 | 8,284 | (8) | 9,576.5 | 1,292.5 F | 0.30 | 387.8 F |
| S2 | 7,535 | (5) | 5,985.3 | 1,549.7 A | 0.50 | 774.9 A |
| S3 | 3,334 | (3) | 3,591.2 | 257.2 F | 0.40 | 102.9 F |
| Total | 19,153 | | 19,153.0 | | | 284.2 A |

**Direct materials yield variance:**

Standard cost of input per kg 6.1/16 = £0.38125.

| 15,408 kg of output | should use (× 10/9) | 17,120 of input materials (kg) |
|---|---|---|
| | did use | 19,153 of input materials (kg) |
| Yield variance (in kg) | | 2,033  (A) of input materials (kg) |

| Standard price per kg | £0.38125 |
|---|---|
| Yield variance (in £) | £775.1  (A) |

**Materials usage variance:**

Usage variance = Yield variance + Mix variance

= 775.1 A + 284.2 (A)

= £1,059.3A

*Tutorial note:* Proof of usage variance

Actual production of 15,408kgs required input of (10/9) × 15,408 = 17,120 kgs. This can be divided into standard usage for each material.

|  |  | Standard usage kg | Actual usage kg | Usage variance kg | Standard price per kg £ | Usage variance £ |
|---|---|---|---|---|---|---|
| S1 | (8) | 8,560 | 8,284 | 276 (F) | 0.30 | 82.8 (F) |
| S2 | (5) | 5,350 | 7,535 | 2,185 (A) | 0.50 | 1,092.5 (A) |
| S3 | (3) | 3,210 | 3,334 | 124 (A) | 0.40 | 49.6 (A) |
|  |  | 17,120 | 19,153 |  |  | 1,059.3 (A) |

(ii) **Labour cost variances**

Standard labour cost for 1 kg of output = £5/(90% of 16) = £5/14.4

= £0.3472 per kg

Rate variance: 6,916 − (1,235 × 5) = £741A

Efficiency variance (1,235 × 5) − (15,408 × 0.3472) = £825A

Total variance = 6,916 − (15,408 × 0.3472) = 825A + 741A = £1,566A.

*Tutorial note:* Alternative methods of calculation

|  |  | £ |  |
|---|---|---|---|
| 1,235 hours | should cost (× £5) | 6,175 | |
|  | did cost | 6,916 | |
| Rate variance |  | 741 | (A) |

|  |  | | |
|---|---|---|---|
| 15,408 units of output | should take (/14.4) | 1,069.72 | hours |
|  | did take | 1,235.00 | hours |
| Efficiency variance (in hours) |  | 165.28 | hours (A) |
| Standard rate per hour |  | £5 | |
| Efficiency variance (in £) |  | £826.4 | (A) |

This is the same amount as calculated by the other method, except with a small rounding difference.

(b) The total mix variance measured in quantity is zero since the expected mix is based on the total quantity actually used and hence the difference between total expected and total actual is nil.

(c) **Analysis of variance for Pan-Ocean Chemicals**

**Circulation:** Pan-Ocean Chemicals: Senior Management

**Author:**

**Date:** xx/xx/xx

**Subject: Variances**

**General**

The appendix to this report (results in part (a)) details mix, yield and usage variances for materials and rate and efficiency variances for labour over the last seven days. The purpose of this report is to explain what is meant by the analysis undertaken and to interpret the results derived.

## Materials variances

Materials variances can be categorised in four ways: usage, mix, yield and price. We are concerned only with mix and yield for the purposes of this report.

The three types of material used to produce Synthon (S1, S2 and S3) are not always used in the same proportions. Whilst it is the intention of the production team to use a constant or standard mix, this is not always achieved. In practice, the proportions of input chemicals used can vary for many reasons, mostly associated with the physical properties of the chemicals (which need not concern us here). To the extent that the standard mix is not used in the production of Synthon, then mix variances arise which simply record to what extent the standard mix has not been followed.

Materials yield variances record the differences arising in what inputs should have been used for the output achieved against what inputs have actually been used. Essentially, yield variances are a description of how efficiently inputs have been used.

The adverse yield variance should give rise to some concern since such results indicate an inefficient use of inputs against what was expected. The adverse variance may have arisen, for example, because of a batch of poor quality input chemicals or because of inefficient working practices which have led to a significant degree of spoilage.

## Labour variances

The labour rate variance has a simple interpretation, in that it reflects changes in the hourly rate paid to workers during the year that are not reflected in the standard cost details. In the case of Pan Ocean, a wage increase from £5 per hour to £5.60 per hour took place. It is possible that the standard rate reflects an average of a variety of rates and that the variance arose because of an unexpected change of higher paid workers undertaking the tasks of lower paid workers. No information is given on the possible mix of rates of pay used.

The labour efficiency variance reflects an assessment of the difference from the standard allocation in the time that was booked to a batch by the workers involved. In other words, the work undertaken on a batch over a weekly period was longer (because the variance was adverse) than that expected in the standard. This may have arisen because of inferior quality of input materials being used, or the introduction of new equipment or procedures.

## Final comments

Variances of any type should be a signal for some sort of investigative action by management. This can involve either looking to see how the variances have arisen or re-assessing the suitability of the standards that have been set. It might have to be accepted that the standard by which materials and labour performance is being measured might not be an accurate one.

Recognition should also be given to the fact that new employees might have been deployed, in which case there will be some inefficiency as they go through the learning curve period. This would also arise in a situation where new chemicals are being used, or new processes to be learnt, such that – again – employees would not be fully familiar with their tasks.

| ACCA marking scheme | | |
|---|---|---|
| *Marking guide* | | *Marks* |
| (a) | Materials usage variance | 1 |
| | Materials mix variance | 3 |
| | Materials yield variance | 3 |
| | Labour rate variance | 2 |
| | Labour efficiency variance | 2 |
| | | 11 |

| | | | |
|---|---|---|---|
| (b) | Explanation of equivalence of total mix variances | | 3 |
| (c) | Explanation of mix and yield variances | 5 | |
| | Up to 2 marks each for identification of possible | | |
| | reasons for the variances calculated in part (a) | | 6 |
| | | | 11 |
| Total | | | 25 |

## 45 CARAT

### Key answer tips

This question is largely a straightforward test of your ability to calculate variances, including materials mix and yield variances, and labour variances when idle time is recorded. However, do not overlook part (d) of the question: there are 7 marks available for a description of the different types of standard cost. The answer here describes a basic, current, attainable and ideal standard. It would also be relevant to answer the question by discussing 'ex post' and 'ex ante' standards, as a means of separating planning and operational variances.

(a)    Standard cost and standard contribution

| | £ | £ |
|---|---|---|
| Standard sales price | | 12.00 |
| Material A: (2.5 × £1.70) | 4.25 | |
| Material B: (1.5 × £1.20) | 1.80 | |
| Labour: (0.45 × £6.00) | 2.70 | |
| | | 8.75 |
| Standard contribution | | 3.25 |

*Calculation of variances*

(i)    *Sales variances*

| | £ | |
|---|---|---|
| 48,000 units should sell for (× £12) | 576,000 | |
| They did sell for | 580,800 | |
| Sales price variance | **4,800** | **(F)** |

| | Units | |
|---|---|---|
| Budgeted sales volume | 50,000 | |
| Actual sales volume | 48,000 | |
| Sales volume variance | 2,000 | (A) |

| | | |
|---|---|---|
| Standard contribution/unit | £3.25 | |
| Sales volume contribution variance | **£6,500** | **(A)** |

(ii)    *Materials variances*

| **Material A price variance** | £ | |
|---|---|---|
| 121,951 kg should cost (× £1.70) | 207,317 | |
| They did cost | 200,000 | |
| Material A price variance | **7,317** | **(F)** |

| **Material B price variance** | | £ |
|---|---|---|
| 67,200 kg should cost (× £1.20) | | 80,640 |
| They did cost | | 84,000 |
| Material A price variance | | **3,360**   (A) |

*Mix variance*

The standard mix is 2.5kg of A for each 1.5kg of B, i.e. 62.5% Material A and 37.5% Material B.

| | Actual quantities used kg | | Actual quantities in standard mix kg | Mix variance kg | Standard price £ | Mix variance £ |
|---|---|---|---|---|---|---|
| Material A | 121,951 | (62.5%) | 118,219 | 3,732 (A) | 1.70 | 6,344 (A) |
| Material B | 67,200 | (37.5%) | 70,932 | 3,732 (F) | 1.20 | 4,478 (F) |
| | 189,151 | | 189,151 | | | 1,866 (A) |

| | | 48,000 units should use kg | Actual quantities in standard mix kg | Yield variance kg | Standard price £ | Yield variance £ |
|---|---|---|---|---|---|---|
| Material A | (× 2.5 kg) | 120,000 | 118,219 | 1,781 (F) | 1.70 | 3,027 (F) |
| Material B | (× 1.5 kg) | 72,000 | 70,932 | 1,068 (F) | 1.20 | 1,282 (F) |
| | | | | | | 4,309 (F) |

***Tutorial note:*** It is unusual to be required to separate the yield variance into an amount for each of the materials individually, but this is what the question asks for. The yield variance would normally be calculated as a single total figure, as follows.

The standard cost per kg of material for A and B together is:

(£4.25 + £1.80)/(2.5kg + 1.5kg) = £6.05/4kg = £1.5125 per kg.

| | kg |
|---|---|
| 48,000 units of ZP should use (× 4kg) | 192,000 |
| They did use | 189,151 |
| Total yield variance | 2,849   (F) |

| | |
|---|---|
| Standard cost per kg | £1.5125 |
| Material yield variance | **£4,309**   (F) |

(iii)   *Labour variances*

| | £ |
|---|---|
| 19,200 hours should cost (× £6.00) | 115,200 |
| They did cost | 117,120 |
| Material A price variance | **1,920**   (A) |

*Idle time variance* = (19,200 – 18,900) hours = 300 hours (A).

At the standard rate per hour, the idle time variance =

300 hours (A) × £6.00 = **£1,800 (A).**

| **Labour efficiency variance** | *Hours* | |
|---|---|---|
| 48,000 units of ZP should take (× 0.45 hours) | 21,600 | |
| They did use | 18,900 | |
| Total yield variance | 2,700 | (F) |
| Standard rate/hour | £6 | |
| Labour efficiency variance | **£16,200** | **(F)** |

(b)  Budgeted contribution = 50,000 units × £3.25 = £162,500.

Budgeted gross profit = £162,500 - £62,500 = £100,000.

| | £ | £ | £ | |
|---|---|---|---|---|
| Budgeted gross profit | | | 100,000 | |
| Budgeted fixed production overhead | | | 62,500 | |
| Budgeted contribution | | | 162,500 | |
| Sales volume contribution variance | | 6,500 (A) | | |
| Sales price variance | | 4,800 (F) | | |
| | | | 1,700 | (A) |
| Actual sales less standard variable cost of sales | | | 160,800 | |
| Variable cost variances: | (F) | (A) | | |
| Material A price | 7,317 | | | |
| Material B price | | 3,360 | | |
| Material B mix | | 6,344 | | |
| Material A mix | 4,478 | | | |
| Material A yield | 3,027 | | | |
| Material B yield | 1,282 | | | |
| Labour rate | | 1,920 | | |
| Labour idle time | | 1,800 | | |
| Labour efficiency | 16,200 | | | |
| | 32,304 | 13,424 | 18,880 | (F) |
| Actual contribution | | | 179,680 | |
| Budgeted fixed production overhead | | 62,500 | | |
| Fixed production overhead expenditure variance | | 1,500 (A) | | |
| Actual fixed production overhead | | | 64,000 | |
| Actual gross profit | | | 115,680 | |

(c)  The **favourable material A price variance** indicates that the actual price per kilogram was less than standard. Possible explanations include buying lower quality material, buying larger quantities of material A and thereby gaining bulk purchase discounts, a change of supplier, and using an out-of-date standard.

The **adverse material A mix variance** indicates that more of this material was used in the actual input than indicated by the standard mix. The favourable material price variance suggests this may be due to the use of poorer quality material (hence more was needed than in the standard mix), or it might be that more material A was used because it was cheaper than expected.

The **favourable material A yield variance** indicates that more output was produced from the quantity of material used than expected by the standard. This increase in yield is unlikely to be due to the use of poorer quality material: it is more likely to be the result of employing more skilled labour, or introducing more efficient working practices.

It is only appropriate to calculate and interpret material mix and yield variances if quantities in the standard mix can be varied.

It has also been argued that calculating yield variances for each material is not useful, as yield is related to output overall rather than to particular materials in the input mix. A further complication is that mix variances for individual materials are inter-related and so an explanation of the increased use of one material cannot be separated from an explanation of the decreased use of another.

The **unfavourable labour rate variance** indicates that the actual hourly rate paid was higher than standard. Possible explanations for this include hiring staff with more experience and paying them more (this is consistent with the favourable overall direct material variance), or implementing an unexpected pay increase. The **favourable labour efficiency variance** shows that fewer hours were worked than standard. Possible explanations include the effect of staff training, the use of better quality material (possibly on Material B rather than on Material A), employees gaining experience of the production process, and introducing more efficient production methods. The **adverse idle time variance** may be due to machine breakdowns; or a higher rate of production arising from more efficient working (assuming employees are paid a fixed number of hours per week).

(d)    The **theory of motivation** suggests that having a clearly defined target results in better performance than having no target at all, that targets need to be accepted by the staff involved, and that more demanding targets increase motivation provided they remain accepted. It is against this background that basic, ideal, current and attainable standards can be discussed.

A **basic standard** is one that remains unchanged for several years and is used to show trends over time. Basic standards may become increasingly easy to achieve as time passes and hence, being undemanding, may have a negative impact on motivation. Standards that are easy to achieve will give employees little to aim at.

**Ideal standards** represent the outcome that can be achieved under perfect operating conditions, with no wastage, inefficiency or machine breakdowns. Since perfect operating conditions are unlikely to occur for any significant period, ideal standards will be very demanding and are unlikely to be accepted as targets by the staff involved as they are unlikely to be achieved. Using ideal standards as targets is therefore likely to have a negative effect on employee motivation.

**Current standards** are based on current operating conditions and incorporate current levels of wastage, inefficiency and machine breakdown. If used as targets, current standards will not improve performance beyond its current level and their impact on motivation will be a neutral one.

**Attainable standards** are those that can be achieved if operating conditions conform to the best that can be practically achieved in terms of material use, efficiency and machine performance. Attainable standards are likely to be more demanding than current standards and so will have a positive effect on employee motivation, provided that employees accept them as achievable.

| ACCA marking scheme | | Marks |
|---|---|---|
| (a) | Sales volume contribution variance | 1 |
| | Sales price variance | 1 |
| | Material price variances | 1 |
| | Material mix variances | 2 |
| | Material yield variances | 2 |

|  |  |  |
|---|---|---|
|  | Labour rate and efficiency variances | 1 |
|  | Idle time variance | <u>1</u> |
|  | Marks available | <u>9</u> |
|  | Maximum awarded | <u>8</u> |
| (b) | Budgeted gross profit | 1 |
|  | Budgeted contribution | 1 |
|  | Fixed production overhead expenditure variance | 1 |
|  | Actual gross profit | 1 |
|  | Format of operating statement | <u>1</u> |
|  |  | <u>5</u> |
| (c) | Material price, mix and yield variances | 3 |
|  | Labour rate and efficiency variances | <u>2</u> |
|  |  | <u>5</u> |
| (d) | Basic standard | 1 |
|  | Ideal standard | 2 |
|  | Current standard | 2 |
|  | Attainable standard | <u>2</u> |
|  |  | <u>7</u> |
| Total |  | <u>25</u> |

## 46   FOOD MANUFACTURER

### Key answer tips

You are given an original budget, followed by some post-budget planning changes, and then actual figures. This should lead you into thinking along the lines of planning and operational variances. However, four things point towards these being required as part of the discussion in (c) rather than as an explicit part of the variance analysis in (b):

- the question states that the original budget is to be used as a reference point

- there is no detail about the changes to the methods of working

- there is no mention of planning and operational variances in requirement (b)

- the budget prepared in (a) is based upon the original figures.

So parts (a) and (b) are standard budget/variance analysis computations. Whilst the examiner has incorporated some of his workings in the discussion in (c), you are best advised to set these out clearly following your answer to (b).

It is in part (c) that you should make use of the information regarding post-budget planning changes. Start with an overall summary of the picture painted by the analysis in (b), then look at individual variances, tying them in to the changes where possible. You must also address the specific areas required by the question, interrelationships and overheads.

(a)   Actual sales were £1,080,000, but the sale price was (× 4.50/5.00) of the budgeted price. The actual sales at the budgeted price were therefore £1,080,000 × (5.00/4.50) = £1,200,000.

|  | Flexed budget | | Actual | | Variance |
|---|---|---|---|---|---|
| Units | 240,000 | | 240,000 | | |
|  | £000 | £000 | £000 | £000 | £000 |
| Sales | | 1,200 | | 1,080 | 120 A |
| Ingredients (40%) | 480 | | 520 | | 40 A |
| Labour and energy (10%) | <u>120</u> | | <u>110</u> | | 10 F |
|  | | <u>600</u> | | <u>630</u> | |
| Contribution | | 600 | | 450 | |
| Fixed overheads | | <u>300</u> | | <u>340</u> | 40 A |
| Profit | | <u>300</u> | | <u>110</u> | <u>190</u> A |

*Note:* The answer only specifically required the flexible budget (flexed budget).

(b) *Workings*

| | |
|---|---|
| Budgeted ingredients cost | £400,000 |
| Price per kg | £0.40 |
| Budgeted kg (400,000/0.40) | 1,000,000 |
| Kg of ingredients in each pack | 5 |
| Budgeted number of packs (1,000,000/5) | 200,000 |
| Actual sales by volume | Sales = £1,080,000a £4.50/pack = 240,000 packs |

Actual ingredients used £520,000/£0.375 per kg = 1,386,667 kg.

| | kg |
|---|---|
| 240,000 packs should use (× 5) | 1,200,000 |
| but did use | 1,386,667 |
| Usage variance | 186,667 kg (A) |

| | |
|---|---|
| Standard price per kg | £0.40 |
| Usage variance in £ | £74,667 (A) |

| | £ |
|---|---|
| 1,386,667 kg should cost (× £0.40) | 554,667 |
| but did cost | 520,000 |
| Ingredient price variance | 34,667 F |

An overall reconciliation of profit is as follows:

| | £000 | £000 | |
|---|---|---|---|
| Budget profit | | 200.0 | |
| Sales volume contribution variance | | 100.0 | F |
| Budget profit for actual sales | | 300.0 | |
| Sales price variance | 120.0 A | | |
| Ingredient usage variance | 74.7 A | | |
| Ingredient price variance | 34.7 F | | |
| Labour and energy variance | 10.0 F | | |
| Overhead expenditure variance | 40.0 A | | |
| | | 190.0 | A |
| Actual profit | | 110.0 | |

(c) **Commentary**

The budgeted **sales volume** was 200,000 packs, whereas 240,000 packs were actually sold, a volume increase of 20%. The material, labour and energy costs are dealt with as totally variable costs. This results in the contribution margin (using the original budget) being £2.50 per pack (£1,000,000–£400,000–£100,000)/200,000. It can be seen that the increased volume earned £100,000 extra standard contribution (40,000 × £2.50) compared to the original budget. The **price reduction** of 50p per pack, however, resulted in lower sales revenue - and lower profits by £120,000. It would be useful to examine the sales price and volume variances together because of the interrelationship between them. The price reduction will have had an impact on the volume sold and this, which was probably anticipated, should be noted by the management. This marketing tactic of trading off price and volume (moving along the demand curve) does not appear to have been entirely successful, but we have no information about the experiences of other manufacturers of similar products. There could have been an unexpected downturn of the whole market. For example, the position could have been worse if the company had not decided to reduce the price. To investigate further they should, perhaps, look outside the organisation for more market intelligence.

The actual total **cost of material** exceeded that which was planned by £40,000. It is possible to analyse this difference further from the information supplied. The price reduction obtained was worth £34,667, a favourable variance. A substantial adverse usage variance of £74,667 occurred. The purchasing department would appear to have succeeded in making purchases of ingredients at favourable prices. If, however, after further investigation the ingredient usage variance is found to be due to waste caused by poorer quality purchases, this has been a false economy. This is a further example of possible interrelationships among variances and should be noted to inform future decisions on ingredient sourcing. It is not appropriate from current information to jump to conclusions about poor quality ingredients; theft or an error in the figures collected could be the cause. If, however, the ingredients are of a poorer quality then there may also be long-term repercussions in subsequent sales of these or other products, another example of interrelationships between the variances which should be borne in mind.

The labour and energy costs show a small favourable variance so the changed method of working has made a difference, providing these are completely variable costs. The actual costs incurred were more than the original budget, but less than the budget when it is flexed for the increased volume. From the information given, it is not possible to isolate labour and energy variances separately. Nor is it possible to identify rate and efficiency variances for these variable costs.

The actual **fixed overheads** were greater than the budget by £40,000. The detailed expenses should be consulted to identify any reasons for cost differences, to judge whether the costs are controllable and what action is needed, or whether the budget should be revised. Reduction of fixed overheads in the short-term may be particularly problematic. Scope to 'manage' the fixed costs (see expenditure variance) may occur when there is some potential to renegotiate prices or use resources more efficiently, perhaps resulting in some resources being disposed of (including staffing economies). However, some of the fixed costs may be uncontrollable in the short-term, for example, the rates applied to premises cannot change unless some premises are vacated. Such changes cannot be made immediately, and there may therefore be a lag in any economies in this area. The company is attempting to increase market share through increased sales, and although this should result in a greater total contribution to overall costs, this in itself does not reduce costs.

## 47    LINSIL

### Key answer tips

It is easy to get confused by part (a) of this question. Planning variances should compare the original standard cost (the 'ex ante' standard) with the revised standard cost (the 'ex post' standard). Operational variances should compare actual costs with the revised standard cost. In this question, the variances have not been calculated in this way, and we would take the view that they are incorrectly calculated. However, the question asks you to show how the variances *have been* calculated, not how they *should* be calculated.

If you can work out the solution to part (a), the rest of the question is more straightforward. Part (b) asks for traditional variance calculations, part (b) asks about the reasons for separating planning and operational variances, and part (d) asks about the factors to consider in deciding whether or not to investigate a variance – all basic study text topics.

(a)     **Revised standard costs**

| After 3% price increase: | direct material price | 2.30 × 1.03 = | £2.369/kg |
| After savings of 5%: | direct material usage | 3.00 × 0.95 = | 2.85 kg/unit |
| Adding 4% wage increase: | direct labour rate | 12.00 × 1.04 = | £12.48/hour |
| Adding back 10% decrease: | direct labour hours | 1.25/0.90 = | 1.3889 hrs/unit |

### Planning variances

*Direct materials*

Actual usage = 122,000 units × 2.80 kg = 341,600 kg.

Actual direct materials costs = 341,600 kg × £2.46/kg = £840,336.

| *Direct materials price* | £ | |
|---|---|---|
| Original standard: 341,600 kg should cost (× 2.30) | 785,680 | |
| Revised (ex post) standard: 341,600 kg should cost (× 2.369) | 809,250 | |
| Direct materials price planning variance | 23,570 | (A) |

| *Direct materials usage* | kg | |
|---|---|---|
| Original standard: 122,000 units should use (× 3.00) | 366,000 | |
| Revised (ex post) standard: 122,000 units should use (× 2.85) | 347,700 | |
| Direct materials usage planning variance in kg | 18,300 | (F) |
| Standard rate per kilogram (balancing figure) | £2.30 | |
| Direct materials usage planning variance in £ | £42,090 | (F) |

The standard rate per kilogram used to calculate the usage planning variance is the original (ex ante) standard price of £2.30. This is unusual, but has been used in this case.

*Direct labour*

Actual hours worked = 122,000 units × 1.30 hours /unit = 158,600 hours.

Actual direct labour costs = 158,600 hours × £12.60/hour = £1,998,360.

| *Direct labour rate* | £ | |
|---|---|---|
| Original standard: 158,600 hours should cost (× 12) | 1,903,200 | |
| Revised standard: 158,600 hours should cost (× 12.48) | 1,979,328 | |
| Direct labour rate planning variance | 76,128 | (A) |

| *Direct labour efficiency* | hours | |
|---|---|---|
| Original standard: 122,000 units should take (× 1.25) | 152,500 | |
| Revised standard: 122,000 units should take (× 1.3889) | 169,446 | |
| Direct labour efficiency planning variance in hours | 16,946 | (A) |
| Standard rate per hour (balancing figure) | £12 | |
| Direct labour efficiency planning variance in £ | £203,333 | (A) |

The standard rate per hour used to calculate the efficiency planning variance is the original (ex ante) standard rate of £12.00. This is unusual, but has been used in this case.

### Operational variances

*Direct materials*

| *Direct materials price* | £ | |
|---|---|---|
| 341,600 kg should cost (× 2.369) | 809,250 | |
| They did cost | 840,336 | |
| Direct materials price operational variance | 31,086 | (A) |

| *Direct materials usage* | kg | |
|---|---|---|
| 122,000 units should use (× 2.85) | 347,700 | |
| They did use | 341,600 | |
| Direct materials usage operational variance in kg | 6,100 | (F) |
| Standard rate per kilogram (balancing figure) | £2.30 | |
| Direct materials usage operational variance in £ | £14,030 | (F) |

The standard rate per kilogram used to calculate the usage operational variance is the original (ex ante) standard price of £2.30. This is most unusual, but has clearly been used in this case.

*Direct labour*

| | £ |
|---|---|
| *Direct labour rate* | |
| 158,600 hours should cost (× 12.48) | 1,979,328 |
| They did cost | 1,998,360 |
| Direct labour rate operational variance | 19,032 (A) |

| | hours |
|---|---|
| *Direct labour efficiency* | |
| 122,000 units should take (× 1.3889) | 169,446 |
| They did take | 158,600 |
| Direct labour efficiency operational variance in hours | 10,846 (F) |
| Standard rate per hour (balancing figure) | £12 |
| Direct labour efficiency operational variance in £ | £130,133 (F) |

The standard rate per hour used to calculate the efficiency operational variance is the original (ex ante) standard rate of £12.00. This is most unusual, but has clearly been used in this case.

(b) The direct material and direct cost variances based on the standard cost data applied during the three-month period can be found by adding the relevant planning and operational variances.

Direct material price variance = £23,570 (A) + £31,086 (A) = £54,656 (A)

Direct material usage variance = £42,090 (F) + £14,030 (F) = 56,120 (F)

Direct labour rate variance = £76,128 (A) + £19,032 (A) = £95,160 (A)

Direct labour efficiency variance = £203,333 (A) + £130,133 (F) = £73,200 (A).

*Alternative calculations*:

| | £ |
|---|---|
| *Direct materials price* | |
| 341,600 kg should cost (× 2.30) | 785,680 |
| They did cost | 840,336 |
| Direct materials price variance | 54,656 (A) |

| | kg |
|---|---|
| *Direct materials usage* | |
| 122,000 units should use (× 3) | 366,000 |
| They did use | 341,600 |
| Direct materials usage variance in kg | 24,400 (F) |
| Standard rate per kilogram | £2.30 |
| Direct materials usage variance in £ | £56,120 (F) |

*Direct labour*

| | £ |
|---|---|
| *Direct labour rate* | |
| 158,600 hours should cost (× 12) | 1,903,200 |
| They did cost | 1,998,360 |
| Direct labour rate variance | 95,160 (A) |

| | hours |
|---|---|
| *Direct labour efficiency* | |
| 122,000 units should take (× 1.25) | 152,500 |
| They did take | 158,600 |
| Direct labour efficiency variance in hours | 6,100 (A) |
| Standard rate per hour | £12 |
| Direct labour efficiency variance in £ | £73,200 (A) |

(c)     If an operating statement had been prepared which did not take into account the changes that were needed to keep the standard cost data relevant, it would have reported the direct material and direct labour variances calculated in part (b). These variances contain both controllable and uncontrollable elements. For the variances to be more useful, these elements can be reported separately.

Each variance was separated into a planning variance and an operational variance. As a general rule, planning variances are not controllable, whereas operational variances could be controllable. Managers cannot be held responsible for variances over which they have no control and so their attention is focused on operational variances. For example, the operating statement shows that the labour efficiency variance consists of an adverse planning variance of £203,333 but a favourable operational variance of £130,133. If the controllable and uncontrollable elements had not been separated, an adverse variance of £73,200 would have been reported.

The planning variances indicate where investigation may result in an improvement in the planning and budgeting process. For example, if it could reasonably have been expected that a wage increase would be agreed at the start of the budget period, the anticipated increase should have been incorporated. The reason for the omission of the 3% increase in direct material price should be investigated: was it a case of forgetfulness or were budget figures not checked before the budgets were sent for approval?

(d)     The following factors might be considered in deciding whether to investigate a variance.

**Size**

Larger cost savings are likely to arise from taking action to correct large variances and a policy could be established of investigating all variances above a given size. Size can be linked to the underlying variable in percentage terms as a test of significance: for example, a policy could be established to investigate all variances of 5% or more.

**Adverse or favourable**

It is natural to concentrate on adverse variances in order to bring business operations back in line with budget. However, whether a variance is adverse or favourable should not influence the decision to investigate. The reasons for favourable variances should also be sought, since they may indicate the presence of budgetary slack or suggest ways in which the budgeting process could be improved. Favourable variances may also indicate areas where the budget is easy to achieve, suggesting that the motivational effect of a budget could be improved by introducing more demanding targets.

**Cost versus benefits**

If the expected cost of investigating a variance is likely to exceed any benefits expected to arise from its correction, it may be decided not to investigate.

**Historical pattern of variances**

A variance which is unusual when compared to historical patterns of variances may be considered worthy of investigation. Statistical tests of significance may be used to highlight such variances.

**Reliability and quality of data**

If data is aggregated or if the quality of the measuring and recording system is not as high as would be liked, there may be uncertainty about the benefits to arise from investigation of variances.

**Cumulative variances over time**

A variance might be investigated if the cumulative variances over time suggest that there is a continuing trend of averse (or favourable variances). The size of the variance in each period might not on its own be sufficient to justify investigation, but the continuing trend might indicate an underlying cause for the variances that should be investigated.

| ACCA marking scheme | | Marks |
|---|---|---|
| (a) | Revised standard costs | 3 |
| | Calculation of planning variances | 4 |
| | Calculation of operational variances | 4 |
| | | 11 |
| (b) | Direct material price variance | 1 |
| | Direct material usage variance | 1 |
| | Direct labour rate variance | 1 |
| | Direct labour efficiency variance | 1 |
| | | 4 |
| (c) | Controllable and uncontrollable variances | 2 |
| | Discussion of calculated variances | 3 |
| | | 5 |
| (d) | Up to 2 marks for each factor discussed | 5 |
| Total | | 25 |

## 48 MERMUS PLC

(a) The flexed budget will be based on the actual activity level of 90,000 units.

| | £ | £ |
|---|---|---|
| Sales: £950,000 × 90/95 = | | 900,000 |
| Cost of sales | | |
| Raw materials: 133,000 × 90/95 = | 126,000 | |
| Direct labour: 152,000 × 90/95 = | 144,000 | |
| Variable production overheads: 100,700 × 90/95 | 95,400 | |
| Fixed production overheads | 125,400 | |
| | ———— | |
| | | 490,800 |
| | | ———— |
| | | 409,200 |
| | | ———— |

(b) Raw materials cost total variance = 126,000 – 130,500 = £4,500 (Adverse)

Direct labour cost total variance = 144,000 – 153,000 = £9,000 (Adverse)

Fixed overhead absorption rate = 125,400/28,500 = £4.40 per machine hour

Standard machine hours for actual production = 28,500 × 90/95 = 27,000 hrs

Standard fixed overhead (actual production) = 27,000 × 4.4 = £118,800

Fixed overhead absorbed on actual hours = 27,200 × 4.4 = £119,680

Fixed overhead efficiency variance = 118,800 – 119,680 = 880 (Adverse)

Fixed overhead absorbed on actual hours = 27,200 × 4.4 = £119,680

Fixed overhead absorbed on budgeted hours = 28,500 × 4.4 = £125,400

Fixed overhead capacity variance = 119,680 – 125,400 = £5,720 (Adverse)

Budgeted overhead expenditure = £125,400

Actual overhead expenditure = £115,300

Fixed overhead expenditure variance = 125,400 – 115,300 = £10,100 (Favourable)

(c)    **Raw materials cost variance**

The budgeted raw material cost for production of 95,000 units was £1.40 per unit (133,000/95,000) but the actual raw material cost for production of 90,000 units was £1.45 per unit (130,500/90,000). The raw material cost per unit may have increased either because more raw material per unit was used than budgeted, or because the price per unit of raw material was higher than budgeted. Calculation of the raw material price and usage sub-variances would indicate where further explanation should be sought.

**Fixed overhead efficiency variance**

The fixed overhead efficiency variance measures the extent to which more or less standard hours were used for the actual production than budgeted. In this case, a total of 27,200 machine hours were actually used, when only 27,000 standard machine hours should have been used. The difference may be due to poorer production planning than expected or to machine breakdowns.

**Fixed overhead expenditure variance**

The fixed overhead expenditure variance measures the extent to which budgeted fixed overhead differs from actual fixed overhead. Here, actual fixed overhead is £10,100 less than budgeted. This could be due to an error in forecasting fixed production overheads such as rent and power costs, or to a decrease in fixed production overheads, such as changing to a cheaper cleaning contractor.

(d)    Key purposes of a budgeting system that could be discussed include planning, co-ordination, communication, control, motivation and performance evaluation. Students were required only to discuss three key purposes.

**Planning**

One of the key purposes of a budgeting system is to require planning to occur. Strategic planning covers several years but a budget represents a financial plan covering a shorter period, i.e. a budget is an operational plan. Planning helps an organisation to anticipate key changes in the business environment that could potentially impact on business activities and to prepare appropriate responses. Planning also ensures that the budgeted activities of the organisation will support the achievement of the organisation's objectives.

**Co-ordination**

Many organisations undertake a number of activities which need to be co-ordinated if the organisation is to meet its objectives. The budgeting system facilitates this co-ordination since organisational activities and the links between them are thoroughly investigated during budget preparation, and the overall coherence between the budgeted activities is reviewed before the master budget is agreed by senior managers. Without the framework of the budgeting system, individual managers may be tempted to make decisions that are not optimal in terms of achieving organisational objectives.

**Communication**

The budgeting system facilitates communication within the organisation both vertically (for example between senior and junior managers) and horizontally (for example between different organisational functions). Vertical communication enables senior managers to ensure that organisational objectives are understood by employees at all levels. Communication also occurs at all stages of the budgetary control process, for example during budget preparation and during investigation of end-of-period variances.

### Control

One of the most important purposes of a budgeting system is to facilitate cost control through the comparison of budgeted costs and actual costs. Variances between budgeted and actual costs can be investigated in order to determine the reason why actual performance has differed from what was planned. Corrective action can be introduced if necessary in order to ensure that organisational objectives are achieved. A budgeting system also facilitates management by exception, whereby only significant differences between planned and actual activity are investigated.

### Motivation

The budgeting system can influence the behaviour of managers and employees, and may motivate them to improve their performance if the target represented by the budget is set at an appropriate level. An inappropriate target has the potential to be demotivating, however, and a key factor here is the degree of participation in the budget-setting process. It has been shown that an appropriate degree of participation can have a positive motivational effect.

### Performance evaluation

Managerial performance is often evaluated by the extent to which budgetary targets for which individual managers are responsible have been achieved. Managerial rewards such as bonuses or performance-related pay can also be linked to achievement of budgetary targets. Managers can also use the budget to evaluate their own performance and clarify how close they are to meeting agreed performance targets.

| ACCA marking scheme | | Marks |
|---|---|---|
| (a) | Sales and raw materials | 1 |
| | Direct labour and variable overheads | 1 |
| | Fixed overheads | 1 |
| | Flexed budget | 1 |
| | | 4 |
| (b) | Raw material total cost variance | 1 |
| | Direct labour total cost variance | 1 |
| | Fixed overhead absorption rate | 1 |
| | Fixed overhead efficiency variance | 2 |
| | Fixed overhead capacity variance | 2 |
| | Fixed overhead expenditure variance | 1 |
| | | 8 |
| (c) | Raw material total cost variance | 2 |
| | Fixed overhead efficiency variance | 2 |
| | Fixed overhead expenditure variance | 2 |
| | | 6 |
| (d) | Up to 3 marks per key function discussed | 9 |
| | Maximum | 7 |
| Total | | 25 |

## 49    BRK

(a)    Calculation of standard profit

Budgeted machine hours = $(10,000 \times 0.3) + (13,000 \times 0.6) + (9,000 \times 0.8) = 18,000$ hours

Overhead absorption rate = $81,000/18,000 = £4.50$ per machine hour

| Product | B (£) | R (£) | K (£) |
|---|---|---|---|
| Direct material | 5.40 (3 × 1.80) | 4.10 (1.25 × 3.28) | 4.85 (1.94 × 2.50) |
| Direct labour | 3.25 (0.5 × 6.50) | 5.20 (0.8 × 6.50) | 4.55 (0.7 × 6.50) |
| Fixed production overhead | 1.35 (0.3 × 4.50) | 2.70 (0.6 × 4.50) | 3.60 (0.8 × 4.50) |
| Standard cost | 10.00 | 12.00 | 13.00 |
| Selling price | 14.00 | 15.00 | 18.00 |
| Standard profit | 4.00 | 3.00 | 5.00 |

Budgeted sales quantity in standard mix at standard profit:

| Product | Quantity | Standard profit | £ |
|---|---|---|---|
| B | 10,000 | £4 | 40,000 |
| R | 13,000 | £3 | 39,000 |
| K | 9,000 | £5 | 45,000 |
| | 32,000 | | 124,000 |

Average standard profit per unit = $124,000/32,000 = £3.875$ per unit

Actual sales quantity in actual mix at actual selling price less standard cost:

| Product | Quantity | Actual selling price less standard cost | £ |
|---|---|---|---|
| B | 9,500 | (14.5 – 10.0) | 42,750 |
| R | 13,500 | (15.5 – 12.0) | 47,250 |
| K | 8,500 | (19.0 – 13.0) | 51,000 |
| | 31,500 | | 141,000 |

Actual sales quantity in actual mix at standard profit:

| Product | Quantity | Standard profit | £ |
|---|---|---|---|
| B | 9,500 | £4 | 38,000 |
| R | 13,500 | £3 | 40,500 |
| K | 8,500 | £5 | 42,500 |
| | 31,500 | | 121,000 |

Actual sales quantity in standard mix at standard profit:

Using the average standard profit per unit calculated earlier: 31,500 x 3.875 = £122,062

Sales price variance = 141,000 – 121,000 = £20,000 (F)
Sales volume profit variance = 121,000 – 124,000 = £3,000 (A)
Sales mix profit variance = 121,000 – 122,062 = £1,062 (A)
Sales quantity profit variance = 122,062 – 124,000 = £1,938 (A)

| Reconciliation | £ | £ | £ |
|---|---|---|---|
| Budgeted sales at standard profit | | | 124,000 |
| Sales price variance | | 20,000 (F) | |
| Sales mix profit variance | 1,062 (A) | | |
| Sales quantity profit variance | 1,938 (A) | | |
| Sales volume profit variance | | 3,000 (A) | |
| | | | 17,000 (F) |
| Actual sales at actual price less standard cost | | | 141,000 |

(b) The sales mix profit variance explains how the change in sales mix contributed to the sales volume profit variance. It compares the actual sales quantity in the actual mix with the actual sales quantity in the standard mix, valued at the standard profit per unit.

The adverse variance calculated in part (a) using the average standard profit per unit was £1,062, indicating that the actual sales mix contained more lower-margin products and fewer higher-margin products. The changes in the sales mix can be shown in tabular form, as follows.

| Product | Standard mix | Actual mix | Difference | Standard profit | £ |
|---|---|---|---|---|---|
| B | 9,844 | 9,500 | (344) | £4 | 1,376 (A) |
| R | 12,797 | 13,500 | 703 | £3 | 2,109 (F) |
| K | 8,859 | 8,500 | (359) | £5 | 1,795 (A) |
| | 31,500 | 31,500 | | | 1,062 (A) |

The difference column shows that more of Product R, with the lowest standard profit of £3 per unit, was sold than was budgeted for. Less of Products B and K, with the higher standard profits per unit, were sold than budgeted for. Calculation of the individual mix variances for Products B, R and K does not offer information which is any more useful than that contained in the 'difference' column.

Sales mix profit variance has significance only when products are inter-related and these relationships are taken into account at the planning stage. If the products sold are not inter-related, the mix variance offers no useful information, since it incorrectly implies that a possible cause of the sales volume profit variance is a change in the mix1. In fact, only deviations from the planned volumes for individual products need to be investigated if products are not inter-related. In this case the products are substitutes and so are inter-related. The individual sales mix profit variances may therefore be useful.

(c) A standard costing system requires preparation of standard costs, comparison of standard costs with actual costs, investigation of variances and instigation of corrective action if needed, and review of standard costs on a regular basis. Standard costs are predetermined unit costs arising under efficient operating conditions. Standard costing can be applied to repetitive or common operations where the input to produce a required output can be clearly specified.

**Preparation of standard costs**

Standards are required for amount of materials, labour and services required to perform a particular operation, and cost standards are compiled from the standard costs of the individual operations needed to produce a given product. The quantities and costs needed for each standard can be derived using the engineering approach or through the analysis of historical records.

The engineering approach requires a detailed study of each operation so that the materials, labour and equipment used in the operation can be verified by observation, for example by using time and motion studies.

Analysis of historical records can be carried out using quantitative analysis, including the high-low method, scattergraphs and regression analysis. Standards are set by these methods by averaging historical data and so there is a danger that past inefficiencies may be perpetuated. This approach to standard setting is widely used in practice[2].

### Variance analysis

Variances obtained by comparing standard costs with actual costs form the basis of cost control and support the use of responsibility accounting. A wide range of variances can be calculated, depending in part on the costing system employed. The causes of individual variances can be investigated if a variance is deemed to be significant, in order to inform the instigation of appropriate corrective action where necessary. Both favourable and adverse variances should be investigated, since useful information can be derived from both.

### Review of standard costs

Standard costs must be reviewed and updated if they are to retain their relevance to an organisation. The review should consider changes in the prices of inputs such as labour and materials as well as changes in working practices and production methods. The exception to this is the basic standard, which is left unchanged for long periods of time so that trends over time can be established. However, basic standards are not commonly used. It is more usual to find ideal, current and attainable standards being used and these all need regular review.

| ACCA marking scheme | | | |
|---|---|---|---|
| | | *Marks* | |
| (a) | Overhead absorption rate | 1 | |
| | Standard costs and standard profits | 3 | |
| | Sales price variance | 2 | |
| | Sales volume profit variance | 2 | |
| | Sales mix profit variance | 2 | |
| | Sales quantity profit variance | 2 | |
| | Profit reconciliation | 1 | |
| | | | 13 |
| (b) | Significance of sales mix profit variance | 3 | |
| | Comment on individual mix variances | 1 | |
| | | | 4 |
| (c) | Elements of a standard costing system | 2-3 | |
| | Preparation of standard costs | 2-3 | |
| | Variance analysis | 2-3 | |
| | Review of standards | 2-3 | |
| | Maximum | | 8 |
| Total | | | 25 |

# BUDGETING, BUDGETARY CONTROL AND DECISION-MAKING

## 50    ALL PREMIER SERVICES PLC

(a)    (i)

|  | X | Y | Z |
|---|---|---|---|
| Number of beds | 60 | 40 | 45 |
| Fee per bed per night £ | 225 | 200 | 170 |
| Assumed occupancy % | 65 | 80 | 100 |
| Occupied beds | 39 | 32 | 45 |
| Number of nights per week | 7 | 7 | 7 |

**Budgeted profit and loss statement per week**

|  | X | Y | Z | Total |
|---|---|---|---|---|
| Occupied beds | 39 | 32 | 45 |  |
|  | £ | £ | £ | £ |
| **Income** (see working 1) | 61,425 | 44,800 | 53,550 | 159,775 |
| Variable costs (working 2) | 16,305 | 11,892 | 14,215 | 42,412 |
| Fixed costs (60:40:45) – working 3 | 52,676 | 35,117 | 39,507 | 127,300 |
| **Total costs** | 68,981 | 47,009 | 53,772 | 169,712 |
| Income less costs | (7,556) | (2,209) | (172) | (9,937) |
| Cost per occupied bed | 1,769 | 1,469 | 1,194 |  |

*Workings*

(W1)    *Income*

X: 39 beds × £225/night × 7 nights = £61,425

Y: 32 beds × £200/night × 7 nights = £44,800

Z: 45 beds × £170/night × 7 nights = £53,550

(W2)    *Variable costs*

Total variable costs = £42,412.

Total income = £159,775.

Variable costs are therefore 0.26544829 of income.

(W3)    *Fixed costs*

Fixed costs = £127,300/145 beds = £877.931/bed.

(ii)

|  | X | Y | Z |
|---|---|---|---|
| Number of beds | 60 | 40 | 75 |
| Fee per bed per night £ | 225 | 200 | 170 |
| Assumed occupancy % | 80 | 95 | 100 |
| Occupied beds | 48 | 38 | 75 |
| Number of night per week | 7 | 7 | 7 |
| Price per bed per night | £336 | £266 | £525 |

**Budgeted profit and loss statement per week**

|  | X | Y | Z | Total |
|---|---|---|---|---|
| **Income** (working 4) | 75,600 | 53,200 | 89,250 | 218,050 |
| Variable costs (working 5) | 20,068 | 14,122 | 23,691 | 57,881 |
| Fixed costs (working 6) | 43,646 | 29,097 | 54,557 | 127,300 |
| **Total costs** | 63,714 | 43,219 | 78,248 | 185,181 |
| Income less costs | 11,886 | 9,982 | 11,002 | 32,869 |
| Cost per occupied bed | 1,327 | 1,137 | 1,043 | |

*Workings*

(W4) *Income*

X: 48 beds × £225/night × 7 nights = £75,600

Y: 38 beds × £200/night × 7 nights = £53,200

Z: 75 beds × £170/night × 7 nights = £89,250

(W5) *Variable costs*

Total variable costs = £57,881.

Total income = £218,050.

Variable costs are therefore 0.26544829 of income.

(W6) *Fixed costs*

Total number of beds = 60 + 40 + 75 = 175.

Fixed costs = £127,300/175 beds = £727.4286/bed.

(b)  (i)  **Ward Z patients from Wards X and Y**

The patients in Ward Z are existing patients and do not represent new admissions. For that reason, Ward Z only exists as a further outlet for Wards X and Y. This implies a degree of dependency in operations. Decisions concerning Ward Z cannot therefore be separated from the decisions concerning X and Y. It may well be the case that, given the hospital is private and presumably subject to competition, patients may choose All Premier Services because of the facilities offered in Ward Z that might be available elsewhere.

(ii)  **The relevance of the allocation bases**

Given that fixed overheads must be incurred irrespective of occupancy, then the fact that costs are allocated to unoccupied beds, irrespective of occupancy, is probably the correct approach. On the other hand, variable overheads are allocated on a fee earned per bed basis. The incorporation of fees into the allocation of variable overheads might reflect the fact that wards X and Y deal with patients with different medical conditions and costs. The fees charged by the hospital reflect this fact. The adjustment for occupancy through the fees earned allocation base reflects the fact that variable overheads relate directly to the consumption of additional resources when beds are occupied. For this reason, it is probably an appropriate allocation base.

(c)  The characteristics of a **responsibility accounting system** imply a well-organised system of budgetary control, such that individuals are personally accountable for their budget centres and there is a monitoring system which facilitates performance evaluation. The components of a well-organised system of control are:

1   A **hierarchy of budget centres** which mirror the lines of reporting within an organisation.

2   A **defined purpose to the budget centre** such that attached costs and revenues have an interpretation associated with the budget centre. Thus, if costs are

rising in catering services and this is a budget centre, then a course of action can be devised which outlines alternatives to the way current catering facilities are delivered.

3    **Cost and revenues** associated with a budget centre then become **the responsibility of the budget holder** to the extent that the budget holder can influence how the costs and revenues behave.

The **difficulties associated with non-profit organisations** are that the requirements for responsibility accounting are not easily met.  For example:

1    Non-profit organisations often do not have clearly defined objectives or the objectives may be multiple.  For example, local government offers a wide range of public services for which there are only fairly imprecise objectives.  To the extent that objectives are unclear, then responsibility will be hard to define because there is no clear link between inputs and outputs (objectives).

2    Many non-profit making organisations do not charge for their services and hence budget centres are then left monitoring rather that controlling costs.  For example, hospital resources are consumed according to clinical decisions, but budget holders are often not medical staff.

3    Value for money performance measures are sometimes used in the public sector that rely on measures relating to economy and efficiency.  Whilst economy and efficiency may be measured in money terms, effectiveness may not be.  Thus, non-financial objectives may be set off which may not be comparable between budget centres or to any overall objective.

4    Public services are often characterised by a high level of fixed costs over which there is little discretion or room to change.  Hence, responsibility is harder to define because change is difficult to implement

| ACCA marking scheme | | | | |
|---|---|---|---:|---:|
| | | | *Marks* | |
| (a) | (i) | calculation of costs incurred per bed in each ward | 5 | |
| | (ii) | calculation of costs incurred per bed in each ward | 5 | |
| | | | | 10 |
| (b) | (i) | detailed comment that ward z is serviced from wards x and y | 2 | |
| | (ii) | detailed comment of relevance of allocation bases | 3 | |
| | | | | 5 |
| (c) | | Up to 2 marks each for detailed points on responsibility accounting. | 6 | |
| | | Up to 2 marks each for detailed points on non-profit organisations | 6 | |
| | | Presentation and quality of argument | 2 | |
| | | Maximum marks available | 14 | |
| | | Maximum marks awarded | | 10 |
| Total | | | | 25 |

# 51    ACRED LIMITED

## Key answer points

Part (a) of the question calls for a lot of calculations and a clear presentation of the budgeted figures. You need to be well-organised to complete the solution within the time available. Note that part (a) of the question is worth just 13 marks, only one half of the total marks for the question. You should therefore beware of spending too much time getting the figures right in part (a) leaving yourself insufficient time to answer part (b) – which should be reasonably straightforward to answer.

(a)  (i)  **Acred Ltd: Production budget for 6 months to end of December 20X4**

| | July units | Aug units | Sept units | Oct units | Nov units | Dec units |
|---|---|---|---|---|---|---|
| Sales | 10,000 | 11,000 | 12,000 | 13,000 | 14,000 | 15,000 |
| Stock increase | 200 | 200 | 200 | 200 | 200 | 0 |
| Production | 10,200 | 11,200 | 12,200 | 13,200 | 14,200 | 15,000 |

(ii)  **Acred Ltd: Cash budget for 6 months to end of December 20X4**

| | July £ | Aug £ | Sept £ | Oct £ | Nov £ | Dec £ |
|---|---|---|---|---|---|---|
| **Receipts (W2)** | | | | | | |
| Cash sales | 30,000 | 33,000 | 36,000 | 39,000 | 42,000 | 45,000 |
| Credit sales | 90,000 | 90,000 | 99,000 | 108,000 | 117,000 | 126,000 |
| | 120,000 | 123,000 | 135,000 | 147,000 | 159,000 | 171,000 |
| **Payments** | | | | | | |
| Materials (W3) | 48,480 | 51,360 | 56,160 | 60,960 | 65,760 | 70,080 |
| Labour (W4) | 18,360 | 20,160 | 21,960 | 23,760 | 25,560 | 27,000 |
| Direct expenses (W5) | 12,240 | 13,440 | 14,640 | 15,840 | 17,040 | 18,000 |
| Fixed o'hds (W6) | 22,000 | 22,000 | 22,000 | 22,000 | 22,000 | 22,000 |
| Advertising | - | 95,000 | - | - | - | - |
| Interest | - | - | 30,000 | - | - | - |
| | 101,080 | 201,960 | 144,760 | 122,560 | 130,360 | 137,080 |
| **Receipts less payments** | 18,920 | (78,960) | (9,760) | 24,440 | 28,640 | 33,920 |
| **Opening cash** | 50,000 | 68,920 | (10,040) | (19,800) | 4,640 | 33,280 |
| **Closing cash** | 68,920 | (10,040) | (19,800) | 4,640 | 33,280 | 67,200 |

*Workings*

(W1) **Sales budget for 6 months to end of December 20X4**

| | June | July | Aug | Sept | Oct | Nov | Dec |
|---|---|---|---|---|---|---|---|
| Sales (units) | 10,000 | 10,000 | 11,000 | 12,000 | 13,000 | 14,000 | 15,000 |
| Sales price | £12 | £12 | £12 | £12 | £12 | £12 | £12 |
| Revenue (£) | 120,000 | 120,000 | 132,000 | 144,000 | 156,000 | 168,000 | 180,000 |

(W2) **Sales receipts**

| | June | July | Aug | Sept | Oct | Nov | Dec |
|---|---|---|---|---|---|---|---|
| Sales revenue | 120,000 | 120,000 | 132,000 | 144,000 | 156,000 | 168,000 | 180,000 |
| Cash sales (25%) | 30,000 | 30,000 | 33,000 | 36,000 | 39,000 | 42,000 | 45,000 |
| Credit sales (75%) | 90,000 | 90,000 | 99,000 | 108,000 | 117,000 | 126,000 | 135,000 |

(W3) **Material purchases**

| | June | July | Aug | Sept | Oct | Nov | Dec |
|---|---|---|---|---|---|---|---|
| Production (units) | 10,000 | 10,200 | 11,200 | 12,200 | 13,200 | 14,200 | 15,000 |
| Materials for production (kg) | 20,000 | 20,400 | 22,400 | 24,400 | 26,400 | 28,400 | 30,000 |

| | £ | £ | £ | £ | £ | £ | £ |
|---|---|---|---|---|---|---|---|
| Materials for production | 48,000 | 48,960 | 53,760 | 58,560 | 63,360 | 68,160 | 72,000 |
| | | | | | | | |
| Half delivered in month | 24,000 | 24,480 | 26,880 | 29,280 | 31,680 | 34,080 | |
| Closing stock delivered | 24,480 | 26,880 | 29,280 | 31,680 | 34,080 | 36,000 | |
| Total purchases in month | 48,480 | 51,360 | 56,160 | 60,960 | 65,760 | 70,080 | |
| Payable in | July | Aug | Sept | Oct | Nov | Dec | |

(W4) **Payments for labour**

Calculation of labour cost: production units × £1·80 per unit

(W5) **Payments for direct expenses**

Calculation of direct expenses: production units × £1·20 per unit

(W6) **Payments for fixed overheads**

Calculation of cash fixed overheads: £34,000 − £12,000 = £22,000 per month

Depreciation is excluded as a non-cash item.

(b) A **periodic budget** is one that is drawn up for a full budget period, such as one year. A new budget will not be introduced until the start of the next budget period, although the existing budget may be revised if circumstances deviate markedly from those assumed during the budget preparation period.

A **continuous or rolling budget** is one that is revised at regular intervals by adding a new budget period to the full budget as each budget period expires. A budget for one year, for example, could have a new quarter added to it as each quarter expires. In this way, the budget will continue to look one year forward. Cash budgets are often prepared on a continuous basis.

The advantages of periodic budgeting are that it involves less time, money and effort than continuous budgeting. For example, frequent revisions of standards could be avoided and the budget-setting process would require managerial attention only on an annual basis.

A major advantage of continuous budgeting is that the budget remains both relevant and up to date. As it takes account of significant changes in economic activity and other key elements of the organisation's environment, it will be a realistic budget and hence is likely to be more motivating to responsible staff. Another major advantage is that there will always be a budget available that shows the expected financial performance for several future budget periods.

It has been suggested that if a periodic budget is updated whenever significant change is expected, a continuous budget would not be necessary. Continuous budgeting could be used where regular change is expected, or where forward planning and control are essential, such as in a cash budget.

(c) **Budget bias (budgetary slack)** occurs when managers aim to give themselves easier budget targets by understating budgeted sales revenue or overstating budgeted costs.

Cost control using budgets is achieved by comparing actual costs for a budget period with budgeted or planned costs. Significant differences between planned and actual costs can then be investigated and corrective action taken where appropriate.

Budget bias will lead to more favourable results when actual and budgeted costs are compared. Corrective action may not be taken in cases where costs could have been reduced and in consequence inefficiency will be perpetuated and overall profitability reduced.

Managers may incur unnecessary expenditure in order to protect existing budget bias with the aim of making their jobs easier in future periods, since if the bias were detected and removed, future budget targets would be more difficult to achieve. Unnecessary costs will reduce the effectiveness of cost control in supporting the achievement of financial objectives such as value for money or profitability.

Where budget bias exists, managers will be less motivated to look for ways of reducing costs and inefficiency in those parts of the organisation for which they bear responsibility. The organisation's costs will consequently be higher than necessary for the level of performance being budgeted for.

| ACCA marking scheme | | | | Marks |
|---|---|---|---|---|
| (a) | (i) | Sales budget | | 1 |
| | | Stock increase | | 1 |
| | | Production budget | | 1 |
| | (ii) | Cash sales | | 1 |
| | | Credit sales | | 1 |
| | | Material costs | | 3 |
| | | Labour costs | | 1 |
| | | Direct expenses and overheads | | 1 |
| | | Marketing expenditure | | 1 |
| | | Interest payment | | 1 |
| | | Closing balance | | 1 |
| | | | | 13 |
| (b) | | Discussion of periodic budgeting | | 3 |
| | | Discussion of continuous budgeting | | 4 |
| | | | | 7 |
| (c) | | Meaning of budget bias | | 1 |
| | | Cost control | | 1 |
| | | Consequences of budget bias | | 3 |
| | | | | 5 |
| Total | | | | 25 |

## 52   SYCHWEDD PLC

### Key answer tips

In part (a) a machine hour rate needs total budgeted overheads for the period (given in the question) and total machine hours budgeted to be worked. The latter is determined from budgeted product activity levels (here, production = sales) and machine hours by products (here given in terms of hours per 1,000 kg).

In part (b) the computations required are not complex, but there are a lot of numbers to work through. You need to make sure you set out your answer in such a way that the examiner can award marks for method even if you make the odd slip here and there. Set up a proforma statement first, ensuring you can identify the contribution line as well as profit, then use separate workings where necessary to compute the figures. These should be referenced in to your statement.

In part (c) it is a temptation to think that by the time you have worked your way through the data for the first two parts, you're virtually there, and it needs only a quick note or two for this part. When there are this many marks involved, this is a dangerous strategy. At the very least, as the question specifically refers to the sales trend, you can assess what is happening to each product in this respect. Consider both the sales volumes and the resulting contributions, as you have this information for both periods. On the whole, you should be ignoring fixed costs in your analysis as they are absorbed on a relatively arbitrary basis. Then look for any other points worthy of mention – e.g. high proportion of material costs.

(a)

| **Period 2** | | *Machine group 1* | | *Machine group 2* |
|---|---|---|---|---|
| *Product* | | | | |
| R   (10,000 × 75 machine hours per 1,000) | | 750 | (10 × 80) | 800 |
| S   (25,000 × 30 machine hours per 1,000) | | 750 | (25 × 110) | 2,750 |
| T   (50,000 × 50 machine hours per 1,000) | | 2,500 | (50 × 50) | 2,500 |
| *Budgeted machine hours* | | 4,000 | | 6,050 |
| Overheads (given) | | £40,800 | | £68,365 |
| Machine hour rate | | £10.20 | | £11.30 |

(b)

| **Period 2** | *Product profitability analysis* | | |
|---|---|---|---|
| | *Product R* | *Product S* | *Product T* |
| Kilos of sale | 10,000 | 25,000 | 50,000 |
| Sale price per kg | £10 × 1.10 = £11 | £10 | £9 |
| | £ | £ | £ |
| Sales | 110,000 | 250,000 | 450,000 |
| Direct materials (W1) | 45,080 | 127,400 | 306,250 |
| Variable labour and overheads (see W2) | 5,650 | 12,500 | 16,000 |
| Sales commission at 4% | 4,400 | 10,000 | 18,000 |
| Variable cost | 55,130 | 149,900 | 340,250 |
| Contribution | 54,870 | 100,100 | 109,750 |
| Fixed overheads (see W3) | 16,690 | 38,725 | 53,750 |
| Budgeted net profit | 38,180 | 61,375 | 56,000 |

***Workings***

(W1) **Materials**

Product R: £4,508 × (10,000/1,000) = £45,080

Product S: £5,096 × (25,000/1,000) = £127,400

Product T: £6,125 × (50,000/1,000) = £306,250.

(W2) **Variable labour and overheads**

| | *Direct labour hours:* | | | | *Products* | | |
|---|---|---|---|---|---|---|---|
| | *R* | *S* | *T* | | *R* £ | *S* £ | *T* £ |
| *Machine group* | | | | *Labour and overhead rate per hour* | | | |
| 1 | 30 : | 10 : | 20 | £7.50 | 225 | 75 | 150 |
| 2 | 40 : | 50 : | 20 | £8.50 | 340 | 425 | 170 |
| Cost per 1,000 kg | | | | | 565 | 500 | 320 |
| Number of batches (sales/1,000) | | | | | 10 | 25 | 50 |
| Variable labour and overheads | | | | | £5,650 | £12,500 | £16,000 |

(W3) **Fixed overheads**

| Machine group | Machine hours | | | Machine hour rate (see (a)) | Products | | |
|---|---|---|---|---|---|---|---|
| | R | S | T | | R £ | S £ | T £ |
| 1 | 75 : | 30 : | 50 | £10.20 | 765 | 306 | 510 |
| 2 | 80 : | 110 : | 50 | £11.30 | 904 | 1,243 | 565 |
| Fixed overhead cost per 1,000 kg | | | | | 1,669 | 1,549 | 1,075 |
| Number of batches (see above) | | | | | 10 | 25 | 50 |
| Fixed overheads | | | | | £16,690 | £38,725 | £53,750 |

The net profit figures have been calculated using absorption costing, i.e. absorbing fixed overheads into the product costs. This method uses arbitrary bases for apportionment, such as floor area, number of employees etc.

The fixed overhead recovery rate uses machine hours (i.e. it is an output-based measure) when in fact a lot of the fixed overheads tend to vary more with time than output. Absorption costing is an attempt to ensure that costs are recovered. It does not attempt to provide accurate and realistic product costs. The marginal costing contribution approach only includes those costs which vary with output, i.e. the variable costs. By indicating the amount that each product contributes towards the recovery of the fixed overheads and profit, marginal cost is considered to be a more appropriate costing method for decision-making purposes.

(c)     At the outset, it should be noted that the budgets are only estimates and that the assumptions on which they were based could change. They provide targets against which the actual performance can be compared as and when the information becomes available.

For decision-making purposes, management need to use a contribution approach and also assess **where the product is in its life cycle**.

The sales of product R are expected to fall. If this continues in the future, the product will be in the **decline stage of its life cycle** and a time could come when its contribution would not cover the fixed overheads assigned to it, meaning that they would have to be recovered out of the contributions generated by the other products.

Product S, if it continues to remain static in terms of the sales demand would appear to have **reached its peak**. However, there should be a significant increase in period two in its contribution, possibly resulting from increased efficiency, improved productivity and cost reductions.

Product T could well be into its **growth stage**, with an anticipated 25% increase in volume planned for period two. Here also the selling price is expected to remain unchanged and increases in efficiency should help to increase the contribution per kilo from £1.89 to around £2.20.

The management need to consider what action they can take to reverse the trends in products S and T and search for new products.

Management also needs to be made aware of the very high proportion of material costs. The material cost for all products as a percentage of the total cost is over 73%. This high level of investment in materials should make inventory management a very high priority. In order to reduce material costs and expensive holding costs, management will need to monitor and review the situation at frequent intervals. They could consider actions which would reduce waste (for example, better design/production methods) or reduce the cost (for example, by using substitutes).

## 53  PRIVATE HOSPITAL

(a)  **For the year to 31 May 20X3:**

Actual patient days = £4.4 million/£200 per day = 22,000.

Bed occupancy = 22,000/(80 beds × 365 days) = 0.75 or 75%.

| Profit/(Loss) statement | £ | £ | £ |
|---|---|---|---|
| Total revenue | | | 4,400,000 |
| Variable costs | | | 1,100,000 |
| | | | 3,300,000 |
| | | | |
| Personnel: | | | |
| Supervisors | 4 × £22,000 = | 88,000 | |
| Nurses | 13 × £16,000 = | 208,000 | |
| Assistants | 24 × £12,000 = | 288,000 | (584,000) |
| Fixed charges | | | (1,650,000) |
| Profit | | | 1,066,000 |

In the statement above, the number of patient days exceeded 20,500, so personnel costs are as shown. If the number of patient days is less than 20,500, personnel costs would be:

(4 × £22,000) + (10 × £16,000) + (20 × £12,000) = £488,000.

$$\text{Break-even point(s)} = \frac{\text{Fixed costs}}{\text{Contribution per patient day}}$$

Fixed costs consist of fixed charges and personnel costs for the bands of patient days shown in the question. The **contribution per patient day is £150**, being the charge per day of £200 less the variable cost of £50 per day.

Given the stepped nature of the staffing costs there are three break-even levels which can be calculated.

Two are shown below.

(1)  14,254 patient days [ = (£1,650,000 + £488,000)/£150], and

(2)  14,893 patient days [ = (£1,650,000 + £584,000)/£150]

---

### Examiner's note

Just two break-even points are shown above. The third, and highest, is shown below for reference, but since it is unlikely to apply for the year to May 20X3, it is not required as part of the answer to (a).

---

15,427 patient days [ = (£1,650,000 + £664,000)/£150].

(b)  The changes for the year to 31 May 20X4 are 20 extra beds occupied for 100 days. This has implications for bed capacity and for the patient days, and thus for the variable and fixed costs charged and the personnel employed.

**Budget for year to 31 May 20X4:**

Revised patient days = 22,000 + (100 × 20) = 24,000

Bed occupancy = 24,000/(100 beds × 365 days) = 0.66 or 66%.

It is assumed that since fixed costs are charged on bed capacity, the amount of apportioned fixed costs will now increase by a factor of × 100/80, from £1,650,000 to £2,062,500.

**Revised Profit/(Loss) statement**

|  | £ | £ |
|---|---|---|
| Total revenue | | 4,800,000 |
| Variable costs | | 1,200,000 |
| | | 3,600,000 |
| Personnel | | |
| Supervisors | 4 × £24,200 | 96,800 |
| Nurses | 15 × £17,600 | 264,000 |
| Assistants | 28 × £13,200 | 369,600 |
| | | (730,400) |
| Fixed charges | 100/80 × £1,650,000 | (2,062,500) |
| Profit | | 807,100 |

**Required profit to achieve same profit as in (a) = £1,066,000.**

**Required contribution** = (£1,066,000 + £730,400 + £2,062,500) = £3,858,900

Contribution per patient day = £150.

**Required patient days = (£3,858,900/£150) = 25,726 days per year in 20X4** to achieve the same profit as in 20X3. This calculation uses the highest level of staffing costs.

(c) In the year to May 20X3, the bed occupancy for 100 days was 100% (i.e. 8,000 patient days) and for the remaining 265 days it was 66% (22,000-8,000)/(265 days × 80 beds). Attempting to deal with the 100 days extra demand with 20 extra beds would reduce the overall occupancy from 75% to 66%. To cater for the 2,000 patient days demanded, an extra number of potential patient days of 7,300 (365 × 20) were provided. This usage rate of 27% is a little unrealistic for this business. The extra fixed costs of bed capacity and extra costs of personnel (including the higher employment costs) exceed the extra contribution from patients by £258,900 which shows as a reduction in profit.

If the paediatric unit proceed to provide 2,000 extra patient days in this way, it will suffer a reduced profit of almost 25% after covering the increased employment costs and fixed overhead apportionment. It would have to achieve another 1,726 patient days per year, above the level anticipated for the year to May 20X4, to attain the profit level reported in May 20X3. It could accept the profit reduction in the interests of meeting its other objectives of patient and social welfare, but for a private sector company this seems unlikely. It would require a significant increase in patient occupancy to regain the profit position, assuming no further changes to costs.

A possible alternative course of action would be to account for bed occupancy differently, being more flexible and charging for part of a year. That may involve having beds available to move to areas of high demand as the occasion arises. Alternatively, the hospital could decide to de-emphasise the net profit measure because of the influence of fixed costs, and **focus on contribution rather than profit**. Achieving the 2,000 extra patient days would increase the contribution after personnel costs of £153,600. But this would have the disadvantage of not highlighting the efficient occupation of beds in this unit or, no doubt throughout the whole hospital, which could have adverse repercussions on overall profitability.

**Attention to improved planning of bed occupancy** could offer improvements in terms of increasing overall occupancy. One option, if not already undertaken, would be to prioritise demand for the paediatric unit when it has no empty beds available. This would involve treating the most urgent cases first, rather than first come first served, leaving less urgent cases until demand has fallen away during the remaining 265 days. This would not alter the fact that people were waiting for admission (or the size of the waiting list), though to the extent it was not adopted before, arguably it would improve the overall welfare of society.

(d)   Any business will have a variety of objectives. Some of these will be orientated towards **financial aspects**, for example, achieving sufficient profitability to enable an adequate return to shareholders or staying within a financial budget allocation of revenue. **Social objectives** involve provision of an adequate level of public health and welfare, safety and security education opportunities, and so on.

For many businesses, there is likely to be a conflict between financial and social aspects. In other words, greater financial return can be achieved only at the expense of poorer social provision of the reduced change of meeting social objectives. Alternatively, improved social provision is possible, but the chance of achieving financial objectives may be compromised. This is where management judgement is often needed in balancing the trade-off between these objectives in any given situation.

In the provision of health care, improved quality of care or shorter waiting lists can be achieved if more public sector funding is provided or, in the private sector business, if a smaller profit is earned or higher prices are charged. In education likewise, more can always be spent on employing more teachers, reducing class sizes and improving education, but this will add considerably to the costs incurred. The private sector will generally make provision only where it will achieve adequate financial return. Some aspects of social provision can be perceived to be so important that they are provided by the government, because they are unlikely to be provided in entirety by a profit-seeking business.

| ACCA marking scheme | | Marks |
|---|---|---|
| (a) | Patient days | 1 |
| | Occupancy | 1 |
| | Profit/loss | 2 |
| | Break-even number(s) | 2 |
| | | 6 |
| (b) | Patient days | 1 |
| | Occupancy | 1 |
| | Profit/loss | 2 |
| | Required patient days | 1 |
| | | 5 |
| (c) | Each developed point 2 marks, up to a maximum of: | 6 |
| (d) | Objectives | 1 |
| | Conflict | 1 |
| | Example | 1 |
| | | 3 |
| Total | | 20 |

## 54   PUBLIC SECTOR ORGANISATION

(a)   **Budget preparation**

It would be in line with the principles of modern management if the department manager was encouraged to participate more in setting the budget. In this way, he would be more likely to show commitment to the organisational goals in general and the budget in particular. He is closer to the activity for which the budget is prepared, and so the relevance and accuracy of the budget should be improved. This involvement should extend also to discussion of the form and frequency of the reporting which is to take place for his/her department.

**Activity volume**

The volume of visits undertaken is 20% greater than that budgeted. It is inappropriate to compare the actual costs of visiting 12,000 clients with a budget for 10,000 clients.

Costs such as wages, travel expenses and consumables would be expected to be higher than the fixed budget in these circumstances.

One way to deal with this is to adjust or flex the budget to acknowledge the cost implications of the higher number of visits, or to be aware of it when making any comparison. If a factor of 1.20 is applied to the overall wages budget for permanent and casual staff (i.e. on the assumption that it is a variable cost), the flexed budget £5,040 (£4,200 × 1.2) is greater than the actual cost of £4,900. Taking a similar approach to travel expenses and consumables expenses:

- actual travel expenses are exactly in line with the flexed budget (1,500 × 1.20), but

- the consumables costs seem to be highly overspent (4,000 × on it difficult to predict.

To circulate a report as originally constructed seems to highlight and publicise some invalid comparisons on which inappropriate conclusions may be drawn. It is recommended that for cost control purposes, a report is prepared which compares actual spending with a flexible budget based on the actual activity. This would require an estimate of the variable, fixed and semi-variable nature of the cost items.

**Controllability**

It is possible to question whether all the costs shown need to feature in the report. For example, the allocated administrative costs and equipment depreciation are book entries which do not directly affect the department and are not likely to be controllable by employees of the department. There are, therefore, adverse variances on the report contributing to the overall overspend which are not the responsibility of the departmental manager. The difference between actual and budgeted cost of administration serves no useful purpose in this report, because the manager can take no action to directly influence this. The only justification to include this is if the manager can bring about some pressure to reduce this spending by someone else.

It may be unwise to adopt the guide of a 5% deviation to judge variances. The key is whether a cost is out of control and can be corrected by managerial action. Also, 5% of some values can be significant whilst on others 5% of the total cost might be of little consequence.

**Funding allocation**

The Director is correct in pointing out that 'the department must live within its funding allocation'. It is not like a commercial organisation where more output can result in more revenue and hence more money to spend. Increased funding will only be achieved if this organisation and the department is allocated more funds as a result of national or local government decisions to support an increase in services.

It would be appropriate for the funding allocation to be compared with the flexible budget (based on actual activity) to encourage the managers to be aware of and live within the budget allocation. Ways can always be found to spend more money, and so authority structures must be in place to ensure that requests to spend have been budgeted and appropriately funded. Hence the organisational arrangements which authorised the increased visits would be examined.

The nature of the activity for which the budget is being developed should not be lost sight of. It is more complex to deal with budget decisions related to the welfare needs of society than those for a typical manufacturing firm. There are no clear input-output relationships in the former, and hence it is difficult to judge what is justifiable spending for the department compared with other departments and public sector organisations.

## Other aspects

One possible outcome from discussion over the appropriate form of report would be the use of **non-financial measures**. The total staff hours worked, client satisfaction and size of the potential client population are all examples of extensions to the reporting procedure which would help to place the results in context.

The style of the approach adopted by the Director may show some lack of behavioural insight. The despatch of a memo to deal with a prototype report may result in lower staff morale and increased tension in the Homecare department. This may lead to inappropriate future decisions on spending and budget 'game playing' within the department. It may, of course, be a conscious decision of the Director to place the manager in the position of having to reduce spending to the allocated level.

Although this is the first month's report, in the future it may be helpful to use an additional column of the report to show the **year-to-date figures**. This would help to **identify trends** and assist discussion of whether costs are being controlled over the longer term. To show future results for only one month may be insufficient; for example, the repairs to equipment may not follow a regular pattern and this would be revealed if cumulative data existed.

(b)     Traditional budgeting, sometimes called incremental budgeting, takes a current level of spending as a starting point. Discussion then takes place on any extra expenditure or what, of the current expenditure, to cut. **Zero Based Budgeting (ZBB)** is an approach which takes nothing for granted, and which requires justification of all expenditure. This technique would not suit expenditure planning in line departments of a manufacturing company because clear relationships of input and output will exist and be defined by standard values. In less clearly defined areas such as service departments or non-profit orientated businesses, ZBB might have some value if selectively applied.

ZBB would involve describing all of the organisation's activities in a series of **decision packages**, for example, visit frequency, level of eligibility for visit, type of support (medical care, food preparation, wash and clean, shopping needs etc). The **packages can then be evaluated and ranked**: what is essential, highly desirable, desirable and so on. The resources would be allocated according to the packages selected, discussion could also take place between other departments so that a wider allocation of funding is brought into the discussion. Once the budget is set the packages are adopted up to the spending level indicated, this is the cut-off point.

It is possible that economies and increased efficiency could result if departments were to justify all the expenditure, and not just incremental expenditure. It is argued that if expenditure were examined on a cost/benefit basis, a more rational allocation of resources would take place. Such an approach would force managers to make plans and **prioritise their activities** before committing themselves to the budget. It should achieve a more structured involvement of departmental management and should improve the quality of decisions and management information, enabling such questions as: Should this be done?, At what quality/quantity?, Should it be done this way?, What should it cost?

ZBB may not be simple and easy to install, could be expensive in time and effort to analyse all expenditure and difficult to establish priorities for the activities or decision packages. Managers are often reluctant to commit themselves to ZBB because they believe they already do it. Critics of ZBB have asserted that no real change in funding allocation takes place as a result of the exercise. However, any system which encourages managers to examine, and communicate about, their spending and performance levels must be useful providing it does not prevent individuals fulfilling their other duties and responsibilities.

## 55   ZERO BASED BUDGETING

### Introduction

(a)   Zero Based Budgeting (ZBB) is a method of budgeting that re-examines, at each budgeting exercise, whether the budgeted activity is to be funded at any level. Hence, the budgeting exercise begins at a **zero or nil cost base**. It is a device that is particularly useful when an organisation is unsure if its costs are at the most efficient levels. Most efficient costs are not the same as minimum levels, since very low costs might impinge on service or product quality. The purpose of ZBB is to overcome inefficient forms of budgeting that might lead to **slack practices**, which consume more resources than the most effective and efficient organisations face.

(b)   There are a series of steps that would ordinarily be taken in order to implement an effective ZBB system.

### The questioning of why expenditure needs to be incurred

The development of a questioning attitude to activities that incur costs is the first step to ensuring that costs are kept to most efficient levels. It is important to recall that ZBB, in the short term, can only change costs over which the organisation has short-term control. Longer-term, or period costs, can only be changed over a longer horizon. Taxes and other regulatory costs cannot be the focus of ZBB because they are difficult to influence.

Thus ZBB can be immediately effective where costs can be related to identifiable activities. The questions that might emerge in such situations are as follows:

Can costs associated with an activity be isolated? If costs cannot be identified to a particular activity to a degree that provides management with confidence that they can change the costs then there is little point in applying ZBB techniques to the cost.

An even more basic question is to ask how important the activity is to the business and what, if the costs can be identified, is the total cost saving that might result should the activity be stopped. In this respect, it is important to identify effects on costs elsewhere in the business. If the activity to be stopped absorbed fixed costs, then the fixed costs will have to be re-apportioned without absorption to the activity that is to be stopped. Moreover, there may be joint costs such that stopping one activity may have an uncertain effect on joint costs incurred with another activity.

Is the activity in question the cheapest way of providing the service or contribution to production? Thus, it is important not to ask simply if the costs relating to the activity are the most efficient, but are there alternatives that might reduce costs still further and still maintain a given level of service or production.

A more fundamental question about conducting ZBB processes is whether the benefits of employing ZBB outweigh the costs. It is important to appreciate that conducting a ZBB exercise is not a costless process if, as will inevitably be the case, management time is consumed.

### How a decision is made as to which activities should be provided with a budget?

Budgeted activities should be capable of being monitored and controlled. If an activity is recognised as a budget centre, and is going to be subject to a ZBB process, then it is important that management undertake the task of monitoring costs in relation to activity and taking corrective action when appropriate. Thus, if an activity consumes resources and is capable of being monitored and controlled then it should be provided with a budget. This will then make the activity subject to ZBB processes.

'Decision packages' are sometimes referred to in the context of ZBB and activities. These relate to how activities can be described when thinking about how ZBB can be used to judge an activity. There are two types of decision activity:

1    **Mutually exclusive decisions**: When ZBB assessments are made of an activity, alternative courses of action are sometimes benchmarked against existing activities. A choice is then made over which activity might be the preferable course of action. The preferred choice will involve budgeted information, but may also involve other factors such as product quality and service level provision.

2    **Incremental decisions**: ZBB assessments are often related to the level of activity within a budget centre. Thus, there will be a minimum level of activity that provides the essential level of product or service. This is often referred to as the **'base' activity**. Further levels of activity are then incremental and, subject to correctly identifying and isolating the variable costs related to an activity, ZBB assessments can be made separately of both the base and the incremental activities. This division might then provide management with an understanding of the degree of flexibility the organisation has.

**What questions should be asked when budgeted activities need to be ranked to allocate scarce resources?**

The allocation of scarce resources is a key management task. Scarce resources will have to be allocated to the activities of a business in terms of providing appropriate labour and materials, along with any other costs related to an activity. Whilst ZBB is most often applied to support activities the technique can also be applied to a production process.

Some sorting of **ranking** will have to be applied in order to determine which activities are funded by a budget against those that are not. The key question for budgeting purposes relates to:

1    defining the appropriate decision package (as described above)

2    the importance of the activity in relation to the organisation in terms of:

    –    support for the organisation's objective (for example, maximising shareholder wealth)

    –    support for other service or product activities

3    how the ranking system is to be used:

    –    are all activities to be funded above a certain rank, or

    –    is there a scaling of funds allocated against funds requested as determined by the rank, or

    –    is there a combination of methods?

Essentially, a judgement has to be made by management of the benefit of the activity to the organisation. Theoretically, this is best achieved by determining deprival value. In practice, deprival values are difficult tools and some level of arbitrary judgement has to take place in which non-financial factors might play a significant role.

(c)    **Critical assessment of the use of Zero Based Budgeting as a tool that might be used to motivate employees**

The motivation of employees is one of the most difficult tasks facing management since the problems are complex and not always referable to financial performance indicators. To the extent that employees are not responsive to financial performance indicators then ZBB is going to be less effective as a device to motivate employees.

The problem of employee motivation is one of achieving goal congruence with the organisational objectives. ZBB can be useful in this respect as a method of tackling the problem of incentivising employees to achieve targeted performance when a clear understanding of the activities and their related decision packages is essential for the management tasks of monitoring and controlling an activity.

**In this respect ZBB has the following advantages**

1   It ensures that only forward looking objectives are addressed. This limits the potential for historical abuses in budget-setting to be established. Employees can be set targets that are consistent with the future objectives of the organisation.

2   Building 'budget slack' is minimised because, in principle, the entire costs of an activity are reviewed at each budget-setting stage. Employees are then set realistic targets that relate to activity levels that are the most efficient.

3   Managers are made to understand, as part of the ZBB process, the activity itself. This reduces tension between those who decide (management) and those who have to implement manager decisions. Claims that management do not really understand the nature of an activity are thus reduced.

4   ZBB encourages flexibility in employees since they know that, potentially, activities may be stopped. Flexibility induces goal consistency by enabling incentive schemes to reflect activity. In other words, employees are more likely to be responsive to management directives if they are aware and trust that the budget setting process encourages and supports payments that are responsive to flexibility.

(d)   **The advantages of encouraging employee participation in budget-setting**

Generally, participative budget-setting will result in:

1   An informed budget-setting process, such that management are aware of the detail of budgeted activities as provided by the people who work daily within the budgeted activity.

2   Avoiding the criticism that budgets are unrealistic.

3   Reducing the adverse effects of budget imposition when difficult management decisions have to be made (e.g. staff reduction).

4   Employees become aware and more involved in the management activities of the organisations. To the extent that they become more aware, then a greater understanding of the needs of the organisation as a whole is reached.

5   Co-ordination within an activity might be improved. If activities are jointly budgeted, or are part of the same process, then co-ordination between activities might be improved.

6   Budgetary slack may be reduced as management become more aware of the operational activities within an activity.

7   Achievable budgets are more likely to be set.

8   When budgets are not met management are more likely to have a deeper knowledge of the operational issues involved.

9   There is less risk that budgets will be undermined by subordinates.

| ACCA marking scheme | | |
|---|---|---|
| | | *Marks* |
| (a) | 2 marks for references to budgetary slack/ efficient costs | 4 |
| (b) | 2 marks for each point relating to framing questions | up to 3 |
| | 2 for references to decision packages | up to 3 |

| | | | |
|---|---|---|---|
| | For reference to importance of activity to organisation | 2 | |
| | For reference to ranking | 2 | |
| | Available | 10 | |
| | Maximum awarded | | 8 |
| (c) | Up to 2 marks for each detailed point on motivation | | 6 |
| (d) | 1 mark for each detailed point on advantages of ZBB | max | 7 |
| Total | | | 25 |

## 56   ROLLING BUDGETS

### Key answer tips

In part (a), even if you can't remember exactly what a rolling budget is, the question itself makes this fairly clear. Give a concise explanation of how such a budget is prepared, and then think about its advantages - again, even if you haven't specifically learnt these, you should be able to come up with some common sense ideas.

In part (b) in the introduction to the data in the question, it refers to 'the cost behaviour' of each cost item. This should alert you to the possibility that some will be fixed costs (which should be obvious), some will be purely variable (change proportionately with volume) and some will be semi-variable (change with volume, though not proportionately). You thus need to determine the fixed and variable elements of the costs from the Q1 to Q3 data, and apply these to Q4.

In part (c) this budget is prepared for three different production levels, using the Q4 unit and fixed costs computed in (b). Note that as the stock adjustment is at a standard cost, not necessarily matching that used in valuing Q4 production, you cannot simply use the sales volume to get cost of sales directly.

In part (d), given both the requirement to produce your answer in summary form only and the number of marks you have for this and comment, you need to think before launching into long repetitious revised budgets. Basically, if you produce the extra 8,000 units instead of using stock, the profit will be charged with the extra actual variable cost instead of the standard full factory cost for these units. The difference between these costs gives you most of the profit difference. You then need to recognise the impact of the bonus - which helps with the discussion part that follows.

(a)   Accounting budgets are typically prepared for the year ahead, each year being divided into months or quarters. A company can then monitor its progress as the year passes. A variation and extension of the annual budget is to regularly add a further quarter to a budget as the immediate quarter passes, so that a full budget year is always in view. This approach is called a **rolling or continuous budget**. As Q1 progresses, Q2 is reviewed and revised in some detail, at the same time the budget for the other quarters are reviewed and updated.

Benefits of this approach are that management can always have in front of them plans for a full year. This will emphasise the longer term focus of the organisation. It also ensures that managers are constantly thinking about planning for the future and the validity of these plans. It keeps planning at the front of the manager's mind all of the year, not just at the annual budget round. As a result of this it is likely that the actual performance is being compared with a more realistic target than if the budget was prepared only once a year.

(b)   The costs are variable, semi-variable or fixed. It is necessary to determine the cost behaviour from Q1–Q3, then adjust this for Q4.

| | Q1 – Q3 | | Q4 | | |
|---|---|---|---|---|---|
| | *Variable costs* £ | *Fixed costs* £ | *Variable costs* £ | | *Fixed costs* £ |
| Material (W1) | 2.5 | - | 2.75 | | - |
| Labour (W2) | 5.0 | 80,000 | 5.00 | | 80,000 |
| Factory overhead (W3) | 1.5 | 140,000 | 1.50 | (+ 5%) | 147,000 |
| Admin overhead | - | 30,000 | - | | 30,000 |
| Selling overhead (W4) | 0.5 | 20,000 | 0.50 | (+ 5%) | 21,000 |

**Workings:**

(W1)

$$Material\ Q1 = \frac{£50,000}{20,000} = £2.5 \text{ per unit in } Q1-Q3 \text{ Material costs will be}10\%$$

higher in Q4, i.e. £2.75.

(W2) *Labour*

Calculate variable cost per unit and fixed labour costs using the high-low method.

| | £ |
|---|---|
| Total labour cost of 40,000 units | 280,000 |
| Total labour cost of 20,000 units | 180,000 |
| Variable labour cost of 20,000 units | 100,000 |
| | |
| Variable labour cost/unit | £5 |

Substituting:

| | £ |
|---|---|
| Total labour cost of 40,000 units | 280,000 |
| Variable labour cost of 40,000 units (× £5) | 200,000 |
| Fixed labour costs | 80,000 |

These costs will not change, since rate increases will be offset by productivity improvements.

(W3) *Factory overhead*

Calculate the variable cost per unit and fixed costs using the high-low method.

| | £ |
|---|---|
| Total cost of 40,000 units | 200,000 |
| Total cost of 20,000 units | 170,000 |
| Variable cost of 20,000 units | 30,000 |
| | |
| Variable cost/unit | £1.50 |

Substituting:

| | £ |
|---|---|
| Total cost of 40,000 units | 200,000 |
| Variable cost of 40,000 units (× £1.50) | 60,000 |
| Fixed costs | 140,000 |

These fixed costs will increase by 5% in Quarter 4.

*Selling overhead* (based on sales)

Calculate variable cost per unit and fixed costs using the high-low method.

| | £ |
|---|---|
| Total cost of 34,000 units | 37,000 |
| Total cost of 30,000 units | 35,000 |
| Variable cost of 4,000 units | 2,000 |
| | |
| Variable cost/unit | £0.50 |

Substituting:

|  | £ |
|---|---|
| Total cost of 30,000 units | 35,000 |
| Variable cost of 30,000 units (× £0.50) | 15,000 |
| Fixed costs | 20,000 |

These fixed costs will increase by 5% in Quarter 4.

(c) Required reduction in stock in Quarter 4 = the amount by which production in Quarters 1 – 3 (90,000 units) exceeded sales (82,000 units). The reduction in stock levels will therefore be 8,000 units, and the production volume should be lower than the sales volume by this amount.

**Flexible budget profit statements**

|  | *Low* 000s | *Most likely* 000s | *High* 000s |
|---|---|---|---|
| Sales | 38 | 44 | 50 |
| Production | 30 | 36 | 42 |
|  | £000 | £000 | £000 |
| Material (£2.75 per unit produced) | 82.5 | 99.0 | 115.5 |
| Labour (see working) | 230.0 | 260.0 | 295.0 |
| Factory overhead | 192.0 | 201.0 | 210.0 |
| (£147,000 + £1.50 per unit produced) |  |  |  |
| Admin. overhead | 30.0 | 30.0 | 30.0 |
| Selling overhead | 40.0 | 43.0 | 46.0 |
| (£21,000 + £0.50 per unit sold) |  |  |  |
| Costs | 574.5 | 633.0 | 696.5 |
| Add decrease in stock (8,000 × £13) | 104.0 | 104.0 | 104.0 |
| Cost of sales | 678.5 | 737.0 | 800.5 |
| Sales (at £18/unit) | 684.0 | 792.0 | 900.0 |
| Profit | 5.5 | 55.0 | 99.5 |

*Working: Labour costs*

When production is 30,000 units: (30,000 × £5) + £80,000 = £230,000.

When production is 36,000 units: (36,000 × £5) + £80,000 = £260,000.

When production is 42,000 units: (42,000 × £5) + (2,000 × £2.50) + £80,000 = £295,000.

(d) The change in profit will be caused by the change in costs as a result of greater production, rendering the stock adjustment undertaken for the quarter (based on absorption costing principles) unnecessary. Change in costs = 8,000 units × variable production cost £9.25 = £74,000. (Variable production cost per unit, see above, = £2.75 + £5 + £1.50 = £9.25).

| Production (000s units) | 38 | 44 | 50 |
|---|---|---|---|
|  | £000 | £000 | £000 |
| Extra variable production costs | 74 | 74 | 74 |
| Additional bonus (see note) | – | 10 | 25 |
| Extra costs: | 74 | 84 | 99 |
| Stock adjustment |  |  |  |
| (Reduction in cost of sales) | 104 | 104 | 104 |
| Increase in profit | 30 | 20 | 10 |

*Note:*

Bonus: At 44,000 = 4,000 × 50% of £5 per unit

Bonus: At 50,000 = 10,000 × 50% of £5 per unit.

Under the assumption of a simple linear relationship of variable costs to volume, the only extra costs for 8,000 units are the variable production costs which are £9.25 per unit. For any volume above 40,000 units there is also the bonus payment to incorporate. If the budgeted production volume is made equal to sales then the stock level at the start of quarter four will remain at the end. There is no need for a stock adjustment. Put another way, the adjustment made in part (c) above can be added back. The above table shows the profit increase which will occur for the three volume levels.

Under the original volume prediction (and absorption costing principles), quarter four was being charged with fixed overhead contained in the opening stock value in addition to the fixed overhead of the period. Such overhead being transferred to that quarter from earlier accounting periods where production exceeded sales. With the revised stocking policy, the production for quarter four is equal to the sales of the quarter, and this fixed overhead is, in effect, being passed into the following year.

Regarding **managerial motivation and production levels**, it is apparent that the reported profit levels, under absorption costing, respond to changes in the levels of production. We have seen that during a quarter, an increase in the production results in an increase in the reported profit. This presents the possibility of opportunistic behaviour by managers wishing to enhance the level of profit being reported in any one period. They may deliberately over-produce, compared to prevailing sales demand, this production would be held in stock to be sold later, and reported profits would increase. This action would occur if they were placed in a position of needing to achieve a target profit for their bonus or performance appraisal purposes. It may be storing up trouble for the future however, because future production may have to be cut back in order to allow stock levels to be reduced. It would really only be justified if, for example, future sales were expected to be so high that they could not be met by the existing production capacity.

## 57 STORRS PLC

(a) The centred moving averages can be compared with actual sales for each quarter in order to determine the seasonal variations.

| Quarter | Actual sales £000 | Centred moving average £000 | Seasonal variation £000 |
|---|---|---|---|
| **20X1** | | | |
| Quarter 3 | 3,400 | 3,200.0 | 200.0 |
| Quarter 4 | 3,000 | 3,300.0 | (300.0) |
| **20X2** | | | |
| Quarter 1 | 3,100 | 3,375.0 | (275.0) |
| Quarter 2 | 3,900 | 3,450.0 | 450.0 |
| Quarter 3 | 3,600 | 3,562.5 | 37.5 |
| Quarter 4 | 3,400 | 3,687.5 | (287.5) |

The average seasonal variations and the residual error term can now be calculated (although with a limited amount of historical data).

| | Quarter 1 £000 | Quarter 2 £000 | Quarter 3 £000 | Quarter 4 £000 | Total £000 |
|---|---|---|---|---|---|
| 20X1 | - | - | 200.00 | (300.00) | |
| 20X2 | (275.0) | 450.0 | 37.50 | (287.50) | |
| Average | (275.0) | 450.0 | 118.75 | (293.75) | Nil |

Since the residual error term is nil, there is no need to net this off against the average seasonal variations. The average trend of the centred moving averages is (3,687.5 – 3,200)/5 = £97,500. This means that in our model, it is assumed that there is an upward trend in sales, with the underlying trend in sales increasing by £97,500 each quarter.

The sales for Quarter 3 of 20X3 can now be forecast.

| | | | £ |
|---|---|---|---|
| Centred moving average, Q4 of 20X2 | | | 3,687,500 |
| Trend growth for 3 quarters | = | 3 × 97,500 = | 292,500 |
| Trend line sales, Q3 of 20X3 | | | 3,980,000 |
| Seasonal variation | | | 118,750 |
| **Forecast sales, Q3 of 20X3** | | | **4,098,750** |

The sales for Quarter 4 of 20X3 can also be forecast.

| | | | £ |
|---|---|---|---|
| Centred moving average, Q4 of 20X2 | | | 3,687,500 |
| Trend growth for 4 quarters | = | 4 × 97,500 = | 390,000 |
| Trend line sales, Q3 of 20X3 | | | 4,077,500 |
| Seasonal variation | | | (293,750) |
| **Forecast sales, Q4 of 20X3** | | | **3,783,750** |

Both forecasts are higher than those made by the Sales Director (7.0% more for the Quarter 3 forecast and 5.1% for the Quarter 4 forecast). This may be because the Sales Director built some slack into his forecasts, or because the forecasts were made using data prior to the current year (although applying the additive model to earlier sales data does not support this).

(b) The **additive model** assumes that the trend and seasonal variations are independent of each other, and that an increasing trend is not linked to increasing seasonal variations. There is no evidence of an increasing trend in the sales of Storrs plc, and in such circumstances use of the additive model may be acceptable.

The model assumes that the historical pattern of the trend and the seasonal variations will continue in the future. This may not happen for a number of reasons, for example because of unexpected events occurring or because of changes in consumer preferences. The forecast sales figures should be compared with the expectations and opinions of sales staff, who may have a more detailed knowledge of likely sales and market factors.

The reliability of the forecasting method is linked to the amount and accuracy of the data analysed. Since only two years of data has been considered, the forecast is unlikely to be reliable. The reliability of the forecast will also decrease as the forecasting period increases, but the forecast period here is only six months.

(c) With the **top-down approach to budget-setting**, budgets are imposed by senior management. This has the advantage that budgets are more likely to support the strategic objectives of the company, and the operations of different divisions are more likely to be co-ordinated. It may be an appropriate form of budget-setting in small organisations, where senior managers are likely to have a detailed knowledge of all aspects of the business, or in situations where close control of planned costs is called for, such as business start-up or difficult economic conditions. It also has the advantage of decreasing the amount of time taken, and the resources consumed, by budget preparation.

There are number of difficulties with the top-down approach, making it likely that it will not regularly be used in isolation.

- Staff may be demotivated if they have not been involved in the formulation of budgets that produce targets they are expected to achieve, especially if their rewards and incentives are linked to their performance against budget.

- This reduction in motivation could result in strategic objectives and organisational goals being less than fully supported at the operational level, with company performance and profitability suffering as a result.

- Initiative and innovation could also be lost as staff simply 'work to budget', rather than making creative suggestions for improving performance that they feel are unlikely to be rewarded, or form part of future plans.

The **bottom-up approach to budget-setting** implies that functional and other junior managers participate in the preparation of budgets. This approach is likely to lead to more realistic and more co-ordinated budgets than the top-down approach if these managers have a more detailed knowledge of the operations and markets of the organisation. It is also likely to be useful in large, established companies where the complexity of the budget-setting process calls for detailed input from lower levels of the organisation. This approach will also lead to higher levels of motivation and commitment, since managers will have contributed towards the targets against which their performance will be measured.

There are a number of difficulties with the bottom-up approach.

- It can be more time-consuming than the top-down approach because of the larger number of participants in the budget-setting process.

- Participants may become dissatisfied if their budget proposals are subsequently amended by senior managers.

- Managers may introduce an element of budgetary slack into their budget estimates, giving them a 'zone of comfort' in reaching budget targets. Any variances between planned and actual performance are then likely to be favourable ones.

The bottom-up approach also requires detailed planning and co-ordination of the budget-setting process, perhaps supported by a budget manual.

The top-down and bottom-up approaches represent two extremes of the budget-setting process. In practice, a compromise or **negotiated approach** is likely to be used, with senior management reviewing and amending the budget proposals of junior or operational managers in the light of the organisation's strategic plan, and junior or operational managers negotiating amendments to aspects of the budget they find unacceptable.

| ACCA marking scheme | | |
|---|---|---|
| | | *Marks* |
| (a) | Calculation of seasonal variances | 2 |
| | Calculation of average seasonal variations | 1 |
| | Consideration of residual error term | 1 |
| | Sales forecasts for quarter 3 and quarter 4 | 2 |
| | Discussion and explanation | 2 |
| | | 8 |
| (b) | Discussion of trend and seasonal variations | 2 |
| | Historical pattern may not be repeated | 2 |
| | Amount of data used in the analysis | 1 |
| | | 5 |
| (c) | Discussion of top-down budgeting | 6 |
| | Discussion of bottom up budgeting | 6 |
| | | 12 |
| Total | | 25 |

## 58    BUDGET BEHAVIOUR

### Key answer tips

Part (a) should not present much difficulty, requiring a discussion of four purposes of budgeting, a list of at least six of which should be imprinted on your mind!  However, you should not just reproduce the 'heading' in your list - expand it out with a couple of sentences.

Part (b) needs a bit of careful thought and planning to first of all decide exactly what it is you are being asked, and then how to answer it. The key word here is *behavioural* - do not discuss other problems of budgetary control, even if you do know a lot more about them! The best approach to a structured answer might be to think (1) what are the behavioural factors to take account of (target setting, motivation, participation etc) (2) how would they ideally be incorporated into the system and (3) what are the practical problems that may arise?

(a)    An answer should cover four purposes from the six provided below.

**Planning**

The budget is a major short-term planning device placing the overall direction of the company into a quarterly, monthly and, perhaps, weekly focus. It ensures that managers have thought ahead about how they will utilise resources to achieve company policy in their area.

**Control**

Once a budget is formulated a regular reporting system can be established so that the extent to which plans are, or are not, being met can be established. Some form of management by exception can be established so that deviations from plans are identified and reactions to the deviation developed if desirable.

**Co-ordination**

As organisations grow the various departments benefit from the co-ordination effect of the budget. In this role budgets ensure that no one department is out of line with the action of others. They may also hold in check anyone who is inclined to pursue his or her own desires rather than corporate objectives.

**Communication**

The construction of the budget can be a powerful aid to defining or clarifying the lines of horizontal or vertical communication within the enterprise. Managers should have a clearer idea of what their responsibilities are, what is expected of them, and are likely to work better with others to achieve it.

**Performance evaluation**

When budgets are 'tailored' to a department or manager they become useful tools for evaluating how the manager or department is performing. If sales targets are met or satisfactory service provided within reasonable spending limits then bonus or promotion prospects are enhanced.

**Motivation**

The value of a budget is enhanced still further if it not only states expectations but motivates managers to strive towards those expectations. This is more likely achieved if a manager has had some involvement in the budget construction, understands its implications and agrees it is fair and controllable by him/her.

(b)    If budgetary control is to be successful, attention must be paid to behavioural aspects, i.e. the effect of the system on people in the organisation and vice versa. The following are some of the points which should be borne in mind:

## Budget difficulty

It is generally agreed that the existence of some form of target or expected outcome is a greater motivation than no target at all. The establishment of a target, however, raises the question of the degree of difficulty or challenge of the target. If the performance standard is set too high or too low then sub-optimal performance could be the result. The degree of budget difficulty is not easy to establish. It is influenced by the nature of the task, the organisational culture and personality factors. Some people respond positively to a difficult target others, if challenged, tend to withdraw their commitment.

## Budgets and performance evaluation

The emphasis on achievement of budget targets can be increased, but also the potential for dysfunctional behaviour, if the budget is subsequently used to evaluate performance. This evaluation is frequently associated with specific rewards such as remuneration increases or improved promotion prospects. In such cases it is likely that individuals will concentrate on those items which are measured and rewarded neglecting aspects on which no measurement exists. This may result in some aspects of the job receiving inadequate attention because they are not covered by goals or targets due to the complexity of the situation or the difficulty of measurement.

## Managerial style

The use of budgets in evaluation and control is also influenced by the way they are used by the superior. Different management styles of budget use have been observed, for example:

*Budget constrained* – placing considerable emphasis on meeting budget targets

*Profit conscious* – where a balanced view is taken between budget targets, long-term goals and general effectiveness

*Non-accounting* – where accounting data is seen as relatively unimportant in the evaluation of subordinates.

The style is suggested to influence, in some cases, the superior/subordinate relationship, the degree of stress and tension involved and the likelihood of budget attainment. The style adopted and its implications are affected by the environment in which management is taking place. For example, the degree of interdependency between areas of responsibility, the uncertainty of the environment and the extent to which individuals feel they influence results are all factors to consider in relation to the management style adopted and its outcomes.

## Participation

It is often suggested that participation in the budget process and discussion over how results are to be measured has benefits in terms of budget attitude and performance. Views on this point are varied however, and the personality of the individuals participating, the nature of the task (narrowly defined or flexible) and the organisation structure influence the success of participation. But a budget when carefully and appropriately established can extract a better performance from the budgetee than one in which these considerations are ignored.

## Bias

Budgetees who are involved in the process from which the budget standards are set are more likely to accept them as legitimate. However, they may also be tempted to seize the opportunity to manipulate the desired performance standard in their favour. That is, they may make the performance easier to achieve and hence be able to satisfy personal goals rather than organisational goals. This is referred to as incorporating 'slack' into the budget. In this context there may be a relationship between the degree of emphasis placed on the budget and the tendency of the budgetee to bias the budget content or circumvent its control.

Any organisational planning and control system has multiple objectives but primary amongst these is encouraging staff to take organisationally desirable actions. It is never possible to predict with certainty the outcomes of all behavioural interaction however it is better to be aware of the various possible behavioural implications than to be ignorant of them.

## 59    NOT-FOR-PROFIT ORGANISATIONS

(a)    Not-for-profit (NFP) organisations such as charities deliver services that are usually limited by the resources available to them. It may be possible neither to express their objectives in quantifiable or measurable terms, nor to measure their output in terms of the services they deliver. The financial focus in NFP organisations is therefore placed on the control of costs.

(i)    **Selection of cost units**

A cost unit for a NFP organisation is a unit of service for which costs are ascertained. These cost units will be used to assess the efficiency and effectiveness of the organisation. The problem for a NFP organisation is that it may not have easily identifiable cost units, and it may not be possible to identify costs with specific outputs. Once appropriate cost units have been identified, however, they can be used to provide cost control information. Examples of costs units used by an NFP organisation are patients, wards, drug treatment programmes, bed-nights and operations, which are all used by a hospital.

(ii)    **The use of performance measures to measure output and quality**

Where output for a NFP organisation can be quantified, targets can be set and performance against these targets can be measured. In a university, for example, targets could be set in terms of the number of students graduating with a first-class degree, the number of students in a tutorial group, and the percentage of students who complete a degree course having started it. Information could easily be gathered to enable an assessment of the University's performance compared to agreed, budgeted or imposed targets.

Measuring performance in terms of quality is not so easy. It may be possible to use a surrogate or substitute performance measure if a quality cannot be directly measured. For example, the efficiency of hospital outpatient treatment could be measured by the average length of the queue for treatment. The quality of a University course could be assessed by a composite weighting of responses to individual student questionnaires.

(iii)    **Comparison of planned and actual performance**

It is likely that a NFP organisation will have a budget that details expected levels of income (for example from donations and investments) and expenditure (for example on staff wages, continuing programmes, fixed overheads and planned purchases). The use and application of costing principles and information here is no different than in a profit-making organisation. Planned performance can be compared to actual performance, income and cost variances calculated and investigated, and corrective action taken to remedy under-performance.

Where objectives cannot be specified in terms of quantifiable targets, costing information will serve no purpose and assessment of actual performance with planned performance will need to be undertaken from a more subjective perspective.

(b)     Zero-based budgeting requires that activities be re-evaluated as part of the budget process so that each activity, and each level of activity, can justify its consumption of the economic resources available. This is in contrast to incremental budgeting, where the current budget is increased to allow for expected future conditions. Zero-based budgeting prevents the carrying forward of past inefficiencies that can be a feature of incremental budgeting and focuses on activities rather than departments or programmes. Each activity is treated as though it was being undertaken for the first time and is required to justify its inclusion in the budget in terms of the benefit expected to be derived from its adoption.

The first step in zero-based budgeting is the formulation of decision packages. These are documents which identify and describe a given activity or group of activities in detail. The base package represents the minimum level of activity that is consistent with the achievement of organisational objectives. Incremental packages describe higher levels of activity which may be delivered if they are acceptable from a cost-benefit perspective.

Following the formulation of decision packages, they are evaluated by senior management and ranked by decreasing benefit to the budgeting organisation. Resources should then be allocated, theoretically at least, to decision packages in order of decreasing marginal utility until all resources have been allocated.

Advantages claimed for zero-based budgeting are that it eliminates the inefficiencies that can arise with incremental budgeting, that it fosters a questioning attitude towards current activities and that it focuses attention on the need to obtain value for money from the consumption of organisational resources.

Value for money is important in not-for-profit (NFP) organisations, where the profit motive found in the private sector is replaced by the need to derive the maximum benefits from limited resources available. Providers of funds to NFP organisations expect to see their cash being used wisely, with as much as possible being devoted to the achievement of organisational aims. For this reason, NFP organisations emphasise cost control and the need for economy in the selection of resources, efficiency in the consumption of resources and effectiveness in the use of resources to achieve organisational objectives (i.e. value for money).

Zero-based budgeting can therefore be applied in a NFP organisation to analyse its activities and the services it provides into decision packages, with a view to ranking them on a cost-benefit basis relative to organisational aims and objectives. In has been noted that zero-based budgeting can be applied more effectively in service-based rather than manufacturing organisations and so it may be ideally suited to a NFP organisation such as a charity.

(c)     Activity-based budgeting (ABB) would need a detailed analysis of costs and cost drivers so as to determine which cost drivers and cost pools were to be used in the activity-based costing system. However, whereas activity-based costing uses activity-based recovery rates to assign costs to cost objects, ABB begins with budgeted cost-objects and works back to the resources needed to achieve the budget.

Once the budgeted activity levels have been determined, the demand for resource-consuming activities is assessed from an organisational perspective. The resources needed to provide for these activities are then assessed and action taken to ensure that these resources are available when needed in the budget period.

The budgeted activity levels are determined in the same way as for conventional budgeting in that a sales budget and a production budget are drawn up. ABB then determines the quantity of activity cost drivers (e.g. number of purchase orders, number of set-ups) needed to support the planned sales and production. Standard cost data would be compiled that included details of the activity cost drivers required to produce a product or number of products.

The resources needed to support the budgeted quantity of activity cost drivers would then be determined (e.g. number of labour hours to process purchase orders, number of maintenance hours needed to complete set-ups). This resource need would then be matched against the available capacity (i.e. number of purchase clerks to process purchase orders) to see whether any capacity adjustment were needed.

One advantage suggested for ABB is that organisational resources are allocated more efficiently due to the detailed cost and activity information obtained by implementing an ABB system. Another advantage of ABB is that it avoids the pitfalls of incremental budgeting due to its detailed assessment of the activities and resources needed to support planned sales and production. In ABB the costs of support activities are not seen as fixed costs to be increased by annual increments, but as depending to a large extent on the planned level of activity.

| ACCA marking scheme | | | |
|---|---|---|---|
| | | | *Marks* |
| (a) | Features of a not-for-profit organisation | | 1 |
| | Selection of cost units | | 3-4 |
| | Use of performance measures | | 3-4 |
| | Comparison of planned and actual performance | | 3-4 |
| | | Maximum | 10 |
| (b) | Zero-based budgeting and incremental budgeting | | 1 |
| | Decision packages | | 2 |
| | Ranking decision packages | | 2 |
| | Allocating resources | | 1 |
| | Zero-based budgeting and NFP organisations | | 2 |
| | | | 8 |
| (c) | Explanation of activity-based budgeting | | 2 |
| | Need for detailed analysis of costs and activities | | 1 |
| | Stages in activity-based budgeting | | 2-3 |
| | Advantages of activity-based budgeting | | 2-3 |
| | | Maximum | 7 |
| Total | | | 25 |

# PERFORMANCE MEASUREMENT

## 60   INDEX

(a)   A weighted index is an index which represents the change in a set of prices or quantities (rather than a single price or quantity), and reflects the fact that certain items are of greater importance than others.

If the index is a price index, constant quantities are used as the weights. Alternatively, if the index is a quantity index, constant prices are used as the weights.

The weights may be base year values (a Laspeyre index) or current year values (a Paasche index).

(b)   (i)   Base weighted sales price index for Period 4 based on Period 1:

*Working*

Prices in period 4 are the $P_n$ prices for the index.

$P_n$ = Product A    13,770 ÷    16,200 = £0.85
       Product B    80,542 ÷    57,530 = £1.40
       Product C    40,905 ÷    22,725 = £1.80

|           | $p_0 \times q_0$ |                          |        |
|-----------|------------------|--------------------------|--------|
| Product A | 15,352           | $0.85 \times 20,200 =$   | 17,170 |
| Product B | 61,584           | $1.40 \times 51,320 =$   | 71,848 |
| Product C | 16,848           | $1.80 \times 10,400 =$   | 18,720 |
|           | 93,784           |                          | 107,738 |

|           |   | $p_n \times q_0$ |
|-----------|---|------------------|

Index $= (\sum p_n \times q_0 / \sum p_0 \times q_0) \times 100$

$$= \frac{107,738}{93,784} \times 100$$

$$= 114.9$$

(ii) Current weighted sales quantity index for Period 4 based on Period 3:

|           | $p_n \times q_n$ |                          |         |
|-----------|------------------|--------------------------|---------|
| Product A | 13,770           | $0.85 \times 15,100 =$   | 12,835  |
| Product B | 80,542           | $1.40 \times 57,300 =$   | 80,220  |
| Product C | 40,905           | $1.80 \times 15,960 =$   | 28,728  |
|           | 135,217          |                          | 121,783 |

|           |   | $p_n \times q_0$ |
|-----------|---|------------------|

Index $= (\sum p_n \times q_n / \sum p_n \times q_0) \times 100$

$$= \frac{135,217}{121,783} \times 100$$

$$= 111.0$$

# 61 WINDERMERE

**Key answer tips**

This is a standard type of divisional assessment question: ROCE used as the performance measure, bonuses for meeting target ROCE, schemes to improve ROCE - some actually profitable but showing poor results, some short term manipulation to improve reported results but not in the long term interests of the company. There is one useful note in the question - there is central control of cash - it is always useful to assume this otherwise an investment will have no effect on a division's net assets (fixed assets rise, bank balance falls). You will need to make an assumption about what is meant by 'cost savings' in (i), pre or post depreciation, but state your assumption. The requirement of (a) provides you with a useful structure for your answer, although some initial general comments on the use of ROCE might help. Don't anticipate (b) in your answer to (a).

(a) **Assessment of four year-end proposals**

Two general comments are of relevance to all four proposals:

- With ROCE based on NBV of assets employed there is an incentive to under-invest, to improve ROCE by 'reducing the bottom line' rather than 'increasing the top line' in the ratio.

- When ROCE-based assessment is linked to a bonus scheme there is a greater incentive to make ROCE appear satisfactory irrespective of the true commercial merit of an operation of project.

(i) **The works manager - new equipment**

An investment at the end of the year will increase capital employed without providing the opportunity to earn any of the savings forecast. ROCE is likely to fall from 14.6% to:

$$\frac{£120,000}{£820,000 + £100,000} \times 100 = 13.0\%$$

Without knowing the depreciation policy, it is not possible to state the effect of this proposal on 19X2 ROCE.

The project itself may well be viable. If 15% can be taken as the division's cost of capital and the £18,000 are net annual cash inflows, the NPV is:

£18,000 × 5.847 – £100,000 = £5,246.

The project has a positive NPV and should be accepted.

Under the same assumptions and assuming straight line depreciation of £6,667 p.a. the ROCE at the end of the first year would be:

$$\frac{18,000 - £6,667}{£100,000 - £6,667} \times 100 = 12.1\%$$

This is less than the target, but that is a failure of the ROCE method and the method of depreciation used. (In the final year the project's ROCE would be £11,333 ÷ £0 = infinity).

There are no ethical issues at stake, but a number of management issues as introduced above and discussed in (b).

(ii) **The chief accountant - delay payments to creditors**

The effect of non-payment of creditors at the year end is to decrease assets by £42,000 and reduce profit by £1,000. ROCE will move from 14.6% to:

$$\frac{£120,000 - £1,000}{£820,000 - £42,000} \times 100 = 15.3\%$$

The required target has been achieved.

This proposal will have no effect on 20X2 ROCE.

The longer term effect is that the company has lost £1,000 and saved one month's interest on £42,000. The cost of this proposal is therefore 1/42 = 0.024 per month, or:

$$[(1.024)^{12} - 1] \times 100 = 32.6\% \text{ per year.}$$

This makes the scheme appear rather costly.

The company do not want to get a reputation for being poor payers, suppliers may withhold goods and it may become difficult to obtain further credit.

The ethics of deferring payment of debt, which is commercially non-viable, in order to earn a bonus, needs questioning.

(iii) **The sales manager - bring forward completion of order**

The effect of this transaction would be to increase profit by either £6,000. As work in progress changes to debtors in the accounting records, capital employed would increase by £6,000 (since debtors includes profit, but work in progress includes cost only). ROCE would change from 14.6% to:

(£120,000 + £6,000)/(£820,000 + £6,000)

= £126,000/£826,000

= 0.153 or 15.3%.

This proposal achieves the desired ROCE.

This proposal will reduce 20X2 profit by £6,000, because it has the effect of bringing profit forward from 20X2 to 20X1.

Looking at the transaction without regard to year-end performance, £1,500 has been spent with no benefit to cash inflows, although the balance sheet will look more impressive.

This is another example of dysfunctional decisions based on a form of assessment and related remuneration scheme that encourages manipulation of year end accounts.

As with the previous proposal, the ethics of taking a commercially unsound decision, in order to secure a bonus, should be challenged.

(iv) **The head of internal audit - closing a regional plant**

This proposal would have a dramatic effect on capital employed, immediately reducing it by £90,000. The effect on profit would be a fall of £50,000 through redundancy and a rise of £30,000 profit on sale of assets. However, none of these would be included in trading profit (since they are presumably non-recurring) and so ROCE would increase to:

$$\frac{£120,000}{£820,000 - £90,000} \times 100 = 16.4\%$$

This easily achieves the required standard.

Without knowing the depreciation policy, or the life of the assets, the effect of this proposal on 20X2 ROCE cannot be determined.

The loss of £12,600 p.a. for 15 years comes from a net disinvestment of £120,000 – £50,000 = £70,000. The PV of the lost profit (ignoring the possibility of 'profit' of £12,600 being increased by depreciation of £90,000 ÷ 15 = £6,000 to £18,600) for 15 years at 15% is

£12,600 × 5.847 = £73,672.

This suggests that the plant should be retained in order to earn these profits. (ROCE appraisal has been ignored.)

Sacking people to improve ROCE despite the move being against the long-term benefit of the business is unethical. The analysis has also excluded any possible loss of business in other parts of the division from customers inconvenienced by this particular closure.

(b) **Remedial action by company finance director**

Many of the problems above come from the use of return on capital employed (ROCE) based on year end figures which encourages under-investment and manipulation. Possible solutions include:

- Change to Residual Income (RI) when divisions will be rewarded for making wise long-term investment decisions.

- Use DCF methods for assessing capital projects. This overcomes the short-term view taken by using ROCE. Performance can then be assessed by seeing whether the cash flow projections used to assess a project are achieved in reality.

- If there is an insistence on the use of ROCE, it can be improved by:

  - using average capital employed figures rather than year-end ones;

  - using gross book values rather than net-book values;

  - changing depreciation methods to ensure that ROCE does not improve just by retaining assets whose book value steadily falls.

- Ensure central approval of investment (and disinvestment) budgets and controls to check that commitments are met.

- Central control of payments to creditors and collection of debtors.

- If the above is too 'interventionist' lay down guidelines for payments and collection periods.

- The Divisional Manager deserves a reprimand for 'window dressing' although he is trying to make his accounts look better in a way that will not only boost his bonus but will also appeal to outside analysts.

- The importance of ethical considerations in decision-making should be emphasised to Divisional management.

- Change the bonus scheme and pay each manager a fair day's salary for doing a fair day's work without the troublesome complication of a bonus scheme.

## 62   KDS LTD

(a)   **Divisional administrator's proposal**

*Effect on 20X5 ROCE*

It will have been assumed in arriving at the 31/12/X5 net assets that the trade creditor will have been paid. Reversing this assumption has the effect of increasing liabilities and has no effect on assets, as cash is excluded. Thus net assets will be reduced by £90,000 (to £4,310,000).

Whether the £2,000 late payment penalty is accounted for in 20X5 or 20X6 will depend to some extent on the company's accounting policy. The accruals concept would, however, lean towards it being accounted for in 20X5. Thus operating profits would be reduced by £2,000 (to £647,000).

The new ROCE would thus be $\dfrac{£647,000}{£4,310,000} \times 100 = 15.01\%$

Thus the target will have been achieved and bonuses paid. This is, of course, no indication of improved performance, but simply an arithmetical anomaly arising as a result of one side of the transaction being ignored in the calculation. In fact, the finance cost of the late payment is extremely high:

Pay £2,000 to delay payment of £90,000 by 12 days: cost = $\dfrac{£2,000}{£90,000} \times 100 = 2.22\%$

Converting this 12 day cost to an equivalent annual cost gives $(1.0222)^{365/12} - 1 = 95\%$

*Longer term effects*

There would be no quantifiable long term effects, although relationships with the creditor may be adversely affected by the late payment.

**The works manager's proposal**

*Effect on 20X5 ROCE*

Assuming no depreciation charge in 20X5, net assets would be increased by the cost of the new assets, £320,000 (to £4,720,000), and operating profits would be unaffected.

The new ROCE would thus be $\dfrac{£649,000}{£4,720,000} \times 100 = 13.75\%$

This represents a reduction of ROCE in the short term.

*Longer term effects*

In 20X6 and beyond, the full impact of the cost savings and depreciation charge would be felt - operating profits would be increased by a net £(76,000 - 40,000) = £36,000. Net assets value will be increased, but the increase will be smaller each year as the asset is depreciated.

In 20X6, the equipment's own ROCE would be $\dfrac{£36,000}{£(320,000 - 40,000)} \times 100 = 12.86\%$

This will still not help the division to achieve its target of 15%, although it does exceed the company's cost of capital and thus may be desirable overall.

However, by the end of 20X7, the equipment WDV will be £(320,000 - 80,000) = £240,000, giving a ROCE of 15%, exactly on target. As it increases above this level it will help the division to achieve its overall target.

This illustrates one of the major problems with using book values for assets in performance measures - as the assets get older, they appear to give better performance. This can have the effect of deterring managers from replacing assets even though this may be of benefit in the long term through cost savings (as above), increased productivity etc.

(b) Residual income (RI) is an absolute measure of performance, and is arrived at by deducting a notional interest charge at the company's cost of capital on the net assets. Appraising the two divisions' performance forecasts under this method would have the following results:

|  | 20X5 operating profit | Interest charge (12% net assets) | Residual income |
|---|---|---|---|
|  | £ | £ | £ |
| Division K | 649,000 | 528,000 | 121,000 |
| Division D | 120,000 | 57,600 | 62,400 |

The performance rankings of the two divisions are now apparently reversed. However, the RIs of the two divisions are not directly comparable - whilst Division K has produced nearly twice the level of RI than that of Division D, the net asset base required to do this is over nine times as large. RI cannot be meaningfully used to compare investments of differing sizes, as ROCE can.

One could also question the use of the company's average cost of money in computing the notional interest charge. The two divisions have been set a target well above this - this may be because they are considered riskier than average. If 15% had been used in the computation, Division K would have negative RI, whilst Division D has positive RI- reflecting the same information as the ROCE, that K is not achieving its target return.

The RI uses the same principles for establishing profit and asset values as the ROCE, and thus shares the same problems. As assets get older and their WDV falls, the imputed interest falls and RI rises.

However, RI can be of greater benefit than ROCE in management decision making. Management may only feel inclined to undertake new investment if doing so improves their performance measure. For example, Division D currently enjoys a ROCE of 25% and its manager may only consider new projects that give a return at least as good as this (although this may depend upon the particular structure of the bonus scheme - a fixed bonus provided the target of 15% is reached may not provoke such an attitude).

However, the RI measure will improve with new investment, ie increase, provided the investment's returns are at least covering the rate used in computing the notional interest (12% or 15%). This will ensure that projects that are worthwhile from the company's point of view will also be seen as such by the divisional manager (goal congruence).

In summary, RI has advantages and disadvantages over ROCE as a performance measure, and both suffer from common valuation problems. One of these can be used as part of a package of performance indicators - market share, productivity, employee satisfaction, technological advancement etc - but neither is perfect in isolation.

(c)     **Non-financial performance measures**

As mentioned above, financial measures taken in isolation are unlikely to tell the whole story of a division's or company's performance. They must be put into context, taking account of the circumstances in which they were achieved - new products being introduced, market changes, technological changes, competitors moves, availability of resources etc.

For example, one might question why the two divisions in KDS are apparently performing at such different levels. Whilst quality of management may well be a contributory factor, it is unlikely to explain a difference of over 10 percentage points in ROCE.

The age profile of assets used should be considered, as discussed above. Division K may have recently invested in new machinery, possibly in response to technological advances. Not to do so would put them at a disadvantage over their competitors, and thus is for long term benefit. The industry of the much smaller Division D may be more static, requiring less asset changes.

Performance relative to the market and competitors should be considered (market share, product leadership etc) and the degree of innovation achieved. Level of complaints received may also be monitored.

Finally, employee measures are relevant when assessing the effectiveness of a manager - labour turnover, staff morale, manager's relationships with both subordinates and superiors. The level of job satisfaction felt by employees at all levels is an important consideration in the plan for achievement of company objectives.

## 63   PROPOSALS FOR DIVISION X

(a)     The calculations of manager's bonus are shown in the following table.

| Year 1 | Year 2 | Year 3 | Total | |
|---|---|---|---|---|
| Original draft | £15,625 | £13,500 | Nil | £29,125 |
| Project (i) - W1 | £15,625 | £13,250 | £20,375 | £49,250 |
| Project (ii) -W2 | Nil | Nil | £25,000 | £25,000 |
| Project (iii) - W3 | £12,500 | £16,000 | £16,875 | £45,375 |

*Workings*

For each 1% by which ROCE exceeds 10%, the bonus is increased by 2.5% of £50,000, i.e. by £1,250.

(W1)  **Project (i)**

| | Year 1 | Year 2 | Year 3 |
|---|---|---|---|
| PBIT | £3.0m | £2.7m | £4.4m |
| Asset base | £24m | £25.5m | £27m |
| ROI | 12.5% | 10.6% | 16.3% |
| | £ | £ | £ |
| Basic bonus @ 25% of salary | 12,500 | 12,500 | 12,500 |
| Additional bonus | 3,125 | 750 | 7,875 |
| Total bonus | 15,625 | 13,250 | 20,375 |

*Note*

Additional bonus Year 1 = 2.5 × £1,250 = £3,125

Additional bonus Year 2 = 0.6 × £1,250 = £750

Additional bonus Year 3 = 6.3 × £1,250 = £7,875

(W2) **Project (ii)**

|  | Year 1 | Year 2 | Year 3 |
|---|---|---|---|
| PBIT | £2.0m | £1.7m | £6.4m |
| Asset base | £24m | £25m | £26m |
| ROI | 8.3% | 6.8% | 24.6% |
|  | £ | £ | £ |
| Basic bonus @ 25% of salary | 0 | 0 | 12,500 |
| Additional bonus | 0 | 0 | 12,500 |
| Total bonus | 0 | 0 | 25,000 |

*Note:*

Additional bonus Year 3 = (ignoring the bonus cap) 14.6 × £1,250 = £18,250, but total bonus capped at 50% of £50,000 = £25,000.

(W3) **Project (iii)**

|  | Year 1 | Year 2 | Year 3 |
|---|---|---|---|
| PBIT | £2.4m | £3.2m | £3.5m |
| Asset base | £24m | £25m | £26m |
| ROI | 10.0% | 12.8% | 13.5% |
|  | £ | £ | £ |
| Basic bonus @ 25% of salary | 12,500 | 12,500 | 12,500 |
| Additional bonus | 0 | 3,500 | 4,375 |
| Total bonus | 12,500 | 16,000 | 16,875 |

*Note:*

Additional bonus Year 2 = 2.8 × £1,250 = £3,500

Additional bonus Year 3 = 3.5 × £1,250 = £4,375

The manager is likely to be influenced in his choice of projects by the personal rewards he can expect from them. In this case, he would favour Project (i) with total bonuses of £49,250, and Project (iii) with total bonuses of £45,375 over the three-year period. Both the first draft plan and adoption of Project (ii) are less attractive from this perspective. Moreover, this view is reinforced by the fact that most weight is likely to be given to bonuses achievable in the short term: on this basis Project (ii) is easily the least attractive, since no bonuses will arise until Year 3.

These considerations illustrate a common problem of bonus systems, namely that they may not achieve goal congruence. In the present case, Project (ii) is the most attractive from the organisation's point of view because its NPV is higher than the alternatives. However, because of its impact on the manager's own bonus Project (ii) is unlikely to be favoured. Indeed, from the manager's point of view it is the project with the lowest NPV that appears most attractive.

(b) (i) The calculations of the manager's bonuses are shown in the following table.

|  | Year 1 | Year 2 | Year 3 | Total |
|---|---|---|---|---|
| Original draft (W1) | £12,000 | £4,000 | Nil | £16,000 |
| Project (i) | £12,000 | £3,000 | £25,000 | £40,000 |
| Project (ii) - W2 | Nil | Nil | £25,000 | £25,000 |
| Project (iii) - W3 | Nil | £14,000 | £18,000 | £32,000 |

*Workings*

(W1)  **Original draft**

|  | Year 1 | Year 2 | Year 3 |
|---|---|---|---|
| PBIT | £3.0m | £2.7m | £2.4m |
| Interest at 10% on asset base | £2.4m | £2.5m | £2.6m |
| Residual income | £0.6m | £0.2m | Nil |
| Bonus at 2% | £12,000 | £4,000 | Nil |

(W2)  **Project (ii)**

|  | Year 1 | Year 2 | Year 3 |
|---|---|---|---|
| PBIT | £2.0m | £1.7m | £6.4m |
| Interest at 10% on asset base | £2.4m | £2.5m | £2.6m |
| Residual income | Nil | Nil | £3.8m |
| Bonus at 2% (limited to £25,000) | Nil | Nil | £25,000 |

(W3)  **Project (iii)**

|  | Year 1 | Year 2 | Year 3 |
|---|---|---|---|
| PBIT | £2.4m | £3.2m | £3.5m |
| Interest at 10% on asset base | £2.4m | £2.5m | £2.6m |
| Residual income | Nil | £0.7m | £0.9m |
| Bonus at 2% | Nil | £14,000 | £18,000 |

(ii)  Overall, the bonuses work out less generously under this scheme. However, the manager's preference is unaffected:  he still benefits most from Project (i), followed by Project (iii). Once again, Project (ii) is the least attractive from his point of view.

It is noticeable that a different result would have been achieved if the 'cap' were removed from the manager's bonus. In this case, the large returns eventually arising from Project (ii) might well influence him to select this as his first preference. It would lead to a potential bonus of £76,000 in Year 3.  However, the fact that this potential is to be realised only in Year 3, with no bonuses at all in Years 1 and 2, might still be a deterrent.

(c)  The calculations and comments already made illustrate the basic conflict between the goals of the manager and the goals of the organisation. Under either version of the bonus scheme the manager does better by selecting the projects which are least attractive to the organisation. The conflict arises because the organisation wishes to maximise NPV, whereas the manager wishes to maximise ROI or RI.

The obvious approach to solving this problem is to base the manager's bonus on a measure which benefits the organisation, in other words to align the bonus with NPV rather than with ROI or RI. The basis of this change would be to focus on cash flows (the determinant of NPV) rather than on accounting measures (the determinant of ROI or RI).

Further, the bonus scheme should also encourage a long-term perspective by being based on cash flows over the life of the projects selected.

# Section 4

# ANSWERS TO SCENARIO-BASED QUESTIONS

## 1 FRANTIC LTD

(a) (i) **Creditor policy**

**Tutorial note**

By paying creditors after one month instead of after two months, the company will earn a discount of 1.5%. This means that by 'investing' 98.50 one month earlier in the payment of creditors, it will 'earn' 1.50, by not having to pay 100 one month later. The question is asking what the 'return on investment' would be from earning 1.50 by investing 98.50 for one month, expressed as an annualised yield.

The establishment of creditor payment policy involves a comparison of interest rates with the number of days credit in relation to the cash discount available.

Taking the discount yields a return of:

$$\frac{\text{Discount \%}}{(100 - \text{Discount \%})} \times \frac{365}{(\text{Final date} - \text{Discount date})}$$

$$\frac{1.5}{98.5} \times \frac{365 \text{ days}}{(60 \text{ days} - 30 \text{ days})}$$

= 0.1853 or 18.53%. This is more than the discount rate the company uses (i.e. the company's cost of capital). A one-month payment policy should therefore be preferred.

**Alternative method of calculation:**

|  | No discount £ | With discount £ |
|---|---|---|
| Payment to supplier (per engine) | 1,300.0 | 1,280.5 |
| Loss of interest on investing £1,280.5 for (60 – 30) = 30 days: | | |
| = 1,280.5 × (30/365) × 15% | – | 15.8 |
| Total cost | 1,300.0 | 1,296.3 |

Taking the discount costs less.

**Examiner's note**

This can be checked as: [(1,300 – 1,280.5) × (365/30)]/1,280.5 = 18.52%.

(ii) **Stock evaluation without early settlement discounting**

Annual production (demand) = 800 cars = 800 engines.

Cost of ordering = cost of delivery = £1,200.

Annual stock holding cost = 22% × £1,300 = £286.

EOQ ignoring volume discounts =

$$\sqrt{\frac{2 \times \text{delivery cost} \times \text{annual demand}}{\text{annual holding cost per unit}}}$$

$$\sqrt{\frac{2 \times 1,200 \times 800}{286}}$$

= 81.93 or 82 whole units.

At this batch ordering level, a quantity discount of 2% would apply. The annual holding cost would therefore be 22% × 98% x £1,300 = £280.28. Re-working the previous calculation with the quantity discount gives:

$$\sqrt{\frac{2 \times 1,200 \times 800}{280.28}}$$

= 82.77 or 83 whole units.

Hence the choice facing Frantic Ltd is between ordering 83 units and getting a 2% discount, or 250 units, which is the minimum purchase quantity needed to get a 3% discount.

**Evaluation for an order quantity of 83:**

|  |  | £ |
|---|---|---|
| Total purchase costs: | £1,300 × 98% × 800 = | 1,019,200 |
| Holding costs: | 83/2 × £280.28 = | 11,632 |
| Order costs: | (800/83) × £1,200 = | 11,566 |
| Total annual costs: |  | 1,042,398 |

**Evaluation for an order quantity of 250:**

|  |  | £ |
|---|---|---|
| Total purchase costs: | £1,300 × 97% × 800 = | 1,008,800 |
| Holding costs: | 250/2 × 22% × 97% × £1,300 = | 34,678 |
| Order costs: | (800/250) × £1,200 = | 3,840 |
| Total annual costs: |  | 1,047,318 |

Difference in costs: Buying in quantities of 250 is cheaper by £4,920 each year.

**The optimal policy** is to order in quantities that minimises total costs, which in this case is to **order in batches of 83 engines**.

---

### Examiner's note

An alternative answer takes an incremental cost approach, and compares the incremental costs or savings from ordering in batches of 250 compared to ordering in batches of 83. The initial assumption is that the company orders in batches of 83. This approach is shown below.

|  | £ | £ |
|---|---|---|
| Saving in purchase price by buying 250: (800 × 1% × £1,300) |  | 10,400 |
| Saving in ordering costs by buying in batches of 250: |  |  |
| [(800 × 1,200)/83] − [(800 × 1,200)/250] |  | 7,726 |
| Total cost savings |  | 18,126 |
| Holding costs with order quantity of 250 (above) | 34,677 |  |
| Holding costs with order quantity of 83 (above) | 11,631 |  |
| Additional holding costs from ordering in batches of 250 |  | 23,046 |
| Increased costs arising from ordering 250 units |  | 4,920 |

The same conclusion is reached as above. The optimal policy is to order 83 engines at a time.

(iii) **Debtors**

**Tutorial note**

This part of the question is similar to (a)(i), except here the question is whether to offer an early settlement discount, whereas in (a)(i) the question was whether to accept an early settlement discount.

Offering the discount implies an interest cost of:

$$\frac{\text{Discount \%}}{(100 - \text{Discount \%})} \times \frac{365}{(\text{Final date} - \text{Discount date})}$$

$$\frac{2}{98} \times \frac{365 \text{ days}}{(60 \text{ days} - 30 \text{ days})}$$

$$= 24.8\%$$

This is more than the discount rate the company uses (i.e. more than the company's cost of capital). It is therefore **not worthwhile**.

**Alternative method of solution**

For every £100 worth of debtors:

|  | No discount £ | With discount £ |
|---|---|---|
| Receipt from debtor | 100.0 | 98.0 |
| Interest on investing £98 for (60 – 30) = 30 days: |  |  |
| = 98 × (30/365) × 15% | – | 1.2 |
| Total income | 100.0 | 99.2 |

Hence, it is not worthwhile to offer the discount.

(b) As stated in solution (a)(ii), the optimal policy is to order 83 engines at a time. This involves ordering 800/83 = 9.64 times per year. A production schedule can be drawn-up to assess when the orders would be made. If this is undertaken the following ordering schedule would result:

| Month | 1 | 2 | 3 | 4 | 5 | 6 | 7 | 8 | 9 | 10 | 11 | 12 |
|---|---|---|---|---|---|---|---|---|---|---|---|---|
| Car production[1] | 66.7 | 66.7 | 66.7 | 66.7 | 66.7 | 66.7 | 66.7 | 66.7 | 66.7 | 66.7 | 66.7 | 66.7 |
| Orders placed | 83 | 83 | 83 | 83 | 83 | | 83 | 83 | 83 | 83 | | 83 |
| Stock at month-end | 16 | 32 | 48 | 64 | 80 | 13 | 29 | 45 | 61 | 77 | 10 | 26 |

[1] Fractional production allowed and reflected in work in progress

Thus, no orders are placed in the sixth month. This does not have any implications for the six month cash flow since creditors will be paid with one month delay (as determined by the answer to part (a)(i)).

**Cash flow for first six months:**

| Month | 1 | 2 | 3 | 4 | 5 | 6 |
|---|---|---|---|---|---|---|
| *Receipts* | | | | | | |
| Cash sales (note 1) | 1,416,667 | 1,416,667 | 1,416,667 | 1,416,667 | 1,416,667 | 1,416,667 |
| Credit sales (note 1) | 1,062,500 | 1,062,500 | 1,416,667 | 1,416,667 | 1,416,667 | 1,416,667 |
| **Total income** | 2,479,167 | 2,479,167 | 2,833,334 | 2,833,334 | 2,833,334 | 2,833,334 |
| | | | | | | |
| *Payments* | | | | | | |
| Capital costs | | | 3,200,000 | | | |
| Engine costs (note 2) | 97,500 | 104,156 | 104,156 | 104,156 | 104,156 | 104,156 |
| Other expenses (note 3) | 1,841,667 | 1,841,667 | 1,841,667 | 1,841,667 | 1,841,667 | 1,841,667 |
| Fixed costs | 18,000 | 18,000 | 18,000 | 22,000 | 22,000 | 22,000 |
| **Costs net of overdraft** | 1,957,167 | 1,963,823 | 5,163,823 | 1,967,823 | 1,967,823 | 1,967,823 |
| | | | | | | |
| **Receipts less payments** | 522,000 | 515,344 | (2,330,489) | 865,511 | 865,511 | 865,511 |
| Opening bank balance | (25,000) | 496,687 | 1,012,031 | (1,318,458) | (469,428) | 390,215 |
| Overdraft interest (note 4) | (313) | - | - | (16,481) | (5,868) | - |
| Closing bank balance | 496,687 | 1,012,031 | (1,318,458) | (469,428) | 390,215 | 1,255,726 |

***Notes:***

(1) Monthly sales = 800/12 units. Cash sales are 50% of 800/12 × £42,500 = £1,416,667. Credit sales are the same in each month, but customers take two months' credit. Receipts from credit sales in months 1 and 2 are as stated in the question.

(2) Engine cost payments. Month 1 payment is given in the question. The company will take a bulk purchase discount of 2% and an early settlement discount of 1.5%. Cash paid in subsequent months = quantity purchased in previous month × 98.5% of 98% of £1,300 = £104,156 per month.

(3) Other expenses are 65% × monthly sales = 65% × (800/12) × £42,500 = £1,841,667.

(4) Assumption = Overdraft costs are calculated as (1/12) × 15% × opening bank balance. (Other bases of calculation are acceptable such as interest calculated on average balances.)

(c)                                              **Report**

To:                 Managing Director and Senior Management Team

From:

Date:            xx/xx/xx

**Subject:**       **Cash budgeting**

**Introduction**

This report addresses a number of key issues concerning Frantic's cash flow position and has four elements which are of immediate concern to Frantic.

**How cash flow problems arise**

It is important first to **distinguish between profitability and cash availability**. The key idea relates to insolvency since even profitable companies can face insolvency if cash positions are not properly managed.

Thus cash positions require management to avoid the difficulties associated with cash shortages. Cash shortages are likely to arise in a number of situations. The following is not an exhaustive list, but is likely to represent the most common. Cash flow problems can arise due to:

(i)    Sustained losses in the business such that cash resources have been drawn-down

(ii)   Difficulties in dealing with inflating costs combined with an inability to raise sales prices proportionately

(iii)  Overtrading and inadequate financing of growth. This is very common with new businesses which are not able to finance working capital requirements sufficiently. Generally, such problems are associated with under-capitalised businesses and a lack of recognition that working capital requirements require a large base of long-term capital funding

(iv)   Seasonal trading against ongoing costs. This situation arises where income from sales is variable according to the time of year but fairly even monthly outgoings have to be met;

(v)    Unplanned one-off large items of expenditure. This may arise, for example, as a result of a break down of a large piece of machinery, and

(vi)   Poor credit management.

The importance and impact of each item will depend on a number of factors.

Thus, losses may be sustained for a period without a liquidity problem, depending on how large cash resources are, whether in the form of positive bank balances or the availability of overdraft facilities.

Suffering cost inflation at a higher rate than prices can be raised is not sustainable in the long-run. The importance of this may depend on the capability of the business to implement cost savings, or to diversify markets where prices could be increased.

Overtrading is a problem of forecasting and planning for adequate long-term capital. The idea is that growth should be within available resources.

Seasonal trading requires careful cash management and the extent to which cash resources can be smoothed over the year.

Unplanned major items of expenditure may be important if alternative sources of finance are not available, such as leasing.

**Methods of easing cash shortages**

There are several techniques for offsetting the short-term effects of cash shortages. In the long-term, however, the adequacy of cash has to be addressed. Thus, for example, cash shortages may be alleviated by the following.

(i)    **Postponement of expenditure** where feasible. This would not be feasible in the payment of staff wages, but might be in relation to replacing an old piece of equipment that is still working.

(ii)   **Accelerating cash inflows.** For example, by more effective use of credit collection, better credit control, improved early payment incentives, or even the factoring of debt.

(iii)  **Sale of redundant assets** either before or after any necessary re-organisation. This may involve the sale of a building where accommodation can be centralised. Other assets may be sold on a sale and lease-back basis, although careful consideration will have to be given to the net benefits arising from this.

(iv)   **Re-negotiation of supplier terms or overdraft arrangements.** In particular, bank debt may be mortgaged or secured to access lower rates. Suppliers may agree to lower prices or longer terms if negotiated agreements can be formalised such that a certain level of purchases are made over a period of time.

The importance of each item will depend on the degree of flexibility that Frantic has in its financial structure and agreements. The room for manoeuvre may be limited, but a thorough review of all possibilities is likely to yield at least a number of options. Furthermore, the impact of each potential response depends on how efficient Frantic has been in arranging its affairs in the first place. Finally, none of the items listed will have a sustained impact if the core problem is not identified and dealt-with.

**Managing cash resources**

A variety of methods might be of use in managing resources. The particular tool chosen will depend on its reliability and appropriateness. Appropriateness, in turn, will be governed by the underlying assumptions of the technique employed. Some of the methods that may be used to managed cash resources are listed below:

(i)     **Inventory approach to cash management**. This method views cash in the same way as engine stock such that EOQ models may be employed. In such circumstances, cash is viewed as an asset with costs associated with it that should be minimised so as to determine what level of cash balances should be held. Thus, decreases or increases in cash balances can be determined according to planned growth, the time value of money and the costs of obtaining new funds.

(ii)    The **Miller-Orr model** recognises that cash balance requirements are likely to fluctuate and that active management is required in responding to these fluctuations. In particular, attention is paid to the variability (or variance) of cash flows, interest rates and the transaction costs of adjusting cash balances. It is the variability of cash balances that is crucial to understanding cash management since this will depend directly on understanding how Frantic's operations (fundamentally, sales and production) vary. For a volatile business, it is likely that large cash balances will need to be kept. Miller-Orr suggest a simple formula to estimate this although the formula itself is limited by the assumptions on which it rests.

(iii)   **Probability approaches** recognise a degree of uncertainty in predicting cash balances and allow for a range of outcomes to occur. If the assessment of such probabilities is accurate then cash resources can be put in place in readiness for the predicted events. The method is not wholly reliable in situations where the number of potential outcomes is small, since unfeasible expected outcomes may be predicted by using a probability approach.

(iv)    Cash management is also about **managing surplus cash**. The response of management should depend on whether the surplus is large and how long it is likely to exist. If the balance is large and is likely to remain, then management have a duty to look for appropriate investment opportunities or else refund the investors with a special dividend, for example. Smaller cash balances can be actively managed via short term deposits.

**A centralised treasury function**

Treasury departments are normally a feature of larger companies than Frantic, although it is perhaps beneficial to consider the benefits of such departments to assess what practices might reasonably be adopted. Essentially, treasury centralisation is an issue concerned with economies of scale. The benefits of treasury departments are numerous and include the following.

(i)     Consolidating bank accounts to create either a single account through which all cash resources are managed or a virtual single account with automatic offset between different accounts. Such an approach maximises deposit interest, which is typically higher on larger cash balances for positive balances whilst minimising overdraft costs for negative balances.

(ii) Borrowings can be arranged in bulk thus accessing lower rates.

(iii) Foreign exchange management is improved. In the same way that cash balances are effectively consolidated, foreign currency payments and receipts of all the divisions in the company can be amalgamated, and cash inflows and outflows in each currency set off against each other. This can reduce the need for expensive hedging agreements. Foreign exchange risk consolidation is common in practice.

(iv) Treasury expertise can be developed within a single department, thus enhancing the quality of resource management generally.

(v) Precautionary cash balances, when centralised, are likely to be lower than when considered on an individual account basis.

<table>
<tr><th colspan="4">ACCA marking scheme</th><th>Marks</th></tr>
<tr><td>(a)</td><td>(i)</td><td colspan="2">Calculation of discount rate implied in the early settlement<br>Decision on payment period</td><td>2<br>1<br><br>3</td></tr>
<tr><td></td><td>(ii)</td><td colspan="2">Calculation of basic EOQ (ignoring discounts)<br>Evaluation of purchase costs with discounts<br>Decision on optimal policy</td><td>1<br>4<br>1<br><br>6</td></tr>
<tr><td></td><td>(iii)</td><td colspan="2">Calculation of discount rate implied in the early settlement<br>Decision on payment period</td><td>2<br>1<br><br>3</td></tr>
<tr><td>(b)</td><td></td><td colspan="2">Defining frequency of orders<br>Consideration of scheduling of orders<br>Preparation of cash budget in accordance with answer to part (a)<br>Identification of overdraft costs</td><td>1<br>4<br>9<br>4<br><br>18</td></tr>
<tr><td>(c)</td><td></td><td colspan="2">2 marks each for identification and elaborated examples of how cash problems arise. Up to a maximum of:<br>2 marks each for identification and elaborated examples of easing cash shortages. Up to a maximum of:<br>2 marks each for identification and elaborated examples of how cash resources may be managed. Up to a maximum of:<br>2 marks each for identification and elaborated examples of the benefits of a treasury function. Up to a maximum of:<br>Quality of presentation of report</td><td>4<br><br>4<br><br>4<br><br>6<br>2<br><br>20</td></tr>
<tr><td>Total</td><td></td><td></td><td></td><td>50</td></tr>
</table>

## 2 JACK GEEP

(a)

| | High demand £ | Medium demand £ | Low demand £ | Expected demand £ |
|---|---|---|---|---|
| February | 22,000 × 0.05 | 20,000 × 0.85 | 19,000 × 0.1 | 20,000 |
| March | 26,000 × 0.05 | 24,000 × 0.85 | 23,000 × 0.1 | 24,000 |
| April | 30,000 × 0.05 | 28,000 × 0.85 | 27,000 × 0.1 | 28,000 |
| May | 29,000 × 0.05 | 27,000 × 0.85 | 26,000 × 0.1 | 27,000 |
| June | 35,000 × 0.05 | 33,000 × 0.85 | 32,000 × 0.1 | 33,000 |

| | January £ | February £ | March £ | April £ | May £ | June £ |
|---|---|---|---|---|---|---|
| **Receipts** | | | | | | |
| Capital | 150,000 | | | | | |
| Cash sales (W1) | | 2,000 | 2,400 | 2,800 | 2,700 | 3,300 |
| Credit sales (W1) | | | 8,775 | 10,530 | 12,285 | 11,846 |
| | | | | 9,000 | 10,800 | 12,600 |
| | 150,000 | 2,000 | 11,175 | 22,330 | 25,785 | 27,746 |
| | | | | | | |
| **Payments** | | | | | | |
| Fixed assets | | 200,000 | | 50,000 | | |
| Labour (W3) | 6,300 | 7,560 | 8,820 | 8,505 | 10,395 | 10,395 |
| Materials (W3) | | 4,200 | 5,040 | 5,880 | 5,670 | 6,930 |
| Overheads (W3) | | | 2,100 | 2,520 | 2,940 | 2,835 |
| Fixed costs | 7,000 | 7,000 | 7,000 | 7,000 | 7,000 | 7,000 |
| Consultant | | 12,000 | | | | |
| | 13,300 | 230,760 | 22,960 | 73,905 | 26,005 | 27,160 |
| | | | | | | |
| **Net cash flow** | 136,700 | (228,760) | (11,785) | (51,575) | (220) | 586 |
| **Opening balance** | 0 | 136,700 | (92,060) | (103,845) | (155,420) | (155,640) |
| | | | | | | |
| **Closing balance** | 136,700 | (92,060) | (103,845) | (155,420) | (155,640) | (155,054) |

### Workings

#### (W1) Cash from sales

| | January £ | February £ | March £ | April £ | May £ | June £ |
|---|---|---|---|---|---|---|
| Cash sales (10%) | | 2,000 | 2,400 | 2,800 | 2,700 | 3,300 |
| Credit sales: | | | | | | |
| $(90\% \times 0.5 \times 0.975)$ | | | 8,775 | 10,530 | 12,285 | 11,846 |
| $(90\% \times 0.5)$ | | | | 9,000 | 10,800 | 12,600 |

#### (W2) Variable production costs (£600 per £1,000 of sales)

| | January £ | February £ | March £ | April £ | May £ | June £ |
|---|---|---|---|---|---|---|
| Cost of sales | 12,000 | 14,400 | 16,800 | 16,200 | 19,800 | 19,800 |
| Defects (5%) | 600 | 720 | 840 | 810 | 990 | 990 |
| Total | 12,600 | 15,120 | 17,640 | 17,010 | 20,790 | 20,790 |

#### (W3) Production cash flows (see (W2))

| | January £ | February £ | March £ | April £ | May £ | June £ |
|---|---|---|---|---|---|---|
| Labour (3/6 of total) | 6,300 | 7,560 | 8,820 | 8,505 | 10,395 | 10,395 |
| Materials (2/6 of total) | | 4,200 | 5,040 | 5,880 | 5,670 | 6,930 |
| Overheads (1/6) | | | 2,100 | 2,520 | 2,940 | 2,835 |

*Tutorial note*: Materials paid one month in arrears and variable overheads two months in arrears.

(b) *Note:* Only the cash flows for sales and labour are required. The remainder of the cash budget is provided to prove the figures supplied in the question.

The basic point is that high demand cannot be satisfied with a just-in-time stock management system.

|  | Medium demand £ | Low demand £ | Expected sales £ |
|---|---|---|---|
| February | 20,000 × 0.9 | 19,000 × 0.1 | 19,900 |
| March | 24,000 × 0.9 | 23,000 × 0.1 | 23,900 |
| April | 28,000 × 0.9 | 27,000 × 0.1 | 27,900 |
| May | 27,000 × 0.9 | 26,000 × 0.1 | 26,900 |
| June | 33,000 × 0.9 | 32,000 × 0.1 | 32,900 |

|  | January £ | February £ | March £ | April £ | May £ | June £ |
|---|---|---|---|---|---|---|
| **Receipts** |  |  |  |  |  |  |
| Capital | 150,000 |  |  |  |  |  |
| Cash sales (W4) |  | 1,990 | 2,390 | 2,790 | 2,690 | 3,290 |
| Credit sales (W4) |  |  | 8,731 | 10,486 | 12,241 | 11,802 |
|  |  |  |  | 8,955 | 10,755 | 12,555 |
|  | 150,000 | 1,990 | 11,121 | 22,231 | 25,686 | 27,647 |
| **Payments** |  |  |  |  |  |  |
| Fixed assets |  | 200,000 |  | 50,000 |  |  |
| Labour (W6) |  | 6,269 | 7,529 | 8,789 | 8,474 | 10,364 |
| Materials (W6) |  |  | 4,179 | 5,019 | 5,859 | 5,649 |
| Overheads (W6) |  |  |  | 2,090 | 2,510 | 2,930 |
| Fixed costs | 7,000 | 7,000 | 7,000 | 7,000 | 7,000 | 7,000 |
| Consultant |  | 12,000 |  |  |  |  |
|  | 7,000 | 225,269 | 18,708 | 72,898 | 23,843 | 25,943 |
| **Net cash flow** | 143,000 | (223,279) | (7,587) | (50,667) | 1,843 | 1,704 |
| **Opening balance** | 0 | 143,000 | (80,279) | (87,866) | (138,533) | (136,690) |
| **Closing balance** | 143,000 | (80,279) | (87,866) | (138,533) | (136,690) | (134,986) |

*Workings*

(W4) **Cash from sales**

|  | February £ | March £ | April £ | May £ | June £ |
|---|---|---|---|---|---|
| Cash sales (10%) | 1,990 | 2,390 | 2,790 | 2,690 | 3,290 |
| Credit sales: |  |  |  |  |  |
| (90% × 0.5 × 0.975) |  | 8,731 | 10,486 | 12,241 | 11,802 |
| (90% × 0.5) |  |  | 8,955 | 10,755 | 12,555 |

(W5) **Variable production costs** (£600 per £1,000 of sales)

|  | February £ | March £ | April £ | May £ | June £ |
|---|---|---|---|---|---|
| Cost of sales | 11,940 | 14,340 | 16,740 | 16,140 | 19,740 |
| Defects (5%) | 597 | 717 | 837 | 807 | 987 |
| Total | 12,537 | 15,057 | 17,577 | 16,947 | 20,727 |

**(W6) Production cash flows** (see (W5))

|  | February £ | March £ | April £ | May £ | June £ |
|---|---|---|---|---|---|
| Labour (3/6 of total) | 6,269 | 7,529 | 8,789 | 8,474 | 10,364 |
| Materials (2/6 of total) |  | 4,179 | 5,019 | 5,859 | 5,649 |
| Overheads (1/6) |  |  | 2,090 | 2,510 | 2,930 |

*Tutorial note:* Materials paid one month in arrears and variable overheads two months in arrears.

*Tutorial note:* A quicker method is merely to deduct 63 from each of the totals in requirement (a) as the loss of sales is constant.

(c)   The introduction of just-in-time stock management for finished goods has a number of benefits:

(1)   It significantly improves the short-term liquidity of the business with a maximum financing requirement of £138,533 rather than £155,640. There is also a more rapidly improving deficit thereafter, with the balance falling to £134,986 by the end of June. In the longer term, however, there is continued loss of profitability due to lost sales when demand is high.

The primary reason for this is the reduced investment in stock that is tying up cash. Under the original proposal there is surplus stock amounting to the next month's sales which means production is necessary at an earlier stage thereby using up cash resources.

(2)   Interest costs and stock holding costs are saved by reduced stock levels, thereby adding to profit.

(3)   There already appears to be a just-in-time stock management policy with respect to raw materials and work in progress and such a policy for finished goods would be consistent with this.

There are, however, a number of problems with just-in-time stock management in these circumstances:

(1)   When demand is higher than expected, the additional sales are lost as there is insufficient production to accommodate demand above the mean expected level. This is because no stock is carried. This, however, amounts to only £100 per month of sales on average, which may be a price worth paying in return for improved liquidity in terms of a reduced cash deficit.

(2)   In addition to losing contribution there may be a loss of goodwill and reputation if customers cannot be supplied. They may go elsewhere not just for the current sale but also for future sales if Mr Geep is seen as an unreliable supplier. This results from the fact that customers demand immediate delivery of orders.

(3)   Just-in-time management of stock relies upon not just reliable timing and quantities but also reliable quality. The number of defects can be planned if it is constant, but if they occur irregularly this presents an additional problem.

(4)   If production in each month is to supply demand in the same month, this relies on the fact that demand parallels production within the month. If the majority of demand is at the beginning of each month this would cause problems without a level of safety stock, given that prompt delivery is expected by customers.

A number of compromises between the two positions would be possible:

(1)   Stock could be held sufficient to accommodate demand when it was high. This amounts to only an extra £2,000 at selling values thus an extra £1,200 at variable cost. This is significantly lower than a whole month's production but would accommodate peak demand.

(2)   Liquidity is very important initially as the business attempts to become established. Therefore minimal stocks could be held in the early months, with perhaps slightly increased stocks once the business and its cash flows become established.

(d)                                   **REPORT**

**To:**      Mr J Geep

**From:**    An Accountant

**Date:**    xx/xx/xx

**Subject: Liquidity and financing**

(i)      **The extent of financing required**

Sales are uncertain with high, low and medium estimates of demand. This of itself gives some uncertainty but the reliability and probability of these estimates will need to be established by appropriate market research. If sales are lower than expected then any bank finance will take longer to repay, thus increasing the amount of finance needed and the proportion of longer-term finance.

If just-in-time stock management is not implemented, the maximum finance requirement is £155,640.

After July 20X3 the expected net cash inflow will be constant (ignoring any further purchases of fixed assets) as follows:

|  | £ | £ |
|---|---|---|
| Sales | | 33,000 |
| Discounts: $(33,000 \times 0.9 \times 0.025)$ | | (742) |
| Labour | (9,900) | |
| Material | (6,600) | |
| Variable overheads | (3,300) | |
| Allowance for defects | (19,800) $\times 1.05$ | (20,790) |
| Fixed costs | | (7,000) |
| Net cash inflow | | 4,468 |

Thus, to pay off a loan of £155,054 it would mean payments over 35 months (155,054/4,468) would have to take place, ignoring interest charges. Any variation in these estimates would, however, affect the amount of the financing needed.

In addition to uncertain trading results affecting the amount of future financing, there will be a requirement to finance future capital investment as the business expands. This is likely to be a major financing need, depending on the rate of expansion.

The levels of the drawings, taxation and interest charges will also extend the amount of finance needed, as these items were not included in the cash budget presented.

(ii)     **Short- and long-term financing mix**

In forming a new business, there is no business history to present to the bank. Consequently, there is additional uncertainty, which will need to be considered before any finance is likely to be forthcoming, either of a short-term or a long-term nature.

If there is a good relationship with the bank, an overdraft might be possible for the entire financing requirement, but an overdraft facility from a bank is uncommitted. There is a risk of it being payable immediately on demand. If planned cash flows did not turn out as expected, the bank may get nervous and possibly withdraw credit facilities.

A medium-term loan would also be possible to meet the entire financing requirement. This has the advantage of security in that it cannot be recalled unless there is a breach in the terms (breach of covenant). Most likely such funding would come from a bank, the issue of debentures being entirely out of the question on the grounds of size. Other considerations would be the term of the loan, security required, the interest rate, and covenants.

Another possible form of finance include leasing which can be regarded as a quasi-loan if entering into a long-term contract. However, other considerations may apply such as variability of rental terms, transfer of risk, residual value of asset, cancellation rights, amount of rentals, and the period of the lease agreement.

A further option would be for Mr. Geep to put in more ownership capital, perhaps secured on the equity in his house.

A mixture of these various forms of finance would be most likely.

The precise mix will depend upon a number of factors (although some of these may also influence the total amount of finance needed):

(1) The ability and willingness of Mr. Geep to supply funds initially and additionally if plans do not turn out as expected.

(2) A loan would require some security. The company has few assets to use as security as there does not appear to be any property, the machinery has a low net realisable value and there is little stock (which is normally poor security anyway). An overdraft may also require security, but may place increased emphasis on the cash-generating potential of the business to make appropriate repayments. Ultimately, however, this is an unlimited business and Mr. Geep's personal assets, and particularly the equity in his house, will act as security.

(3) Other costs are necessary including the drawings of the owner Mr. Geep and interest charges. These will reduce the ability of the business to repay any loan and thus extend the period of repayments in excess of the above estimate of 35 months.

(4) There may be more restrictive covenants in a loan agreement than an overdraft, because an overdraft is repayable on demand, and thus the bank needs less protection from other clauses in the contact. The documentation for an overdraft, unlike a longer-term loan, is fairly short and simple.

(5) Overdraft interest is only payable on the balance outstanding, thus if major inflows occur this will reduce interest costs.

(6) The difference between short- and long-term interest rates may influence the relative charges on an overdraft or a medium-term loan.

(7) The purpose of the finance is also likely to affect the form of finance. For example, if funds are required to finance fixed assets then it might be appropriate to use long-term finance to match the long-term usage of the asset.

(iii) **Working capital management**

It has already been seen (in answer (b)) that a reduction in stock due to the introduction of just-in-time stock management can improve liquidity and reduce any cash deficit. The same principle can be applied to reductions in other elements of working capital.

Some of the same arguments also apply, however, in that while liquidity may be improved there could be offsetting disadvantages in terms of lost profitability or increased risk.

**Debtors**

Giving two months' credit creates a significant level of debtors that need financing.

If sales are £33,000 per month, the cash flow needed to fund the debtors will be:

| | £ |
|---|---|
| Sales with one month's credit (£33,000 × 90% × 50% × 0.975) | 14,479 |
| Sales with two month's credit (£33,000 × 90% × 50% × 2m) | 29,700 |
| Total | 44,179 |

This is a significant proportion of the maximum financing requirement.

Whether the credit terms themselves can be changed may depend on the credit terms of competitors when set alongside the other conditions of sale. If the business is out of line with competitors, lost sales may result. A balance may therefore need to be struck between liquidity and profitability.

In terms of debt collection, it would appear that all debtors are expected to pay on time so there is little that can be done in this area given the current credit terms.

Accelerated payment could be encouraged by a higher cash discount but this is expensive, particularly as customers who would pay within one month anyway would also receive a greater reduction in price without any benefit to the business.

Invoice discounting and debt factoring may be alternative sources of financing, but these can be expensive and in the particular circumstances of the business, where there are expected to be no late payers or bad debts, it might seem inappropriate to use outside assistance.

**Creditors**

It may be possible to delay payment to creditors in respect of materials and variable overheads. This may, however, damage relationships with suppliers and this might be significant for a new business.

| ACCA marking scheme | | |
|---|---|---|
| | | *Marks* |
| (a) | Demand forecasts | 2 |
| | Production cash flows | 5 |
| | Sales cash flows | 4 |
| | Fixed cost cash flows | 1 |
| | Consultant cost cash flows | 1 |
| | Capital investment cash flows | 1 |
| | Fixed asset cash flows | 1 |
| | Bank balances | 2 |
| (b) | Sales | 4 |
| | Labour | 2 |
| (c) | 2 marks for each explained point | 6 |
| (d) | Up to 2 marks for each explained point | 18 |
| | Report format | 2 |
| Total | | 50 |

## 3    DOE LIMITED

### Key answer tips

For part (a) of the question, remember to present the answer in a report format. To provide an answer, you need to make it clear that you understand what overtrading is (trying to carry on too much business with insufficient long-term finance) and what the symptoms of overtrading might be (raid increase in sales, increases in current assets financed largely or entirely by current liabilities, growing bank overdraft, deteriorating current ratio and acid test ratio). These symptoms are evident in the figures for Doe Limited.

Part (b) tests your ability to evaluate the costs of using a factor to collect debts and provide factor finance. However, although the factor will provide a without recourse (non-recourse) service, no information is provided about the benefits that might arise from savings in bad debts. This should be mentioned in your answer. Part (c) calls for a broader consideration of debt collection policies and procedures.

Parts (d) and (e) are a good test of your understanding of DCF techniques, and you should check how long it takes you to write an answer. The two parts of the question together are only worth 15 marks, and you need to work quickly to complete the question within the time allowed.

(a)                                          **REPORT**

To:    The Board of Doe Limited

From: Accountant

Date: xx/xx/xx

Subject:  **Is the company overtrading?**

1    **Introduction**

This report presents my findings regarding the suggestion made at the last board meeting that our company is overtrading. Overtrading is also known as under capitalisation, and occurs when the volume of trade is not supported by an adequate supply of capital. Overtrading can lead to liquidity problems that can cause serious difficulties if they are not dealt with promptly.

2    **Signs of overtrading**

There are a number of generally recognised signs that a company may be overtrading. These are considered, together with relevant financial data from Appendix 1, in the following paragraphs.

*Rapid increase in turnover*

The forecast financial statements for 20X3 show that our turnover is expected to increase by 25% during the year.

*Rapid increase in current assets*

Current assets are expected to rise by 27%, slightly more than the increase in turnover.

*Increase in stock days and debtor days*

Debtor days are expected to increase from 110 to 121 days, with a 38% increase in total debtors, but stock days are not expected to increase, but to fall from 265 days to 238 days. Nevertheless, a 19% increase in stocks is anticipated.

*Increased reliance on short-term finance*

Reserves are expected to increase by £100,000 whereas total assets are expected to increase by £1,400,000. The expansion of our business activity is therefore based primarily on an expansion of short-term finance (trade creditors and overdraft). Creditor days will increase from 177 to 190 days, while in relative terms creditors will increase by 42% – more than the expected rise in turnover (25%) and in our overdraft (20%).

*Decrease in current ratio and quick ratio*

The current ratio is expected to fall very slightly from 1·04 to 1·03, but the quick ratio is not expected to fall, but to increase from 0.44 to 0.47.

However, any interpretation of these ratios should reflect the fact that different industries have different working capital needs. Sector average data can be useful here.

3    **Comparison with sector averages**

Any conclusion about the signs of overtrading needs to be put in the context of the normal values of accounting ratios for other companies in the industry, as indicated by the sector averages. However, it should be recognised that averages exist because no two companies are identical, even when in the same business sector, and the following discussion should be read with this in mind.

The increasing trend of debtor days away from the sector average of 100 days is clearly a cause for concern. If our level of debtors was brought into line with the sector average our financing need would fall by £477,000 (£2.75m × 21/121), which is equivalent to 17% of our forecast overdraft. The decrease in stock days is encouraging, although forecast stock days remain 13% higher than the sector average, indicating the possibility of further improvement.

There is clear evidence of an increased reliance on short-term finance. The trend of creditor days is increasing away from the sector average of 120 days and the forecast of 190 days is a very worrying 58% more than the average. This represents £940,000 (£2.55m × 70/190) more in trade finance that our company is carrying compared to a similar company in our business sector. On this evidence, it is likely that our suppliers will begin to press for earlier settlement in the near future and this will add to the pressure already being exerted by our bank.

The quick ratio is expected to increase but will still be 15% below the sector average, while the current ratio is expected to be 25% lower than the average. The low current and quick ratios reflect the increased reliance of our company in comparative terms on short-term sources of finance.

4    **Conclusion on overtrading**

Most of the evidence suggests that our company is moving into an overtrading situation, although the evidence is not conclusive. Current pressure from our bank to reduce our overdraft serves to highlight the fact that our company needs to reduce its reliance on short-term finance, whether trade finance or overdraft finance. Improved working capital management could reduce the level of investment in debtors, and to a lesser extent perhaps in stocks, which would ease our financial difficulties. However, more drastic measures than this will be needed to deal with our reliance on short-term finance. Although the size of the reduction in the overdraft required by the bank is not known at present, simply reducing trade credit to an average level would need £1m of additional finance. Factoring of debtors has been suggested as a source of working capital finance and it is certainly true that this would produce an immediate injection of cash that could decrease our overdraft and lower our average trade credit period. A further consideration is that our company has no long-term debt and given our continuing growth, this source of finance also deserves serious consideration.

**Appendix 1: Financial analysis**

| | | | |
|---|---|---|---|
| Growth in turnover | = | (8,300 – 6,638)/6,638 = 0.25 or 25% | |
| Growth in current assets | = | (5,950 – 4,700)/4,700 = 0.27 or 27% | |
| Increase in overdraft | = | (2,750 – 2,300)/2,300 = 0.20 or 20% | |
| Increase in trade creditors | = | (2,550 – 1,800)/1,800 = 00.42 or 42% | |

| | | 20X3 | | 20X2 |
|---|---|---|---|---|
| Stock turnover (days) | 365 × 3,200/4,900 | 238 days | 365 × 2,700/3,720 | 265 days |
| Debtor days | 365 × 2,750/8,300 | 121 days | 365 × 2,000/6,638 | 110 days |
| Creditor days | 365 × 2,550/4,900 | 190 days | 365 × 1,800/3,720 | 177 days |
| Current ratio | 5,950/5,800 | 1.03 | 4,700/4,500 | 1.04 |
| Quick ratio | 2,750/5,800 | 0.47 | 2,000/4,500 | 0.44 |

(b) (i) **Evaluation of factor's offer using overdraft interest rate of 6%**

| | £ |
|---|---|
| Cost of financing with the factor | |
| 80% of £8.3 million × 90/365 × 8% | 130,981 |
| 20% of £8.3 million × 90/365 × 6% | 24,559 |
| | 155,540 |
| Current cost of financing debtors | |
| £2,750,000 × 6% | 165,000 |
| *Saving in finance costs with factor* | 9,460 |
| *Saving in administration costs* | 15,000 |
| | 24,460 |
| *Factor's fee* (£8.3 million × 1%) | (83,000) |
| *Net cost of factoring* | (58,540) |

On this analysis, the factor's offer is not financially acceptable. The offer was on a non-recourse basis, however, and the information given does not refer to any reduction in bad debts. If bad debts are currently more than 0.7% of turnover (£58,540/£8.3m), the factor's offer might become financially attractive.

**Evaluation of factor's offer using medium-term bank loan rate of 10%**

As the overdraft must be reduced anyway, the 10% interest cost of the medium-term bank loan could be seen as the opportunity cost of not accepting the factor's offer. An alternative evaluation of the factor's offer could be as follows:

| | £ |
|---|---|
| Cost of financing with the factor | |
| 80% of £8.3 million × 90/365 × 8% | 130,981 |
| 20% of £8.3 million × 90/365 × 10% | 40,932 |
| | 171,913 |

| | |
|---|---:|
| Current cost of financing debtors £2,750,000 × 10% | 275,000 |
| | ———— |
| Saving in finance costs with factor | 103,087 |
| Saving in administration costs | 15,000 |
| | ———— |
| | 118,087 |
| Factor's fee (£8.3 million × 1%) | (83,000) |
| | ———— |
| Net benefit from factoring | 35,087 |
| | ———— |

On this analysis, in view of the high interest rate on the bank loan, the factor's offer is financially acceptable, even before considering any reduction in bad debts.

(ii) The following benefits of factoring are commonly identified.

**Factor finance**

The factoring company will advance up to 80% of the face value of invoices raised. This would create a one-off improvement in cash flow and allow Doe Ltd to pay its trade creditors promptly and perhaps take advantage of any early payment discounts available. It would also allow Doe Ltd to finance its growth from sales rather than by seeking external finance.

**Reduces administration costs**

The factor would take over the administration of Doe Ltd's sales ledger, allowing a reduction in administration costs in the longer term.

**Factor expertise**

In the areas of credit analysis and debtor collection, the expertise of the factor is likely to be higher than Doe Ltd's, leading to lower bad debts and more efficient collection of amounts owed by debtors.

**Credit protection**

If the factoring is with recourse, Doe Ltd will be effectively insured against the possibility of bad debts, although this will be included in the factor's fee.

(c) No information has been provided on the current methods used by Doe Ltd to manage its debtors and so this answer is in general terms.

**Credit analysis: granting credit**

Potential credit customers should be carefully screened using such methods as trade references, bank references, credit reports from credit reference agencies, and analysis of financial statements. The extent of the credit analysis should depend on the size of the initial order as well as the potential for repeat business. Credit analysis can improve debtor management by reducing the incidence of bad debts, slow payers and troublesome customers.

**Terms of trade**

Doe Ltd should negotiate agreed terms of trade with its customers in order to encourage prompter payment. These terms of trade may offer discounts for early payment, which apart from cash flow benefits will reduce the likelihood of late payments and bad debts.

### Credit control

Once credit has been extended it is important to ensure that customers abide by agreed terms of trade. Regular checks on customer accounts, for example using an aged debtor analysis, can direct attention to overdue accounts or those close to their credit limit. Statements of account should be mailed to debtors on a regular basis in order to remind them of their outstanding debts. Late payers should be contacted by telephone to enquire after the reason for the delay in settling their accounts. A policy of charging interest on overdue accounts might be considered in order to encourage prompt payment.

### Debt collection

The company should have an agreed policy or procedure for dealing with accounts in default. This policy should be included in the terms of trade so that customers are aware of the steps the company is likely to take if payment is not made on time. The company could decide, for example, to take legal action to recover debts more than one month old. However, the benefit of such action must always exceed the cost incurred.

### Factoring and invoice discounting

The cash flow and other benefits of factoring were discussed earlier. Invoice discounting also offers cash flow advantages. With invoice discounting, selected invoices of good quality are sold in exchange for an advance of up to 80% of face value. The balance, less a fee charged by the invoice discounter, is received when the invoices are settled.

(d)  It is appropriate to use the after-tax cost of borrowing as the discount rate since Doe Ltd is clearly in a tax-paying situation and hence is in a position to claim the tax benefits of lease payments and capital allowances.

Care must be taken when determining the timing of cash flows, since financial evaluation models seek to represent the real world. As lease payments are made on the first day of Doe Ltd's accounting period, it is appropriate to treat them for discounting purposes as though they occur at the end of the previous accounting period. However, the tax benefits of lease payments will occur in the accounting period following that in which payment is made. Similarly, it is appropriate to treat the purchase cost on 1 January of the first year of use as being made at year 0 for discounting purposes, even though the tax benefit from the first capital allowance will arise in year 2, i.e. in the accounting period following the one in which payment is made.

### Capital allowances and associated tax benefits:

| Start of Year | Written down value of asset | Capital allowance (25%) | Tax benefit (30%) | Tax benefit cash flow in Year |
|---|---|---|---|---|
| | £ | £ | £ | |
| 1 | 365,000 | 91,250 | 27,375 | 2 |
| 2 | 273,750 | 68,437 | 20,531 | 3 |
| 3 | 205,313 | 51,328 | 15,398 | 4 |
| 4 | 153,985 | 38,496 | 11,549 | 5 |
| 5 | 115,489 | | 34,647 | 6 |

### Evaluation of borrowing to buy:

| Year | | Cash flow | Discount factor at 7% | Present value |
|---|---|---|---|---|
| | | £ | | £ |
| 0 | Capital expenditure | (365,000) | 1.000 | (365,000) |
| 2 | Tax savings | 27,375 | 0.873 | 23,898 |

| Year | | Cash flow £ | Discount factor at 7% | Present value £ |
|---|---|---|---|---|
| 3 | Tax savings | 20,531 | 0.816 | 16,753 |
| 4 | Tax savings | 15,398 | 0.763 | 11,749 |
| 5 | Tax savings | 11,549 | 0.713 | 8,234 |
| 6 | Tax savings | 34,647 | 0.666 | 23,075 |
| | Net present value | | | (281,291) |

The cost of borrowing to buy the machine is £281,291.

**Evaluation of leasing**

| Years | | Cash flow £ | Discount factor at 7% | Present value £ |
|---|---|---|---|---|
| 0 – 4 | Lease rentals | (77,250) | 4.387 | (338,896) |
| 2 – 6 | Savings in tax payments | 23,175 | 3.832 | 88,807 |
| | Net present value | | | (250,089) |

*Notes:*

Discount factor, years 0 – 4 = 1.000 + 3.387 = 4.387

Discount factor, years 2 – 6 = 4.767 – 0.935 = 3.832.

The cost of leasing is £250.089.

Leasing has the lower cost by £31,202 and is therefore preferred to borrowing.

(e)  The optimum price will be the one that maximizes total contribution over the five-year life of the new machine. (Taxation and the time value of money are ignored, as required by the question.)

**Sales price of £70 per unit**

Contribution per unit = £70 – £42 = £28 per unit.

Sales growth is 20% per annum.

| Year | 1 | 2 | 3 | 4 | 5 |
|---|---|---|---|---|---|
| Sales volume (units) | 10,000 | 12,000 | 14,400 | 17,280 | 20,000 |
| Contribution (£/unit) | 28 | 28 | 28 | 28 | 28 |
| Total contribution (£) | 280,000 | 336,000 | 403,200 | 483,840 | 560,000 |

Year 5 sales volume is limited to the maximum capacity of the new machine.

Total contribution over the five years is £2,063,400

**Sales price of £67 per unit**

Contribution per unit = 67 – 42 = £25 per unit.

Sales growth is 23% per annum.

| Year | 1 | 2 | 3 | 4 | 5 |
|---|---|---|---|---|---|
| Sales volume (units) | 11,000 | 13,530 | 16,640 | 20,000 | 20,000 |
| Contribution (£/unit) | 25 | 25 | 25 | 25 | 25 |
| Total contribution (£) | 275,000 | 338,250 | 416,050 | 500,000 | 500,000 |

Sales volume is restricted in years 4 and 5.

Total contribution over the five years is £2,029,300.

## Conclusion

The sales price of £70 per unit appears to be marginally preferable on the basis of total contribution. The incremental fixed production overheads will be the same irrespective of which sales price is selected and so may be omitted from the analysis.

| | | ACCA marking scheme | Marks |
|---|---|---|---|
| (a) | | Explanation of overtrading | 1 |
| | | Symptoms of overtrading | 2 |
| | | Calculation of relevant ratios | 4 |
| | | Discussion of evidence for overtrading | 3 |
| | | Conclusion and format | 2 |
| | | | 12 |
| (b) | (i) | Change in level of debtors | 1 |
| | | Reduction in cost of financing | 1 |
| | | Cost of advance by factor | 1 |
| | | Administration savings | 1 |
| | | Factor's fee | 1 |
| | | Net cost of factor's offer | 1 |
| | | Discussion | 1 |
| | | | 7 |
| | (ii) | Up to 2 marks for each detailed advantage | 8 |
| (c) | | Up to 3 marks for each way discussed | 8 |
| (d) | | Capital allowances | 2 |
| | | Tax effects of capital allowances | 1 |
| | | Evaluation of cost of borrowing to buy | 2 |
| | | Lease payments | 1 |
| | | Tax effects of lease payments | 1 |
| | | Evaluation of cost of leasing | 1 |
| | | Evaluation of leasing versus borrowing to buy | 1 |
| | | | 9 |
| (e) | | Sales volumes | 2 |
| | | Annual contributions | 2 |
| | | Total contributions | 1 |
| | | Conclusion | 1 |
| | | | 6 |
| Total | | | 50 |

## 4    NESPA

### Key answer tips

Parts (a) to (c) of the question should be straightforward, although cash flows must be adjusted for inflation, and in part (b) the effect of capital allowances on cash flows must also be calculated. The difficulty with these sections of the question is completing all the calculations accurately within the time available. When answering part (d), don't overlook the second part of the question, about Nespa's views of investment appraisal methods.

For part (e), there are several methods commonly considered to assess project risk and uncertainty, such as sensitivity analysis, probability analysis, risk-adjusted discount rates, certainty equivalents and range estimates. The question asks for a discussion of just two methods, although three methods are discussed in this solution.

Part (f) should be straightforward, but it is important to refer to the question scenario in your answer, rather than writing in general terms about alternative sources of finance.

(a)  *Assumption*: It is assumed that the inflation rate of 3% in prices and variables costs applies from Year 1 onwards.

**Strategy 1**

| Year | 1 | 2 | 3 | 4 | 5 |
|---|---|---|---|---|---|
| Demand (units) | 100,000 | 105,000 | 110,250 | 115,762 | 121,551 |
| Selling price (£/unit) | 8.00 | 8.00 | 8.00 | 8.00 | 8.00 |
| Variable cost (£/unit) | 3.00 | 3.00 | 2.95 | 2.95 | 2.90 |
| Contribution (£/unit) | 5.00 | 5.00 | 5.05 | 5.05 | 5.10 |
| Inflation factor at 3% per year | 1.03 | 1.0609 | 1.0927 | 1.1255 | 1.1593 |
| Inflated contribution (£/unit) | 5.15 | 5.30 | 5.52 | 5.68 | 5.91 |
| Total contribution (£) | 515,000 | 556,500 | 608,580 | 657,528 | 718,366 |
| 10% discount factors | 0.909 | 0.826 | 0.751 | 0.683 | 0.621 |
| PV of contribution (£) | 468,135 | 459,669 | 457,044 | 449,092 | 446,105 |

**Total PV of strategy 1 contributions** = £2,280,045 or approximately £2,280,000.

*Strategy 2*

| Year | 1 | 2 | 3 | 4 | 5 |
|---|---|---|---|---|---|
| Demand (units) | 110,000 | 126,500 | 145,475 | 167,296 | 192,391 |
| Selling price (£/unit) | 7.00 | 7.00 | 7.00 | 7.00 | 7.00 |
| Variable cost (£/unit) | 2.95 | 2.90 | 2.80 | 2.70 | 2.55 |
| Contribution (£/unit) | 4.05 | 4.10 | 4.20 | 4.30 | 4.45 |
| Inflation factor at 3% per year | 1.03 | 1.0609 | 1.0927 | 1.1255 | 1.1597 |
| Inflated contribution (£/unit) | 4.17 | 4.35 | 4.59 | 4.84 | 5.16 |
| Total contribution (£) | 458,700 | 550,275 | 667,730 | 809,713 | 992,738 |
| 10% discount factors | 0.909 | 0.826 | 0.751 | 0.683 | 0.621 |
| PV of contribution (£) | 416,958 | 454,527 | 501,465 | 553,034 | 616,490 |

**Total PV of strategy 2 contributions** = £2,542,474 or approximately £2,542,000.

Strategy 2 is preferred as it has the higher present value of contributions.

(b)  Evaluating the investment in the new machine using internal rate of return:

| Year | 0 £ | 1 £ | 2 £ | 3 £ | 4 £ | 5 £ |
|---|---|---|---|---|---|---|
| Contribution | | 458,700 | 550,275 | 667,730 | 809,713 | 992,738 |
| Fixed costs | | (114,400) | (118,976) | (123,735) | (128,684) | (133,832) |
| Taxable profit | | 344,300 | 431,299 | 543,995 | 681,029 | 858,906 |
| Taxation at 30% | | (103,290) | (129,390) | (163,199) | (204,309) | (257,672) |
| | | 241,010 | 301,909 | 380,796 | 476,720 | 601,234 |
| Capital allowance tax benefits (see note) | | 112,500 | 84,375 | 63,281 | 47,461 | 142,383 |
| Profit after tax | | 353,510 | 386,284 | 444,077 | 524,181 | 743,617 |

*Note: capital allowances and tax benefits*

| Year | | £ |
|---|---|---|
| 1 | 25% × £1,500,000 × 30% tax rate | 112,500 |
| 2 | 75% of Year 1 amount | 84,375 |
| 3 | 75% of Year 2 amount | 63,281 |
| 4 | 75% of Year 3 amount | 47,461 |
| | | 307,617 |
| 5 | Balancing amount | 142,383 |
| Total | £1,500,000 × 30% tax rate | 450,000 |

| | | | | | | |
|---|---|---|---|---|---|---|
| Cash flows | (1,500,000) | 353,510 | 386,284 | 444,077 | 524,181 | 743,617 |
| 10% discount factors | 1.000 | 0.909 | 0.826 | 0.751 | 0.683 | 0.621 |
| Present values | (1,500,000) | 321,341 | 319,071 | 333,502 | 358,016 | 461,786 |

NPV at 10% = £293,716

| | | | | | | |
|---|---|---|---|---|---|---|
| Cash flows | (1,500,000) | 353,510 | 386,284 | 444,077 | 524,181 | 743,617 |
| 20% discount factors | 1.000 | 0.833 | 0.694 | 0.579 | 0.482 | 0.402 |
| Present values | (1,500,000) | 294,474 | 268,081 | 257,121 | 252,655 | 298,934 |

NPV at 20% = (£128,735)

IRR = 10% + [ 293,716 / (293,716 + 128,735)] × (20 – 10)% = 17%.

Since the internal rate of return is greater than the company's cost of capital of 10%, the investment is financially acceptable.

(c)    Evaluating the investment using return on capital employed:

Annual depreciation charge = £1,500,000/5 = £300,000

| Year | 1 | 2 | 3 | 4 | 5 |
|---|---|---|---|---|---|
| | £ | £ | £ | £ | £ |
| Contribution | 458,700 | 550,275 | 667,730 | 809,713 | 992,738 |
| Fixed costs | (114,400) | (118,976) | (123,735) | (128,684) | (133,832) |
| Depreciation | (300,000) | (300,000) | (300,000) | (300,000) | (300,000) |
| Annual PBIT | 44,300 | 131,299 | 243,995 | 381,029 | 558,906 |

Total profit before interest and tax (PBIT) over five years = £1,359,529.

Average investment = £1,500,000/2 = £750,000

Average annual accounting profit = £1,359,529/5 = £271,906

Return on capital employed = (£271,906/ £750,000) × 100% = 36%.

Since the return on capital employed is greater than the hurdle rate of 20%, the investment is financially acceptable.

(d)    Internal rate of return (IRR) is a discounted cash flow investment appraisal method that calculates the discount rate which causes the net present value of an investment to become zero. An investment project is acceptable if it has an IRR greater than the cost of capital of the investing company. It uses cash flows rather than accounting profits in the evaluation of an investment project. It also takes account of the time value of money, the concept that the value of a given sum of money decreases over time due to the opportunity cost of selecting one investment rather than the best available alternative. IRR considers all cash flows over the life of an investment project and always gives correct advice, provided that investment projects being compared are not mutually exclusive.

Return on capital employed (ROCE) is also called accounting rate of return. Unlike IRR, ROCE uses average annual accounting profit before interest and tax in the evaluation of investment projects, expressing this as a percentage of the amount of capital invested. The decision as to whether a project is acceptable is made by comparing project ROCE with a target ROCE, such as a company's current ROCE.

The problem with using accounting profit rather than cash flow is that only cash flow (and not profit) is linked directly to an increase in company value. ROCE also ignores the time value of money. Because it averages accounting profit over the life of the project, the amount of profit in a given year is irrelevant; ROCE therefore ignores the timing of accounting profits.

ROCE also suffers from definition problems as there are several definitions in common use and so care must be taken to ensure comparisons are made using identical definitions. Capital invested can be defined as initial capital invested or average capital invested, but other definitions are met in practice.

Both IRR and ROCE offer a relative measure of return in percentage terms, a feature that is seen as attractive to managers who may have difficulty in interpreting the absolute measure of value offered by net present value. A relative measure of return ignores the size of the initial investment, however, and so should not be relied on as a sole measure of investment worth.

Academically, IRR is preferred to ROCE because it takes account of the time value of money, uses cash flows, and compares the return on investment projects with the cost of capital of a company.

Nespa's use of several investment appraisal methods is, however, common in practice as few companies rely on a single investment appraisal method.

The company is correct in its belief that NPV measures the potential increase in company value of an investment project, since theoretically the stock market value of a company increases by the total NPV of projects undertaken. This is correct as long as the capital market is efficient and information about new investment projects is made available to it.

It is possible that a high IRR offers a margin of safety for risky projects and it can be interpreted in this way. However, calculation of IRR is not a substitute for an assessment of project risk.

Nespa's decision rule for ROCE is flawed, in that if used continually it could eventually run out of investment projects that meet its hurdle rate (its existing before-tax ROCE). This hurdle rate could increase with each successive project accepted, causing the company to reject projects that would have been acceptable in a previous period. However, it is important to recognise that not all costs associated with the capital budgeting process are included in investment appraisal and that such costs will reduce the existing ROCE. The sunk cost of Nespa's market research is one example, and another would be infrastructure costs that increase on a stepped basis as a result of cumulative project investment. The existence of such costs offers a partial justification for Nespa's ROCE decision rule.

(e)    In assessing project risk it is important to be clear about the meaning of risk. From an academic perspective, risk refers to a set of circumstances regarding a given decision to which probabilities can be assigned. This distinguishes risk from uncertainty, which implies that it is not possible to assign probabilities to future events. In practice, the two terms are often used interchangeably, but the distinction is a useful one for the purposes of analysis and discussion.

(*Note:* Three methods of analysis are described here. Only two are required for a solution. A discussion of (1) certainty equivalents and (2) range estimates would be equally acceptable.)

### Sensitivity analysis

This method measures the change in project NPV arising from a fixed change in each project variable, or measures the change in each project variable required to make the NPV zero. Only one project variable is changed at a time. The key or critical project variables are the ones to which the NPV is most sensitive, or the ones where the smallest change results in a zero NPV.

Knowledge of the key project variables allows managers to confirm the strength of their underlying assumptions, thereby increasing their confidence that the forecast NPV will be achieved. It also allows managers to monitor these variables closely when the project is implemented as a way of ensuring success. However, sensitivity analysis does not indicate the likelihood of a change occurring in a given project variable and so, strictly speaking, does not assess project risk at all.

### Probability analysis

This involves the assessment of the probabilities of future events linked to an investment project. If these events are general circumstances, the technique is called scenario analysis. For example, an assessment might be made of the outcome of an investment project under poor, moderate and good economic conditions, and the probability of each economic state arising assessed.

An alternative approach is to assess the likelihood of particular values of project variables occurring, so that a probability distribution for each variable can be determined. This leads to the technique called simulation or the Monte Carlo method, which results in a probability distribution for the project NPV.

With both approaches it is therefore possible to determine the expected net present value (ENPV) based on all possible outcomes, and the probability of a negative or zero NPV. The problem with probability analysis is that in practice it is difficult to determine the probabilities to be attached to future events. An inescapable element of subjectivity is likely to exist in probability estimates.

### Risk-adjusted discount rates

One technique under this heading is the assignment of investment projects to one of a set of risk classes, and each risk class has a different discount rate. The assessment of risk depends here on the classification of the project: for example, asset replacements projects are considered to be low risk, while new product launches may be placed in a high risk category. The discount rate applied increases with the risk class to which a project is assigned. One problem with this technique is that there may be no academic justification for the discount rate assigned to each risk class, so that there is no explicit link between risk and required rate of return.

An alternative approach is to increase the discount rate by an amount that reflects the perceived risk of an investment project, i.e. to add a risk premium reflecting project risk. While this can be done on a rule of thumb basis, so that a different discount rate is used for each project, it would be preferable to use a technique that assesses project risk and derives a required rate of return based on that assessment. (*Note*: Such techniques are outside the syllabus.)

(f) Since Nespa has been listed on a stock exchange for some time, it will be able to access the capital market for new finance if it wishes. It can therefore consider issuing debt securities, such as debentures or loan stock, issuing shares to existing shareholders via a rights issue, issuing shares to new investors, a bank loan, and leasing. However, Nespa is a medium-sized company, and it is therefore doubtful whether the company would be able to access the domestic or international bond markets to issue debt securities. Equity finance, bank loans or lease finance seem the most practical alternatives.

Nespa should consider the following factors.

**Amount of finance needed**

Although the director suggests that equity finance is appropriate given the amount of finance needed, the amount alone does not rule out other financing methods. It would be sensible to review the effect of the new finance on the company's capital structure and cost of capital, to consider the relative issue costs of different sources of finance, and to assess the effect on the company of any change in financial risk.

**Cost of capital**

If Nespa can reduce its average cost of capital, this will increase its overall value. The information that its interest cover is higher than similar companies points to its competitors having proportionately more debt in their capital structures, a view supported by Nespa's return on capital employed being close to the sector average.

It is also worth noting that, since Nespa's average cost of capital (and hence its cost of equity) is 10%, and since equity is more expensive than debt, the cost of debt finance is certain to be less than 10%. The tax efficiency of debt will reduce the effective cost to Nespa even further, implying that debt finance at a cost of 6% or less is available; the cost will be even lower for secured debt. From this discussion it may be concluded that an issue of debt may well be in the best interests of Nespa's shareholders.

**Security**

Nespa appears to have an adequate supply of fixed assets to offer as security for an issue of new debt.

**Interest cover and earnings**

Nespa should also consider the volatility of its profit before interest and tax. Debt finance would not be as attractive if this volatility is high. This is because with gearing in the capital structure, profits after tax (= earnings) are even more volatile than profits before interest and tax.

The existence of similar companies with lower interest cover indicates that competitors may be comfortable with higher levels of debt than Nespa.

**Maturity**

Nespa should match the maturity of the finance with the life of the purchased asset, although no indication of the useful economic life of the new machine is provided.

**Leasing**

Clear advice cannot be given because we lack detailed financial information on the company. It may be worth considering leasing as an alternative to outright purchase, but this decision would depend on an assessment of relevant costs and benefits. For example, under an operating lease the lessor would be responsible for maintenance and servicing, but the cost of this would be reflected in the annual lease payments.

The least likely alternative in the circumstances described appears to be equity finance. While this financing choice keeps financial risk low, it does not appear to offer any other advantages to shareholders.

| ACCA marking scheme | | |
|---|---|---|
| | | *Marks* |
| (a) | Variable costs | 2 |
| | Contribution | 2 |
| | Inflated contribution | 2 |
| | Present value of overall contribution | 2 |
| | Selection of contribution-maximising strategy | <u>1</u> |
| | | <u>9</u> |

| | | | |
|---|---|---|---:|
| (b) | | Inflated fixed costs | 1 |
| | | Taxable profit | 1 |
| | | Tax liabilities | 1 |
| | | Capital allowance tax benefits | 3 |
| | | Net present values | 2 |
| | | Calculation of internal rate of return | 2 |
| | | Omission of cost of market research | 1 |
| | | Recommendation | 1 |
| | | | 12 |
| (c) | | Annual depreciation | 1 |
| | | Average accounting profit | 1 |
| | | Average investment | 1 |
| | | Return on capital employed | 1 |
| | | Recommendation | 1 |
| | | | 5 |
| (d) | | Discussion of IRR | 3 |
| | | Discussion of ROCE | 3 |
| | | Discussion of company's views | 2 |
| | | | 8 |
| (e) | | Discussion of risk and uncertainty | 1 |
| | | Discussion of risk assessment methods | 7 |
| | | | 8 |
| (f) | | Effect of listed company status | 1 |
| | | Discussion of debt finance | 4 |
| | | Discussion of other forms of finance | 3 |
| | | | 8 |
| Total | | | 50 |

## 5    SPENDER CONSTRUCTION PLC

(a)    (i)    **Operational gearing** may be defined as a measure of the impact of a change in sales on Earnings Before Interest and Taxation (EBIT). The following formula can be used to calculate the level of operational gearing for a unit output level of Q:

Level of operational gearing at point Q = $\dfrac{Q(P - VC)}{Q(P - VC) - FC}$

Q    = Units of output

P    = Selling price per unit

VC    = Variable cost per unit

FC    = Total fixed costs

The numerator in the formula represents total contribution. The denominator represents EBIT (total earnings before interest and taxation).

Hence, for any given level of output the **level of operational gearing** =

**Contribution/EBIT**.

A company's level of operational gearing is dependent on the ratio of fixed to variable costs and the current level of profit. If a company has a high level of fixed costs, then beyond the break-even point, an increase in the volume of sales will lead to a high percentage increase in profit. However, the percentage increase declines as the size of the profit continues to grow. Applying the formula shown above to the 20X0 financial statements for Spender plc, we can compute the current level of operational gearing within the company:

Operational gearing = $\dfrac{\text{Contribution}}{\text{EBIT}}$

For 20X0:

| | |
|---|---|
| Variable selling and distribution costs | = £348,000 - £100,000 |
| | = £0.248 million. |
| Variable administration costs | = £8.250 m - £7 m (fixed) |
| | = £1.250 million |
| Contribution | = Sales – Variable costs |
| | = £55.258m – (41.827m + 0.248m + 1.250m) |
| | = £11.933m |
| EBIT | = £4.833m |
| Operational gearing | = 11,933/4.833 |
| | = 2.47 |

(ii) **Financial gearing** is measured by comparing a company's use of long-term debt finance relative to equity. The higher the proportion of debt finance, the higher the level of gearing. Financial gearing affects the sensitivity of the profit attributable to equity (profit after interest and tax) to changes in EBIT. Using debt as a source of finance commits a company to the payment of debt interest which, for any given level of operating profit, erodes the amount of profit attributable to equity investors. However, once operating profits are sufficient to cover the interest payments due, all additions to operating profit will be fully attributable to equity investors.

Textbooks contain a number of different formulae for financial gearing. They include the following alternatives:

(1) $\dfrac{\text{Long - term interest bearing debt} + \text{preference share capital}}{\text{Equity plus reserves}}$

(2) $\dfrac{\text{Long - term interest bearing debt} + \text{preference share capital}}{\text{Total long - term capital}}$

(3) $\dfrac{\text{Profit before interest}}{\text{Profit after interest}}$

A further variation on the formula might be applied which includes short-term interest bearing debt in the numerator. In this way financial gearing is then measuring the proportion of total borrowing relative to total capital, rather than just the proportion of long-term loans in the total capital base.

It is useful to note the differences between the formulae. The first two differ only in relation to the denominator, but this has the effect of altering the resulting figure for financial gearing. This can be illustrated by reference to Spender plc.

Using formula (1) in respect of the 20X0 financial statements.

| | |
|---|---|
| Financial gearing | $= \dfrac{1,200}{12,452}$ |
| | = 0.0964 or 9.64% |

Using formula (2):

$$\text{Financial gearing} = \frac{1,200}{13,652}$$

$$= 0.0879 \text{ or } 8.799\%$$

The second figure is lower because the denominator is larger. This means that care must be taken in interpreting figures for financial gearing to ensure that there is consistency in the formula chosen for the calculation. Finally, applying formula (3), which uses figures from the profit and loss account (as opposed to the balance sheet), and so is more consistent with the operational gearing calculation done earlier, we get:

$$\text{Financial gearing} = \frac{\text{Profit before interest}}{\text{Profit after interest}}$$

$$= \frac{4,833}{4,506}$$

$$= 1.07$$

Formula (3) yields a very different result to the other two, and so serves to underline further the need for caution in interpretation of gearing figures.

Financial gearing is sometimes referred to as 'second tier' gearing because it affects the profit going to equity but not until the impact of operational gearing has already affected the level of EBIT. This means that if a company trades with a high level of operational gearing, EBIT is already highly sensitive to changes in sales revenue. If this is then combined with the potential for further erosion of the returns to equity as a result of large debt interest payments (caused by high financial gearing) then the overall risk to equity investors is high. This overall effect is most important to investors, and means that attention needs to be given to a company's level of operational and financial gearing in combination.

Spender's fixed costs (which are £7,100,000 excluding interest payments) equal over 12.5 % of sales, compared with the industry average of just 7%. The potential risk of this high operational gearing level lies in the sales volatility that is often associated with construction firms. The industry is very sensitive to the state of the economy, and an economic downturn can hit sales quite dramatically. Under such circumstances, and with an operational gearing level of 2.47, Spender plc could find that a 10% fall in sales from current levels would cause a drop of almost 25% in operating profit. It is worth noting, however, that this gearing level will come down next year as a result of increased sales and reduced fixed costs. It is probably in recognition of this sensitivity of profits to changes in sales that the company has chosen to keep its level of financial gearing relatively low at 1.07.

Spender's financial gearing cannot be compared with that of the industry because the relevant information is not available. The lower level helps to limit the potential impact of sales changes on the profit available to equity, and so limits the overall risk to equity investors. Nonetheless, Spender plc must be regarded as a somewhat risky choice for equity investors and the example clearly demonstrates how a company needs to think about how it mixes its levels of financial and operating gearing in such a way as to limit the risk to equity shareholders.

(b) The additional working capital required is expected to rise in line with sales (note 6 in the question), i.e. growth of 15%.

To estimate the required increase in working capital, the net current asset figure in the balance sheet should be adjusted to exclude the overdraft and VAT bill, plus tax and dividends payable. Only stocks plus debtors minus trade creditors should be affected by the increase in sales volume.

|  | £000 | £000 |
|---|---|---|
| Net current assets in balance sheet |  | 7,852 |
| Add back: |  |  |
| Overdraft | 2,000 |  |
| VAT bill | 450 |  |
| Corporation tax payable | 1,352 |  |
| Dividends payable | 1,520 |  |
|  |  | 5,322 |
| Adjusted working capital figure |  | 13,174 |

Working capital needed in 20X1 $= 1.15 \times$ (Net current assets in 20X0)

$= 1.15$ (£13.174 million)

$= £15.15$ million.

This represents an increase of £1.98 million (i.e. £13.174 × 0.15).

In addition to the capital expenditure investment of £7 million, this gives an extra funding requirement of £8.98 million. This may be raised either from external or internal sources. Internal funding will come from operations and the anticipated cash flow from operations can be estimated from the profit and loss account for 20X0 and the additional information in the question.

The profit and loss account for 20X0 shows cash inflows from operations equal to £4.956 million (i.e. £4.506 million plus £450,000 VAT), and after adjusting for depreciation this gives an operating cash flow of £5.391 million. The net cash available for investment within the business can thus be calculated as follows:

|  | £000 | £000 |
|---|---|---|
| Operating profit, 20X0 |  | 4,833 |
| Depreciation |  | 435 |
| Cash from operations |  | 5,268 |
| *Cash outflows* |  |  |
| Tax | (1,352) |  |
| Interest payments | (327) |  |
| Dividends | (1,520) |  |
| Other payments | (2,500) |  |
|  |  | (5,699) |
| Net reduction in cash |  | (431) |

The total funding requirement equals £8.98 million. In 20X0, the company would not have been able to meet any of this funding requirement from its operating activities. This suggests that in 20X1, it might be unable to meet any of its additional funding requirements from operating cash flows. (Note. The estimate excludes any allowance for additional cash required to pay higher debenture interest due to new borrowing, or the dividends planned for 20X1 - although these may be funded out of future profits.)

(c) In considering whether to replace short-term with long-term borrowing, Spender plc needs to look at the current structure of its balance sheet and its forecast capital requirements. The current level of financial gearing in the company is relatively low. Converting short- into long-term borrowing will affect the level of financial gearing slightly as calculated in (a)(1), and (a)(2), but the impact on the gearing measure in (a)(3) will depend upon relative short-term and long-term interest rates. The main factors that Spender plc need to consider are the need for flexibility in access to short-term funding and the relative cost and risk of alternative funding sources.

The **overdraft facility** offers the advantage of flexibility, but the cost is relatively high if the funds are borrowed on a semi-permanent basis. In other words, if Spender plc does not expect to utilise its overdraft except for brief periods throughout the year, it may be prudent and cheaper to retain it. On the other hand, if the overdraft is being used to finance 'permanent' working capital within the business, and Spender plc is regularly borrowing at close to the overdraft limit, then it may be prudent to convert the borrowing into a long-term loan. **As a general rule, long-term finance is slightly cheaper**, and given that the company is already having to raise funds for other purposes, the marginal cost of raising an additional £2 million would be small. As a general principle, it is a good idea for companies to **divide working capital requirements into temporary and permanent**, with the funding for these being short-term or long-term respectively. The forecasts suggest that Spender plc will be experiencing rising sales, and an associated high level of cash generation, although this will be linked to a related increase in its need for working capital. By converting the overdraft into a long-term loan, the company can leave itself renewed access to short-term borrowing whilst reducing the average cost of its working capital funding by an increased use of long-term money. The only time when it might not be sensible to convert the overdraft is if economic forecasts suggested that interest rates are expected to fall dramatically in the near future. In such a case, it would make sense to wait until interest rates had bottomed out before converting the overdraft.

(d)    Number of shares currently in issue = 8 million (i.e. £4m/£0.50).

EPS in 20X0 = 39.4 pence (i.e. £3.154m/8m).

Dividend per share in 20X0 = 19 pence (i.e. £1.520 million/8 million).

In comparing a rights issue and a debenture issue as alternative funding sources, it is important to take account of the effect of each alternative on the returns to ordinary shareholders, and the level of risk to those shareholders. It is reasonable to assume that if we are asking shareholders to accept a higher level of risk (operational or financial) then they will expect to receive an increase in their returns in compensation. The two alternative methods of funding affect only the level of financial risk in the company. The debenture issue will increase the level of financial gearing whilst the rights issue will reduce the level of financial gearing. As at December 20X0 the financial gearing of Spender Construction was 1.07. In selecting the most appropriate source of funding, therefore, consideration must be given as to whether such changes would be acceptable to the equity shareholders. A comparison of the forecast EPS under both types of funding is useful in assessing the likely shareholder response. Care must be taken, however, in interpreting the forecast, because only one year's data is available.

### Forecast profit and loss account, Spender Construction, Year ending 31 December 20X1

|  |  | With debenture issue £000 | With rights issue £000 |
|---|---|---:|---:|
| Turnover | (£55,258 × 1.15) | 63,547 | 63,547 |
| Cost of sales | 0.98 × (£41,827 × 1.15) | 47,139 | 47,139 |
| Gross profit | | 16,408 | 16,408 |
| Selling and dist'n costs | (£248 × 1.15) + 100 | 385 | 385 |
| Administration costs | (1,250 × 1.15) + (7,000 − 500) | 7,938 | 7,938 |
| Operating profit | | 8,085 | 8,085 |
| Interest charges | (10% of 1,200) + 280 + (10% of 7,000) | 1,100 | 400 |
| Profit before tax | | 6,985 | 7,685 |
| Corporation tax (30%) | | 2,096 | 2,306 |
| Profit after tax | | 4,889 | 5,379 |
| Dividend | 25p × 8,000/ 25p × 9,333 | 2,000 | 2,333 |
| Retained profit | | 2,889 | 3,046 |

| *Assuming debenture is issued:* | *Assuming rights issue* |
|---|---|
| *Forecast EPS,* | *Forecast EPS,* |
| *Year ending 31 December 20X1* | *Year ending 31 December 20X1* |
| EPS = 4,889/8,000 = 61.1 pence | EPS = 5,379/9,333 = 57.6 pence |
| Change in EPS = 55.1% growth | Change in EPS = 46.2% growth |

The figures show that if the sales targets are achieved, the **EPS will grow faster if debenture financing is selected**, but in both instances the growth is substantial. This is largely because profits are already sufficiently high to meet the interest payments required and so, helped substantially by other changes, such as the fixed cost savings, all increases in profit (net of tax) can accrue to equity investors. The rights issue generates a smaller EPS because the number of shares in issue has been increased by 1.33 million, and so the equity earnings are shared more widely. In either case the shareholders benefit from a growth of EPS which exceeds the rate of growth of sales. However, if sales were to fall, then EPS would fall at a rate greater than the drop in sales, again because of the leverage effect. This risk from additional borrowing must be acknowledged and explained to shareholders.

If shareholders are looking for rapid growth of earnings, it is marginally preferable to fund the investment with the debenture issue. However the **effect** of this choice **on shareholder risk** needs to be taken into account, because Spender's financial gearing will be increased by the debenture issue. Whether shareholders will accept the higher risk or not depends to some extent on industry and economic forecasts. If the outlook for the construction industry is good, then shareholders are likely to accept such a proposal; conversely if the future prospects look poor then the rights issue is the safer choice. The attractiveness of the higher returns from using debenture finance needs to compensate for the marginal additional risk created by the issue, and given that the use of debentures yields an EPS 6% greater than if the rights issue is made then it is likely that this is the case.

In addition to financial considerations, Spender plc should also take into account the **organisational aspects of the two financing alternatives**, including the speed of issue, issue costs, and prevailing stock market conditions. Rights issues will tend to be slower to arrange and complete than a debenture issue, but rights do offer the advantage that the issue costs may be kept low as it is not a requirement (though it is usual practice) for them to be underwritten. At the same time, debentures may be easier to sell if the stock market is volatile or on a bear run.

In conclusion, the debenture issue should be the chosen source of funding if market forecasts indicate rising future sales and earnings. The rights issue should be the chosen source of finance if the directors believe that shareholders are highly risk averse, and would prefer to avoid any additional financial gearing, and that stock market conditions are favourable to such an issue.

(e)   **Dividend cover** is calculated by dividing the profit available to equity by the total dividend payable, and it measures the extent to which equity investors can view their dividend as being 'secure'. As the level of cover rises, so does the security of the dividend, inasmuch as equity investors can still expect there to be sufficient profit available to pay the dividend. A high dividend cover offers a reasonable certainty that dividend levels can be maintained, but it should also lead investors to question how the retained profits are being utilised. By definition, a high dividend cover implies that a large proportion of profits are being retained within the business, and unless these funds are being invested wisely, the equity investor may be better off if the cash is paid out to shareholders, who can then re-invest it elsewhere to earn a better rate of return.

For Spender plc, the forecast profit available to equity (from (d)) if the debentures are issued equals £4.889m and the dividend forecast for the year is £2m. This gives a dividend cover of:

4.889/2 = 2.44 times.

This means that over half of the profit is being retained for re-investment. If the re-investment can be expected to maintain the profit growth achieved between 20X0 and 20X1, then investors have little to worry about. If, however, Spender plc gives little indication of how it intends to use this money, then shareholders should be concerned that dividend cover is perhaps a little high.

## 6  STADIUM EATS

### Key answer tips

In part (a) there are 10 marks, so you need to spend a little time thinking of various issues that may be discussed. You have very little detail in the profit and loss account (indeed, this is one point to raise), so you are expected to look at the broad figures  - level of turnover, margins etc - and then comment on the feasibility of achieving these for a brand new enterprise, and possible impact on the existing business. Some of your criticisms cannot be taken into account when redrafting the profit and loss, but some sensible assumptions are needed as regards turnover and margins to produce revised (lower) figures.

Part (b) gives you a chance to display your general knowledge of gearing before having to relate it to the scenario. Don't stint on your explanation of the meaning of capital gearing - the marks allow you to give a little detail about different definitions and which types of debt may be included etc. You then need to consider the impact of high gearing levels on both lenders and equity investors.

In part (c) you need to apply what you have discussed in general terms in (b) to the data and circumstances of the question. Make it clear which definition of gearing you are using in your calculations. You cannot come to any firm conclusions without any benchmarks for comparison, but you can discuss particular aspects of the restaurant business that may affect the impact of the gearing level.

In part (d) you can initially recall your sources of finance 'checklist', but before writing about any of them, you must think whether they will apply in this particular context. And don't forget the all important source - equity - that appears to be perhaps most appropriate in this case.

In part (e) there are two parts to this requirement - a general discussion on the AIM, followed by the specific factors to be considered in obtaining a listing. The latter actually carries more marks, and should not be skimped on.

(a)  The forecast covers only the first trading year. This is unlikely to be representative of the longer-term trading position of the business, and a forecast over a three- to five-year period would be more appropriate.

The question indicates that the forecast is loosely based on the current Stadium Eats figures. There would in fact appear to have been some questionable assumptions made in constructing the forecast.

Firstly, a sales target of £600,000 (well in excess of the current sales of £425,000) might be considered rather ambitious for the first year. It is unrealistic to assume sales will be close to equivalent to those of the original restaurant within such a short time. Furthermore, it may be that some customers simply switch from eating at Stadium Eats to eating at the new location. The forecast makes no mention of the sales for the overall operation, and the possible interdependence of sales between the two outlets.

The figures given in the forecast are lacking in any detail. There is insufficient information and no comparative data to show sales trends over time. It is impossible to learn anything about the costs of the restaurant from the information given. A detailed breakdown of costs by type, and over time, would be very helpful. The operating profit margin is difficult to appraise without further information on the average rate for similar restaurant businesses, but seems excessive when compared with the margin currently achieved. A forecast cash flow would also be useful.

The forecast may also be criticised for failing to take account of the likely need to employ new managerial staff to take responsibility for the existing outlet, in order to free up the partners to concentrate on the new site.

Working on sales in Stadium Eats at present, annual turnover is equal to £2,833 per cover (£8,500 × 50 weeks/150 covers). The estimate for the new restaurant is equal to £3,333 per cover per annum (£600,000/180 covers). Taking a pessimistic view, sales of perhaps just £1,500 per cover per annum might be assumed, and this would give a turnover of only £270,000, instead of the forecast £600,000.

The current operating profit margin is 11%. If this margin is achieved on the forecast sales of £600,000, operating profit would be just £66,000, as compared to the £135,000 figure for operating profit that is in the forecast. This figure assumes management drawings are maintained at just £22,000 each.

Re-working the forecast to use an adjusted sales figure, and maintaining the 11% net margin gives:

|  | £ |
|---|---|
| Sales | 270,000 |
| Operating profit | 29,700 |
| Less interest | (18,000) |
| Profit before tax | 11,700 |

In practice, it is likely that the lower turnover (compared with the existing outlet) will lead to a reduction in net margin, leading to an even lower operating profit and lower profit before tax. If the margin is reduced to 10%, the operating profit (on sales of £270,000) would be £27,000, and the profit before tax just £9,000.

This is a great deal lower than the forecast, and significantly alters the potential viability of the business; hence the need for a longer term forecast set of figures.

(b) **Capital gearing** refers to the extent to which a company is funded by fixed return finance as opposed to equity. Two different formulae may be used when measuring capital gearing.

*Formula 1*

Capital gearing = Debt plus preference share capital/Equity

This measures the ratio of fixed return capital to equity finance within a business.

*Formula 2*

An alternative formula, commonly used, measures the proportion of fixed return capital in relation to the total capital of a business. The formula is as follows:

Capital gearing = Debt + preference share capital/Total long-term capital

In both cases, debt may be measured as either long-term debt, or all interest bearing debt. Clearly the gearing level will vary depending on the formula selected, and the type of debt included, but in all cases the level of gearing rises as the proportion of fixed return finance increases. It is not possible to specify a precise dividing line between high gearing and low gearing. Gearing is a relative measure, and should be assessed in terms of the gearing levels of comparable companies in the same business sector. Companies in different industrial sectors may exhibit very different levels of capital gearing.

The level of gearing is of interest to a bank that is lending to a business, because it reflects the extent to which the owners of the business are risking their own capital relative to that of the bank. At the same time, the bank will recognise that increased loan finance, which is not matched by an increase in equity investment, will lead to an increase in capital gearing. As the level of debt increases, if sales figures decline or are static, businesses may find it increasingly difficult to meet the interest payments due on the debt. The bank will therefore look for an increase in cash flows from operations to help to pay any incremental interest due on new borrowing. One problem, however, is that gearing does not measure cash flows.

The equity investor should be cautious of highly-geared companies, because the return on equity in such a business will be very sensitive to changes in profit before interest. When gearing is high, and interest payments are also high, a dramatic fall in the profit before interest figure may result in a collapse in the profit attributable to equity. Equally, a large rise in pre interest profit may lead to a surge in the profit attributable to equity, if earnings were already more than sufficient to meet interest payments. In summary, high gearing is of concern to the equity investor because it increases the volatility of the return on equity.

(c)     **Using the first formula for capital gearing:**

Long-term debt/ Equity = 195/176          = 1.108 or 110.8%

or

Interest-bearing debt/ Equity  = 195/176   = 1.108 or 110.8%

In this case, the absence of short-term interest-bearing debt means that the gearing calculation gives the same result for both calculations.

Alternatively, using the second formula:

Long-term debt/Total long-term capital = 195/371  = 0.526 or 52.6%

or

Interest-bearing debt/Total long-term capital = 195/371 = 0.526 or 52.6%

As before, the fact that long-term debt is the only form of interest bearing debt results in the same value for gearing using either definition.

The gearing level appears quite high, inasmuch as debt is a significant source of funding for the business, although the bulk of the debt is of a long-term nature and is secured against property. The restaurant business is a volatile one, subject to changing tastes, and sales volatility needs to be taken into account when analysing financial gearing. For most businesses in a volatile market, the risk of falling sales means that high levels of debt can leave a business facing difficulties in meeting its interest payments. The restaurant business, however, is cash generating when compared with other types of business that are dependent on credit sales. In view of this, the new restaurant should have fewer problems in servicing interest payments. Nonetheless, if the owners wish to limit their risk, it may be advisable to reduce the level of gearing to below one (depending on the formula used), so that a sharp drop in sales would not threaten the long-term survival of the business. It is often the case that banks will only be prepared to lend to small businesses on the basis of 'matching funds' i.e. £100 loan per £100 equity. As the gearing is in this case already over one, the owners would be unable to increase their borrowing if the matched funds approach was used.

The adjusted profit and loss account given in answer to (a) shows interest cover is poor. This would serve to confirm that gearing is uncomfortably high.

Furthermore, the figures do not reveal the true level of indebtedness and risk for the proprietors, who are in fact borrowing £75,000 in order to purchase their equity stake. For them the company is a very risky venture.

(d) The accounts clearly indicate that the business should seek out new equity investors, rather than further borrowing. However, the ease of attracting such investors will depend on the forecast profitability and medium-term growth potential of the business. In order to attract investors, Stadium Eats would need to prepare a Business Plan which included detailed profit and loss forecast, balance sheet forecast and cash flow forecast, together with information on company strategy and marketing plans. Such a plan could then be studied by potential investors, in order to make their own estimates of the potential of the business, and the risk that they would be taking in buying an equity stake.

Possible sources of such finance might include Business Angels, Venture Capital Trusts or wealthy relatives/individuals looking to obtain tax relief via an Enterprise Investment Scheme. It is possible that Stadium Eats could encourage customers to sign up as investors in return for discount vouchers on meals. Business Angels will be individuals who are used to dealing with small businesses, and might have some expertise to offer. Some Business Angels will request a seat on the Board of Directors in order to monitor the progress of their investment. Venture Capital Funds vary widely in size, from small regional funds (often part financed by local authorities) through to large-scale funds operating as investment trusts, and raising investment finance through the issue of shares to the general public.

Equity is not the sole source of funding which that might be available. If the restaurant is located in an economic development area, such as an inner city or rural community, then there may be job creation grants/soft loan funds provided by local or central government. In certain areas, a limited amount of grant finance is also available via the European Union.

(e) AIM is the Alternative Investment Market, which is a junior stock market operated by the London Stock Exchange. AIM serves as the market place in the UK where smaller companies can raise equity capital. The issue costs and annual registration fees are much lower than for the main stock exchange, and the investors are more likely to be looking for higher risk investments. As relatively new and fast growing businesses, many AIM companies choose to retain a large proportion of their profits, and so they offer low dividend yields to potential investors. The attraction of such investments lies in the potential for substantial capital gains if the business is successful.

Amongst the factors to be considered when seeking a stock market quotation are:

- Does the company need a large-scale injection of equity?

- Public quotation involves greater reporting requirements and openness.

- A stock market quotation increases take-over risks, because shareholdings are more widely spread.

- The owners are likely to see a reduction in the scale of their shareholding, and perhaps lose overall control.

- Are growth rates sufficient to give potential investors their required rate of return?

# 7    WATER SUPPLY SERVICES PLC

(a) Rental costs based on projected sales. Sales growth at 15% per annum.

| Period: | 1 | 2 | 3 | 4 | 5 |
|---|---|---|---|---|---|
| Demand (units): | 110,000 | 126,500 | 145,475 | 167,296 | 192,391 |
| Existing capacity: | 80,000 | 80,000 | 80,000 | 80,000 | 80,000 |
| Extra capacity required: | 30,000 | 46,500 | 65,475 | 87,296 | 112,391 |
| Number of machines required: | 1 | 2 | 2 | 2 | 3 |
| Rental costs (£): | 22,000 | 44,000 | 44,000 | 44,000 | 66,000 |

### Unit variable costs

|  | £/unit |
|---|---|
| Labour (45+64) | 109.00 |
| Material A costs | 23.85 |
| Material B costs (5 x 12·45) | 62.25 |
| Variable overheads | 10.00 |
| Unit variable costs | 205.10 |

### Incremental cash flow schedule:

| Year: | 0 | 1 | 2 | 3 | 4 | 5 |
|---|---|---|---|---|---|---|
| Units: | | 110,000 | 126,500 | 145,475 | 167,296 | 192,391 |
| Incremental units: | | 30,000 | 46,500 | 65,475 | 87,296 | 112,391 |
| | £000 | £000 | £000 | £000 | £000 | £000 |
| Variable costs (at £205.10 per unit) | | (6,153) | (9,537) | (13,429) | (17,904) | (23,051) |
| Additional fixed costs | | | | | (50) | (50) |
| Machine rentals | | (22) | (44) | (44) | (44) | (66) |
| Allowable costs | | (6,175) | (9,581) | (13,473) | (17,998) | (23,167) |
| Incremental revenue (allowable costs + 25%) | | 7,719 | 11,976 | 16,841 | 22,498 | 28,959 |
| Capital costs | (7,500) | | | | (30) | |
| Working capital | (1,158) | (638) | (730) | (849) | (969) | 4,344 |
| Net cash flow | (8,658) | 906 | 1,665 | 2,519 | 3,501 | 10,136 |
| | | | | | | |
| Discount factor at 20% | 1.000 | 0.833 | 0.694 | 0.579 | 0.482 | 0.402 |
| PV | (8,658) | 755 | 1,156 | 1,459 | 1,688 | 4,075 |
| NPV | + 475 | | | | | |

### Decision: project is worthwhile

*Tutorial note*: workings for working capital

| Year | 15% of sales value | Total working capital | Increase in working capital |
|---|---|---|---|
| 1 (start of year 0) | 15% of 7,719 | 1,158 | 1,158 |
| 2 (start of year 1) | 15% of 11,976 | 1,796 | 638 |
| 3 (start of year 2) | 15% of 16,841 | 2,526 | 730 |
| 4 (start of year 3) | 15% of 22,498 | 3,375 | 849 |
| 5 (start of year 4) | 15% of 28,959 | 4,344 | 969 |
| 6 (start of year 5) | | 0 | (4,344) |

(b)

## Report

| | |
|---|---|
| **To:** | Board of Directors |
| **From:** | Accountant |
| **Date:** | xx/xx/xx |
| **Subject:** | **Aspects of capital investment appraisal** |

### Limitations of the five-year period of analysis

A number of limitations to the analysis potentially arise:

1   The approach does not take account of future benefits/costs after five years either continuing or new.

2   No information on contract length from the Water Authorities, which may be longer than five years.

3    Other, cheaper, resources may be available over a longer period e.g. it may be cheaper to buy machines rather than rent them.

4    Analysis does not take account of the potential for physical site capacity increases that may become available after five years.

**Problems and difficulties associated with forecasting**

We have relied to a great extent on the forecasting of data in order to provide an evaluation of the proposal. Not all the components are forecast: for example, we will know that we are able to recover agreed costs. However, to the extent that components are forecast, there exists the **potential for error** in our evaluation which, of course, leads to uncertainty in our conclusions. In particular, the following problems are evident at this stage:

1    Uncertainty increases with the length of time forecast. That is, the further into the future, the less able we are to predict with accuracy because our initial assumptions may be wrong and small errors at the beginning magnify subsequently as the forecast becomes increasingly irrelevant to what is actually happening to the key variable in question. For example, we may have not predicted general inflation rates correctly, and this could have a large impact on our labour costs.

2    Project complexity: The more variables we have to forecast, the less likely we are to be accurate. This problem has an unknowable outcome if there are a large number of variables to forecast, the uncertainty concerning the two components can have two effects:

-    The larger the number of components to forecast, the greater the difficulty in determining project outcome. Forecasting so many components can lead to errors because the scale of the problem is large.
-    By forecasting many components, we assume a relationship between the components which is also a forecast. This relationship may change. For example, the relationship of production variable overheads to units produced may change. Currently, they are related to the amount of materials used. If we use forecasts based on these assumptions, then we also assume that the relationship between materials used and overheads absorbed is constant. This may not be the situation if the type of materials change.

3    The background information may change. What happens, for example, if a new competitor enters the market? This effect will be alleviated to the extent that we have an agreed contract. There are other factors that could have a significant effect, given enough time to materialise. For example, technological change could have an impact on our industry. In particular, social change may be relevant if consumers begin to demand even higher quality water supplies, which would inevitably affect our costs.

4    There is always the random component that could distort our forecasts. However, an alternative view would suggest that such random components are really an admission of lack of skill in forecasting. The best forecasters attempt to anticipate all eventualities.

**Choice of an appropriate discount rate**

The difficulty with choosing a discount rate rests on whether the correct rate for the risk/return has been derived. A number of factors are relevant here.

1    The position of the Water Authorities as single customer. The business is potentially at risk if the Water Authorities choose to look elsewhere for their water supplies. This may mean that a higher discount rate is more appropriate.

2    The financing of the capacity expansion. This may have an impact on the discount rate if the debt/equity mix of the company is significantly altered. A number of factors are relevant here:

(a)    Higher gearing is likely to induce higher costs of equity.

(b)    Higher equity financing may reduce the cost of equity, but increase the overall WACC if we move off our minimum WACC.

3    A lower discount rate may be more appropriate to the extent that a long-term contract implies secure income streams.

4    Different components of the cash flows may have different variability and it may therefore not be appropriate to discount them all at the same rate.

**Any non-quantifiable factors you feel might influence the decision to accept the proposal**

Net present value methods are only assessments of factors that we can quantify. There may be non-quantifiable factors that also have an impact on any decision we make. Some of these may be:

1    It is important to keep our only customer happy and therefore a high standard of general service is important.

2    Future contracts are likely to depend on agreeing to the proposal. Hence, future benefits may emerge which are currently hard to quantify.

3    The continuance of the existing business relationship with the Water Authorities may position the company to expand and provide water to other sectors of the economy.

4    The existing and proposed contracts secure continued employment for personnel. This is important in a labour market that may be experiencing shortages and where key personnel are difficult to replace.

(c)    In year 5, demand will be 192,391 units.

In year 6, demand will be 15% higher:

1.15 × 192,391 = 221,250 units.

| | |
|---|---:|
| Hence, the 1st quarter forecast is based on: | 221,250 |
| Average demand per quarter is therefore (× 3/12): | 55,312 |
| Applying the 1st quarter adjustment of − 8% gives: | |
| (− 8% × 55,312) | (4,425) |
| Hence, demand in the 1st quarter is projected to be: | 50,887 |

The difficulty faced by the company is that the demand level is beyond its capacity of 200,000 units. It is reasonable to assume steady water production throughout the year, in which case maximum output capacity for the 1st quarter is only 50,000 units.

(d)    (i)    **Components of the linear equation:**

816,000:    This might represent the initial level of fixed costs

205.1:    This represents the impact of a change in the variable x. In cost equations such as the one indicated, x would normally represent the level of output and, hence, for every unit change in output, total costs will rise by £205.1.

x:    This is likely to represent the number of units produced.

(ii)    As outlined in the question, fixed costs are not constant over all activity levels. In fact, it would be more appropriate to describe them as stepped fixed costs. When costs are described as stepped-fixed they are constant only over a range of output, but make step changes at certain points in capacity. The problems for estimation of fixed costs under such circumstances are two-fold:

–    The equation does not take into account capital investment required which will be occasional, as in the question, and assumes the costs incurred will be continuous (or annual as in the question): the linear equation cannot deal with non-yearly costs in an easy manner.

–    Ascertaining an appropriate absorption rate for overheads which, in itself, is a forecast.

| ACCA marking scheme | | |
|---|---|---|
| | | *Marks* |
| (a) | Unit forecasts | 2 |
| | Rental costs | 2 |
| | Incremental units | 1 |
| | Unit variable costs | 3 |
| | Variable cost cash flows | 1 |
| | Fixed cost cash flows | 1 |
| | Revenues | 3 |
| | Capital costs | 1 |
| | Working capital | 3 |
| | Use of correct discount factors | 1 |
| | Correct NPV | 1 |
| | Investment decision | 1 |
| | | 20 |
| (b) | 1 mark each for detailed points, limitations of 5 years | up to 4 |
| | Up to 2 marks each for difficulties with forecasting | up to 8 |
| | Up to 2 marks each for discount rate problems | up to 8 |
| | 1 mark each for non-quantifiable factors | up to 4 |
| | Maximum marks available | 20 |
| (c) | Projection of year 6 demand | 1 |
| | Quarterly adjustment | 1 |
| | 1st quarter projection | 1 |
| | Comment | 2 |
| | | 5 |
| (d) (i) | 1 mark each for explanation of each component | up to 2 |
| (ii) | 1 mark for each point made | up to 3 |
| | Marks available | 5 |
| Total | | 50 |

## 8    TOWER RAILWAYS PLC

(a)    **Data**

| | |
|---|---|
| After-tax discount rate (%) | 10 |
| Tax rate (%) | 30 |
| Contribution/sales ratio (%) | 35 |
| Therefore variable costs as a proportion of sales (%) | 65 |
| Occupancy rate (%) | 60 |
| Number of carriages | 8 |
| Passenger numbers per carriage | 55 |
| Number of trips | 10 |
| Average price per passenger (£) | 12 |
| Annual days travelling/operating | 340 |

*Assumption*: It is assumed that tax cash flows occur in the same year as the benefit, allowance or cost to which they relate.

| Capital allowances calculations, Year to: | 31 Dec X3 | 31 Dec X4 | 31 Dec X5 | 31 Dec X6 | 31 Dec X7 |
|---|---|---|---|---|---|
| | £000 | £000 | £000 | £000 | £000 |
| Tax written down value | 5,000 | 3,750 | 2,812 | 2,109 | 1,582 |
| Writing down allowance (25%) | 1,250 | 938 | 703 | 527 | |
| Sale proceeds | | | | | 500 |
| Balancing allowance | | | | | 1,082 |
| Tax saving (30%) | 375 | 281 | 211 | 158 | 325 |

**Capital projections**

| | Year 0 | Year 1 | Year 2 | Year 3 | Year 4 |
|---|---|---|---|---|---|
| | £000 | £000 | £000 | £000 | £000 |
| Initial investment and proceeds | (5,000) | | | | 500 |
| Capital allowances | 375 | 281 | 211 | 158 | 325 |
| Net capital flows | (4,625) | 281 | 211 | 158 | 825 |
| Discount factor at 10% | 1.000 | 0.909 | 0.826 | 0.751 | 0.683 |
| PV of capital flows | (4,625) | 256 | 174 | 119 | 563 |
| **NPV of capital flows** | **(3,513)** | | | | |

**Projected annual revenue** = 60% occupancy × 8 carriages × 55 passengers (carriage capacity) × £12 ticket price × 10 trips per day × 340 days = £10,771,200.

**Annual operating cash surplus, years 1 – 5**

| | £000 |
|---|---|
| Expected revenue | 10,771 |
| Variable costs (65%) | (7,001) |
| Contribution | 3,770 |
| Additional fixed costs (cash spend) | (1,000) |
| Incremental net cash income, pre-tax | 2,770 |
| Tax (30%) | (831) |
| Post-tax annual cash flows | 1,939 |

**Loss of revenue from long-standing contract**

= £250,000 each year, before tax, in perpetuity

= £175,000 each year after tax in perpetuity.

The Present Value of £1 each year in perpetuity at a discount rate of 10% = £1/0.10 = £10, i.e. the discount factor for the perpetual annual cash flow is 10.

| Years | Cash flow item | Cash flow £000 | Discount factor at 10% | Present value £000 |
|---|---|---|---|---|
| 1 - 5 | Post-tax additional profits | 1,939 | 3.791 | 7,351 |
| 1 in perpetuity | Post-tax loss of revenue | (175) | 10.000 | (1,750) |
| | | | | 5,601 |
| | PV of capital cash flows | | | (3,513) |
| | **NPV of project** | | | 2,088 |

*Decision: The contract is worthwhile*

(b)   The project will cease to be viable if the NPV falls by more than £2,088,000 and becomes negative.

This would happen if the Present Value of the annual operating profits fell by more than £2,088,000. A reduction in the average price charged would affect revenue and annual contribution, but would not affect fixed costs.

On the basis of the estimates in part (a), the expected annual contribution is £3,770,000 before tax. After tax, this is (× 70%) £2,639,000.

The discount factor at 10% for years 1 – 5 is 3.791.

In the estimates in part (a), the contribution for the five years, allowing for tax, therefore has a present value of:

£2,639,000 × 3.791 = £10,004,449.

If this value fell by £2,088,000, it would fall in percentage terms by (2,088,000/10,004,449) × 100% = 20.87%.

To reduce the NPV to zero, given no other changes in the estimated values, would therefore require a fall in price of about 20.87% or £2.50, from £12 to £9.50.

(c)   (i)

|  | £000 |
|---|---|
| PV of capital cash flows (given in the question) | (9,220) |
| PV of lost annual revenue in perpetuity | (1,750) |
| PV of extra operating profits, as estimated in (a) | 7,351 |
| NPV of the project for part (c) | (3,619) |

A similar analysis can be made as in part (b), except that we need to calculate the occupancy rate at which the project would just break even. This requires an increase in the PV of extra operating profits in years 1-5 by at least £3,619,000.

The PV of the after-tax additional contribution was calculated, on the basis of the original estimates, as £10,004,449 (see above). For these to increase by £3,619,000 would mean an increase in percentage terms of (3,619/10,004.449) × 100% = over 36%.

Given no other changes in the estimates, this would require an **increase in the occupancy rate** from 60% to (60 × 1.36) 81.6%, say 82%.

(ii)   The PV of the annual post-tax additional annual operating profits of £1,939,000 for years 1-5 is £7,351,000 (see earlier).

If the project could continue after year 5 earning additional post-tax cash flows of £1,939,000 each year, the project would achieve an NPV of 0 when the PV of the operating profits is (£7,531,000 + £3,619,000) = £10,970,000.

Given annual post-tax operating profits of £1,939,000, these would have a PV of £10,970,000 when the cumulative annual discount factor at 10% is (10,970,000/1,939,000) 5.658.

Examining the DCF annuity table under the 10% column for a figure closest to 5.658 we find the project length, expressed in whole years, should be at least 9 years long (at 9 years the annuity figure is 5.759).

(d)                                    **REPORT**

**Circulation**:       Chairman, Tower Railways

**Author**:

**Date**:              xx/xx/xx

**Subject**:          **Business Risk for Tower Railways plc**

**Introduction**

In the light of the possibility of an extension to the contract to services the main railway line this report makes an assessment of the background and specific risk relating to the project.

### What is meant by business risk

1    **Basic description**: Risk is related to the lack of certainty of future outcomes and is fundamentally related to decision making, such as the project proposed, in that business decisions are always taken against a background of risk. Because of that, it becomes important to understand the risk exposure that exists. At a basic level risk is positively associated with return in that the higher the return we expect from a project, the higher the degree of risk it is likely to be exposed to.

2    **Chance and probability**: Risk is associated with chance or probability in ways that allow us to quantify the degree of risk we face. This is particularly relevant to businesses that face variability in projected outcomes, for example, so that a fairly clear idea can be formed of the profit impact of risk. In the contract extension facing Tower Railways, project outcome has been assessed using NPV techniques that assume cash flows are certain (without risk). However the cash flows are dependent on projections of future passenger occupancy, prices charged, implicit zero inflation, the relation of variable costs to sales, discount rates, constant tax rates and so on. In fact, every component of the calculation is subject to risk, because we cannot be certain of ensuring that the figures we use will actually arise when the time comes or even at the time we project. Under such circumstances, we can only estimate the most likely figures and the most likely times, and accept that we may be wrong on either or both counts.

3    **Time**: Risk is also related to the length of time the projections extend. There is an important distinction at this point between constant risk and increased exposure. For example, we may assume that passenger occupancy stays constant at 60% and we may feel that there is a risk associated with being wrong in this project by a factor of –1% or + 1% each year. Whilst risk might remain constant at + or -1% each year, it is feasible that after five years, projected passenger occupancy could be less than 55% over 65%. Compounding effects of risk on risk over successive periods means that risk exposure grows without having to alter the risk percentage faced.

4    **Negative and positive variability**: Another important point relates to risk being both a good or bad thing. Risk, in the context of NPV projections, relates to variability of returns, both positive and negative. Thus, while you may not welcome negative variability in income, you would welcome it in relation to costs. Thus, risk is not only related to unwelcome outcomes, although it is often misperceived as such.

5    **Uncertainty**: Risk can also arise but may be unforeseen. This is perhaps the most important aspect in that, whilst we may be able to anticipate variability in income, we may not anticipate fully the risk we are exposed to or the form it will take (variability in sales revenues may be more than we anticipate for example). This is the hardest aspect of risk to judge.

### Methods of estimating the degree of business risk

Because risk affects decisions in such a fundamental way, businesses attempt to estimate risk as a way of putting in place contingency plans and/or evaluating if the project is likely to produce a profitable outcome. This is usually incorporated into NPV decisions in a number of ways:

1    **Sensitivity analysis**: This is one method which is widely used by which an assessment may be made of how responsive a project's NPV is to changes in its components. Thus, an idea may be gained of to what extent prices charged for a good or service have to reduce by before a zero NPV is produced. This technique can be applied to any cost, including initial capital costs, and also to

the discount rate. Sensitivity is normally expressed as a percentage. Some of the difficulties associated with the techniques are as follows:

- The analysis can only deal with changes in one key factor at a time. It cannot deal with multiple changes in NPV components which may well arise.

- No idea is given in sensitivity analysis of the likelihood of occurrence of a key variable changing to the extent to produce a zero NPV. In other words, it measures the percentage change required to produce a catastrophic result, but does not indicate if this has a low, medium or high chance of occurring.

- As with any risk assessment, sensitivity analysis is only a guide. It cannot tell managers how important such a risk exposure is to the company. In order to assess this, the attitude of the managers to risk needs to be determined. In other words, a high return/high risk company will want to be exposed to more risk than a low return/low risk company.

### Examiner's note

Discussions of CAPM and Certainty Equivalents could be included in this list. Whilst beyond the syllabus, appropriate references to these subjects would have been rewarded.

2    **Probability analysis:** This approach attempts to use measures which indicate just how variable cash flows are. It addresses one of the key criticisms of the sensitivity approach, in that it provides an idea of how much variability is likely, whereas sensitivity analysis indicates the room for manoeuvre without an assessment of the likelihood that any such event will arise. Probability analysis is essentially a weighted average approach, where the averages are determined by pre-set probabilities. By doing this, expected cash flows emerge based on the most likely outcomes. The degree of variability of the expected outcomes may be estimated from the standard deviation of the net present value. It is in this calculation that we at least get some idea of the degree of risk a project is exposed to, which can be expressed in terms of a range of NPVs. The important drawback of this approach is that a good idea of what probability weights to use must first be established. This can never be determined with 100% accuracy for project cash flows that arise in the future simply because the future is uncertain and so are the probabilities.

3    **Decision trees:** This is similar to a probability approach, in that it relies on weighting future cash flows by probabilities to arrive at an overall average. The distinctive feature of decision trees is that certain cash flow outcomes can be made contingent on certain previous ones arising. Decision trees are most useful in expressing, in a systematic manner, the different project outcomes that may emerge. Formally, the technique is no different to that of using compound probabilities and hence the criticisms of probabilities apply here also.

4    **Simulation models:** This method allows management to vary changes in the different cash flows simultaneously. As such it gives an idea of the variability in project cash flows overall by allowing changes in many of the outcomes. It can only give an idea, since the number of changes allowed can be quite large and, when compounded together, the number of different combinations become unmanageable in terms of trying to interpret what is going on. The key advantage of this technique is that it allows an idea of the most likely range of project outcomes that could possible emerge. However, the technique requires many computations to be carried out.

### Methods of reducing business risk

Risk can only be reduced to the extent that management can control events. Risks associated with uncontrolled events cannot be manipulated. There are a variety of ways the management can respond to risky situations:

- Undertake short payback projects. This is related to the fact that risk exposure increases with time because of its compounding effect even though the degree of risk may remain constant (this point is explained above).

- Avoid risky projects. If riskless projects are undertaken then only a risk free return could be expected. This may not satisfy shareholders.

- Ensure proper evaluations of risk are undertaken so that unnecessary exposure to risk is avoided.

- Employ risk avoidance project selection strategies. Management should not undertake high risk projects simultaneously, which might produce undesirable risk exposure to the business as a whole.

- Combine projects to diversify risk.

| | | | Marks | |
|---|---|---|---|---|
| | **ACCA marking scheme** | | | |
| (a) | Calculation of capital allowance | | 3 | |
| | Omission of apportionment overheads | | 1 | |
| | Projected revenues | | 2 | |
| | Variable costs | | 1 | |
| | Incremental overheads | | 1 | |
| | Tax on net revenues | | 1 | |
| | NPV of revenues | | 1 | |
| | NPV of lost contribution net of tax | | 2 | |
| | Capital investment and disposal | | 1 | |
| | Incorporation of capital allowances in cash flow | | 1 | |
| | NPV of capital flows | | 1 | |
| | Total NPV of new project | | 1 | |
| | Use of correct discount factors | | 1 | |
| | Investment decision | | 1 | |
| | | | | 18 |
| (b) | Calculation of correct sensitivity | | | 4 |
| (c) | (i) Calculation of increase in occupancy | | 4 | |
| | (ii) Calculation of increase in contract length | | 4 | |
| | | | | 8 |
| (d) | Up to 2 marks each for detailed points on what is meant by risk | | 6 | |
| | Up to 3 marks each for detailed points relating to estimating risk | | 12 | |
| | Up to 2 marks each for detailed points on to how to reduce risk | | 6 | |
| | Presentation and quality of argument | | 2 | |
| | Maximum available | | 26 | |
| | Maximum awarded | | | 20 |
| Total | | | | 50 |

## 9 AMBER PLC

(a) ***Tutorial* note:** The train company provides a daily return service, so there are two single journeys each day.

The expected number of passengers per journey using the service is dependent on the demand at each particular exchange rate.

At €1.52/£1: expected demand      = (500 + 460 + 420)/3

                                      = 460

At €1.54/£1: expected demand = (550 + 520 + 450)/3

= 506.67 (rounded)

At €1.65/£1: expected demand = (600 + 580 + 500)/3

= 560

The expected demand is therefore:

= (0.2) (460) + (0.5) (506.67) + (0.3) (560)

= 92 + 253.33 + 168

= 513.33 per train journey

= 1,026.67 per day (outward and return journeys).

(b)    *Workings*

45% of passengers use the catering service, spending £4.50 per head on average. Two journeys are run daily, for 360 days per year. This gives:

*Annual revenue*    = 0.45 × 1,026.67 × £4.50 × 360

= £748,440

*Daily revenue*    = £748,440/360 = £2,079 per day (= less than £2,200 per day).

| **Variable costs** | | £ |
|---|---|---|
| Direct material (55% of revenue) | = (0.55) (£748,440) | 411,642 |
| Variable overhead (12% of revenue) | = (0.12) (£748,440) | 89,813 |
| Total variable costs | | 501,455 |
| **Fixed costs** | | |
| Labour: Year 1 | = (0.10) (£748,440) | 74,844 |

Rising by 5% per year; this gives:

Year 2: £78,586
Year 3: £82,516
Year 4: £86,641
Year 5: £90,973

| Purchase/store management and insurance | = 0.05 (£748,440) | 37,422 |
|---|---|---|

With out-sourcing

If the service is out-sourced, there will be a saving of (£18,000 + £3,000) = £21,000 in purchasing/store management and insurance costs:

| Purchase and insurance with out-sourcing (£37,422 - £21,000) | 16,422 |
|---|---|

| Contract cost per year = £250 per day × 360 days | 90,000 |
|---|---|

Gross catering receipts are less than £2,200 per day on average, therefore the 5% commission does not apply.

**Cash flows: in-house option**

| Year | 1 | 2 | 3 | 4 | 5 |
|---|---|---|---|---|---|
| | £ | £ | £ | £ | £ |
| Sales | 748,440 | 748,440 | 748,440 | 748,440 | 748,440 |
| Variable costs | (501,455) | (501,455) | (501,455) | (501,455) | (501,455) |
| Contribution | 246,985 | 246,985 | 246,985 | 246,985 | 246,985 |
| Labour costs | (74,844) | (78,586) | (82,516) | (86,641) | (90,973) |
| Purchase and insurance | (37,422) | (37,422) | (37,422) | (37,422) | (37,422) |
| Asset purchase/sale | - | (500,000) | - | - | 280,000 |
| Net cash flow | 134,719 | (369,023) | 127,047 | 122,922 | 398,590 |
| Discount factor at 12% | 0.893 | 0.797 | 0.712 | 0.636 | 0.567 |
| Present value | 120,304 | (294,111) | 90,457 | 78,178 | 226,001 |

**Net present value = £220,829**

**Cash flows: contract out option**

| Year | 0 | 1 | 2 | 3 | 4 | 5 |
|---|---|---|---|---|---|---|
| | £ | £ | £ | £ | £ | £ |
| Contract fee payable | | (90,000) | (90,000) | (90,000) | (90,000) | (90,000) |
| Asset sale | 650,000 | | | | | |
| Fixed costs | - | (16,422) | (16,422) | (16,422) | (16,422) | (16,422) |
| Net cash flow | 650,000 | (106,422) | (106,422) | (106,422) | (106,422) | (106,422) |
| Discount factor at 12% | 1.000 | 0.893 | 0.797 | 0.712 | 0.636 | 0.567 |
| Present value | 650,000 | (95,035) | (84,818) | (75,772) | (67,684) | (60,341) |

**Net present value £266,350**

This option thus offers an NPV which is £45,521 greater than the in-house option, which means that profits could be increased by contracting out the catering service.

Contracting out the catering service is thus the preferred alternative and it is recommended that Amber plc accept the tender from the outside supplier.

(c)   The financial effect can be assessed by comparing the present value of the additional costs incurred with the present value of the incremental contribution.

*Workings*

| | |
|---|---|
| Additional staff training cost each year | £10,000 |
| Discount factor at 12% for years 1 - 5 | 3.605 |
| Present value of the additional training expense | £36,050 |

| | |
|---|---|
| The additional contribution amounts to 10% per year for years 1 - 5 | £24,699 each year |
| Discount factor at 12% for years 1 - 5 | 3.605 |
| Present value at 12% per year | £89,040 |

The net present value of the additional investment in staff training is therefore £89,040 less £36,050. This means that the net present value can be increased by £52,990 by retaining the service in-house, but increasing demand via improved services.

This additional net present value is greater than the £45,521 that can be achieved by switching to an outside provider for the catering service. The decision to contract out is therefore changed.

However, Amber plc must be wary of the fact that the difference between the in-house and the contracted-out service is only £7,469 i.e. (£52,990 - £45,521). The advantage is therefore relatively insignificant. Perhaps more importantly, if demand can be increased by as much as ten per cent for the relatively small investment of £10,000 per year (less than 2% of current variable costs), this suggests that Amber plc should perhaps look more closely at the possible opportunities for increasing the contribution from the in-house catering service, before choosing to contract out. If demand is very sensitive to both price and quality, it may require little investment to make the catering service very profitable.

The gains from investing internally, however, must be weighed against the potential gains to be earned from higher demand for a contracted-out service. The additional information shows that the company will receive 5% of gross sales receipts once daily sales exceed £2,200. At present sales are at £2,079 and so, if the external contractor was able to raise demand by 10%, Amber plc would receive 5% of the new annual revenue i.e. £41,164 without incurring any additional expense. The choice, therefore, of whether to use the outside supplier or keep the service in-house is very much dependent on the anticipated levels of future demand.

(d)   The **main limitation of making demand forecasts** lies in the fact that their **reliability is unknown**. Most forecasts are based on a mix of historical information and expectations in relation to relevant influential variables. For example, the exchange rate forecasts, where the highest probability is attached to a rate of €1.54/£1, is likely to be based on the statistical pattern of historical exchange rates (including the standard deviation) such that €1.54/£1 constitutes the most frequently-observed rate. This does not necessarily mean, however, that the rate will be similar in the future – history does not always repeat itself.

Another limitation relates to the **nature of the data being forecast**. Weather forecasts are notoriously unreliable, because nature is such an uncontrollable force. Even if the UK weather has been hot, on average, for the past five years, this does not imply that this will be the case in the future. The factors which dictate the weather are uncontrollable and consequently to a large degree unpredictable.

The forecast also runs into problems because it **seeks to link two unrelated variables**. The state of the weather is totally independent of the exchange rate, and vice versa, and they can only be linked in the way suggested by the table if the range of alternative observations is restricted. This is ultimately a distortion of a reality which is far more complex.

(e)   There are numerous **non-financial factors** which may be relevant to a decision to contract out, and the type of factors are likely to be dependent on the process/service which is the subject of the decision. Amongst the most important of the non-financial considerations will be the impact of any decision on the company's **competitive position**. For example, in the case of Amber plc, if the on-train catering facility is of a sufficiently high standard, it may attract new clientele to use their trains, thereby giving Amber plc a competitive advantage. The opposite may also be the case. In other words, the **strategic impact of a decision** needs to be taken into account, in addition to the directly measurable financial effects.

Another factor that should be taken into account is the question of **management control over service quality**. Once a service moves 'out of house', the only control mechanism that remains with the purchasing company might be a variety of penalties, the extreme one being termination of the contract. If the service remains inside the company, it may be easier to change things in response to changing customer needs. In other words, contracting out may be linked to a reduction in the level of management control.

**Staff morale** might be affected by contracting out, and any such possible effects should be carefully considered. Staff in departments that remain in-house might begin to feel threatened and view their service as the next on the 'hit list' for external contracting. It is important for managers to help allay such fears, and make clear the criteria on which any future outsourcing decisions will be based.

Other non-financial factors which may be useful to consider include:

- Environmental effects, such as changes in food packaging policies

- The terms of any contract for outside supply, and the willingness of the supplier to respond to changes in market demand as and when necessary

- The capability of the business to manage the external supply process. If a large number of contracts are in place, this can possibly become a logistical headache.

## 10   SPRINGBANK PLC

(a)   *Working W1*

**Calculation of tax benefits of capital allowances**

| Year | Tax written-down value of asset £ | Writing down allowance – WDA (25%) £ | Tax saving due to WDA (30%) £ |
|---|---|---|---|
| 1 | 3,000,000 | 750,000 | 225,000 |
| 2 | 2,250,000 | 562,500 | 168,750 |
| 3 | 1,687,500 | 421,875 | 126,563 |
| 4 | 1,265,625 | 316,406 | 94,922 |
| 5 | 949,219 | | 284,766 |

(balancing allowance in Year 5)

These figures for tax savings will be rounded to the nearest £1,000.

**Calculation of net present value of proposed investment**

| Year | 0 £000 | 1 £000 | 2 £000 | 3 £000 | 4 £000 | 5 £000 |
|---|---|---|---|---|---|---|
| Sales | | 2,750 | 2,750 | 2,750 | 2,750 | 2,750 |
| Production costs | | (1,100) | (1,100) | (1,100) | (1,100) | (1,100) |
| Admin/dist'n expenses | | (220) | (220) | (220) | (220) | (220) |
| Net revenue | | 1,430 | 1,430 | 1,430 | 1,430 | 1,430 |
| Tax payable at 30% | | (429) | (429) | (429) | (429) | (429) |
| Tax benefits from WDAs (W1) | | 225 | 169 | 127 | 95 | 285 |
| Working capital | (400) | | | | | 400 |
| Machinery | (3,000) | | | | | |
| Project cash flows | (3,400) | 1,226 | 1,170 | 1,128 | 1,096 | 1,686 |
| Discount factor at 12% | 1.000 | 0.893 | 0.797 | 0.712 | 0.636 | 0.567 |
| Present value | (3,400) | 1,095 | 932 | 803 | 697 | 956 |

*The net present value is approximately £1,083,000.*

This analysis makes the following assumptions:

(1)   The first tax benefit occurs in Year 1, the last tax benefit occurs in Year 5

(2)   Cash flows occur at the end of each year.

(3)   Inflation can be ignored.

(4)   The increase in capacity does not lead to any increase in fixed production overheads.

(5)   Working capital is all released at the end of Year 5

(b)    *Tutorial note:* The method of reaching a solution depends on whether it is assumed that the working capital investment varies with the volume of sales, or whether it is a fixed amount at £400,000. The solution here makes the assumption, preferred by the examiner, that the investment in working capital varies with the volume of sales.

### *Solution*

Some costs and benefits would be fixed amounts. These are the cost of the investment and the tax benefits from the writing down allowances. The present value of these tax benefits is as follows.

| Year | Tax benefit (see (W1)) £000 | Discount factor at 12% | Present value £000 |
|------|------|------|------|
| 1 | 225 | 0.893 | 200.9 |
| 2 | 169 | 0.797 | 134.7 |
| 3 | 127 | 0.712 | 90.4 |
| 4 | 95 | 0.636 | 60.4 |
| 5 | 285 | 0.567 | 161.6 |
|   |   |   | 648.0 |

*After-tax profit from units sold*

Variable administration and distribution expenses per unit = 220,000/5,500 = £40 per unit

Net revenue from additional units sold, before tax = £500 – £200 – £40 = £260 per unit.

Net revenue from additional units sold, after tax = 70% of £260 = £182.

Let the volume of annual sales be V units.

The present value of after-tax profits from selling V units each year for 5 years (years 1 – 5) = £182V × 3.605 (at a discount rate of 12%).

*Working capital*

It is assumed that the amount of working capital investment varies with the volume of annual sales.

Incremental working capital per unit = 400,000/5,500 = £72.73 per unit.

The net present value of the working capital investment is therefore:

| Year | Cash flow £000 | Discount factor at 12% | Present value £000 |
|------|------|------|------|
| 0 | (72.73V) | 1.000 | (72.73V) |
| 5 | 72.73V | 0.567 | 41.24V |
| Net PV of cost |   |   | 31.49V |

### **The NPV of the project is zero when**:

$(3,000,000) + 648,000 + 656.11V – 31.49V = 0$

$624.62V$

$= 2,352,000$

$V = 3,765$ units.

Current annual sales are 10,000 units (£5,000,000/£500).

To achieve breakeven will therefore require an increase in annual sales of 37.65% (3,765/10,000).

This is about 32% (1,735/5,500) less than the expected increase in sales volume.

(c)    (i)

| | | | |
|---|---|---|---|
| The current gearing of Springbank plc | = | (3.5m/4m) × 100 | = 87.5% |
| Total debt after issuing £3.4m of debt | = | 3.5m + 3.4m | = £6.9m |
| **New level of gearing** | = | (6.9m/4m) × 100 | = 172.5% |

| | | | £ |
|---|---|---|---|
| Current annual debenture interest | = | 3.5m × 0.10 | = 350,000 |
| Current interest on overdraft | = | 400,000 − 350,000 | = 50,000 |
| Annual interest on new debt | = | 3.4m × 0.08 | = 272,000 |
| **Expected annual interest** | | | 672,000 |

| | | | |
|---|---|---|---|
| Current profit before interest and tax | | | £1.5m |
| **Current interest cover** | = | 1.5m/0.4m | = 3.75 times |

With the investment, annual profits before tax will increase by £1.43 million (see answer (a)).

Assuming straight-line depreciation, **additional depreciation** = £600,000 per year (£3,000,000/5 years).

| | | | |
|---|---|---|---|
| Current profit before interest and tax | = | (1.5 + 1.43 − 0.6) m | £2.33m |
| **Expected interest cover** | = | 2.33m/0.672m | = 3.47 times |

This is lower than the current interest cover, assuming no change in overdraft interest.

Thus, Springbank's **gearing** is expected to rise from slightly below the sector average of 100% to significantly more than the sector average. Springbank's **interest cover** is likely to remain at a level lower than the sector average of four times, and will be slightly reduced assuming no change in overdraft interest.

(ii)    **Ratio calculations**

| | 20X1 | | 20X2 | |
|---|---|---|---|---|
| ROCE | 1,750/7,120 | 24.6% | 1,500/7,500 | 20% |
| Net profit margin | 1,750/5,000 | 35% | 5,000/7,500 | 30% |
| Asset turnover | 5,000/7,120 | 0.70 | 5,000/7,500 | 0.67 |
| Current ratio | 2,000/1,280 | 1.56 | 2,150/1,150 | 1.87 |
| Quick ratio | 1,000/1,280 | 0.78 | 980/1,150 | 0.85 |
| Stock days | 365 ×1,000/3,000 | 122 days | 365 × 1,170/3,100 | 138 days |
| Debtors ratio | 12 × 900/5,000 | 2.2 months | 12 × 850/5,000 | 2 months |
| Sales/working capital | 5,000/720 | 6.9 | 5,000/1,000 | 5 |
| Debt/equity | 3,500/3,620 | 96.7% | 3,500/4,000 | 87.5% |
| Interest cover | 1,750/380 | 4.6 | 1,500/400 | 3.75 |

The **return on capital employed** of Springbank has declined as a result of both falling net profit margin and falling asset turnover: while comparable with the sector average of 25% in 20X1, it is well below the sector average in 20X2. The problem here is that turnover has remained static while both cost of sales and investment in assets have increased.

Despite the fall in profitability, both **current ratio** and **quick ratio** have improved. This is due mainly to the increase in stock levels and the decline in current liabilities, the composition of which is unknown. However, the current ratio remains below the sector average. The increase in both stock levels and **stock days**, together with the fact that stock days is now 53% above the sector average, may indicate that current products are becoming harder to sell, a conclusion supported by the failure to increase turnover and the reduced profit margin. The expected increase in sales volume is therefore likely to be associated with a new product launch, since it is unlikely that an increase in capacity alone will be able to generate increased sales. There is also the possibility that the static sales of existing products may indicate that sales will decline in the future.

The decrease in the **debtors' ratio** is an encouraging sign, but the interpretation of the decreased **sales/working capital ratio** is uncertain. While the decrease could indicate less aggressive working capital management, it could also indicate that trade creditors are less willing to extend credit to Springbank, or that stock management is poor.

The **gearing** of the company has fallen, but only because reserves have been increased by retained profit. The **interest cover** has declined since interest has increased and operating profit has fallen. Given the constant long-term debt, the increase in interest, although small, could indicate an increase in overdraft finance.

Ratio analysis offers evidence that the financial performance of Springbank plc has been disappointing in terms of sales, profitability and stock management. It may be that the management of Springbank see the increase in capacity as a cure for the company's declining performance.

(iii)    Since the investment has a positive NPV it is acceptable in financial terms. The danger highlighted by the analysis of recent financial performance is that existing sales may generate a declining contribution towards meeting interest payments in the future. However, sensitivity analysis shows the proposed expansion is robust in terms of sales volume, since a 31% - 32% reduction below the forecast increase in sales is needed to eliminate the positive NPV. The proposed expansion is therefore acceptable, but the choice of financing is critical.

Springbank should be able to meet future interest payments if the cashflow forecasts for the increase in capacity are sound. However, no account has been taken of expected **inflation**, and both sales prices and costs will be expected to change. There is also an underlying **assumption of constant sales volumes**, when changing economic circumstances and the actions of competitors make this assumption unlikely to be true. More detailed financial forecasts are needed to give a clearer indication of whether Springbank can meet the additional interest payments arising from the new debentures. There is also a danger that managers may focus more on the short-term need to meet the increased interest payments, or on the longer-term need to replace the machinery and redeem the debentures, rather than on increasing the wealth of shareholders.

**Financial risk** has increased from a balance sheet point of view and this is likely to have a negative effect on how financial markets view the company. The cost of raising additional finance is likely to rise, while the increased financial risk may lead to downward pressure on the company's share price. The current debentures represent 54% of fixed assets and after the new issue of debentures, this will rise to 73% of fixed assets. The assets available for offering as security against new debt issues will therefore decrease, and continue to decrease as fixed assets depreciate.

No information has been offered as to the **maturity of the new debenture issue**. If the matching principle is applied, a medium term maturity of five to six years is indicated. However, the 10% debentures are due for redemption in 20X7 and it would be unwise to have two significant redemption calls so close to each other.

On the basis of the above discussion, careful thought needs to be given to the maturity of any new issue of debentures and it may be advisable to use debt finance to meet only part of the financing need of the proposed capacity expansion. Alternative sources of finance such as equity and leasing should be considered.

(d)  Financing the investment by an issue of ordinary shares could offer several advantages to Springbank plc. Gearing would fall to 47% (3.5/7.4), less than half of the sector average of 100%, rather than increasing to significantly more than the sector average. Interest cover would increase to 5.8 (2.33/0.4) from 3.75, compared to a sector average of 4. The financial risk faced by the company would thus be reduced, making it a more attractive investment prospect on the stock market. This could have a positive effect on the company's share price.

Ordinary shares do not carry a commitment to make regular payments such as interest on debt, giving Springbank plc a degree of flexibility in rewarding shareholders in financial terms. This must be balanced against the common desire of shareholders for a regular and increasing dividend.

Ordinary shares are permanent capital since they do not need to be repaid. Springbank plc would thus avoid the need to find funds for redemption that would arise if it issued debentures.

Because the fixed assets of the company would increase but its burden of long-term debt would be unchanged, Springbank would find it easier to raise additional debt in the future. This could be useful when the need arises to redeem the existing debentures in 20X7.

| ACCA marking scheme | | |
|---|---|---:|
| | | *Marks* |
| (a) | Calculation of capital allowances | 2 |
| | Calculation of tax benefits | 1 |
| | Calculation of net revenue | 1 |
| | Calculation of tax on net revenue | 1 |
| | Inclusion of tax benefits | 1 |
| | Treatment of working capital | 1 |
| | Capital investment | 1 |
| | Calculation of project cash flows | 1 |
| | Use of correct discount factors | 1 |
| | Calculation of NPV | 1 |
| | | 11 |
| (b) | Formulation of algebraic solution | 1 |
| | Calculation of sales volume giving zero NPV | 2 |
| | Expression of volume change in relative terms | 1 |
| | | 4 |
| (c) (i) | Calculation of current gearing | 1 |
| | Calculation of expected gearing | 1 |
| | Calculation of current interest cover | 1 |
| | Calculation/discussion of expected interest cover | 2 |
| | Comparison with sector averages | 1 |
| | | 6 |
| (ii) | Calculation of relevant ratios | 8 |
| | Comment on recent financial performance | 5 |
| | | 13 |
| (iii) | Comment of acceptability of expansion | 2 |
| | Ability to meet future interest payments | 2 |
| | Maturity of new debentures | 2 |
| | Financial Risk and asset backing | 2 |
| | Comment on acceptability of proposed finance | 2 |
| | | 10 |
| (d) | Up to 2 marks for each detailed advantage | 6 |
| Total | | 50 |

## 11 THE INDEPENDENT FILM COMPANY

### Key answer tips

Part (a) is a standard DCF computation, and a well organised and laid out answer should gain high marks. The best layout is probably a horizontal one, with columns for each year. Start by annotating the list of costs for those that have to be multiplied up by 3, and those that are increasing. Set up a proforma computation table, and put in all the operating cash flows first (including effects of increases etc). Sales will be based on an expected value. The tax is very simple here, as there are no capital allowances, so you just need to multiply the net cash flow by 33% and delay it by one year.

Be very careful in part (b) - you are being asked to discuss the use of *expected values* in investment appraisal, not DCF. A simple example, such as that shown in the examiner's answers, is not essential, but helps to illustrate the limitations.

The success or otherwise of your answer in part (c) (i) hangs upon whether you know what a profitability index (PI) is! Using it to decide between projects in a capital rationing situation is a form of key factor analysis - equivalent to using contribution per unit of scarce resource in product mix problems. Whilst a quick example of the calculation of the index is useful, with a brief explanation of its use, you probably wouldn't have time to go into the detail the examiner has in his answer.

Parts (c)(ii) and (iii) - don't worry if you are not confident about your answer to (a), you should still use your answer here to get the project's PI. The examiner will be looking for understanding of its application, not necessarily the right answer! Note that here, a bit of trial and error is needed to decide the optimal investment plan, as the projects are non-divisible (so you can't go for all of Y and ¾ of the filmmaking company project, as the PI ranking would indicate). This difficulty gives you your first point for (iii); then you need to think of 2 or 3 more.

Part (d) is a fairly straightforward discussion.

(a)

| **Cash flows  (£000)** | | | | *Year* | | | |
|---|---|---|---|---|---|---|---|
| | *0* | *1* | *2* | *3* | *4* | *5* | *6* |
| Purchase of company | (400) | | | | | | |
| Legal/professional | | (20) | (20) | (20) | (20) | (20) | |
| Lease rentals | | (12) | (12) | (12) | (12) | (12) | |
| Studio hire | | (540) | (540) | (702) | (702) | (702) | |
| Camera hire | | (120) | (120) | (120) | (120) | (120) | |
| Technical staff (+ 10% p.a.) | | (1,560) | (1,716) | (1,888) | (2,077) | (2,285) | |
| Screenplay (+ 15% p.a.) | | (150) | (173) | (199) | (229) | (263) | |
| Actors' salaries (+ 10% p.a.) | | (2,100) | (2,310) | (2,541) | (2,795) | (3,074) | |
| Costumes/wardrobe | | (180) | (180) | (180) | (180) | (180) | |
| Non-production staff wages | | (60) | (66) | (73) | (80) | (88) | |
| Set design | | (450) | (450) | (450) | (450) | (450) | |
| 'Lost income' from office accommodation | | (20) | (20) | (20) | (20) | (20) | |
| Sales (+ 5% p.a.) | - | 5,900 | 6,195 | 6,505 | 6,830 | 7,172 | |
| Cash flow before tax | (400) | 688 | 588 | 300 | 145 | (42) | |
| Tax (33%) | - | - | (227) | (194) | (99) | (48) | 14 |
| Net cash flow | (400) | 688 | 361 | 106 | 46 | (90) | 14 |
| Discount factor at 14% | 1.000 | 0.877 | 0.769 | 0.675 | 0.592 | 0.519 | 0.456 |
| | | | | | | | |
| P.V. of net cash flow £000 | (400) | 603 | 278 | 72 | 27 | (47) | 6 |

**NPV = £539,000**

(b)    An **expected value** is calculated by using forecast probabilities to weight the values of alternative outcomes and thus compute an arithmetic mean for the overall expected result. There are three main problems with the use of expected values for making investment decisions:

(i) The **investment may only occur once**. It is certainly very unlikely that there will be the opportunity to repeat the investment many times. The average of the anticipated returns will thus not be observed.

(ii) Attaching probabilities to events is a **highly subjective** process. In investment decisions, probability may often be used in relation to sales forecasts derived from market research. The subjectivity involved in setting probabilities means that the judgements may be incorrect, even though the Net Present Value for the investment may be highly sensitive to changes in the probability distribution.

(iii) The **expected value does not evaluate the range of possible NPV outcomes**.

The limitations of expected values can be demonstrated by means of a simple example. Suppose that an individual places a £10 bet with a colleague that it will rain within the next 24 hours. The weather forecast predicts the likelihood of rain with the 24-hour period at 60%. The expected value of the bet can thus be calculated as: $(0.6 \times £10) - [0.4 \times (£10)] = £2$. In reality, the expected value can never be observed, because the person will never be just £2 better off, only £10 richer or poorer depending on the success of the bet.

(c) (i) A **profitability index** for an investment project may be defined as the ratio of the net present value of the cash flows relative to the capital invested. The formula is thus:

$$\frac{\text{NPV of cash flows}}{\text{Capital investment}} = \text{profitability index}$$

For example, an investment which yields an NPV of £250,000 as a result of an investment of £100,000 would yield a profitability index of 2.5.

In cases where companies do not have unlimited funds available for investment, the profitability index can be used as the criterion for rationing of the scarce available capital where investments can be assumed to be divisible (i.e. any amount can be invested up to the desired level). Projects with the highest profitability index will be selected first, and selection will continue until all available funds have been used up.

For example, suppose that the NPV of two projects is calculated, based on a common discount rate, and Project A yields an NPV of £150,000 whilst Project B yields an NPV of £50,000. The yield per £ invested can be calculated if project costs are known.   If Project A cost £20,000 then the yield per £ invested is £7.5. In contrast, if Project B costs £5,000, then the yield per £ is higher at £10. This means that B is the preferred investment and capital should be allocated accordingly.

Suppose then that a company had £15,000 available for investment, then the optimal investment strategy is to put £5,000 into Project B and the balancing £10,000 into Project A. The net yield will then be as follows:

| | |
|---|---|
| £5,000 × £10 per £ | = £50,000 |
| £10,000 × £7.5 per £ | = £75,000 |
| Total yield | = £125,000 |
| Profitability index | $= \dfrac{125}{15}$ |
| | = 8.33 |

In this way, the company has maximised the Net Present Value per £ invested. A key assumption, however, is that investments are divisible can be split (i.e. that it is possible to invest in a proportion of an investment and earn the same proportion of the total expected returns).

(ii) Purchase of the film production company yields an NPV of £539,000 on an investment of £400,000. This gives a profitability index of 539/400 = 1.35.

**Investment X**

NPV = $(200 \times 0.877) + (200 \times 0.769) + (150 \times 0.675) + (100 \times 0.592) + (100 \times 0.519) + (100 \times 0.456) - 200 = 387$

Profitability index     = 387/200

                                  = 1.94

**Investment Y**

NPV = $(80 \times 0.877) + (80 \times 0.769) + (40 \times 0.675) + (40 \times 0.592) + (40 \times 0.519) + (40 \times 0.456) - 100 = 121$

Profitability index     = 121/100

                                  = 1.21

*Note:* Profitability indices may also be calculated as Present Value of Cash Inflows/Initial Outlay instead of Net Present Value/Initial Outlay. The ranking will remain the same regardless of the formula used. The profitability index cannot be applied in this case because of non-divisibility.

The choices available are:

- X plus Y at a cost of £300,000 and yielding an NPV of £508,000.

- Purchase of the company costing £400,000 and yielding an NPV of £539,000.

If the objective is to maximise the sum of the Net Present Values, which can be achieved subject to the budget constraint, then the optimal investment strategy is to purchase the film production company.

(iii) There are several problems with using the profitability index as the basis for profit selection under capital rationing.

First, as has been shown above in the answer to (ii), the method is of limited use if projects are indivisible, because it ignores the opportunity to maximise the sum of the net present values from all projects.

Secondly, the criterion for selection is relatively simplistic in nature, and takes no account of the potential strategic value of individual projects. In the case of the Independent Film Company, for example, we have no information about the nature of investments X and Y. It is however clear that the investment in a film-making business involves some vertical integration of the company's activities and this may be important to its future survival in the industry. The discounted cash flow for the purchase shows that it yields a positive return, and is thus a viable investment, even if it offers a lower rate of return than project X. The use of a Profitability Index effectively takes no account of strategic considerations.

A third problem with the approach relates to the fact that it is of limited use when projects have differing cash flow patterns. The index selects purely on the basis of NPV per £ invested, but the pattern of cash flows from projects will vary. This means that in multi-period rationing it is possible for the project with the highest index to be the slowest in generating returns. The cash flow pattern of returns may, however, be important to a company as it will affect the timing and availability of funds for future investment.

Finally, the profitability index ignores the absolute size of individual projects. An investment may yield an index of 10, but the sum invested is just £5,000. By contrast, an investment with an index of 3, and hence less attractive on this criterion, may involve the investment of £500,000. An absolute return of £50,000 is clearly less attractive then one of £1.5 million, but comparison of the alternatives is not straightforward in practice. The company should look at all the alternatives open to it, within the bounds of the capital available, and maximise the total NPV that can be achieved. The most useful tool for this type of analysis is linear programming, which allows maximisation of an objective subject to specified constraints, but this assumes divisibility of projects.

(d)     The **tax treatment of capital purchases** can affect an investment decision because where tax relief is available, the tax benefits serve to reduce the effective cost of an investment. For example, suppose that a company estimates the net present value of a two-year project to be £10,000, but that this is in the absence of any capital allowances being available on capital purchase. If the government then introduces 100% first year allowances, the company can use the allowances claimed on purchases to offset its corporation tax liability. If capital purchases totalled £15,000 and tax was payable at a rate of 30%, the cash impact of the capital allowances would be (£15,000 x 0.30) or £4,500 in reduced tax liabilities. This represents an increase in the NPV. The impact on NPV will be less marked where the capital allowances take the form of writing down allowances instead of a large first year allowance, but the general effect is the same.

Clearly the example given above is an extreme case, but it illustrates the fact that on potentially marginal projects, it is possible that tax benefits could serve to convert a negative NPV into one which is positive. For this reason, capital allowances on investments can be viewed as a tool of government economic policy. If the economy is suffering from low levels of industrial investment, then an increase in the level of allowances can be used to encourage such investment.

Obviously the tax treatment of capital purchases will only affect investment decisions in cases where the investing company is able to take advantage of the reliefs available. For loss making companies or those with tax liabilities below the threshold of the tax relief created by allowances, the situation is more complex, and investment decisions may be made irrespective of the tax position. Similarly, there may be some investments which are being made for strategic reasons, and which would be made regardless of the tax treatment of capital purchases. It is therefore oversimplifying the situation to argue that higher tax allowances will definitely lead to an increase in industrial investment.

## 12   SASSONE PLC

(a)     **Planning direct material usage variance:**

$10,000 \times (5.0 - 5.3) \times 7.50 = £22,500$ (A)

Operational direct material usage variance:

$[(10,000 \times 5.3) - 54,400] \times 7.50 = £10,500$ (A)

If the Production Director is correct in his claim that the standard material usage needs to be revised to 5.3 kg/unit, then 68% of the direct material variance of £33,000 is due to the use of an out-of-date standard. The Production Director is therefore correct in stating that most of the variance is due to an out-of-date standard, but he cannot avoid responsibility for the operational usage variance of £10,500.

Standards need to be revised regularly in order that they remain relevant for costing and control purposes. The Production Director's claim must be investigated and the material usage standard revised if the claim is found to be true and a revision is deemed to be necessary.

Providing planning and operational variances as a result of ex post variance analysis will enable more accurate assessment f managerial performance by identifying controllable and uncontrollable variances. Managers cannot be held responsible for uncontrollable variances, whether positive or negative in nature. Providing planning and operational variances will also reduce the frequency of revisions to standards.

(b) **Machine One**

| Year | 0 | 1 | 2 | 3 | 4 | 5 |
|---|---|---|---|---|---|---|
| | £ | £ | £ | £ | £ | £ |
| Initial investment | (238,850) | | | | | |
| Maintenance | | (10,000) | (13,000) | (16,000) | (19,000) | (22,000) |
| 11% discount factor | 1.000 | 0.901 | 0.812 | 0.731 | 0.659 | 0.593 |
| | (238,850) | (9,010) | (10,556) | (11,696) | (12,521) | (13,046) |

Present value of costs = £295,679

Annuity factor for five years at 11% = 3.696

Equivalent annual cost = 295,679/3.696 = £80,000 per year

**Machine Two**

| Year | 0 | 1 | 2 | 3 | 4 |
|---|---|---|---|---|---|
| | £ | £ | £ | £ | £ |
| Initial investment | (215,000) | | | | |
| Maintenance | | (10,000) | (15,000) | (20,000) | (25,000) |
| 11% discount factor | 1.000 | 0.901 | 0.812 | 0.731 | 0.659 |
| | (215,000) | (9,010) | (12,180) | (14,620) | (16,475) |

Present value of costs = £267,285

Annuity factor for four years at 11% = 3.102

Equivalent annual cost = 267,285/3.102 = £86,165 per year

Machine One should be bought as it has the lowest equivalent annual cost.

(c) **Sales volume reaches the maximum capacity of the new machine in Year 4.**

| Year | 1 | 2 | 3 | 4 | 5 |
|---|---|---|---|---|---|
| | £ | £ | £ | £ | £ |
| Sales revenue | 312,000 | 432,000 | 562,500 | 702,000 | |
| Marginal cost | (243,300) | (337,600) | (438,500) | (547,200) | |
| Fixed cost | (10,600) | (11,236) | (11,910) | (12,625) | |
| Maintenance | (10,000) | (15,750) | (22,050) | (28,941) | |
| Taxable cash flow | 48,100 | 68,214 | 90,040 | 113,234 | |
| Taxation | | (14,430) | (20,464) | (27,012) | (33,970) |
| WDA tax benefit | | 16,125 | 12,094 | 9,070 | 27,211 |

| Year | 1 | 2 | 3 | 4 | 5 |
|---|---|---|---|---|---|
| | £ | £ | £ | £ | £ |
| Net cash flow | 48,100 | 69,909 | 81,670 | 95,292 | (6,759) |
| Discount factors | 0.901 | 0.812 | 0.731 | 0.659 | 0.593 |
| | | | | | |
| Present values | 43,338 | 56,766 | 59,701 | 62,727 | (4,008) |

| | £ |
|---|---|
| Sum of present values | 218,594 |
| Initial investment | 215,000 |
| | |
| Net present value | 3,594 |

The positive NPV indicates that the investment in Machine Two is financially acceptable, although the NPV is so small that there is likely to be a significant possibility of a negative NPV.

*Workings*

| Year | 1 | 2 | 3 | 4 |
|---|---|---|---|---|
| Selling price (£/unit) | 10.40 | 10.82 | 11.25 | 11.70 |
| Sales (units/yr) | 30,000 | 40,000 | 50,000 | 60,000 |
| Sales revenue (£/yr) | 312,000 | 432,800 | 562,500 | 702,000 |

| Year | 1 | 2 | 3 | 4 |
|---|---|---|---|---|
| Marginal cost (£/unit) | 8.11 | 8.44 | 8.77 | 9.12 |
| Sales (units/yr) | 30,000 | 40,000 | 50,000 | 60,000 |
| Marginal cost (£/yr) | 243,300 | 337,600 | 438,500 | 547,200 |

| Year | 1 | 2 | 3 | 4 |
|---|---|---|---|---|
| Maintenance (£/yr) | 10,000 | 15,000 | 20,000 | 25,000 |
| Inflated cost (14/yr) | 10,000 | 15,750 | 22,050 | 28,941 |

Writing down allowances and tax benefits

| | Allowances £ | Benefits £ |
|---|---|---|
| Year 1: 215,000 × 0.25 = | 53,750 | 16,125 |
| Year 2: 161,250 × 0.25 = | 40,312 | 12,094 |
| Year 3: 120,938 × 0.25 = | 30,234 | 9,070 |
| | | |
| | 124,296 | |
| Year 4: (215,000 − 124,296) = | 90,704 | 27,211 |
| | | |
| | 215,000 | |

(d)    Total taxable cash flow = (48,100 + 68,214 + 90,040 + 113,234) = £319,588

Total depreciation = £215,000

Total accounting profit = 319,588 − 215,000 = £104,588

Average annual accounting profit = 104,588/4 = £26,147

Average investment = 215,000/2 = £107,500

Return on capital employed = 100 × 26,197/107,500 = 24.3%

ROCE of 24.3% is slightly less than the target ROCE of 25%, indicating that buying the machine is not acceptable with respect to this criterion. However, evaluation using the net present value approach is preferred for investment advice.

(e)   The objectives to which organisational strategy relates depend on the relative power of different stakeholders associated with the company, and on whether objectives are imposed on the organisation by, for example, government or other legislation. Since it is unlikely that the objectives of different stakeholders will coincide, conflict will arise between corporate objectives and management must decide on the extent to which conflicting objectives can be met. In this case, 55% of the company's shares are in the hands of institutional investors and so this shareholder group, if it acts in concert, can wield considerable power over the organisational strategy of Sassone plc. In practice shareholder groups are likely to be fragmented and this fragmentation will reduce the power of Sassone plc's institutional investors.

The primary financial objective of a company is usually stated to be the maximisation of shareholder wealth and Sassone plc has declared publicly that this is one of its objectives. Returns to shareholders can be measured in terms of dividend yield and capital growth, reflecting the attention paid by investors to dividends and increasing share prices. Both dividend yield and capital growth can be measured over a standardised holding period in order to assess shareholder returns.

Some of the institutional shareholders of Sassone have complained that annual dividend payments have not increased at an acceptable rate due to expenditure on environmentally-friendly and socially acceptable projects. This represents a conflict between a financial objective (shareholder wealth maximisation) and a non-financial objective (social welfare). The claim is that unnecessary expenditure has reduced the amount of profits paid out as dividends. It is important for Sassone plc to find the extent to which this view is shared by other institutional shareholders, given the relative size of this shareholder grouping.

This conflict between objectives cannot be resolved by rational argument. It is possible that Sassone plc's support for environmentally-friendly and socially acceptable projects has generated a positive image in the minds of its customers, resulting in increased sales, but this effect cannot be quantified readily. Alternatively, it is possible that sales would be lower if Sassone plc did not support environmentally-friendly and socially acceptable projects, since such behaviour may be expected by its customers. The institutional investors' complaint may therefore be short-sighted, although a comparison between Sassone plc and its competitors may show that its expenditure on socially acceptable and environmentally-friendly projects is larger than necessary. However, the benefit of such projects may arise only in the long term, whereas the complaint by institutional investors indicates a short-term focus.

One of the roles of company managers is therefore to seek to resolve or reduce any conflict between corporate objectives. The fact that institutional investors have threatened to vote against the re-appointment of directors at the next Annual General Meeting signifies that they are resolved to seek change, although in practice they may be unable to gather sufficient votes to achieve their objective. However, company managers must maintain a good relationship with institutional investors, if only because they may wish to seek investor support for a rights issue in the future, and it is likely the complaint will be investigated and an amicable solution found. The key task of management may be to persuade institutional investors to adopt a longer-term view.

(f)   When considering the incremental increase in sales arising from the purchase of the new machine, it was assumed that product costs remained constant in real terms over the life cycle of the product. In fact, the life cycle of the product was ignored and all of the engineering components produced were treated as being identical. In reality, each kind of engineering component is likely to go through the stages of the product life cycle: introduction, growth, maturity and decline. Higher costs are likely to be incurred at the start of the product life cycle due to product development, marketing and promotion. During the growth stage, sales volumes increase and unit cost consequently decreases. During the maturity stage, unit cost initially continues to fall as developmental and promotional costs are recovered and scale economies continue to grow, but eventually competition on price and product differentiation begin to reduce profitability. In the decline stage, sales volumes fall and unit cost increases, further reducing profitability and leading to abandonment or replacement of the product concerned.

Most costing systems report product costs on a periodic basis (e.g. monthly or annually) and fail to track product profitability over the product life cycle. Life cycle costing accumulates actual costs over the product life cycle and allocates research, development, promotion and marketing costs to specific products rather than treating them as general overhead costs. In this way, a clearer picture of estimated life cycle costs and product profitability is gained, and actual life cycle costs can be monitored and compared to budgeted life cycle costs for cost control purposes.

Product pricing should reflect the need to recover costs over the product life cycle. Initially, prices may be set at a level that reflects the captive nature of the initial market (since competitors may not exist), while also considering the need to persuade potential customers to substitute the new product for existing products. During the maturity stage, product prices will decline as companies struggle to maintain market share in the face of increasingly fierce competition. Product prices will continue to fall in the decline stage as the product becomes obsolete and replacements are developed. Sassone plc could incorporate these considerations into the pricing of the engineering components it sells, particularly the need to keep prices competitive during the maturity and decline stages.

Target costing considers the price that ought to be charged in order to achieve a desired market share for a given product and uses this, together with the desired profit margin, as the basis for determining product cost. Target costing can therefore take account of the life cycle of the product rather than just production costs. For new products, the product development team can use this product cost as a target to be met when the product is launched. If the target cost differs from the expected actual cost, the product development team can seek ways to achieve the desired target cost, for example by product and process design. This approach could be useful to Sassone plc since it would discover what product price was needed to achieve the desired market share for a given engineering component, rather than simply adding a mark-up to expected actual cost, and it could use the derived target cost as a way of controlling costs and increasing profitability.

| ACCA marking scheme | | Marks |
|---|---|---|
| (a) | Planning variance | 1 |
| | Operational variance | 1 |
| | Discussion of Production Director's views | 2 |
| | | 4 |
| (b) | Equivalent annual cost of machine 1 | 3 |
| | Equivalent annual cost of machine 2 | 2 |
| | Selection of lowest equivalent annual cost | 1 |
| | | 6 |
| (c) | Sales volume | 1 |
| | Sales revenue | 2 |
| | Marginal costs | 2 |
| | Maintenance costs | 1 |
| | Incremental fixed costs | 1 |
| | Taxation | 2 |

| | | |
|---|---|---|
| | Capital allowances and tax benefits | 4 |
| | Net cash flow | 1 |
| | Discount factors | 1 |
| | Net present value | 1 |
| | Comment | 2 |
| | | 18 |
| (d) | Average annual accounting profit | 1 |
| | Average investment | 1 |
| | Return on capital employed | 1 |
| | Comment on findings | 1 |
| | | 4 |
| (e) | Discussion of stakeholders and objectives | 3-4 |
| | Discussion of conflict between objectives | 4-5 |
| | Discussion relating to Sassone plc | 2-3 |
| | | 10 |
| (f) | Discussion of life cycle costing | 3-4 |
| | Discussion of target costing | 3-4 |
| | Link to Sassone plc | 1 |
| | | 8 |
| Maximum | | 50 |

## 13 ARG CO

(a) NPV calculation for Alpha and Beta

| Year | 1 | 2 | 3 | 4 |
|---|---|---|---|---|
| | £ | £ | £ | £ |
| Sales revenue | 3,585,000 | 6,769,675 | 6,339,000 | 1,958,775 |
| Material cost | (1,395,000) | (2,634,225) | (2,466,750) | (761,925) |
| Fixed costs | (1,000,000) | (1,050,000) | (1,102,500) | (1,157,625) |
| Advertising | (500,000) | (200,000) | (200,000) | |
| Taxable profit | 690,000 | 2,885,450 | 2,569,750 | 39,225 |
| Taxation | (172,500) | (721,362) | (642,438) | (9,806) |
| WDA tax benefit | 250,000 | | | |
| Fixed asset sale | | | | 1,200,000 |
| WC recovery | | | | 1,000,000 |
| Net cash flow | 767,500 | 2,164,088 | 1,927,312 | 2,229,419 |
| Discount factors | 0.885 | 0.783 | 0.693 | 0.613 |
| Present values | 679,237 | 1,694,481 | 1,335,626 | 1,366,634 |

| | £ |
|---|---|
| Sum of present values | 5,075,978 |
| Initial investment | 3,000,000 |
| Net present value | 2,075,978 |

The positive NPV indicates that the investment is financially acceptable.

*Workings*

**Alpha sales revenue**

| Year | 1 | 2 | 3 | 4 |
|---|---|---|---|---|
| Selling price (£/unit) | 31.00 | 31.93 | 32.89 | 33.88 |
| Sales (units/yr) | 60,000 | 110,000 | 100,000 | 30,000 |
| Sales revenue (£/yr) | 1,860,000 | 3,512,300 | 3,289,000 | 1,016,400 |

**Beta sales revenue**

| Year | 1 | 2 | 3 | 4 |
|---|---|---|---|---|
| Selling price (£/unit) | 23.00 | 23.69 | 24.40 | 25.13 |
| Sales (units/yr) | 75,000 | 137,500 | 125,000 | 37,500 |
| Sales revenue (£/yr) | 1,725,000 | 3,257,375 | 3,050,000 | 942,375 |
| Year | 1 | 2 | 3 | 4 |
| Sales revenue (£/yr) | 3,585,000 | 6,769,675 | 6,339,000 | 1,958,775 |

**Alpha direct material cost**

| Year | 1 | 2 | 3 | 4 |
|---|---|---|---|---|
| Material cost (£/unit) | 12.00 | 12.36 | 12.73 | 13.11 |
| Sales (units/yr) | 60,000 | 110,000 | 100,000 | 30,000 |
| Material cost (£/yr) | 720,000 | 1,359,600 | 1,273,000 | 393,300 |

**Beta direct material cost**

| Year | 1 | 2 | 3 | 4 |
|---|---|---|---|---|
| Material cost (£/unit) | 9.00 | 9.27 | 9.55 | 9.83 |
| Sales (units/yr) | 75,000 | 137,500 | 125,000 | 37,500 |
| Material cost (£/yr) | 675,000 | 1,274,625 | 1,193,750 | 368,625 |
| Year | 1 | 2 | 3 | 4 |
| Material cost (£/unit) | 1,395,000 | 2,634,225 | 2,466,750 | 761,925 |

(b)   The evaluation assumes that several key variables will remain constant, such as the discount rate, inflation rates and the taxation rate. In practice this is unlikely. The taxation rate is a matter of government policy and so may change due to political or economic necessity.

Specific inflation rates are difficult to predict for more than a short distance into the future and in practice are found to be constantly changing. The range of inflation rates used in the evaluation is questionable, since over time one would expect the rates to converge. Given the uncertainty of future inflation rates, using a single average inflation rate might well be preferable to using specific inflation rates.

The discount rate is likely to change as the company's capital structure changes. For example, issuing debentures with an interest rate of 9% is likely to decrease the average cost of capital.

Looking at the incremental fixed production costs, it seems odd that nominal fixed production costs continue to increase even when sales are falling. It also seems odd that incremental fixed production costs remain constant in real terms when production volumes are changing. It is possible that some of these fixed production costs are stepped, in which case they should decrease.

The forecasts of sales volume seem to be too precise, predicting as they do the growth, maturity and decline phases of the product life-cycle. In practice it is likely that improvements or redesign could extend the life of the two products beyond five years. The assumption of constant product mix seems unrealistic, as the products are substitutes and it is possible that one will be relatively more successful. The sales price has been raised in line with inflation, but a lower sales price could be used in the decline stage to encourage sales.

Net working capital is to remain constant in real terms. In practice, the level of working capital will depend on the working capital policies of the company, the value of goods, the credit offered to customers, the credit taken from suppliers and so on. It is unlikely that the constant real value will be maintained.

The net present value is heavily dependent on the terminal value derived from the sale of fixed assets after five years. It is unlikely that this value will be achieved in practice. It is also possible that the machinery can be used to produce other products, rather than be used solely to produce Alpha and Beta.

(c)     ARG Co currently has £50m of fixed assets and long-term debt of £10m. The issue of £3m of 9% debentures will increase fixed assets by £2m of buildings and machinery. There seems to be ample security for the new issue.

Interest cover is currently 5.1 (4,560/900) which is less than the sector average, and this will fall to 3.9 (4,560/(900 + 3m × 9%)) following the debenture issue. The new products will increase profit by £440,000 (£690,000 – £250,000 of depreciation), increasing interest cover to 4.3 (5,000/1,170). Although on the low side and less than the sector average, this evaluation ignores any increase in profits from current activities. Interest cover may not be a cause for concern.

Current gearing using debt/equity based on book values of 32% (10,000/30,900) will rise to 42% (13,000/30,900) after the debenture issue. Both values are less than the sector average and ignore any increase in reserves due to next year's profits. Financial risk appears to be at an acceptable level and gearing does not appear to be a problem.

The debentures are convertible after eight years into 20 ordinary shares per £100 debenture. The current share price is £4.00, giving a conversion value of £80. For conversion to be likely, a minimum annual growth rate of only 2.83% is needed ((5.00/4.00)0.125 – 1). This growth rate could well be exceeded, making conversion after eight years a likely prospect. This analysis assumes that the floor value on the conversion date is the par value of £100: the actual floor value could well be different in eight years' time, depending on the prevailing cost of debt.

Conversion of the debentures into ordinary shares will eliminate the need to redeem them, as well as reducing the company's gearing.

The current share price may be depressed by the ongoing recovery from the loss-making magazine publication venture. Annual share price growth may therefore be substantially in excess of 2.83%, making the conversion terms too generous (assuming a floor value equal to par value on the conversion date). On conversion, 600,000 new shares will be issued, representing 23% (100 × 0.6m/2.6m) of share capital. The company must seek the views and approval of existing shareholders regarding this potential dilution of ownership and control.

The maturity of the debentures (12 years) does not match the product life-cycle (four years). This may be caution on the part of the company's managers, but a shorter period could be used.

It has been proposed that £1 million of the debenture issue would be used to finance the working capital needs of the project. Financing all working capital from a long-term source is a very conservative approach to working capital financing. ARG Co could consider financing fluctuating current assets from a short-term source such as an overdraft. By linking the maturity of the finance to the maturity of the assets being financed, ARG Co would be applying the matching principle.

(d)     Calculation of ABC recovery rates

| Cost driver | Alpha | Beta | Total | Cost | Recovery rate |
|---|---|---|---|---|---|
| Floor area (m$^2$) | 3,500 | 6,500 | 10,000 | £505,000 | £50.50/m$^2$ |
| Labour hours | 10,000 | 15,000 | 25,000 | £300,000 | £12/hr |
| Inspections | 3,000 | 3,750 | 6,750 | £67,500 | £10/test |
| Orders | 3,000 | 1,500 | 4,500 | £67,500 | £15/order |
| Maintenance hours | 625 | 1,875 | 2,500 | £26,000 | £10.40/hr |
| Set-ups | 120 | 50 | 170 | £34,000 | £200/set-up |

Activity-based cost apportionment

| Fixed cost | £ | Alpha | Beta |
|---|---|---|---|
| Power, heating, etc. | 505,000 | 176,750 | 328,250 |
| Salaries | 300,000 | 120,000 | 180,000 |
| Inspection costs | 67,500 | 30,000 | 37,500 |
| Order processing | 67,500 | 45,000 | 22,500 |
| Maintenance | 26,000 | 6,500 | 19,500 |
| Set-up costs | 34,000 | 24,000 | 10,000 |
| | 1,000,000 | 402,250 | 597,750 |

Fixed costs for Alpha = 402,250/60,000 = £6·70
Fixed costs for Beta = 597,750/75,000 = £7·97

ARG Co uses a cost plus pricing system and appears from the information provided to use a mark-up of 50% on total cost. The revised total costs for Alpha and Beta are £18.70 and £16.97. Applying a 50% mark-up gives selling prices of £28.05 and £25.45 respectively. On this basis Alpha is over-priced and Beta is under-priced. However, the selling price should also reflect the best price obtainable in the market. This might be higher or lower than any of the prices based on total cost.

(e)     ARG Co will be concerned to protect the sterling value of its expected dollar receipt. The quoted forward rates show that the dollar is weakening against sterling, so that the sterling value of $500,000 dollars will have fallen in three months. ARG Co can enter into a contract now with a bank to exchange its expected dollar receipt in three months time at the current forward rate. Such a contract is called a forward exchange contract and is binding on both the bank and ARG Co. By agreeing to an exchange at the current forward rate, the company will be protected against any further deterioration in the sterling-dollar exchange rate. The sterling value arising from the contract will be $500,000/1.8174 = £275,118.

(f)     A bill of exchange is a means of payment initiated by an exporter. It is signed (accepted) by an importer, signifying agreement to pay the amount on the face of the bill. This payment may either be on demand (sight bill) or on a mutually agreed future date (term bill).

The risk associated with overseas debtors is reduced by bills of exchange since these bills are a liquid short-term financial asset. They can be discounted (sold at less than face value) to a bank in order to provide advance payment of the amount due to be received from overseas debtors. A smaller discount will be charged if the bill of exchange is confirmed (countersigned) by the importer's bank.

Bills of exchange can be also used in conjunction with documentary letters of credit (also known as documentary credits) to reduce export credit risk even further.

**ACCA marking scheme**

| | | *Marks* |
|---|---|---|
| (a) | Sales revenue | 4 |
| | Material costs | 4 |
| | Fixed costs | 1 |
| | Advertising | 1 |
| | Taxation | 2 |
| | Capital allowance tax benefit | 1 |
| | Fixed asset sale | 1 |
| | Working capital recovery | 1 |
| | Present values | 1 |
| | Net present value and comment | 1 |
| | | 17 |
| (b) | Assumptions regarding economic variables | 2 |
| | Fixed costs | 1 |
| | Sales volume | 1 |
| | Working capital | 1 |
| | Terminal value | 1 |
| | | 6 |
| (c) | Evaluation and discussion should consider: | |
| | Security available | |
| | Interest cover | |
| | Gearing | |
| | Convertibility | |
| | Maturity | 8 |
| (d) | ABC recovery rates | 3 |
| | Fixed costs using ABC | 4 |
| | Total costs, selling prices and discussion | 4 |
| | | 11 |
| (e) | Explanation of need to hedge receipt | 2 |
| | Sterling value of forward hedge | 2 |
| | | 4 |
| (f) | Bills of exchange and risk reduction | 2 |
| | Discounting bills of exchange | 2 |
| | | 4 |
| Total | | 50 |

# Section 5

# MOCK EXAM QUESTIONS

## SECTION A – THIS IS COMPULSORY AND MUST BE ATTEMPTED

### 1 NETHERBY PLC

Netherby plc manufactures a range of camping and leisure equipment, including tents. It is currently experiencing severe quality control problems at its existing fully-depreciated factory in the south of England. These difficulties threaten to undermine its reputation for producing high quality products. It has recently been approached by the European Bank for Reconstruction and Development, on behalf of a tent manufacturer in Hungary, which is seeking a UK-based trading partner which will import and distribute its tents. Such a switch would involve shutting down the existing manufacturing operation in the UK and converting it into a distribution depot. The estimated exceptional restructuring costs of £5m would be tax-allowable, but would exert serious strains on cash flow.

Importing, rather than manufacturing tents appears inherently profitable as the buying-in price, when converted into sterling, is less than the present production cost. In addition, Netherby considers that the Hungarian product would result in increased sales, as the existing retail distributors seem impressed with the quality of the samples which they have been shown. It is estimated that for a five-year contract, the annual cash flow benefit would be around £2m pa before tax.

However, the financing of the closure and restructuring costs would involve careful consideration of the financing options. Some directors argue that dividends could be reduced as several competing companies have already done a similar thing, while other directors argue for a rights issue. Alternatively, the project could be financed by an issue of long-term loan stock at a fixed rate of 12%.

The most recent balance sheet shows £5m of issued share capital (par value 50p), while the market price per share is currently £3. A leading security analyst has recently described Netherby's gearing ratio as 'adventurous'. Profit-after-tax in the year just ended was £15m and dividends of £10m were paid.

The rate of corporation tax is 33%, payable with a one-year delay. Netherby's reporting year coincides with the calendar year and the factory will be closed at the year-end. Closure costs would be incurred shortly before deliveries of the imported product began, and sufficient stocks will be on hand to overcome any initial supply problems. Netherby considers that it should earn a return on new investment projects of 15% pa net of all taxes.

### Required:

(a) Is the closure of the existing factory financially worthwhile for Netherby? **(7 marks)**

(b) Explain what is meant when the capital market is said to be information-efficient in a semi-strong form.

If the stock market is semi-strong efficient and without considering the method of finance, calculate the likely impact of acceptance and announcement of the details of this project to the market on Netherby's share price. **(6 marks)**

(c) Advise the Netherby board as to the relative merits of a rights issue rather than a cut in dividends to finance this project. **(8 marks)**

(d) (i) Explain why a rights issue generally results in a fall in the market price of shares.

(ii) If a rights issue is undertaken, calculate the resulting impact on the existing share price of issue prices of £1 per share and £2 per share, respectively. (You may ignore issue costs.) **(7 marks)**

(e) Assuming the restructuring proposal meets expectations, assess the impact of the project on earnings per share if it is financed by a rights issue at an offer price of £2 per share, and loan stock, respectively. **(4 marks)**

(Again, you may ignore issue costs.)

(f) Briefly consider the main operating risks connected with the investment project, and how Netherby might attempt to allow for these. **(8 marks)**

(g) Why would a depressed stock market make a rights issue difficult to accomplish? **(4 marks)**

(h) Explain whether the bond markets might be a viable alternative source of finance for the company. **(6 marks)**

**(Total: 50 marks)**

## SECTION B – TWO QUESTIONS ONLY TO BE ATTEMPTED

## 2 BENLAND PLC

Benland plc manufacture and fit a variety of children's playground equipment. The company at present purchases the rubber particles used in the playground surfacing from an outside supplier, but is considering investing in equipment that would process and shred used vehicle tyres to produce equivalent rubber particles. One tonne of purchased particles is saved per tonne of tyres processed. Disposal of used tyres is becoming an environmental problem, and Benland believes that it could charge £40 per tonne to garages/tyre distributors wishing to dispose of their old tyres. This price would be 20 per cent lower than the cost of the landfill sites currently being used, and so Benland believes that it would face no risk or shortage of supply of what would be a key raw material for the business. The price charged by Benland for tyre disposal (£40 per tonne) remains fixed for the next five years.

The cost to Benland of purchased particles is £3.50 per tonne for each of the next five years, and the price has been contractually guaranteed. If the contract is terminated within the next two years, Benland will be charged an immediate termination penalty of £100,000 which will not be allowed as a tax deductible expense.

The machine required to process the tyres will cost £1.06 million, and it is estimated that at the end of year five the machine will have a second-hand value of £120,000 before selling costs of £5,000.

Sales of the playground surfacing which uses rubber particles are forecast to be £1.2 million in year one, rising by 10% per year until year five but prices will remain constant. The new equipment will result in Benland incurring additional maintenance costs of £43,000 per year.

80,000 tonnes of tyres need to be processed in order to meet the raw material requirement for the forecast sales in year one. Processing costs are estimated at £37 per tonne (excluding additional depreciation and maintenance).

Benland is subject to corporation tax at a rate of 33%, payable one year in arrears. Capital expenditure is eligible for 25% allowances on a reducing balance basis, and sales proceeds of assets are subject to tax. Benland has sufficient profits to fully utilise all available capital allowances.

**Required:**

(a)   Using 12% as the after-tax discount rate, advise Benland on the desirability of purchasing the tyre processing equipment.   **(12 marks)**

(b)   Discuss which cash flows are most important in determining the outcome of the proposed investment and how Benland might seek to minimise the risk of large changes in predicted cash flows.   **(8 marks)**

(c)   Comment on how the project would affect the different stakeholders of Benland.

**(5 marks)**

**(Total: 25 marks)**

## 3   FILLS FOOTBALLS LTD

Fills Footballs Limited is considering the use of debt factoring. Currently, the company's annual turnover is £750,000. All sales are on credit and on average, debtors take 45 days to pay. Bad debts are about 1% of turnover.

A factor has proposed to take on the task of debt collection on a no recourse basis, but would want to administer the sales ledger, for which it would charge an annual fee of 3% of turnover. The factor has expressed the view that it would expect to reduce the average debt collection period to 35 days and to reduce bad debts to 0.25% of sales turnover. The factor would also advance finance to Fills Footballs equal to 80% of uncollected debts, and would charge interest at 9% on the money advanced. Fills Footballs currently has a bank overdraft, on which it is paying interest at 10% per annum. It has been estimated that if the factor takes over the sales ledger administration, Fills Footballs would save annual operating expenses of £20,000.

**Required:**

(a)   Recommend, with supporting calculations, whether the company should take up the debt factor's offer.   **(8 marks)**

(b)   Write a report to management explaining:

(i)   credit control procedures

(ii)   other methods of improving debt collection, if the factor is not used

(iii)   the importance to a company of careful debtor management.   **(17 marks)**

**(Total: 25 marks)**

## 4   FERTICOM PLC

Ferticom Co plc manufactures a range of fertilizers and pesticides for the farming industry. Management have provided you with the following information for a recently developed organic fertilizer, W, that requires traditional methods to produce:

### Standard costs of product W

| Materials | Kilos | Price per kilo £ | Total £ |
|---|---|---|---|
| F | 15 | 4 | 60 |
| G | 12 | 3 | 36 |
| H | 8 | 6 | 48 |
|   | 35 |   | 144 |
| Less: Standard loss | (3) |   |   |
| Standard yield | 32 |   |   |

| Other variable costs per kg of W produced | Hours | Rate per hour | Total |
|---|---|---|---|
| | | £ | £ |
| Labour | 0.4 | 10 | 4.00 |
| Variable overheads | 0.4 | 3 | 1.20 |
| | | | 5.20 |

Budgeted sales for the period were 4,096 kilos at £16 per kilo. There were no budgeted opening or closing stocks of product W.

The actual costs were:

| Materials | Kilos | Price per kilo | Total |
|---|---|---|---|
| | | £ | £ |
| F | 1,680 | 4.25 | 7,140 |
| G | 1,650 | 2.80 | 4,620 |
| H | 870 | 6.40 | 5,568 |
| | 4,200 | | 17,328 |
| Less: Actual loss | (552) | | |
| Actual yield | 3,648 | | |

| | Hours | Rate per hour | Total |
|---|---|---|---|
| | | | £ |
| Labour | 1500 | 10.60 | 15,900 |
| Variable overheads | 1500 | 5.60 | 8,400 |
| | | | 41,628 |

All of the production of W was sold during the period for £16.75 per kilo.

**Required:**

(a) Calculate the following:

    (i) Sales variances. **(2 marks)**

    (ii) Materials price mix and yield variances for each material **(8 marks)**

    (iii) Labour rate and efficiency variances **(2 marks)**

(b) Explain the following variances and suggest reasons why they have arisen:

    (i) Materials mix

    (ii) Materials yield

    (iii) Labour efficiency

    (iv) Sales volume **(8 marks)**

(c) Discuss the factors to be considered in deciding whether a variance should be investigated. **(5 marks)**

**(Total: 25 marks)**

## 5    BUDGET COMPILATION

A product manager has responsibility for a single product and is in the process of submitting data to be compiled into budgets for 20X9. The manager has performance targets set in relation to sales volume, profitability levels and a target cash surplus from the product.

Shown below are the agreed budgeted sales for the product for December 20X8 to May 20X9.

|       | Dec    | Jan    | Feb    | Mar    | April  | May    |
|-------|--------|--------|--------|--------|--------|--------|
| Units | 14,000 | 16,000 | 22,000 | 17,000 | 20,000 | 24,000 |

The company policy is that, at each month end, the closing stock of finished goods should be 25% of the following month's forecast sales and the stock of raw material should be sufficient for 10% of the following month's production. Stock levels currently conform to this policy. One unit of raw material makes one unit of finished stock, there is no wastage.

Raw material purchases are paid for during the month following the month of purchase. All other expenses are paid for as incurred. All sales are made on credit and the company expects cash receipts for 50% of sales in the month of sale and 50% in the following month.

The company operates an absorption costing system which is computed on a monthly basis. That is, in addition to direct costs it recovers each month's fixed and variable manufacturing overhead expenses in product costs using the budgeted production and budgeted expenditure in the month to establish an absorption rate. This cost is used to place a value on the stock holding. Opening stock is valued at the unit cost which was established in the previous month. At 1 January 20X9 finished stock should be assumed at £40 per unit. A flow of cost based on FIFO is assumed.

Sales are made at a price of £58 per unit.

Estimated costs to be used in the budget preparation for the product are:

**Manufacturing costs:**

| | |
|---|---|
| Material | £10.00 per unit produced |
| Variable overhead and labour | £16.00 per unit produced |
| Fixed overhead costs | £210,000 per month |
| (including depreciation of £54,000 per month) | |

**Selling costs:**

| | |
|---|---|
| Variable | £7.00 per unit sold |
| Fixed | £164,000 per month |

### Required:

(a)   Compute the monthly budgeted production and material purchases for January to March 20X9.                                                                            **(6 marks)**

(b)   Prepare a budgeted profit and loss account and a statement of cash receipts and payments for January 20X9.                                                          **(10 marks)**

(c)   Explain briefly the implications of the company's treatment of fixed manufacturing overheads compared to a predetermined overhead rate prepared annually.    **(4 marks)**

(d)   The preparation of budget data may be assisted by the use of a time series. Explain what a time series is and the various components which comprise one.    **(5 marks)**

**(Total: 25 marks)**

# Section 6

# ANSWERS TO MOCK EXAM QUESTIONS

## SECTION A

### 1 NETHERBY PLC

(a) Assuming that the restructuring cost is a revenue item, and that all costs are incurred in year 0, the estimated cash flow profile is:

**Cash flow profile (£m)**

| Item | 0 | 1 | 2 | 3 | 4 | 5 | 6 |
|---|---|---|---|---|---|---|---|
| | | | | *Year* | | | |
| Closure costs | (5.0) | | | | | | |
| Tax saving | | 1.65 | | | | | |
| Cash flow increase | | 2.00 | 2.00 | 2.00 | 2.00 | 2.00 | |
| Tax payment | - | - | (0.66) | (0.66) | (0.66) | (0.66) | (0.66) |
| Net cash flow | (5.0) | 3.65 | 1.34 | 1.34 | 1.34 | 1.34 | (0.66) |
| Discount factor at 15% | 1.000 | 0.870 | 0.756 | 0.658 | 0.572 | 0.497 | 0.432 |
| Present value | (5.0) | 3.18 | 1.01 | 0.88 | 0.77 | 0.67 | (0.29) |

**Net present value    + £1. 22 million**

Hence, the restructuring appears worthwhile.

(b) A semi-strong efficient capital market is one where security prices reflect all publicly-available information, including both the record of the past pattern of share price movements and all information released to the market about company earnings prospects. In such a market, security prices will rapidly adjust to the advent of new information relevant to the future income-earning capacity of the enterprise concerned, such as a change in its chief executive, or the signing of a new export order. As a result of the speed of the market's reaction to this type of news, it is not possible to make excess gains by trading in the wake of its release. Only market participants lucky enough already to be holding the share in question will achieve super-normal returns.

In the case of Netherby, when it releases information about its change in market-servicing policy, the value of the company should rise by the value of the project, assuming that the market as a whole agrees with the assessment of its net benefits, and is unconcerned by financing implications.

Net present value of the project = £1.22m

Number of 50p ordinary shares in issue = £5m × 2 = 10m shares

Increase in market price = £1.22m/10m = 12.2p per share.

---

(Alternatively, the answer could be expressed in terms of Netherby's price-earnings ratio. This would necessitate an assumption about Netherby's sustainable future earnings per share after tax.)

(c)   Arguments for and against making a rights issue include the following:

**For**

(i)    A rights issue enables the company to at least maintain its dividends, thus avoiding both upsetting the clientele of shareholders, and also giving negative signals to the market.

(ii)   It may be easy to accomplish on a bull market.

(iii)  A rights issue automatically lowers the company's gearing ratio.

(iv)   The finance is guaranteed if the issue is fully underwritten.

(v)    It has a neutral impact on voting control, unless the underwriters are obliged to purchase significant blocks of shares, and unless existing shareholders sell their rights to other investors.

(vi)   It might give the impression that the company is expanding vigorously, although this appears not to be the case with Netherby.

**Against**

(i)    Rights issues normally are made at a discount, which usually involves diluting the historic earnings per share of existing shareholders. However, when the possible uses of the proceeds of the issue are considered, the prospective EPS could rise by virtue of investment in a worthwhile project, or in the case of a company earning low or no profits, the interest earnings on un-invested capital alone might serve to raise the EPS.

(ii)   Underwriters' fees and other administrative expenses of the issue may be costly, although the latter may be avoided by applying a sufficiently deep discount.

(iii)  The market is often sceptical about the reason for a rights issue, tending to assume that the company is desperate for cash. The deeper the discount involved, the greater the degree of scepticism.

(iv)   It is difficult to make a rights issue on a bear market, without leaving some of the shares with the underwriters. A rights issue which 'fails' in this respect is both bad for the company's image and may also result in higher underwriters' fees for any subsequent rights issue.

(v)    A rights issue usually forces shareholders to act, either by subscribing direct or by selling the rights, although the company may undertake to reimburse shareholders not subscribing to the issue for the loss in value of their shares. (This is done by selling the rights on behalf of shareholders and paying over the sum realised, net of dealing costs.)

(d)   A rights issue normally has to be issued at a discount in order, firstly, to make the shares appear attractive, but more importantly, to safeguard against a fall in the market price below the issue price prior to closure of the offer. If this should happen, the issue would fail as investors wishing to increase their stakes in the company could do so more cheaply by buying on the open market. Because of the discount, a rights issue has the effect of diluting the existing earnings per share across a larger number of shares, although the depressing effect on share price is partly countered by the increased cash holdings of the company.

The two possible issue prices are now evaluated.

(i)    *A price of £1*

It is assumed that to raise £5m, the company must issue £5m/£1 = 5m new shares at the issue price of £1.

In practice, it is possible that the number of new shares required might be lower than this, as the post-tax cost of the project is less than £5m due to the (delayed) tax savings generated. The company might elect to use short-term borrowing to bridge the delay in receiving these tax savings, thus obviating the need for the full £5m.

Ignoring this argument, the terms of the issue would be '1-for-2' i.e. for every two shares currently held, owners are offered the right to purchase one new share at the deeply-discounted price of £1.

The ex-rights price will be:

[Market value of 2 shares before the issue + cash consideration]/3

= [(2 × £3) + £1]/3 = £7/3 = £2.33

(ii)    *Similarly, if the issue price is £2*, the required number of new shares = £5m/£2 = 2.5m, and the terms will have to be '1 -for-4'

The ex-rights price will be [(4 × £3) + £2]/5 = £14/5 = £2.80.

Clearly, the smaller the discount to the market price, the higher the ex-rights price.

(e)    Ignoring the impact of the **benefits of the new project**:

The rights issue at £2 involves 2.5m new shares.

The EPS was £15m/10m = £1.50p per share.

Hence, EPS becomes $\dfrac{£15m}{10m + 2.5m} = £1.20$

With the debt financing, the interest charge net of tax = [12% × £5m] [1 − 33%] = £0.40m

Hence, EPS becomes $\dfrac{£15m − £0.40m}{10m} = £1.46$

**Allowing for the benefits of the new project**

The annual profit yielded by the proposal, after tax at 33% = (£2m × 0.67) = £1.34m, although the cash flow benefit in the first year is £2m due to the tax delay.

After the rights issue, the prospective EPS will become:

[£15m + £1.34m]/12.5m = £1.31 per share

With debt finance, the financing cost, net of tax relief, of £0.40m pa reduces the net return from the project to (£1.34m − £0.40m) = £0.94m pa.

(In the first year, the cash flow cost will be the full pre-tax interest payment. Thereafter, Netherby will receive annual cash flow benefits from the series of tax savings.)

The EPS will be: £15.94m/10m = £1.59 per share.

Therefore, in terms of the effect on EPS, the debt-financing alternative is preferable, although it may increase financial risk.

(f)    A range of factors could be listed here. Among the major sources of risk are the following:

(i)    *Reliability of supply.* This can be secured by inclusion of penalty clauses in the contract, although these will have to be enforceable. The intermediation of the European Bank for Reconstruction and Development may enhance this.

(ii)   *The quality of the product.* Again, a penalty clause may assist, although a more constructive approach might be to assign a UK-trained total quality management (TQM) expert to the Hungarian operation to oversee quality control.

(iii)  *Market resistance to an imported product.* This seems less of a risk, if retailers are genuinely impressed with the product, and especially as there are doubts over the quality of the existing product.

(iv)   *Exchange rate variations.* Netherby is exposed to the risk of sterling depreciating against the Hungarian currency, thus increasing the sterling cost of the product. There are various ways of hedging against foreign exchange risk, of which use of the forward market is probably the simplest. Alternatively, Netherby could try to match the risk by finding a Hungarian customer for its other goods.

(v)    *Renewal of the contract.* What is likely to happen after five years? To obtain a two-way protection, Netherby might write into the contract an option to renew after five years. If the product requires re-design, Netherby could offer to finance part of the costs in exchange for this option.

(g)    When the stock market is depressed, investors are generally reluctant to buy shares, particularly shares in a new issue, unless there are particularly strong prospects that the company will perform much better than other stock market companies generally. New issues are therefore very few in number.

Rights issues are often underwritten. If institutions that normally act as underwriters are concerned that a new issue will not be successful, and a large number of shares will be left in the hands of the underwriters, they will be reluctant to join the underwriting syndicate.

The company will also be reluctant to issue new shares, particularly if it thinks that its shares ought to be worth more. A large number of new shares would have to be issued to raise the amount of finance required, and this will have a 'dilutive' effect on earnings per share.

(h)    The bond markets outside the US are generally accessible only to fairly large companies. Netherby would seem to be a small company, and so it not certain that it is large and substantial enough to gain the support of a bank that would be willing to lead manage a bond issue on its behalf.

The domestic corporate bond markets are very small in many countries, including the UK, and it is unlikely that the company would be able to make a bond issue in sterling in the UK.

When share prices are depressed, corporate bonds might also be unattractive to investors, particularly if they consider that the companies concerned could be in financial difficulties. For example, in the depressed stock market conditions during 2001/2002, poor economic conditions resulted in falling profits and falling share prices. At the same time, the bond markets were also depressed, and corporate bond yields were high for many companies.

KAPLAN PUBLISHING

## 2    BENLAND PLC

### Key answer tips

Note the types of cash flow that arise and any unusual points that may be missed later – such as the fact that the raw material (tyres) will actually represent an income rather than a cost, the existence of the non-tax-deductible penalty clause, and the fact that seals are rising by 10% wholly due to volume rises (so other volume dependent cash flows will increase by 10% as well). A horizontal layout for the DCF computation is probably best, with workings shown separately, either before or after the main computation. Make and state any necessary assumptions.

In part (b), the requirement to 'discuss' probably excludes detailed sensitivity computations – it is fairly clear which cash flows are most significant. The main marks will be awarded for the discussion on risk management.

(a)    *Workings*

(W1)    Starting from year one, and taking into account the sales increases of 10% per year:

| Year | Receipts from garages £000 | Savings on particles £000 | Tyre processing costs (£39/tonne) £000 | Extra maintenance costs £000 | Total costs £000 |
|---|---|---|---|---|---|
| 1 | 3,200 | 280 (W2) | 2,960 | 43 | 3,003 |
| 2 | 3,520 | 308 | 3,256 | 43 | 3,299 |
| 3 | 3,872 | 339 | 3,582 | 43 | 3,625 |
| 4 | 4,259 | 373 | 3,940 | 43 | 3,983 |
| 5 | 4,685 | 410 | 4,334 | 43 | 4,377 |

(W2)    The savings are one tonne of particles (£3.50 cost) for each tonne of tyres processed 80,00 tonnes are processed in year 1, giving a cost of 80,000 × £3.50 = £280,000. This then rises in line with sales, by 10% each year.

(W3)    **Tax cash flow (excluding capital allowances)**

| Year | 1 £000 | 2 £000 | 3 £000 | 4 £000 | 5 £000 |
|---|---|---|---|---|---|
| Receipts | 3,200 | 3,520 | 3,872 | 4,259 | 4,685 |
| Savings | 280 | 308 | 339 | 373 | 410 |
| Costs | (3,003) | (3,299) | (3,625) | (3,983) | (4,377) |
| Taxable cash flows | 477 | 529 | 586 | 649 | 718 |
| Tax at 33% | (157) | (175) | (193) | (214) | (237) |

(W4)    **Capital allowances and associated tax savings**

Assume purchase of the machine in year 0, and claim of the first capital allowance in the same year. This gives rise to the first cash flow from tax savings on allowances in year one.

| Year | Written down value of asset £000 | Allowance (from preceding year) £000 | Tax saving at 33% £000 |
|---|---|---|---|
| 1 | 1,060 | 265 | 87 |
| 2 | 795 | 199 | 66 |
| 3 | 596 | 149 | 49 |
| 4 | 447 | 112 | 37 |
| 5 | 335 | 84 | 28 |
| 6 | 251 | | |
| 6 | **Balancing allowance, see below** | 136 / 945 | 45 |

|  | £000 |
|---|---|
| WDV at time of sale | 251 |
| Receipts from disposal (120 – 5) | 115 |
| Balancing allowance (in £000) | 136 |

**NPV calculations**

| Year | 0 | 1 | 2 | 3 | 4 | 5 | 6 |
|---|---|---|---|---|---|---|---|
|  | £000 | £000 | £000 | £000 | £000 | £000 | £000 |
| Machine purchase/sale | (1,060) |  |  |  |  | 115 |  |
| Tax savings on WDAs (W4) |  | 87 | 66 | 49 | 37 | 28 | 45 |
| Processing costs (W1) |  | (3,003) | (3,299) | (3,625) | (3,983) | (4,377) |  |
| Savings on particles (W1) |  | 280 | 308 | 339 | 373 | 410 |  |
| Receipts from garages (W1) |  | 3,200 | 3,520 | 3,872 | 4,259 | 4,685 |  |
| Penalty charge | (100) |  |  |  |  |  |  |
| Tax on cash flows (W3) | - | - | (157) | (175) | (193) | (214) | (237) |
| Net cash flow | (1,160) | 564 | 438 | 460 | 493 | 647 | (192) |
| Discount factor at 12% | 1.000 | 0.893 | 0.797 | 0.712 | 0.636 | 0.567 | 0.507 |
| PV of cash flow | (1,160) | 504 | 349 | 328 | 343 | 367 | (97) |

**Net present value = £634,000**

*Note:* = Tax on cash flows excluding capital allowances

The net present value of the investment is positive, and so **it is advisable that Benland purchase the machine**.

(b)     The most important costs are those of the equipment itself and the tyre processing. The final sales volumes and estimated receipts from garages per tonne of tyres recycled are also critical in determining the viability of the investment. A significant change in any of these figures could alter the attractiveness of the investment.

The **purchase price of the equipment** is of critical importance, but this is a one-off cost, and so the time scale of its variability is strictly limited. Once Benland has signed a purchase contract, the cost is fixed. In order to avoid any risk of a price change in the immediate short term, Benland should ask the supplier to provide a fixed price quotation, which remains valid for a prescribed period. As long as the purchase is made within the defined period, the company can be certain of the price to be paid. The second-hand value of the equipment at the end of the investment period is not of great significance, as its estimated present value is just £65,000, or 10% of the net present value.

In order to avoid the **risk of large scale changes in processing costs**, it may be possible for Benland to use engineering calculations to assess the expected processing time, maintenance requirements, and yields per tonne of used tyres. (There is insufficient detail on the question to assess which of these aspects is most important in determining the overall cost.) It may also be possible to obtain general cost information from other users of similar equipment, in order to verify the accuracy of Benland's current estimates. Once production has commenced, statistical process controls can be used to help the company to accurately record the processing time and yields, and the amount of machine downtime can be recorded via job-sheets. In this way changes in costs can quickly be identified. If any costs change by a significant amount Benland may need to revise its NPV forecast, and if necessary look at the feasibility of disinvesting. The cash flow forecast suggests that the investment is feasible partly because processing costs are less than the receipts from garages for used tyre disposal. If this situation were to be reversed, then the viability of the investment may be altered.

**Management of the cash flows from receipts from garages** and other possible suppliers of the used tyres should be more straightforward. If there is a cost advantage to such parties relative to the cost of land-fill, then Benland can be assured of raw material supplies at a predictable cost. The only circumstances under which the revenue may become less certain is if sales of the playground equipment, and hence the company's demand for rubber particles, rose to a level beyond that which could be supplied from existing sources of used tyres. In such a case, the price paid for the tyres may increase, or the company may have to revert to the use of outside suppliers to meet the shortfall in supply. This seems unlikely, but Benland should formally assess the likelihood of sales reaching such high levels, and monitor the company's demand for particles relative to supply, in order to avoid any risk of a sudden large cost increase.

An aspect of the cash flow which is outside the control of Benland, but may nevertheless have a potentially significant effect on the investment's viability, is **the tax position**. The appraisal is based on the assumption of tax allowances granted on the basis of 25% of the reducing balance, and a corporation tax rate of 33%. If either the allowances or the tax rate were to change, the NPV of the investment would be affected. For example, if tax allowances were altered to give a 100% first year allowance, then the cash flow impact of additional tax savings would be considerable. Conversely, if the tax rate is reduced to, say, 25%, then the tax savings created via the capital allowances would be reduced, but so also would the corporation tax payable on profits, and so the NPV would change. Assessing the likelihood of changes in the tax regime is difficult, as tax rates tend to reflect political opinion, but it is highly unlikely that tax rates would be dramatically changed. The tax aspects of the cash flow are important, but they must be viewed as of less significance than the equipment cost, processing costs and revenues already discussed.

Overall, the NPV of the project is sufficiently high to allow for some changes in all of the key variables without the risk of making the project non-viable.

(c)   The project should affect the different stakeholders of Benland as follows:

| Stakeholder | Impact |
|---|---|
| Shareholders | • Wealth should increase by the NPV of the project – i.e. £634,000<br><br>• Risks will increase |
| Society | • More tyres will be recycled, proytecting the environment |
| Customers | • Customers may perceive the quality of the product to increase because it is more environmentally friendly |
| Suppliers | • Existing suppliers of rubber will lose business<br><br>• Garages will get cost savings on tyre disposal |
| Potential investors | • Benland will become more attractive to "green chip" investors, possibly making future financing easier. |

# 3   FILLS FOOTBALLS LTD

(a)   **Current situation**

Investment in debtors = £750,000 × 45/365 = £92,466.

The interest cost of this investment is 10% × £92,466 = £9,247.

| | £ |
|---|---|
| Interest cost of investment in debtors | 9,247 |
| Bad debts (1% of £750,000) | 7,500 |
| Administrative costs: operating expenses | 20,000 |
| Total costs | 36,747 |

**With the factor**

Investment in debtors = 20% of £750,000 × 35/365 = £14,384.

Interest cost of this investment = 10% of £14,384 = £1,438.

Finance provided by factor = 80% of £750,000 × 35/365 = £57,534.

Interest cost of this finance = 9% × £57,534 = £5,178.

| | £ |
|---|---|
| Interest cost of investment in debtors | 1,438 |
| Interest payments on factor finance | 5,178 |
| Administration charge (3% of £750,000) | 22,500 |
| Total costs | 29,116 |

Under the arrangement with the factor, which is on anon-recourse basis, the bad debt losses would be borne by the factor. Bad debts would therefore be zero for the company.

The factor would therefore appear to be cheaper, and from a financial perspective, using the factor would be the better option.

(b)
**Report**

**To**          Management of Fills Footballs

**From:**        Accountant

**Date:**        xxxxxx

**Credit control and debt collection procedures**

**Credit control procedures**

The company is currently losing £7,500 each year from bad debts, which is equivalent to 1% of its annual sales turnover. This level of bad debts might well be within acceptable limits. However, the company should take suitable measures to ensure that its credit control procedures are effective, without being so strict that good customers are deterred from buying from the company.

For existing customers, credit control procedures should consist principally of monitoring the payment record of the customer, and if the customer shows a good track record of paying debts on time, the company should be prepared, at the customer's request, to allow a higher credit limit.

When prospective new customers ask for credit, the problem is to decide whether to agree to give credit and if so, how much. If the amount of credit involved is likely to be small, the company might be willing to take a risk and agree to a limited amount of credit. If the customer asks for fairly extensive credit, it would be appropriate to ask for references, from a bank and from one or two other suppliers to the prospective customer. In some cases, it might even be appropriate to arrange to visit the prospective customer's premises, to gain a first-hand impression of its business.

The company should also have a credit policy, and offer standard credit terms (e.g. 30, 45 or 60 days credit, depending on what is normal in the industry) up to a limited credit limit. As the relationship with the customer develops, better credit terms might be offered.

There is an argument that a prospective new customer needs to be offered generous credit terms, otherwise the company will not win the customer's business. As indicated earlier, however, the company must have a clear policy on how much bad credit risk it is prepared to accept. By offering generous credit terms, the level of bad debts will almost certainly rise, although the volume of sales turnover is likely to rise too. Easy credit terms should not be offered without considering the risk, and setting a tolerable limit on the scale of that risk exposure.

## Alternative methods for improving debt collection

I have been asked to suggest ways of improving debt collection, other than using the services of a factor. This request suggests that you are not satisfied with current debt collection procedures in your company. My comments below are based on the assumption that these are weak and inadequate, although if this were the case, bad debt levels might be higher.

Collecting debts effectively and efficiently is largely a matter of administration and organisation. Invoices should be sent out to customers promptly after the delivery of the goods or services, and the invoice should state the credit terms.

Customers who buy regularly should be sent periodic statements, perhaps monthly, to keep them informed of the current position and the details of the invoices as yet unpaid. More occasional customers should be sent a written reminder if they fail to pay by the due date. If the customer makes a complaint about some detail in the invoice, this should be dealt with promptly: the customer should not have a legitimate excuse for delaying payment!

Late payers should also be monitored by means of an aged debtors list, which should be produced regularly. This is a list of all unpaid debts, grouped according to the time for which they have remained unpaid. When debts are unpaid after a given length of time, and the customer has not responded to a statement or reminder, one or more individuals in the debt collection section should chase payment by telephoning the customer concerned. Contacting the person in the customer organisation who is responsible for payment, and obtaining a promise to pay, often succeeds in extracting payment fairly quickly.

Some customers will remain reluctant or unwilling to pay, in spite of several telephone calls. In such cases, the company should have established procedures for what to do next. The company could have a policy of trying to obtain payment by referring the matter to a higher level in the management hierarchy. Alternatively, the services of a debt collection agency might be used. In some cases, payment might be chased through the courts.

Another approach to improving debt collection, which can be used in addition to improved internal administrative procedures, is to encourage the customer to pay more promptly. There are at least two ways of doing this. One method is to persuade regular customers to pay by bank transfer (in the UK, by BACS) rather than by cheque. The customer could then arrange to pay invoices electronically, by giving an instruction to its bank, as part of its routine 'month end' payments procedures. An alternative method is to encourage early payment by offering early settlement discounts.

## The importance of debtor management

Debtor management is important for several reasons.

- The credit terms offered to customers could be a factor in the customer's decision to buy from the company, or to go to an alternative supplier offering better terms. However, although generous credit terms can help to boost sales, they can also lead to significantly higher bad debt losses. A company has to strike a balance between offering reasonable credit terms to win business, but not so reasonable that the losses exceed the benefits.

- Generous credit terms will result in a larger volume of debtors. Debtors tie up cash, and have to be financed. Proper control over debtors should prevent the investment being larger and more costly than necessary.

- Because debtors tie up cash, an increase in debtors can have important consequences for cash flow. In order to pay their own creditors, companies need cash from their debtors. Profitable companies might suffer a shortage of liquidity by allowing their debtors to increase to an amount higher than they can safely afford.

**Conclusion**

Credit control and debt collection are both elements of debtor management. If you continue to collect debts yourself, without the services of a factor, formulating and applying a clear policy on credit, together with efficient administrative procedures for debt collection, should enable you to manage your credit levels and your debtors effectively.

## 4 FERTICOM PLC

(a) Standard cost and standard contribution per kg

|  | £ | £ |
|---|---|---|
| Standard sales price |  | 16.00 |
| Materials: (144/32) | 4.50 |  |
| Labour: (0.4 × £10.00) | 4.00 |  |
| Variable overheads: (0.4 × £3.00) | 1.20 |  |
|  |  | 9.70 |
| Standard contribution |  | 6.30 |

*Calculation of variances*

(i) *Sales variances*

|  | £ |  |
|---|---|---|
| 3,648 kg should sell for (× £16) | 58,368 |  |
| They did sell for (× £16.75) | 61,104 |  |
| Sales price variance | **2,736** | **(F)** |

|  | Kg |  |
|---|---|---|
| Budgeted sales volume | 4,096 |  |
| Actual sales volume | 3,648 |  |
| Sales volume variance | 448 | (A) |

|  |  |  |
|---|---|---|
| Standard contribution/unit | £6.30 |  |
| Sales volume contribution variance | **£2,822** | **(A)** |

(ii) *Materials price and mix variances*

| **Material F price variance** | £ |  |
|---|---|---|
| 1,680 kg should cost (× £4) | 6,720 |  |
| They did cost | 7,140 |  |
| Material F price variance | **420** | **(A)** |

| **Material G price variance** | £ |  |
|---|---|---|
| 1,650 kg should cost (× £3) | 4,950 |  |
| They did cost | 4,620 |  |
| Material G price variance | **330** | **(F)** |

**Material H price variance** £
870 kg should cost (× £6)          5,220
They did cost                       5,568

Material H price variance          **348**   **(A)**

*Mix variances*

The standard mix is 15 kg of F for 12kg of G and 8kg of H.

| Material | Actual quantities used | Actual total quantity in standard mix | Mix variance | Standard price | Mix variance |
|---|---|---|---|---|---|
|  | kg | kg | kg | £ | £ |
| F | 1,680 | 1,800 | 120 (F) | 4 | 480 (F) |
| G | 1,650 | 1,440 | 210 (A) | 3 | 630 (A) |
| H | 870 | 960 | 90 (F) | 6 | 540 (F) |
|  | 4,200 | 4,200 |  |  | 390 (F) |

*Yield variances*

| | 3,648kg of W should use | Actual quantities in standard mix | Yield variance | Standard price | Yield variance |
|---|---|---|---|---|---|
|  | kg | kg | kg | £ | £ |
| F | 1,710 | 1,800 | 90 (A) | 4 | 360 (A) |
| G | 1,368 | 1,440 | 72 (A) | 3 | 216 (A) |
| H | 912 | 960 | 48 (A) | 6 | 288 (A) |
|  | 3,990 | 4,200 |  |  | 864(A) |

(iii)  *Labour variances*

**Actual hours × actual rate**   = 15,900
1500 × 10.60                                          900(A) rate variance

Actual hours × standard rate   = 15,000
1500 × 10.00                                          408 (A) efficiency variance

Standard hours × standard rate   = 14,592
3,648 × 0.4 × 10

(b)   The variances can be explained as follows:

(i)   *Materials mix*

- The mix variances for F and H are favourable, indicating that proportionately less of these materials have been used. The mix variance for G is adverse, indicating that proportionately more of this material has been used than expected.

- The overall variance is favorable, indicating that the actual mix involved less of the relatively expensive materials F and H, and more of the cheaper material G.

- This could have arisen because of poor budgeting, given that the product W has only recently been developed.

(ii)   *Materials yield*

- The yield variances are adverse indicating that the actual yield was worse than expected, or, equivalently, that more of each type of material was needed than expected.

- This could be because the process of making the new fertilizer is still being learnt by workers, resulting in more waste.

(iii) *Labour efficiency*

- The labour efficiency variance is adverse, indicating that workers took longer than expected to make the fertilizer . This is not surprising, given that one might have expected workers to take longer as they would be unfamiliar with the new process.

- One reason could be that the standard was set assuming a learning rate.

(iv) *Sales volume*

- The sales volume variance is adverse, indicating that less product W was sold than expected.

- Given that no stocks appear to be held, the shortfall in sales is most likely due to the poor yield in production.

- Alternatively, the product is relatively new and may take longer than expected to catch on.

(c) The following factors might be considered in deciding whether to investigate a variance.

**Size**

Larger cost savings are likely to arise from taking action to correct large variances and a policy could be established of investigating all variances above a given size. Size can be linked to the underlying variable in percentage terms as a test of significance: for example, a policy could be established to investigate all variances of 5% or more.

In the current example, the sales volume variance was the largest and might warrant further investigation.

**Adverse or favourable**

It is natural to concentrate on adverse variances in order to bring business operations back in line with budget. However, whether a variance is adverse or favourable should not influence the decision to investigate. The reasons for favourable variances should also be sought, since they may indicate the presence of budgetary slack or suggest ways in which the budgeting process could be improved. Favourable variances may also indicate areas where the budget is easy to achieve, suggesting that the motivational effect of a budget could be improved by introducing more demanding targets.

The labour efficiency variance was adverse as expected, giving less reason to investigate.

**Cost versus benefits**

If the expected cost of investigating a variance is likely to exceed any benefits expected to arise from its correction, it may be decided not to investigate.

With the new product above it is likely that all of the standards would need time to get right. A detailed investigation at this stage may thus prove uneconomic.

**Historical pattern of variances**

A variance that is unusual when compared to historical patterns of variances may be considered worthy of investigation. Statistical tests of significance may be used to highlight such variances.

### Reliability and quality of data

If data is aggregated or if the quality of the measuring and recording system is not as high as would be liked, there may be uncertainty about the benefits to arise from investigation of variances.

### Cumulative variances over time

A variance might be investigated if the cumulative variances over time suggest that there is a continuing trend of averse (or favourable variances). The size of the variance in each period might not, on its own, be sufficient to justify investigation, but the continuing trend might indicate an underlying cause for the variances that should be investigated.

| Marking scheme | | Marks |
|---|---|---|
| (a) | Sales volume variance | 1 |
| | Sales price variance | 1 |
| | Material price variances | 2 |
| | Material mix variances | 3 |
| | Material yield variances | 3 |
| | Labour rate and efficiency variances | 2 |
| | Marks available | 12 |
| | | |
| (b) | Material mix variances | 2 |
| | Material yield variances | 2 |
| | Labour efficiency variance | 2 |
| | Sales volume variance | 2 |
| | | 8 |
| | | |
| (c) | Up to 2 marks for each factor discussed | 5 |
| Total | | 25 |

## 5    BUDGET COMPILATION

### Key answer tips

In part (a) the key is to remember the flow of the budgets - starting with the sales units given, *add* closing stock (finished goods) and *subtract* opening stock to get to production. This will determine materials usage, which then needs to be adjusted for opening and closing stock of raw materials in the same way to arrive at materials purchases.

In part (b) we are looking at one month only, and the main working required is that of closing stock value, incorporating the overhead absorption rate appropriate to that month's production.

In part (c), having used the company's 'monthly' system of overhead absorption in (b), you are now asked to assess its implications. You should start by stating the obvious - that stock value will fluctuate with production levels, even though budgeted overhead for the month is constant - then think how this might affect the information conveyed by the management accounts.

Part (d) is a straightforward textbook explanation of a time series and its components, and should give easy marks.

(a)   **Production budget (units)**

|  | Dec | Jan | Feb | Mar | Apr |
|---|---|---|---|---|---|
| Sales | 14,000 | 16,000 | 22,000 | 17,000 | 20,000 |
| Closing stock | 4,000 | 5,500 | 4,250 | 5,000 | 6,000 |
|  | 18,000 | 21,500 | 26,250 | 22,000 | 26,000 |
| Opening stock | 3,500 | 4,000 | 5,500 | 4,250 | 5,000 |
| Production | 14,500 | 17,500 | 20,750 | 17,750 | 21,000 |

**Purchases budget (units)**

|  | Dec | Jan | Feb | Mar |
|---|---|---|---|---|
| Production | 14,500 | 17,500 | 20,750 | 17,750 |
| Closing stock | 1,750 | 2,075 | 1,775 | 2,100 |
|  | 16,250 | 19,575 | 22,525 | 19,850 |
| Opening stock | 1,450 | 1,750 | 2,075 | 1,775 |
| Purchases | 14,800 | 17,825 | 20,450 | 18,075 |

**Examiner's note**

Columns for January to March only are required in an answer to (a) though you will find that you will need some data from December for the cash budget, as well as the production for April for the purchases budget.

(b)   **Working: Product unit manufacturing cost for January**

|  | £ |
|---|---|
| Material | 10 |
| Variable overhead and labour | 16 |
| Fixed overhead | 12 |
|  | 38 |

*Note:* The fixed overhead rate for January is calculated using the budgeted monthly overhead and production: £210,000/17,500 = £12/unit.

**Budgeted profit and loss account January 20X9 (FIFO stock valuation)**

|  |  | £000 | £000 |
|---|---|---|---|
| Sales | 16,000 × £58 |  | 928 |
| Raw material usage | 17,500 × £10 | 175 |  |
| Variable overhead and lab. | 17,500 × £16 | 280 |  |
| Fixed overhead | 17,500 × £12 | 210 |  |
| Manufacturing cost | 17,500 × £38 | 665 |  |
| Closing stock | (5,500 × £38) | (209) |  |
|  | 12,000 × £38 | 456 |  |
| Opening stock | 4,000 × £40 (cost given) | 160 |  |
| Cost of sales |  |  | 616 |
| Gross profit |  |  | 312 |

*Selling costs*

| | | | |
|---|---|---|---|
| Variable | 16,000 units of sale × £7 | 112 | |
| Fixed | | 164 | |
| | | | 276 |
| Net profit | | | 36 |

**Cash receipts and payments January 20X9**

| | | £000 | £000 |
|---|---|---|---|
| Receipts | | | |
| From December sales | 50% × 14,000 × £58 | | 406 |
| From January sales | 50% × 16,000 × £58 | | 464 |
| Total receipts | | | 870 |
| Payments: | | | |
| Materials (December purchases) | (14,800 × £10) | 148 | |
| Variable overhead and labour | (17,500 × £16) | 280 | |
| Fixed overhead | (210,000 – 54,000 dep'n) | 156 | |
| Variable selling | (16,000 × £7) | 112 | |
| Fixed selling | | 164 | |
| Total payments | | | 860 |
| Receipts less payments in January | | | 10 |

(c)  Under a system of absorption costing, an overhead rate is used to apply overheads to each unit produced. At present the company applies each month's overhead to products based on the budgeted production levels and the budgeted expenditure in each month, which are used to establish **a separate predetermined rate for each month**. As a result, unit overhead costs fluctuate if production levels fluctuate because the fixed overheads are spread over fluctuating volumes.

It can be disconcerting and misleading for production and sales staff to be dealing with product costs which fluctuate on a monthly basis. This is especially so when the fluctuation has not been caused by changes in production efficiency, and it bears no relation to changes in the general market price.

One way to overcome this is to compute an overhead rate which is based on a longer time period, for example quarterly, or a predetermined annual rate as mentioned in the question. This enables large fluctuations in, and extreme values of, product costs to be avoided. This would mean that management would be able to monitor the business volume and overhead costs on which the calculations were based to ensure that over the longer-term the average product costs which were predicted were in fact achieved.

(d)  A **time series** is the name given to a set of observations taken at equal intervals of time in order to obtain an overall picture of what is taking place. For example, monthly sales covering a period of, say, five years. A time series consists of various components, such as trend, cyclical, seasonal and residual components.

To develop this explanation a little further, the **trend component** is the way in which the series appears to be moving over a long interval, after other fluctuations have been smoothed out. The **cyclical component** is the wave-like appearance which occurs in the series when taken over a fairly long period, a number of years. Generally it is caused by the booms and slumps in an industry or trade cycle.

A **seasonal component** is the regular rise and fall of values over specified intervals of time, within say one year. Though the term seasonal is used it does not have to align with seasons, but any regular variations over short time periods. **Residual components** are any other variations which cannot be ascribed to any of those mentioned above, essentially random factors and due to unpredictable causes.

# Section 7

# DECEMBER 2005 EXAM QUESTIONS

## SECTION A – THIS ONE QUESTION IS COMPULSORY AND MUST BE ATTEMPTED

**1    BFD CO**

BFD Co is a private company formed three years ago by four brothers who, as directors, retain sole ownership of its ordinary share capital. One quarter of the initial share capital was provided by each brother. The company has returned a profit in each year of operation as shown by the following financial statements.

**Profit and Loss Accounts for years ending 30 November**

|  | 2005 | 2004 | 2003 |
|---|---|---|---|
|  | £000 | £000 | £000 |
| Turnover | 5,200 | 3,400 | 2,600 |
| Cost of sales | 4,570 | 2,806 | 2,104 |
| Profit before interest and tax | 630 | 594 | 496 |
| Interest | 70 | 34 | 3 |
| Profit before tax | 560 | 560 | 493 |
| Tax | 140 | 140 | 123 |
| Profit after tax | 420 | 420 | 370 |
| Dividends | 20 | 20 | 20 |
| Retained profit | 400 | 400 | 350 |

**Balance Sheets as at 30 November**

|  | £000 | 2005 £000 | £000 | 2004 £000 | £000 | 2003 £000 |
|---|---|---|---|---|---|---|
| Fixed assets |  | 1,600 |  | 1,200 |  | 800 |
| Current assets |  |  |  |  |  |  |
| Stock | 1,450 |  | 1,000 |  | 600 |  |
| Debtors | 1,400 |  | 850 |  | 400 |  |
|  | 2,850 |  | 1,850 |  | 1,000 |  |
| Current liabilities | 2,300 |  | 1,300 |  | 450 |  |
| Net current assets |  | 550 |  | 550 |  | 550 |
|  |  | 2,150 |  | 1,750 |  | 1,350 |
| Ordinary shares (£1 par) |  | 1,000 |  | 1,000 |  | 1,000 |
| Reserves |  | 1,150 |  | 750 |  | 350 |
|  |  | 2,150 |  | 1,750 |  | 1,350 |

BFD Co has an overdraft limit of £1.25 million and pays interest on its overdraft at a rate of 6% per year. Current liabilities consist of trade creditors and overdraft finance in each of the three years.

The directors are delighted with the rapid growth of BFD Co and are considering further expansion through buying new premises and machinery to manufacture Product FT7. This new product has only just been developed and patented by BFD Co. Test marketing has indicated considerable demand for the product, as shown by the following research data.

| Year of operation | 1 | 2 | 3 | 4 |
|---|---|---|---|---|
| Accounting year | 2005/6 | 2006/7 | 2007/8 | 2008/9 |
| Sales volume (units) | 100,000 | 120,000 | 130,000 | 140,000 |

Sales after 2008/9 (the fourth year of operation) are expected to continue at the 2008/9 level in perpetuity.

Initial investment of £3,000,000 would be required in new premises and machinery, as well as an additional £200,000 of working capital. The directors have no further financial resources to offer and are considering approaching their bank for a loan to meet their investment needs. Selling price and standard cost data for Product FT7, based on an annual budgeted volume of 100,000 units, are as follows.

| | £ per unit |
|---|---|
| Selling price | 18.00 |
| Direct material | 7.00 |
| Direct labour | 1.50 |
| Fixed production overhead | 4.50 |

The fixed production overhead is incurred exclusively in the production of Product FT7 and excludes depreciation. Selling price and standard unit variable cost data for Product FT7 are expected to remain constant.

BFD Co expects to be able to claim writing down allowances on the initial investment of £3,000,000 on a straightline basis over 10 years. The company pays tax on profit at an annual rate of 25% in the year in which the liability arises and has an after-tax cost of capital of 12%.

**Average data for companies similar to BFD Co**

| | | | |
|---|---|---|---|
| Net profit margin: | 9% | Creditor days: | 70 days |
| Interest cover: | 15 times | Current ratio: | 2.1 times |
| Stock days: | 85 days | Quick ratio: | 0.8 times |
| Debtor days: | 75 days | Debt/equity ratio: | 40% (using book values) |

**Required:**

(a)  Calculate the net present value of the proposed investment in Product FT7. Assume that it is now 1 December 2005. **(16 marks)**

(b)  Comment on the acceptability of the proposed investment in Product FT7 and discuss what additional information might improve the decision-making process. **(7 marks)**

(c)  BFD Co has received an offer from a rival company of £300,000 per year for 10 years for the manufacturing rights for Product FT7. If BFD Co accepts this offer, it would not be able to manufacture Product FT7 for the duration of the agreement.

**Required:**

Determine whether BFD Co should accept the offer for the manufacturing rights to Product FT7. In this part of the question only, ignore cash flows occurring after the ten-year period of the offer. Assume that it is 1 December 2005. **(6 marks)**

(d)    As the newly-appointed finance director of BFD Co, write a report to the board which discusses whether the company is likely to be successful if it approaches its bank for a loan. Your discussion should include an analysis of the current financial position and recent financial performance of the company.                                             **(16 marks)**

(e)    On the basis that BFD Co decided to invest and manufacture Product FT7, the actual data for the first year of operation (2005/6) is now available and is as follows:

| | |
|---|---|
| Number of units produced and sold | 110,000 |
| Selling price (£ per unit) | 18.20 |
| Direct material (£ per unit) | 7.10 |
| Direct labour (£ per unit) | 1.70 |
| Fixed production overhead (£ per unit) | 4.50 |

**Required:**

Calculate the following variances using marginal costing and absorption costing:

(i)    sales price variance;

(ii)   sales volume profit variance;

and comment on the relative values obtained.                                             **(5 marks)**

**(Total: 50 marks)**

## SECTION B – TWO QUESTIONS ONLY TO BE ATTEMPTED

**2    PERFORMANCE APPRAISAL**

**Required:**

(a)    Identify the types of responsibility centres used in responsibility accounting and discuss how the performance of each responsibility centre type might be measured, including in your discussion examples of controllable and non-controllable factors.
                                             **(12 marks)**

(b)    Critically discuss whether return on investment or residual income should be used to assess managerial performance in an investment centre.                         **(13 marks)**

**(Total: 25 marks)**

**3    LINEACRE CO**

Linacre Co operates an activity-based costing system and has forecast the following information for next year.

| Cost Pool | Cost | Cost Driver | Number of Drivers |
|---|---|---|---|
| Production set-ups | £105,000 | Set-ups | 300 |
| Product testing | £300,000 | Tests | 1,500 |
| Component supply and storage | £25,000 | Component orders | 500 |
| Customer orders and delivery | £112,500 | Customer orders | 1,000 |

General fixed overheads such as lighting and heating, which cannot be linked to any specific activity, are expected to be £900,000 and these overheads are absorbed on a direct labour hour basis. Total direct labour hours for next year are expected to be 300,000 hours.

Linacre Co expects orders for Product ZT3 next year to be 100 orders of 60 units per order and 60 orders of 50 units per order. The company holds no stocks of Product ZT3 and will need to produce the order requirement in production runs of 900 units. One order for components is placed prior to each production run. Four tests are made during each production run to ensure that quality standards are maintained. The following additional cost and profit information relates to product ZT3:

| | |
|---|---|
| Component cost: | £1.00 per unit |
| Direct labour: | 10 minutes per unit at £7.80 per hour |
| Profit mark up: | 40% of total unit cost |

### Required:

(a)   Calculate the activity-based recovery rates for each cost pool.   **(4 marks)**

(b)   Calculate the total unit cost and selling price of Product ZT3.   **(9 marks)**

(c)   Discuss the reasons why activity-based costing may be preferred to traditional absorption costing in the modern manufacturing environment.   **(12 marks)**

**(Total: 25 marks)**

## 4   AGD CO

AGD Co is a profitable company which is considering the purchase of a machine costing £320,000. If purchased, AGD Co would incur annual maintenance costs of £25,000. The machine would be used for three years and at the end of this period would be sold for £50,000. Alternatively, the machine could be obtained under an operating lease for an annual lease rental of £120,000 per year, payable in advance.

AGD Co can claim capital allowances on a 25% reducing balance basis. The company pays tax on profits at an annual rate of 30% and all tax liabilities are paid one year in arrears. AGD Co has an accounting year that ends on 31 December. If the machine is purchased, payment will be made in January of the first year of operation. If leased, annual lease rentals will be paid in January of each year of operation.

### Required:

(a)   Using an after-tax borrowing rate of 7%, evaluate whether AGD Co should purchase or lease the new machine.   **(12 marks)**

(b)   Explain and discuss the key differences between an operating lease and a finance lease.   **(8 marks)**

(c)   The after-tax borrowing rate of 7% was used in the evaluation because a bank had offered to lend AGD Co £320,000 for a period of five years at a before-tax rate of 10% per year with interest payable every six months.

### Required:

(i)   Calculate the annual percentage rate (APR) implied by the bank's offer to lend at 10% per year with interest payable every six months.   **(2 marks)**

(ii)   Calculate the amount to be repaid at the end of each six-month period if the offered loan is to be repaid in equal instalments.   **(3 marks)**

**(Total: 25 marks)**

## 5 THORNE CO

Thorne Co values, advertises and sells residential property on behalf of its customers. The company has been in business for only a short time and is preparing a cash budget for the first four months of 2006. Expected sales of residential properties are as follows.

| Month | 2005 December | 2006 January | 2006 February | 2006 March | 2006 April |
|---|---|---|---|---|---|
| Units sold | 10 | 10 | 15 | 25 | 30 |

The average price of each property is £180,000 and Thorne Co charges a fee of 3% of the value of each property sold. Thorne Co receives 1% in the month of sale and the remaining 2% in the month after sale. The company has nine employees who are paid on a monthly basis. The average salary per employee is £35,000 per year. If more than 20 properties are sold in a given month, each employee is paid in that month a bonus of £140 for each additional property sold.

Variable expenses are incurred at the rate of 0.5% of the value of each property sold and these expenses are paid in the month of sale. Fixed overheads of £4,300 per month are paid in the month in which they arise. Thorne Co pays interest every three months on a loan of £200,000 at a rate of 6% per year. The last interest payment in each year is paid in December.

An outstanding tax liability of £95,800 is due to be paid in April. In the same month Thorne Co intends to dispose of surplus vehicles, with a net book value of £15,000, for £20,000. The cash balance at the start of January 2006 is expected to be a deficit of £40,000.

**Required:**

(a) Prepare a monthly cash budget for the period from January to April 2006. Your budget must clearly indicate each item of income and expenditure, and the opening and closing monthly cash balances.
**(10 marks)**

(b) Discuss the factors to be considered by Thorne Co when planning ways to invest any cash surplus forecast by its cash budgets.
**(5 marks)**

(c) Discuss the advantages and disadvantages to Thorne Co of using overdraft finance to fund any cash shortages forecast by its cash budgets.
**(5 marks)**

(d) Explain how the Baumol model can be employed to reduce the costs of cash management and discuss whether the Baumol cash management model may be of assistance to Thorne Co for this purpose.
**(5 marks)**

**(Total: 25 marks)**

# Section 8

# ANSWERS TO DECEMBER 2005 EXAM QUESTIONS

## SECTION A

### 1 BFD CO

**Key answer tips**

Part (a) asks for a NPV calculation. The first consideration is how to set out your answer as there are cash flows for the first four years and annuities for t=5-∞ and t=1-10. These can be incorporated as separate calculations or you could have had columns for flows 0,1,2,3,4,5-10 and 11-∞. This latter approach would have made part (c) slightly easier. Either way you needed to be particularly careful when calculating the tax flows given the lack of a delay.

In part (b) it is vital that issues are applied to the scenario, making reference to specific figures where possible.

Part (c) is tricky as the calculation to part (a) needs adjusting to remove the impact of cash flows for t= 11-∞.

Part (d) requires a structured approach to ensure a wide range of issues is covered, so a little time spent planning would have been a good idea. Where possible the impact of the loan should be quantified – for example, with the impact on gearing.

In part (e) you are asked to calculate the variances using both marginal and absorption costing so you need to prepare a standard cost under both systems. The required discussion is on the relative values so should be limited to explaining the difference, if any, rather than wider issues such as explaining the causes of the variances.

(a) Net present value evaluation of proposed investment:

|  | 2005/6 £000 | 2006/7 £000 | 2007/8 £000 | 2008/9 £000 |
|---|---|---|---|---|
| Sales revenue | 1,800 | 2,160 | 2,340 | 2,520 |
| Variable costs | 850 | 1,020 | 1,105 | 1,190 |
| Contribution | 950 | 1,140 | 1,235 | 1,330 |
| Fixed costs | 450 | 450 | 450 | 450 |
| Net cash flow | 500 | 690 | 785 | 880 |
| Taxation | 125 | 173 | 196 | 220 |
| After-tax cash flow | 375 | 517 | 589 | 660 |
| 12% discount factors | 0.893 | 0.797 | 0.712 | 0.636 |
| Present values | 335 | 412 | 419 | 419 |

| | £ |
|---|---|
| Sum of present values | 1,585,000 |
| PV of tax benefits | 423,750 |
| PV of cash flows after Year 4 = | 3,498,000 |
| | 5,506,750 |
| *Less* initial investment | 3,200,000 |
| Net present value | 2,306,750 |

**Workings**

| | 2005/6 | 2006/7 | 2007/8 | 2008/9 |
|---|---|---|---|---|
| Sales volume (units) | 100,000 | 120,000 | 130,000 | 140,000 |
| Selling price (£/unit) | 18.00 | 18.00 | 18.00 | 18.00 |
| Sales revenue (£) | 1,800,000 | 2,160,000 | 2,340,000 | 2,520,000 |
| Variable costs (£/unit) | 8.50 | 8.50 | 8.50 | 8.50 |
| Variable costs (£) | 850,000 | 1,020,000 | 1,105,000 | 1,190,000 |

Fixed costs = $4.50 \times 100,000$ = £450,000 per year

Annual writing down allowance = $3,000,000/10$ = £300,000

Annual writing down allowance tax benefits = $25\% \times 300,000$ = £75,000

Ten-year annuity factor at 12% = 5.650

Present value of writing down allowance tax benefits = $75,000 \times 5.650$ = £423,750

Year 4 value of year 5 after-tax cash flows in perpetuity = $660,000/0.12$ = £5,500,000

Present value of these cash flows = $5,500,000 \times 0.636$ = £3,498,000

(b)   From a net present value perspective the proposed investment is acceptable, since the net present value (NPV) is large and positive. However, a large part of the present value of benefits (63%) derives from the assumption that cash flows will continue indefinitely after Year 4. This is very unlikely to occur in practice and excluding these cash flows will result in a negative net present value of approximately £1.2m. In fact the proposed investment will not show a positive NPV until more than seven years have passed.

Before rejecting the proposal, steps should be taken to address some of the limitations of the analysis performed.

*Inflation*

Forecasts of future inflation of sales prices and variable costs should be prepared, so that a nominal NPV evaluation can be undertaken. This evaluation should employ a nominal after-tax cost of capital: it is not stated whether the 12% after-tax cost of capital is in nominal or real terms. Sales price is assumed to be constant in real terms, but in practice substitute products are likely to arise, leading to downward pressure on sales price and sales volumes.

*Constant fixed costs*

The assumption of constant fixed costs should be verified as being acceptable. Sales volumes are forecast to increase by 40% and this increase may result in an increase in incremental fixed costs.

*Constant working capital*

The assumption of constant working capital should be investigated. Net working capital is likely to increase in line with sales and so additional investment in working capital may be needed in future years. Inflation will increase required incremental working capital investment.

*Taxation and capital allowances*

The assumptions made regarding taxation should be investigated. The tax rate has been assumed to be constant, when there may be different rates of profit tax applied to companies of different size. The method available for claiming capital allowances should be confirmed, since it is usual to find a different method being applied to buildings compared to that applied to machinery, whereas in this case they are the same.

*Machine replacement*

The purchase of replacement machinery has been ignored, which seems unreasonable. Future reinvestment in new machinery will be needed and this will reduce the net present value of the proposed investment. Technological change is also possible, bringing perhaps new manufacturing methods and improved or substitute products, and these may affect the size of future cash flows.

*Changes in technology*

Technological change is also possible, bringing perhaps new manufacturing methods and improved or substitute products, and these may affect the size of future cash flows.

*Financing*

The method of financing the proposed investment should be considered. It may be that leasing will be cheaper than borrowing to buy, increasing the net present value and making the project more attractive. The amount of the investment is large compared to the current long-term capital employed by BFD Co and the after-tax cost of capital is likely to change as a result. A lower cost of capital would increase the NPV.

(c)　The offer for the manufacturing rights is for a ten-year period.

Annual after-tax cash flow after Year 4 = £660,000

Present value of this cash flow over six years at 12% = 660,000 × 4.111 = £2,713,260

Present value of post Year 4 cash flows = 2,713,260 × 0.636 = £1,725,633

| | |
|---|---:|
| Sum of present values over 4 years | 1,585,000 |
| PV of tax benefits | 423,750 |
| PV of cash flows from Year 5 to Year 10 = | 1,725,633 |
| | 3,734,383 |
| *Less* initial investment | 3,200,000 |
| Net present value | 534,383 |

This net present value is equivalent to an annual benefit of 534,383/ 5.650 = £94,581

The after-tax value of the offer of £300,000 per year for 10 years = 300,000 × 0.75 = £225,000

In the absence of other information, the offer should be accepted.

An alternative approach is to calculate the present value of the offer:

300,000 × 0.75 × 5.650 = £1,271,250

Since this is greater than the NPV of investing by £737,867, the offer should be accepted.

**Alternative answer to parts (a) and (c)**

| Narrative | 0 | 1 | 2 | 3 | 4 | 5–10 | 11–∞ |
|---|---|---|---|---|---|---|---|
| Sales | | 1,800 | 2,160 | 2,340 | 2,520 | | |
| Var costs | | (850) | (1,020) | (1,105) | (1,190) | | |
| Fixed costs | | (450) | (450) | (450) | (450) | | |
| | | 500 | 690 | 785 | 880 | | |
| Tax | | (125) | (173) | (196) | (220) | | |
| | | 375 | 517 | 589 | 660 | 660 | 660 |
| Invest | (3,200) | | | | | | |
| Tax re WDAs | | 75 | 75 | 75 | 75 | 75 | |
| Net cash flow | (3,200) | 450 | 592 | 664 | 735 | 735 | 660 |
| DF@12% | 1 | 0.893 | 0.797 | 0.712 | 0.636 | 0.636 × 4.111 | 0.322 × 1/0.12 |
| PV | (3,200) | 402 | 472 | 473 | 467 | 1922 | 1,771 |

NPV = £2,307k

NPV (excluding t=11-∞) = 2,307 – 1,771 = £536k

(d)                    **REPORT**

**To:**      The Board of BFD Co

**From:**    Finance Director

**Date:**

**Subject:**   Proposal to seek £3.2 million of Debt Finance

1.  **Introduction**

This report considers whether seeking £3.2 million of debt finance is likely to be successful in the light of our current financial position and recent financial performance.

2.  **Sector Data**

I have obtained some benchmark data relating to companies active in our business sector. The sector data applies to the current year and may not be applicable in previous years.

3.  **Analysis of Financial Data**

Analysis of our financial statements gives the following results.

| | 2002/3 | 2003/4 | 2004/5 | Sector value |
|---|---|---|---|---|
| Turnover growth | 31% | 53% | | |
| Cost of sales growth | 33% | 63% | | |
| Net profit margin | 19% | 17% | 12% | 9% |
| Interest cover | 165 | 17 | 9 | 15 |
| Sales/net working capital | 4.7 | 6.2 | 9.5 | |
| Stock days | 104 | 130 | 116 | 85 |
| Debtor days | 56 | 91 | 98 | 75 |
| Creditor days | 69 | 95 | 90 | 70 |

|  | 2002/3 | 2003/4 | 2004/5 | Sector value |
|---|---|---|---|---|
| Current ratio | 2.2 | 1.4 | 1.2 | 2.1 |
| Quick ratio | 0.9 | 0.7 | 0.6 | 0.8 |
| Gearing (debt/equity ratio) | 4% | 33% | 54% | 40% |

Note: Gearing calculations are based on our average overdraft, as our company has no long-term debt. This seems a reasonable approach to calculating gearing, since our overdraft is a large and increasing one.

### Workings

|  | 2002/3 | 2003/4 | 2004/5 |
|---|---|---|---|
| Annual interest at 6% (£) | 3,000 | 34,000 | 70,000 |
| Overdraft (£) | 50,000 | 567,000 | 1,167,000 |
| Trade creditors (£) | 400,000 | 733,000 | 1,133,000 |

4. **Comment on Financial Position and Performance**

BFD Co has experienced rapid growth in turnover since its formation three years ago, but it has been unable to maintain net profit margin, which has fallen from 19% in 2002 to 12% in 2004. On a positive note, our net profit margin is higher than the sector average, but this may also indicate that a further decrease may arise.

Our growth in turnover has not been matched by growth in long-term finance. Apart from the original equity investment made by the founder directors, growth in long-term finance has been through retained earnings alone. Our company has increasingly relied on short-term finance and over the three-year period the overdraft has grown from £50,000 to £1,167,000. From a financial risk point of view, gearing has increased from 4% to 54% and interest cover has declined from 165 times to nine times. Both ratios are currently worse than the comparable sector average. The average period of time in which we settle with trade creditors has grown from 69 days to 90 days compared to a sector average of 70 days.

The average amount of credit extended by the sector is 75 days but our debtors' ratio has grown from 56 days to 98 days. This has increased the amount of working capital finance we need, as has the growth in stock days from 104 days to 116 days compared to a sector average of 85 days. Funds which are tied up in stocks and debtors decrease profitability.

There is further bad news in the area of working capital management since both our current ratio and quick ratio are less than the current sector average, having declined in each of the past two years.

5. **Effect of Additional Debt Finance on Current Financial Position**

Debt finance of £3.2m would increase gearing on a book value basis from 54% to 203% ((1,167 + 3,200)/2,150), which is five times the sector average. If the overdraft is ignored in calculating gearing it would still be four times the sector average at 158% (3,400/2,150). Assuming interest at a fixed rate of 8%, our interest cover would fall from 9 times to 1.8 times (630/(272 + 70)). This is a dangerously low level of interest cover. We would need to assess whether we could offer security for a loan of this size.

6. **Chances of Success in Application for Debt Finance**

I must advise you that there are signs of overtrading in our recent financial statements and our company is approaching its overdraft limit of £1.25 million.

We will need to obtain further long-term finance regardless of whether our application for a £3.2 million bank loan is successful.

I note that no further equity investment is available from the current directors. It may be in our best interests to address our overall long-term financing needs rather than seeking finance only for the proposed investment in Product FT7 manufacture. Our overall long-term financing need is greater than £3.2 million.

It is my opinion, based on our recent financial performance, our current financial position, and the effect of such a large amount of debt on our capital structure, that an application for a £3.2 million bank loan would not be successful and that alternative sources of finance should be sought. I would be pleased to advise on these if the Board requested.

Yours sincerely,

A.N. Accountant

(e)     Calculation of standard contribution and standard profit

|                           |       | £     |
|---------------------------|-------|-------|
| Selling price             |       | 18.00 |
| Direct material           | 7.00  |       |
| Direct labour             | 1.50  | 8.50  |
| Standard contribution     |       | 9.50  |
| Selling price             |       | 18.00 |
| Direct material           | 7.00  |       |
| Direct labour             | 1.50  |       |
| Fixed production overhead | 4.50  | 13.00 |
| Standard profit           |       | 5.00  |

Sales price variance (marginal costing)
$$= ((18.20 - 8.50) - 9.50) \times 110,000$$
$$= (9.70 - 9.50) \times 110,000 = £22,000 \text{ (F)}$$

Sales price variance (absorption costing)
$$= ((18.20 - 13.00) - 5.00) \times 110,000$$
$$= (5.20 - 5.00) \times 110,000 = £22,000 \text{ (F)}$$

There is no difference between the two sales price variances because this variance depends upon the difference between actual selling price and standard selling price and not on the costing system employed in calculating it.

Sales volume profit variance (marginal costing) = $(110,000 - 100,000) \times 9.50 =$ £95,000 (F)

Sales volume profit variance (absorption costing) = $(110,000 - 100,000) \times 5.00 =$ £50,000 (F)

The sales volume profit variances are different, even though the volume difference is the same, because standard contribution (marginal costing) has a different value to standard profit (absorption costing), since marginal costing excludes production overheads from product cost while absorption costing includes them.

| ACCA marking scheme | | |
|---|---|---|
| | | *Marks* |
| (a) | Sales revenue | 1 |
| | Variable costs | 1 |
| | Contribution | 1 |
| | Fixed costs | 2 |
| | Taxation of operating cash flows | 2 |
| | Present value of income | 1 |
| | Present value of capital allowance tax benefits | 3 |
| | Present value of cash flows after year 4 | 3 |
| | Initial investment and working capital | 1 |
| | Net present value | 1 |
| | | 16 |
| (b) | Acceptability of proposed investment | 2–3 |
| | Discussion of additional information | 4–5 |
| | Maximum | 7 |
| (c) | PV of post Year 4 after-tax cash flows | 2 |
| | NPV of investing over ten years | 1 |
| | Present value comparison of offer with investing | 2 |
| | Discussion and conclusion | 1 |
| | | 6 |
| (d) | Financial analysis | 7–8 |
| | Discussion | 8–9 |
| | Report format | 1 |
| | Maximum | 16 |
| (e) | Sales price variances | 1 |
| | Sales volume variances | 2 |
| | Discussion | 2 |
| | | 5 |
| Total | | 50 |

## 2    PERFORMANCE APPRAISAL

### Key answer tips

A very straightforward discussion of divisional performance appraisal. Be careful in part (a) to link measures to the different types of centres. In part (b) you need to focus on appraising the manager, not the business unit.

(a)    A responsibility centre is part of an organisation for whose activities a manager is deemed to be responsible. The type of responsibility centre depends on the type of activities for which responsibility is carried.

**Cost Centre**

A cost centre or expense centre can be defined as a responsibility centre where a manager is accountable only for costs which are under his control. It is a production or service location for which costs can be identified or accumulated prior to allocation to cost units. Cost centres may be either standard cost centres, where output can be measured and the input needed for a given output can be specified, or discretionary cost centres, where output cannot be measured easily and the relationship between inputs and outputs cannot be specified1. An example of a standard cost centre is a production unit within a factory, while an example of a discretionary cost centre is a health and safety department within a university. A cost centre manager is responsible for the cost of inputs to the organisation. The performance of the manager of a cost centre can be assessed by comparing actual performance with budgeted targets for price, usage and efficiency.

### Revenue Centre

A revenue centre is a responsibility centre where a manager is accountable solely for the revenue generation that is under his control. An example would be a sales team with a target geographical area which is under the control of a sales manager. The manager would have no responsibility for the production cost of the items his team is selling, but has responsibility for meeting sales targets in terms of sales volume, sales revenue or market share. A revenue centre manager has responsibility for the revenue generated by outputs from the organisation. The performance of the manager of a revenue centre can be assessed by comparing actual performance with budgeted targets for price, mix and volume.

### Profit Centre

A profit centre is a combination of a cost centre and a revenue centre where a manager has responsibility for both production costs and revenue generation. The degree of responsibility carried by a manager can be higher with a profit centre than with a cost centre or a revenue centre, and the manager may be responsible for purchasing, production planning, product mix and pricing decisions. The performance of the manager of a profit centre is unlikely to be assessed on the fine detail of cost and revenue data but by the extent to which agreed targets for overall cost, revenue and profit have been achieved.

### Investment Centre

With an investment centre, the manager of a profit centre is given additional responsibility for investment decisions regarding working capital and the purchase and replacement of fixed assets. The manager of an investment centre is likely to be assessed with an aggregate measure that links periodic profit to the assets employed in the period to generate that profit. An example of such an aggregate measure is return on capital employed.

### Controllable and Non-controllable Factors

It is a cardinal principle of responsibility accounting that managers can only be assessed on the cash flows that are under their control. If a manager has no control over a cash flow he cannot influence its size or timing and so cannot be held responsible if either of these values changes. The performance of the manager of a cost centre can thus only be assessed on the controllable costs over which he exercises control. In the case of a production cost centre, the manager may be able to control material usage but could have no influence over the price at which materials are bought by the purchasing department. For the production cost centre manager, material usage is a controllable factor whereas material purchase price is not.

With a revenue centre, a sales manager can be held responsible for generating revenue against agreed sales volume targets but may have no control over the selling price of his products as this is determined by market conditions. In this case sales volume is a controllable factor whereas selling price is not.

The manager of a profit centre will have control of operating costs but will not be able to influence the financing costs arising from investment decisions. The manager may thus have responsibility for operating profit but his performance should not be assessed on profit before tax since interest charges are outside of his control.

The manager of an investment centre could have his performance assessed on profit before tax, but the profit on which he is assessed should exclude non-controllable elements such as overhead costs that he cannot influence, for example allocated head office charges.

(b)     While it is possible to assess the performance of an investment centre such as a division within a company on the basis of the profit it generates, considering profit alone and taking no account of the assets used to generate the profit will provide an incomplete picture of performance. Comparing profit between profit centres is also misleading if assets employed are ignored. Assessment of the performance of an investment centre will usually therefore include a performance measure that relates profit to assets employed. Two such measures are return on investment (ROI) and residual income (RI).

Return on investment expresses controllable profit as a percentage of capital employed. It is thus a relative, rather than an absolute, performance measure and is both widely used and understood. Controllable profit means that non-controllable factors are excluded as far as possible from the profit used in calculating ROI since these will diminish the usefulness of the calculated measure in assessing managerial performance.

Because ROI is a relative measure, it can be used to compare performance between investment centres. ROI also offers a way of assessing the past investment decisions made by an investment centre, since it is measured after these investment decisions have been made. It can thus be used to check that the performance predicted by investment appraisal decisions is in fact being achieved post implementation.

Since ROI assesses investment centre managerial performance on the basis of controllable profit generated, managers will be keen to maximise this as far as possible. The desire to maximise controllable profit can be assisted by the use of performance related pay and similar incentive schemes. But if performance is assessed using ROI, investment centre managers will be as keen to minimise capital employed as they will be to maximise controllable profit. While this can encourage managers to dispose of obsolete equipment and minimise working capital, it can also lead to sub-optimal decisions for the company as a whole.

If managers are assessed using ROI, there will be a disincentive to invest in projects with a ROI that is less than the current ROI of the investment centre. However, these projects should be accepted if the project ROI is greater than the company's cost of capital. In this case, the decision not to invest will not be consistent with the overall objective of maximizing shareholder wealth.

A similar problem arises with asset disposal decisions. Here, a manager assessed using ROI may choose to retain assets with a low written down value since these assets will generate a higher ROI than new, more expensive assets that could be more economical and efficient. This problem highlights the way in which short-term concerns can outweigh longer-term interests when ROI is used to assess managerial performance. It should be noted that ROI can simply increase due to ageing assets rather than from the actions of managers charged with increasing it.

Residual income has been suggested as a way of overcoming some of the perceived shortcomings of ROI as a managerial performance measure. Residual income (RI) is defined as controllable profit less a cost of capital charge on controllable investment. RI is therefore an absolute, rather than a relative, performance measure, which means that comparisons between investment centres cannot be made directly.

The advantage of RI as a performance measure is that the cost of capital charge (or imputed interest charge) is made by reference to the company's cost of capital, so that a positive residual income arises if an existing or proposed investment generates a return greater than the required minimum. Investment centre managers assessed on the basis of RI will therefore choose to accept all projects with a positive RI, increasing the company's overall return. Sub-optimal investment decisions should therefore be reduced or eliminated using RI. Investment centre managers will also be discouraged from retaining ageing and inefficient assets, since replacing such assets by more efficient ones is likely to lead to an increase in residual income.

Overall, it is felt that return on investment is an unsatisfactory way of assessing managerial performance as far as an investment centre is concerned, and that residual income should be used instead. Despite this, ROI appears in practice to be preferred to RI2.

| ACCA marking scheme | | |
|---|---|---|
| | | *Marks* |
| (a) | Responsibility centres | 5–6 |
| | Performance measurement | 4–5 |
| | Controllable and non-controllable factors | 2–3 |
| | Maximum | 12 |
| (b) | Return on capital employed | 7–8 |
| | Residual income | 5–6 |
| | Conclusion | 1 |
| | Maximum | 13 |
| Total | | 25 |

## 3    LINEACRE CO

### Key answer tips

Part (a) is a routine calculation of ABC recovery rates.

In applying these rates in part (b) it is simplest to calculate the total costs for the product before converting to a cost per unit. Care must be taken to distinguish between customer orders and component orders.

Part (c) asks for a discussion of ABC in a modern manufacturing environment and should be familiar ground for most students.

(a)    Activity-based recovery rates are found by dividing the expected cost in each cost pool by the number of cost driver transactions expected during the coming year.

| Cost Pool | Cost | Number of Drivers | ABC Recovery Rate |
|---|---|---|---|
| Production set-ups | £105,000 | 300 set-ups | £350.00 per set-up |
| Product testing | £300,000 | 1,500 tests | £200.00 per test |
| Component supply/storage | £25,000 | 500 component orders | £50.00 per order |
| Customer orders/delivery | £112,500 | 1,000 customer orders | £112.50 per order |

(b)    Production of product ZT3 = $(100 \times 60) + (60 \times 50)$ = 9,000 units per year

Number of production runs = number of set-ups = 9,000/900 = 10 set-ups

Number of product tests = $10 \times 4$ = 40 tests

Number of component orders = number of production runs = 10 orders

Number of customer orders = 100 + 60 = 160 orders

General overheads absorption rate = 900,000/300,000 = £3.00 per direct labour hour

Annual direct labour hours for Product ZT3 = $9,000 \times 10/60$ = 1,500 hours

| Activity | ABC recovery rate | Number of Drivers | Annual cost (£) |
|---|---|---|---|
| Setting up | £350.00 per set-up | 10 set-ups | 3,500 |
| Product testing | £200.00 per test | 40 tests | 8,000 |
| Component supply | £50.00 per order | 10 orders | 500 |
| Customer supply | £112.50 per order | 160 orders | 18,000 |
| | | | 30,000 |
| General overheads = 1,500 × £3.00 per hour = | | | 4,500 |
| Total annual overhead cost | | | 34,500 |

| Total unit cost | £ |
|---|---|
| Components | 1.00 |
| Direct labour = 7.80 × 10/60 = | 1.30 |
| Overheads = 34,500/9,000 = | 3.83 |
| | 6.13 |
| Profit mark up | 2.45 |
| Selling price | 8.58 |

(c) Traditional absorption costing allocates a proportion of fixed overheads (indirect costs) to product cost through an overhead absorption rate, usually based on labour hours, machine hours, or some other volume-related measure of activity. These overhead absorption rates may be factory-wide absorption rates (blanket rates) or, for increased accuracy in determining product cost, departmental absorption rates. In the traditional manufacturing environment, indirect costs constituted a relatively small proportion of total product cost compared to direct costs such as direct material cost, direct labour cost and direct expenses (collectively referred to as prime cost).

**The modern manufacturing environment**

In the modern manufacturing environment, indirect costs constitute a relatively high proportion of total product cost. There are several reasons for this.

Modern manufacturing is characterised by shorter and more frequent production runs rather than continuous or high volume production runs. This increases the frequency of production line set-ups and therefore the total cost arising from set-up activity.

Widespread use of computer control and automation has decreased the importance and use of direct labour. Direct labour cost as a proportion of total cost has therefore declined. This decline has been accelerated by the use of salaried employees rather than staff whose wages depend on production output, transferring labour costs from a direct cost to an indirect cost.

Increased use of just-in-time production methods and customer-led manufacture has led to quality control costs and production planning costs forming a higher proportion of total cost. These costs relate to particular production runs rather than to manufacture as a whole.

**Activities and costs**

Traditional absorption costing, by employing volume-related overhead absorption rates, failed to take account of the relationship between costs, activities and products. The insight at the heart of activity-based costing is that it is activities that incur costs and products that consume activities. Analysis of the way in which products consume activities allows the overhead costs incurred by those activities to be related to product cost using cost drivers derived from those activities rather than using production volume-related overhead absorption rates.

For example, set-up costs under traditional absorption costing could have been allocated to product cost using an overhead absorption rate based on machine hours. This would transfer a disproportionate amount of set-up costs to high volume products, which in fact gave rise to fewer set-ups because of their longer production runs. If set-up costs were transferred using number of set-ups as the cost driver, a fairer allocation of set-up costs would be achieved and products with longer production runs would not be penalised with a disproportionate share of their indirect costs.

### Improved cost control

Activity-based costing can lead to more detailed product cost information because a larger number of ABC cost drivers are likely to be identified in a given manufacturing organisation. An average of fifteen ABC cost drivers tends to be used, compared with one or two overhead absorption rates in traditional absorption costing. This more detailed product cost information can lead to improved cost control, since managers can seek to control costs by controlling the activities that cause the costs to be incurred. Production scheduling, for example, can optimise the number of production runs in order to minimise set-up costs.

### Better information on product profitability

Since product cost information is more accurate, managers have more accurate information on the relative profitability of individual products. This can lead to better decisions on product promotion and pricing, since managers can promote higher margin products while seeking to improve margins on products where margins are lower.

### Activity-based budgeting

Budget planning and formulation can use an activity-based approach to determining the required level of support activities, rather than an incremental approach based on prior year figures. With activity-based budgeting, the required level of production is used to determine the required number of cost driver transactions (e.g. number of set-ups), which in turn are used to determine the level of support activity that must be budgeted for (e.g. number of set-up engineers). In this way managers can seek to identify and eliminate any unnecessary slack in support activities, thereby improving efficiency and profitability.

| ACCA marking scheme | | Marks |
|---|---|---|
| (a) | ABC recovery rates | 4 |
| (b) | Cost drivers for Product ZT3 | 2 |
| | ABC overheads for Product ZT3 | 2 |
| | General overheads for Product ZT3 | 1 |
| | Total overhead per unit | 1 |
| | Direct labour cost | 1 |
| | Standard total unit cost | 1 |
| | Standard selling price | 1 |
| | | 9 |
| (c) | Discussion of relevant issues | 12 |
| Total | | 25 |

## 4    AGD CO

### Key answer tips

Part (a): To evaluate lease v buy the examiner's preferred approach is to perform two separate calculations. A combined approach will also gain credit but be careful of the signs of cash flows. Particular care is needed regarding the tax flows; they are delayed in this question, unlike in Question 1, and the asset would be bought on the first day of a new accounting period. Likewise the lease payments are in advance.

In part (b) ensure you both explain and discuss the differences. This requires you to describe the differences and look at the implications of them.

In part (c) the key is to recognise that there will be ten payments with an interest rate of 5% per six months.

(a)    Evaluation of purchase versus leasing compares the net cost of each financing alternative using the after-tax cost of borrowing.

Borrowing to buy evaluation

|  | Year 0 £000 | Year 1 £000 | Year 2 £000 | Year 3 £000 | Year 4 £000 |
|---|---|---|---|---|---|
| Purchase and sale | (320) |  |  | 50 |  |
| Capital allowance tax benefits |  |  | 24 | 18 | 39 |
| Maintenance costs |  | (25) | (25) | (25) |  |
| Maintenance cost tax benefits |  |  | 8 | 8 | 8 |
| Net cash flow | (320) | (25) | 7 | 51 | 47 |
| Discount factors (7%) | 1.000 | 0.935 | 0.873 | 0.816 | 0.763 |
| Present values | (320) | (23) | 6 | 42 | 36 |

PV of borrowing to buy = –£259,000

**Workings**: Capital allowance tax benefits

| Year | Capital allowance | Tax benefit | Taken in year |
|---|---|---|---|
| 1 | $320,000 \times 0.25 =$ | 80,000 80,000 × 0.3 = 24,000 | 2 |
| 2 | $80,000 \times 0.75 =$ | 60,000 60,000 × 0.3 = 18,000 | 3 |
| 3 | Balancing allowance = | 130,000 130,000 × 0.3 = 39,000 | 4 |

Balancing allowance = (320,000 – 50,000) – (80,000 + 60,000) = £130,000

Leasing evaluation

|  | Year 0 £000 | Year 1 £000 | Year 2 £000 | Year 3 £000 | Year 4 £000 |
|---|---|---|---|---|---|
| Lease rentals | (120) | (120) | (120) |  |  |
| Lease rental tax benefits |  |  | 36 | 36 | 36 |
| Net cash flow | (120) | (120) | (84) | 36 | 36 |
| Discount factors (7%) | 1.000 | 0.935 | 0.873 | 0.816 | 0.763 |
| Present values | (120) | (112) | (73) | 29 | 27 |

PV of leasing = –£249,000

On financial grounds, leasing is to be preferred as it is cheaper by £10,000. Note that the first lease rental is taken as being paid at year 0 as it is paid in the first month of the first year of operation.

An alternative form of evaluation combines the cash flows of the above two evaluations. Because this evaluation is more

complex, it is more likely to lead to computational errors.

Combined evaluation

| | Year 0 £000 | Year 1 £000 | Year 2 £000 | Year 3 £000 | Year 4 £000 |
|---|---|---|---|---|---|
| Purchase and sale | (320) | | | 50 | |
| Capital allowance tax benefits | | | 24 | 18 | 39 |
| Maintenance costs | | (25) | (25) | (25) | |
| Maintenance cost tax benefits | | | 8 | 8 | 8 |
| Lease rentals saved | 120 | 120 | 120 | | |
| Lease rental tax benefits lost | | | (36) | (36) | (36) |
| Net cash flow | (200) | 95 | 91 | 15 | 11 |
| Discount factors (7%) | 1.000 | 0.935 | 0.873 | 0.816 | 0.763 |
| Present values | (200) | 89 | 79 | 12 | 8 |

The PV of –£12,000 indicates that leasing would be £12,000 cheaper than borrowing. The difference between this and the previous evaluation is due to rounding.

(b)   A finance lease exists when the substance of the lease is that the lessee enjoys substantially all of the risks and rewards of ownership, even though legal title to the leased asset does not pass from lessor to lessee. A finance lease is therefore characterised by one lessee for most, if not all, of its useful economic life, with the lessee meeting maintenance and similar regular costs. A finance lease cannot be cancelled, once entered into, without incurring severe financial penalties. A finance lease therefore acts as a kind of medium- to long-term source of debt finance which, in substance, allows the lessee to purchase the desired asset. This ownership dimension is recognised in the balance sheet, where a finance-leased asset must be capitalised (as a fixed asset), together with the amount of the obligations to make lease payments in future periods (as a liability).

In contrast, an operating lease is a rental agreement where several lessees are expected to use the leased asset and so the lease period is much shorter than the asset's useful economic life. Maintenance and similar costs are borne by the lessor, with this cost being reflected in the lease rentals charged. An operating lease can usually be cancelled without penalty at short notice. This allows the lessee to ensure that only up-to-date assets are leased for use in business operations, avoiding the obsolescence problem associated with the rapid pace of technological change in assets such as personal computers and photocopiers. Because the substance of an operating lease is that of a short-term rental agreement, operating leases do not require to be capitalised in the balance sheet, allowing companies to take advantage of this form of 'off-balance sheet financing'[3].

(c)   (i)   The offer of 10% per year with interest payable every six months means that the bank will require 5% every six months. This is equivalent to an annual percentage rate of 10.25% ($100 \times (1.05^2 - 1)$) before tax.

OR

1 + annual rate = $(1 + \text{six monthly rate})^2 = 1.05^2 = 1.1025$

(ii)   To calculate the repayment schedule use:

PV of repayments = PV of amount borrowed

Here we have a simple annuity, so

Instalment (A) × annuity factor = 320,000

where we want an annuity discount factor for ten payments and a rate of 5%.

*Using annuity tables:*

A = 320,000/7.722 = £41,440

An alternative solution can be found using the formula for the present value of an annuity given in the formula sheet, a six-monthly interest rate of 5% and 10 periods of six months over the 5-year period of the loan:

$$320,000 = (A/r) \times (1 - 1/(1 + r)n) = (A/0.05) \times (1 - 1/1.0510)$$

Hence the amount to be paid at the end of each six-month period = A = £41,441

The difference between the two values is due to rounding in the annuity tables.

| ACCA marking scheme | | | Marks |
|---|---|---|---|
| (a) | | Purchase price | 1 |
| | | Sale proceeds | 1 |
| | | Capital allowances | 1 |
| | | Balancing allowance | 1 |
| | | Capital allowance tax benefits | 1 |
| | | Maintenance costs | 1 |
| | | Maintenance cost tax benefits | 1 |
| | | NPV of borrowing to buy | 1 |
| | | Lease rentals | 1 |
| | | Lease rental tax benefits | 1 |
| | | NPV of leasing | 1 |
| | | Selection of cheapest option | 1 |
| | | | 12 |
| (b) | | Explanation and discussion | |
| | | Finance lease | 4–5 |
| | | Operating lease | 4–5 |
| | | Maximum | 8 |
| (c) | | Annual percentage rate | 2 |
| | | Amount of equal instalments | 3 |
| | | | 5 |
| | Total | | 25 |

# 5 THORNE CO

## Key answer tips

In part (a) the key to success is to have clear, logical workings, even if you feel that this slows you down.

In part (b) you should apply your comments to the scenario where possible, bringing in issues such as seasonality, the amount of cash available and likely risk aversion, for example.

Part (c) asks for a more routine discussion of overdraft finance but again your answer should relate to the specific circumstances in the question.

In part (d) the key is to examine the assumptions underlying the Baumol model and see whether they apply to Thorne Co.

(a) **Cash Budget for Thorne Co:**

| Receipts | January £ | February £ | March £ | April £ |
|---|---|---|---|---|
| Cash fees | 18,000 | 27,000 | 45,000 | 54,000 |
| Credit fees | 36,000 | 36,000 | 54,000 | 90,000 |
| Sale of assets | | | | 20,000 |
| Total receipts | 54,000 | 63,000 | 99,000 | 164,000 |
| | | | | |
| Payments | | | | |
| Salaries | 26,250 | 26,250 | 26,250 | 26,250 |
| Bonus | | | 6,300 | 12,600 |
| Expenses | 9,000 | 13,500 | 22,500 | 27,000 |
| Fixed overheads | 4,300 | 4,300 | 4,300 | 4,300 |
| Taxation | | | | 95,800 |
| Interest | | | 3,000 | |
| Total payments | 39,550 | 44,050 | 62,350 | 165,950 |
| | | | | |
| Net cash flow | 14,450 | 18,950 | 36,650 | (1,950) |
| Opening balance | (40,000) | (25,550) | (6,600) | 30,050 |
| Closing balance | (25,550) | (6,600) | 30,050 | 28,100 |

***Workings***

| Month | December | January | February | March | April |
|---|---|---|---|---|---|
| Units sold | 10 | 10 | 15 | 25 | 30 |
| Sales value (£000) | 1,800 | 1,800 | 2,700 | 4,500 | 5,400 |
| Cash fees at 1% (£) | 18,000 | 18,000 | 27,000 | 45,000 | 54,000 |
| Credit fees at 2% (£) | 36,000 | 36,000 | 54,000 | 90,000 | 108,000 |
| Variable costs at 0.5% (£) | | 9,000 | 13,500 | 22,500 | 27,000 |

Monthly salary cost = $(35,000 \times 9)/12 = £26,250$

Bonus for March = $(25 - 20) \times 140 \times 9 = £6,300$

Bonus for April = $(30 - 20) \times 140 \times 9 = £12,600$

(b) The number of properties sold each month indicates that Thorne Co experiences seasonal trends in its business. There is an indication that property sales are at a low level in winter and increase as spring approaches. A proportion of any cash surplus is therefore likely to be short-term in nature, since some cash will be required when sales are at a low level. Even though net cash flow is forecast to be positive in the January, the month with the lowest level of property sales, the negative opening cash balance indicates that there may be months prior to December when sales are even lower.

Short-term cash surpluses should be invested with no risk of capital loss. This limitation means that appropriate investments include treasury bills, short-dated gilts, public authority bonds, certificates of deposit and bank deposits. When choosing between these instruments Thorne Co will consider the length of time the surplus is available for, the size of the surplus (some instruments have minimum investment levels), the yield offered, the risk associated with each instrument, and any penalties for early withdrawal4. A small company like Thorne Co, with an annual turnover slightly in excess of £1m per year, is likely to find bank deposits the most convenient method for investing short-term cash surpluses.

Since the company appears to generate a cash surplus of approximately £250,000 per year, the company must also consider how to invest this longer-term surplus. As a new company Thorne Co is likely to want to invest surplus funds in expanding its business, but as a small company it is likely to find few sources of funds other than bank debt and retained earnings. There is therefore a need to guard against capital loss when investing cash that is intended to fund expansion at a later date. As the retail property market is highly competitive, investment opportunities must be selected with care and retained earnings must be invested on a short- to medium-term basis until an appropriate investment opportunity can be found.

(c)     In two of the four months of the cash budget Thorne Co has a cash deficit, with the highest cash deficit being the opening balance of £40,000. This cash deficit, which has occurred even though the company has a loan of £200,000, is likely to be financed by an overdraft. An advantage of an overdraft is that it is a flexible source of finance, since it can be used as and when required, provided that the overdraft limit is not exceeded. In addition, Thorne Co will only have to pay interest on the amount of the overdraft facility used, with the interest being charged at a variable rate linked to bank base rate. In contrast, interest is paid on the full £200,000 of the company's bank loan whether the money is used or not. The interest rate on the overdraft is likely to be lower than that on long-term debt.

A disadvantage of an overdraft is that it is repayable on demand, although in practice notice is given of the intention to withdraw the facility. The interest payment may also increase, since the company is exposed to the risk of an interest rates increase. Banks usually ask for some form of security, such as a floating charge on the company's assets or a personal guarantee from a company's owners, in order to reduce the risk associated with their lending.

(d)     The Baumol model is derived from the EOQ model and can be applied in situations where there is a constant demand for cash or cash disbursements. Regular transfers are made from interest-bearing short-term investments or cash deposits into a current account. The Baumol model considers the annual demand for cash (D), the cost of each cash transfer (C), and the interest difference between the rate paid on short-term investments (r1) and the rate paid on a current account (r2), in order to calculate the optimum amount of funds to transfer (F). The model is as follows.

$$F = ((2 \times D \times C)/(r1 - r2))0.5$$

By optimising the amount of funds to transfer, the Baumol model minimises the opportunity cost of holding cash in the current account, thereby reducing the costs of cash management.

However, the Baumol model is unlikely to be of assistance to Thorne Co because of the assumptions underlying its formulation. Constant annual demand for cash is assumed, whereas its cash budget suggests that Thorne Co has a varying need for cash. The model assumes that each interest rate and the cost of each cash transfer are constant and known with certainty. In reality interest rates and transactions costs are not constant and interest rates, in particular, can change frequently. A cash management model which can accommodate a variable demand for cash, such as the Miller-Orr model, may be more suited to the needs of the company.

| **ACCA marking scheme** | | |
|---|---|---|
| | | *Marks* |
| (a) | Credit sales | 2 |
| | Cash sales | 1 |
| | Proceeds from asset disposal | 1 |
| | Salaries | 1 |
| | Bonus | 1 |
| | Expenses | 1 |
| | Fixed overheads | 1 |
| | Taxation and interest | 1 |
| | Closing balances | 1 |
| | | 10 |
| (b) | Discussion of factors | 5 |
| (c) | Discussion of advantages and disadvantages | 5 |
| (d) | Discussion of Baumol model | 2–3 |
| | Discussion of applicability in this case | 2–3 |
| | Maximum | 5 |
| Total | | 25 |